State capit... ...p, California, 1882.—*Courtesy the California State Library.*

The Governors of California

———————

Peter H. Burnett to Edmund G. Brown

The
Governors of California

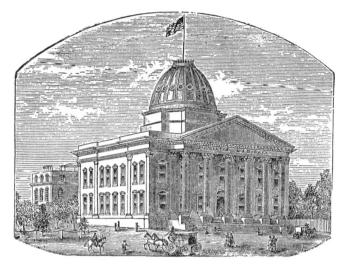

Peter H. Burnett to Edmund G. Brown

By

H. Brett Melendy and Benjamin F. Gilbert

THE TALISMAN PRESS
Georgetown, California   1965

Dedicated to the Governors of California,
their works and achievements,
and to the people of California.

Contents

Illustrations

Preface

Since World War II, the office of California governor has gained prestige and political power with national attention focused upon it. This study traces the historical development of the California governorship from the days of Spanish beginnings to the present. The book chronicles the major political events and economic problems of each administration and analyzes each governor's concept of his role in office. Additionally, little known biographical facts and stories are narrated. A brief background chapter about the pre-statehood governors sets the stage for the separate chapters on each administration from Peter Hardeman Burnett to Edmund Gerald Brown.

Our major purpose is to update a neglected aspect of California history. Besides correcting certain factual errors about the governors, an effort is made to present additional facts and new interpretations. Scholars of United States history have always stressed the importance of the presidents; we hope that California history might now be read with an increased awareness of the governors.

Few books have dealt with the lives and administrations of individual California governors. Actually more serious attention has been paid to the Spanish, Mexican, and United States military governors than to the governors since statehood. The glorification given to the colonial and gold rush periods and the superficiality of California political history explain to a large degree the lack of interest in the governors.

In the nineteenth century Californians were more aware of their governors through reading the histories by Hubert Howe Bancroft, Winfield J. Davis, and Theodore H. Hittell. Hittell's

History of California described the governorship best, but this work, completed in 1897, lacked perspective and covered the governors only through 1887. Moreover, some inaccuracies appeared in these earlier histories, particularly Bancroft's, which subsequent research has corrected. Many California historians in the past have confused Henry Bigler of Sutter's sawmill fame with Governor John Bigler, Senator James A. McDougall with Governor John McDougal, and Washington Allon Bartlett, the alcalde of Yerba Buena, with the later San Francisco mayor and California governor, Washington Bartlett.

This study is intended to be a general survey of the California governors rather than a comprehensive treatment of the thirty-two men. Since recent governors' papers are not available, a complete evaluation of their administrations is impossible. Thus no real effort is made to judge these and we merely state what seems to be major accomplishments. To assist those interested in further study of a particular governor, selected bibliographies follow each chapter. These list manuscripts, if existing and available, contemporary accounts, newspapers, secondary sources, and other materials. Not all sources consulted are listed; for example, only a few important newspaper items are given, although many more were used.

While the basic research was largely completed in California, much material was obtained elsewhere. For the most part the authors relied upon the resources of the Bancroft Library at the University of California, the California State Archives, the California Section of the State Library, the Henry E. Huntington Library, the San Jose State College Library, and the Stanford University Library. Materials were also consulted at the California Historical Society, the Library of Congress, the National Archives, the Yale University Library, and the public libraries of Eureka, Oakland, Pasadena, Sacramento, San Francisco, San Jose, and Stockton.

Among those who especially aided the authors are Dr. George P. Hammond, John B. Tompkins, Robert H. Becker, and Helen H. Bretnor of the Bancroft Library; Allan R. Ottley of the California State Library; Dr. William N. Davis, Jr. of the California State Archives; and Robert L. Lauritzen, Grace London, Christine Simpson, and Mildred B. Nelson of the San Jose State College Library staff. Through correspondence information was obtained from the following depositories: the

Bureau of Governmental Research of the University of California at Los Angeles, the Santa Barbara Public Library, the San Diego Public Library, and the San Joaquin Pioneer Museum. Useful pieces of information were also received from former Governor Goodwin J. Knight, from the late former Governor Culbert L. Olson, and from Hildreth Markham West, daughter of Governor Henry H. Markham.

Governor Edmund G. Brown granted the privilege of an interview at his office in the capitol building, and the late former Governor Culbert L. Olson was interviewed at his Los Angeles home. Robert Waldo Waterman, grandson of Governor Robert W. Waterman, made a much appreciated visit to San Jose to provide significant data.

Several individuals and staffs of depositories outside California assisted in the research. Among these special indebtedness is owed to Judge Charles L. Larson and to the public library of Port Washington, Wisconsin for locating obscure facts about the Wisconsin career of Governor Leland Stanford. Pertinent information concerning various governors was procured from the Archives of DePauw University, Tulane University Library, Illinois State Library, Geneva (Illinois) Historical Society, Sycamore (Illinois) Public Library, Albany (New York) Public Library, Wisconsin State Historical Society, Archives Division of the Indiana State Library, and Miami University in Ohio.

Photographs of all thirty-two governors were made available through the courtesies of the Bancroft Library, California State Library, Governor's Office, and the First Security National Bank of Los Angeles.

The authors express gratitude to the publishers, Robert Greenwood and Newton Baird, for editorial advice.

HOWARD BRETT MELENDY
BENJAMIN FRANKLIN GILBERT

SAN JOSE, MARCH 1, 1965

California Governors from 1769 to 1849

THE OFFICE OF CALIFORNIA GOVERNOR dates back to 1769, and prior to the settlement of California the office existed in Baja California. From 1769 to 1849, California was ruled by Spanish, Mexican, and United States military governors. In this entire pre-statehood period government was primarily undemocratic and unrepresentative.

SPANISH ERA (1769-1822)

Three basic institutions, the mission, presidio, and pueblo, were utilized by the Spaniards in their occupation of California. The mission was primarily a frontier institution, existing in theory for ten years until the process of Christianization and civilizing was completed, whereupon it would be secularized. The presidio was the military unit whereas the pueblo was the civic unit. All three functioned in establishing civil society.

Under the leadership of Father Juan María Salvatierra the Jesuits first occupied Baja California, on October 18, 1697. Loreto was selected as the site for the capital and mother mission. The first military governor, Luis de Torres y Tortolero, was not much more than a captain of the guard. The colony never prospered because of its tortuous terrain and bellicose natives. The seventh governor, Gaspar de Portolá, arrived at Loreto on December 17, 1767, having been ordered to the colony to expel the Jesuits. As captain of dragoons in command of fifty soldiers he carried out this delicate duty in a courteous way. After making an inventory, he gave the mis-

13

sions to the Franciscans in 1768, who had replaced the Jesuits. Then Portolá headed the land expedition of soldiers, missionaries, and colonists which settled Alta California in 1769. Besides Portolá, José de Gálvez, the visitador general, and Father Junípero Serra, were the chief luminaries in the occupation.

Portolá was the first governor of Alta California, serving in 1769 and 1770. In a strict sense he was not governor, for when he left northward, he had been replaced by Matías de Armona. However, before the latter had formally assumed his office, there was an acting governor at Loreto. In actuality Portolá referred to himself as governor of the Californias, reporting directly to the viceroy, and only in theory was he dependent upon the superior military officer at Loreto.

Portolá and Serra marched to San Diego. From there Portolá commanded two significant expeditions northward. Presidios and missions were established at San Diego and Monterey. The primary achievement of his governorship was that California was colonized.

Portolá's actual successors in Alta California were Pedro Fages and then Fernando de Rivera y Moncada, although neither officially possessed the title of governor. However, Felipe de Barri, who resided at Loreto as governor of the Californias from 1770 to 1775, was theoretically the second governor of Alta California. The third governor, Felipe de Neve, resided at Loreto from March 4, 1775, and then at Monterey from February 3, 1777 to September 10, 1782.

In the Spanish era, government was military in character except for the clerical rule of the missions. All functions of government, civil, military, judicial, and economic, were combined in the commandant. The first California code was the Reglamento Provisional of 1773, drafted by Juan José de Echeveste, who had been purchasing agent for the Californias in Mexico City. Instructions issued by Viceroy Antonio María Bucareli y Ursúa to Rivera on August 17, 1773, developed the reglamento further. For example, the relations of Rivera with the governor at Loreto were defined. He was to report to the governor, but the Baja California official could not alter Rivera's measures. In 1776, a decision was reached to have the governor of the Californias reside in Monterey and the lieutenant governor reside in Loreto. Neve was to replace Rivera and on December 25, 1776, Bucareli drafted instructions to Neve. These together with the earlier instructions to Rivera and the Reglamento of 1773 were to be completed by Neve's own reglamento. All of these documents were the basis for governing California until the end of Spanish rule.

Neve's Reglamento provided rules for the presidios and had colonization provisions. The only evidence of political rights was that the pueblos were allowed alcaldes and other municipal officers, to be appointed by the governor for the first two years and afterward to be elected by the inhabitants.

At first California was a part of New Spain and was governed directly by the Viceroy of Mexico. In 1776, it was attached to the commandancia general of the Provincias Internas. Later it was a part of the Provincias Internas of the West and eventually reverted to the viceroy. Laws emanated from the king, in his council of the Indies, to the viceroy, and from him to the governor at Monterey. Laws took effect only as published and communication was slow. Hence the governor possessed virtually autocratic powers.

Neve founded the Pueblo de San José in 1777, the first civic community in California. Among a few of his other achievements were the drafting of a military manual and rules for mail delivery. Before his departure from California, Neve wrote complete instructions for his successor, Pedro Fages, whose second term in office lasted from September, 1782, to April, 1791. Fages is generally considered the fourth governor. His uneventful administration only witnessed gradual development.

The next Spanish governor, José Antonio Roméu, suffered poor health and in 1792, a council held at Monterey selected as governor *ad interim* José Joaquín de Arillaga, the commandant at Loreto and lieutenant governor of the Californias. He first served in this capacity for two years. Then Diego de Borica served as governor from 1794 to 1800. He founded several new missions, improved fortifications at the presidios, founded the pueblo of Branciforte, and established a few secular schools. Arillaga served again as governor *ad interim* from 1800 to 1804 and as constitutional governor from 1804 to 1814. However, it appears that Pedro de Alberni was in command of the four presidios of Alta California from 1800 to 1802, and was followed in this position by José Argüello for four years. Because of their military status the latter two sometimes were referred to as governor.

From 1814 to 1815, José Darío Argüello served as acting governor ruling from Santa Barbara where he had been commandant. The last Spanish governor, Pablo Vincente Solá, served from 1815 to 1822. He was unable to dislodge the Russian intruders at Fort Ross and he had apprehensions about the Americans at the mouth of the Columbia River. During his administration the capital at Monterey was sacked by piratical insurgents in 1818. These events were signs of Spain's developing weakness.

MEXICAN ERA (1822-1846)

In February, 1821, Mexico gained her independence from Spain. Solá also served as first Mexican governor of California. On March 16, 1822, he summoned a junta at Monterey which met on April 9, and agreed to recognize the regency of Emperor Augustín Iburbide. Solá continued in office until November 9, 1822.

In the Mexican era, eleven persons served as governors—two serving two terms, hence making thirteen administrations. The Mexican republic replaced the empire in 1823. By its constitution a federation of nineteen states and four territories was formed. Meanwhile, on November 9, 1822, by action of the electoral junta meeting at Monterey, Luís Antonio de Argüello, having been elected president of the provincial deputación, became by virtue of his office temporary governor of Alta California in place of Solá, who had been elected as deputy to the Mexican congress.

When news of the empire's fall reached California, Argüello called a junta, composed of only military officers, to meet at Monterey on January 7, 1824. This body adopted the Plan de Gobierno which has been called California's first constitution. Although it was nominally the law for one year, it never had any legal force. It stated that the government should be civil and military, vested in one person exercising the functions before prescribed by laws. Early in 1825, Argüello received the federal constitution of Mexico. By its terms both Californias were united into one territory. The constitution made no provision for governing the territories. Yet the Mexican president assumed power to appoint a governor and to allow the deputación, a body representative of local vested interests, to continue.

In 1825, José María de Echeandía, the first "Jefe Politico" and "Commandante General" appointed by the republic, arrived. He failed to administer justice and to enforce military discipline which resulted in considerable civil strife. He moved the capital from Monterey to San Diego causing a conflict between the north and south. On June 1, 1829, Echeandía was relieved of his duties as general commandant of Baja California, but he continued to be civil governor of the two Californias. He was the last Alta California governor to be governor of both Californias.

Upon taking office as president of the republic, General Anastacio Bustamento completed separation of the governments of the Californias on March 8, 1830. He appointed Manuel Victoria as general commandant and civil governor of Alta California. Echeandía was instructed to relinquish office and return to Mexico. However, he remained in California and issued a decree for immediate secularization of the missions. Victoria countermanded this decree and appeared to be strict and tyrannical as he assumed his governorship. He refused to call the territorial deputación whose members he felt would oppose him. Whereas missionaries, merchants, and rancheros tended to support Victoria, others plotted a revolt in San Diego. On December 9, 1831, Echeandía issued a circular letter announcing that he had resumed the offices of civil governor and general commandant. Then the deputación placed Pío Pico in office as temporary civil governor, but Echeandía refused to recognize him. Actually from February 1, 1832 to January 14, 1833, while Echeandía was merely a revolutionary chieftain operating in one district, Agustín V. Zamorano assumed the title of acting general commandant and was in actual possession of the territorial government at Monterey.

After the strife of 1831 and 1832, the people of California welcomed the appointment of a new governor, José Figueroa. His commission was dated May 9, 1832, but he did not reach Monterey until the next year. Figueroa has been regarded as the greatest of the Mexican governors. He performed the difficult task of secularizing the missions. He founded Yerba

Buena and Sonoma and inaugurated the ayuntamiento (council) system of municipal government.

Following Figueroa's death in 1835, constant turmoil occurred in California politics. While internal revolts characterized periods of home rule, the people tended to unite against
the Mexican governors. Additional sectional conflicts developed
between the north and south. Into this confusing picture
American settlers arrived in greater numbers aggravating the
mounting political tempest.

The frequent wavering of the Mexican government between
liberal or federal and conservative or centralist policies also
intensified the turmoil in California. José Castro and then
Nicolás Guitiérrez succeeded Figueroa briefly as governors *ad
interim* until the arrival from Mexico of Mariano Chico. Within three months Chico was expelled and Guitiérrez served again
for a short time until a revolt was led by Juan Bautista
Alvarado and José Castro. On November 7, 1836, the deputación declared California a free and sovereign state until
Mexico should restore its federal constitution. Alvarado was
named governor and Mariano G. Vallejo became military
commandant or actually co-governor.

In August, 1838, Alvarado's position as governor was recognized by Mexico. On December 31, 1842, Alvarado and
Vallejo were replaced by General Manuel Micheltorena, the
last governor legally recognized by Mexico. When Micheltorena fell from power in 1845 as the result of a revolution,
Pío Pico was made civil governor with José Castro serving as
military commandant. Although Pico's exercise of power was
not sanctioned by Mexico, he was the last California governor
of the Mexican era. After the American conquest, José María
Florés and then Andrés Pico served briefly as provisional governors following a native revolt against American rule in
southern California.

In the Mexican era there was a struggle for civil control of
government and a weakening of military institutions as municipal government spread. Furthermore, a legislative authority
emerged. The Alvarado revolution demanded home rule and
brought about a separation of the military and civil. By the
Mexican laws of 1837, operative until the end of the era, the
governor still had despotic powers, but at least partial home
rule had been achieved.

UNITED STATES MILITARY GOVERNORS (1846-1849)

From July 7, 1846 to December 20, 1849, California was ruled by six military governors. The first two were naval officers and the other four were army officers. Some authorities make a distinction between the period prior to the Treaty of Guadalupe de Hidalgo, when Mexican institutions were retained in accordance with international law, and the period after the peace treaty, when Congress delayed providing a government and when Mexican institutions were retained as part of a system of *de facto* provisional government. Although several of the military governors considered themselves civil governors, in reality the military always prevailed over the civil authority. When civil government was established, it was accomplished largely by citizens themselves with the blessings of the military government.

On July 7, 1846, Commodore John Drake Sloat occupied Monterey and began the military conquest of California. In his proclamation he invited the judges, alcaldes, and other civil magistrates to retain their offices. During his sixteen days' command in California, occupation was only extended over the larger northern settlements. He did little to organize military government while several alcaldes who refused to serve under the United States government were replaced by naval officers.

On July 23, Commodore Robert Field Stockton relieved Sloat. After conquering southern California, he issued a proclamation at Los Angeles, on August 23, relating that California belonged to the United States and would be governed as soon as circumstances permitted by officers and laws similar to those of other territories. However, he indicated that until the governor, secretary, and council were appointed, military law would exist and that he would be governor.

Stockton planned to leave California shortly and intended to appoint Major John Charles Frémont as governor, but the Californian uprising delayed his plans. The reconquest was made by Stockton and General Stephen Watts Kearny, who with his troops had arrived overland from Santa Fé. After the Battle of San Pascual, a controversy arose between Stockton and Kearny over the governorship. Both men believed themselves invested with the appropriate authority. On January 16, 1847, Kearny demanded that Stockton cease organizing a civil government. In his reply Stockton refused and announced that he would ask President Polk for Kearny's recall. He also ordered Kearny to consider himself suspended from command of United States forces in California. Frémont also refused to recognize Kearny and on the same day Stockton commissioned Frémont as governor.

Nothing of real significance was achieved by Frémont during his fifty days as governor and his administration was hampered by lack of funds. On March 12, Colonel Philip St. George Cooke appraised the confused situation as follows:

> General Kearny is supreme somewhere up the coast; Colonel Fremont supreme at Pueblo de los Angeles; Commodore Stockton is commander-in-chief at San Diego; Commodore Shubrick the same at Monterey; and I at San Luis Rey; and we are all supremely poor; the government having no money and no credit; and we hold the territory because Mexico is poorest of all.

Frémont disobeyed Kearny and was guilty of insubordination toward his superior officer. Frémont was *de facto* governor, but his control did not extend beyond Los Angeles. On February 12, 1847, Colonel Richard Barnes Mason arrived at San Francisco with definite orders that Kearny was to be governor.

With Kearny's proclamation dated March 1, a period of stable military government soon began. Kearny was governor for three months and he extended his authority as needs arose. By the end of May, he felt that California was under control. He appointed Colonel Mason as governor and returned overland to St. Louis.

At times Mason had difficulty in asserting his authority in local government. In matters affecting the entire province he ruled by proclamation. To assist with his duties Mason appointed William T. Sherman as Assistant Adjutant General and Lieutenant Henry W. Halleck as Secretary of State. All legal and land matters were administered by Halleck, who knew Spanish and international law.

Two events of 1848 greatly influenced military government. First, the gold rush caused desertions of sailors and soldiers, weakening military strength. Second, the peace treaty changed the status of the province and invalidated Mason's laws. As a part of the United States, California was extended rights under the constitution and the laws. Mason questioned his own authority, but continued military government while he and the people awaited action by Congress. However, because of the sectional conflict between the northern and southern states Congress failed to provide civil government for California. In the mining camps self-government evolved and the gold region was virtually independent.

On November 24, 1848, Mason requested to be ordered home, but he was not relieved until five months later, when on April 13, 1849, General Bennett Riley replaced him. Meanwhile, on February 28, General Persifor F. Smith arrived in San Francisco and took command of the Third Division. This consisted of the Tenth Military Department, which included California, and the Eleventh Military Department, which included Oregon Territory. Some writers assert that Smith succeeded Mason as military governor, but Mason remained commanding officer of the Tenth Military Department and Smith considered Mason as governor.

Governor Riley had the problem of maintaining military government when the people were demanding an elected government. At first he decided not to make decisions regarding civil government until Congress acted. However, extra-legal governmental activity in San Francisco and the arrival of news on June 1, 1849, that Congress had adjourned without organizing a territorial government caused Riley to act. On June 3, he issued a proclamation in which he defined the legal status of California and called for a constitutional convention. He said that "in accordance with instructions from the Secretary of War he had assumed the administration of civil affairs in California not as a *military* governor, but as an executive of the existing civil government." Riley also listed the various departments of the *de facto* government and provided for its operation under modified Mexican laws until a state or territorial government could be devised. Although Mexican laws were considered unacceptable by American citizens, the prospect of a state or territorial government made the Riley government tolerable.

Riley's call for a convention was actually unauthorized. His predecessor, Mason, had advised a convention and the people had demanded it. Hence he disarmed the proponents of civil government, retained his authority, and gave unity to the movement for an elected government. The convention met at Monterey on September 1, 1849, and by October 12, had formed a state constitution providing for an American civil governor.

A month later the people ratified it and on December 20, Riley yielded his authority to Peter H. Burnett, ending a period of three and one half years of military government.

As a result of the gold rush, California was able to bypass the usual territorial stage of government. The civil government began its operation without Congressional sanction—but on September 9, 1850, California was admitted as the thirty-first state which has been administered by thirty-two state governors.

BIBLIOGRAPHY

MANUSCRIPTS

"Letter from Stephen Kearny to the Secretary of War, enclosing original papers referring to the interference of Com. Stockton, U.S.N., to enforcement of the execution of the orders of the President of the United States in regard to the Government of Territory of California." Record Group 94, Office of the Adjutant General, Letters Received (The National Archives, Washington, D.C.).

Sloat, John Drake, "Correspondence, 1845-46," (California Historical Society).

Stockton, Robert Field, "Letters and Miscellaneous Material, 1846-1847," (California Historical Society).

"Territorial Papers, California, 1846-1847," (The National Archives, Foreign Affairs Section, Washington, D.C.).

CONTEMPORARY ACCOUNTS

Browne, J. Ross, *Report of the Debates in the Convention of California, on the Formation of the State Constitution* (Washington, D.C., 1850).

California and New Mexico, House of Representatives, 31st Cong., 1st Sess., Ex. Doc. No. 17, (Washington, D.C., 1850).

Hammond George P., ed., *The Larkin Papers* (10 vols., Berkeley, 1951-64).

SECONDARY SOURCES

Barrows, Henry D., "Governor Gaspar de Portolá," *Annual Publication* of the Historical Society of Southern California, III (1896), 15-18.

———, "Governors of California," *ibid.*, VI (1903), 32-37.

———, "Mexican Governors of California," *ibid.*, V, Pt. I (1900), 25-30.

Bayard, Samuel J., *A Sketch of the Life of Com. Robert F. Stockton* (New York, 1856).

Clarke, Dwight L., *Stephen Watts Kearny, Soldier of the West* (Norman, 1961).

Goodwin, Cardinal, *The Establishment of State Government in California, 1846-1850* (New York, 1914).

———, *John Charles Frémont, An Explanation of His Career* (Stanford University Press, 1930).

Grivas, Theodore, *Military Governments in California, 1846-1850* (Glendale, 1963).

Harding, George L., *Don Agustín V. Zamorano* (Los Angeles, 1934),

Hittell, Theodore H., *History of California* (4 vols., San Francisco, 1897-98).

Morrison, Raymond K., "Luís Antonio Argüello: First Mexican Governor of California," *Journal of the West,* II (1963), 193-204, 347-61.

Sherman, Edwin A., *The Life of the Late Rear-Admiral John Drake Sloat* (Oakland, 1902).

Calendar of Events

November 15, 1807	Burnett born at Nashville, Tennessee.
May 8, 1842	Burnett left Missouri overland for Oregon.
1844	Burnett elected member of Legislative Committee of Oregon.
May 15, 1845	Burnett elected Judge of Oregon Supreme Court.
1848	Burnett elected to first Oregon Territorial Legislature.
November 9, 1848	Burnett arrived at Long's Bar, Yuba River.
August, 1849	Burnett appointed by General Riley to Superior Tribunal of California.
November 13, 1849	Burnett elected first Governor of California.
December 20, 1849	Burnett inaugurated as Governor at San Jose.
September 9, 1850	California admitted to statehood.
January 9, 1851	Burnett resigned as Governor and re-entered the legal profession.
1852	Burnett accepted temporary appointment to California Supreme Court.
1852	Burnett served as Sacramento City Councilman.
1857	Burnett appointed by Governor J. Neely Johnson to California Supreme Court.
September, 1858	Burnett elected to short term on supreme court bench.
1863	Burnett succeeded Sam Brannan as President of the Pacific Bank of San Francisco.
1880	Burnett wrote *Recollections and Opinions of an Old Pioneer.*
1880	Burnett resigned as President of the Pacific Bank.
May 17, 1895	Burnett died in San Francisco.

Peter H. Burnett

1ST GOVERNOR—INDEPENDENT DEMOCRAT
BORN: NOVEMBER 15, 1807   DIED: MAY 17, 1895
TERM OF OFFICE: DECEMBER 20, 1849—JANUARY 9, 1851

CALIFORNIA'S FIRST GOVERNOR under the newly adopted state constitution, Peter H. Burnett, appeared before the first legislature at San Jose, the first capital, to take his oath of office in December, 1849. All assembled for that occasion were aware of the importance of this ceremony as well as being uncertain about the immediate future, for this new government was launched without official sanction from the United States Congress. In fact the first legislative session met and adjourned before the question of statehood was settled. Not until September 9, 1850, did Congress confer the status of a state upon California. Nevertheless, Burnett urged these pioneering lawmakers to do their work well and fix brightly the star of the state.

Burnett had been born in Nashville, Tennessee, on November 15, 1807. He spent his youth in Williamson County, Missouri. In the fall of 1826 he returned to Tennessee, settling at Bolivar, Hardeman County, where he worked as a hotel clerk. During 1827 and 1828 he clerked in a country store. In August, 1828, he married Harriet Rogers. The following spring Burnett purchased the store but by 1830 he was in serious financial trouble. Forced out of business, he returned to the Missouri family home in 1832, $700 in debt.

Burnett had 62½ cents in his pockets and a wife and child to support. He undertook the study of law and, after fifteen months of study, was admitted to the bar. About to open a law office in 1834, he instead joined a mercantile partnership. While the firm prospered for a time it failed in the general depression of 1837-1838. Burnett was then about $15,000 in debt. After this failure, he resumed his study of law, reviewing the latest legal works before launching his practice. He also edited the Liberty, Missouri, weekly newspaper, *The Far West*, for which he received no salary but seized this opportunity to improve his writing style. At the same time he joined a debating club to improve his speaking ability.

Burnett's law practice, dealing with mercantile and civil cases, prospered. In 1839, he joined Amos Rees and Alexander W. Doniphan as defense counsels for Joseph Smith, Jr., Sidney Rigdon, Lymon Wight, and other Mormon leaders then in the Liberty jail. When the grand jury found cause for indictment, the defense moved for a change of venue. As the prisoners were being moved, they escaped into Illinois, bringing the case to a close.

In the winter of 1839-40, Burnett was appointed district attorney for a newly created district in western Missouri. By late 1842, he resided in Weston, Platte County, where he happened to read a recent congressional report about Oregon. The lure of free land, the prospect of ridding himself of his debts, and the hope of improving Mrs. Burnett's failing health led Burnett to decide to move to Oregon. He first sought the consent of his creditors with the understanding that he would repay his debts. Obtaining their approval, he immediately set to work organizing a wagon train. He then resigned as district attorney —the first of several resignations during his life.

The Burnett family left Weston on May 8, 1842, with two oxen teams and one two-horse wagon. The use of oxen by this train was a new experiment in crossing the plains. At the Kansas River on June 1, the company officially organized, electing Burnett captain. However, the company proved too difficult for him to manage and he resigned on June 8.

By October 10, 1843, the train had arrived in Oregon Territory. Burnett proceeded on to Vancouver arriving there November 7. Soon he was helping lay out the town of Linnton, named in honor of Senator Lewis Linn of Missouri who had in 1838 urged American occupation of Oregon. Burnett and his colleagues mistakenly believed Linnton to be the navigable head of the Willamette River. He resided in Linnton until May, 1844. Although he had no prior experience as a farmer, he resolved to make the most of the opportunity to acquire good land. Moving west from Linnton to the Tualatin Plains he purchased a claim but had a difficult time making his farm productive.

The Oregonians, faced with the question of organizing a provisional government, had in July, 1843, voted approval of organic laws for the territory. The continuing influx of settlers made revision of the laws imperative. Burnett, first opposed to the idea of a provisional government, changed his mind on the ground that some organization was needed to protect the rights of the inhabitants. He was elected one of the nine-member 1844 Legislative Committee of Oregon.

This committee created a new governmental organization, comprising an executive, a House of Representatives, and a Supreme Court Judge. The committee also proposed that the former plan of voluntary taxation give way to optional taxation, which provided that if a man did not pay his taxes, he lost his right to vote and his protection under territorial law. Burnett carried this idea with him to California to be proposed in part to the first legislature. Under Burnett's guidance, an act was passed prohibiting the importation, distillation, and bartering of ardent spirits in Oregon with a system of fines established for enforcement.

Throughout his public career in Oregon and California, Burnett opposed the bringing of slaves and free Negroes into these two areas. In June, 1844, he introduced a measure to the Legislative Committee providing that slavery be prohibited in Oregon and slaves already in residence be removed within three years. At the end of that time, any slaves still there would be set free. All free Negroes and mulattoes had to remove themselves from the territory. Persons failing to do so would be brought to trial and, if found guilty, would receive not less than twenty and not more than thirty-nine lashes by the county constable. If they were still in Oregon after six months, they were liable to the same punishment. The Legislative Committee passed this act, but so much public criticism arose over the punishment feature that at the December meeting Burnett moved to repeal the sections dealing with whipping. In lieu of this, he proposed that any free Negroes or mulattoes found guilty by trial of remaining in the territory be hired out to the lowest bidder for work. The bidder obligated himself to remove such a person from Oregon after the expiration of service.

The bidder was under a $1,000 bond subject to forfeiture in the event of failure to abide by the law.

Burnett based his anti-Negro views on the assumption that while a person born in a certain community had the natural right of residence there, he was not entitled as a matter of right to reside in another community. If another community denied the privilege of residence, it did not deny a right but only refused a favor asked. In his 1880 *Recollections and Opinions of An Old Pioneer* Burnett stated that he had opposed slavery as injurious to both races involved.

While a member of the 1844 Legislative Committee, Burnett gained experience in proposing ideas for creating a new government. He showed willingness to experiment with the structure of government and gathered ideas that later aided him as governor of California. His active role in Oregon was remembered by those Oregonians in the California gold fields when they helped elect the first governor in 1849. Some historians of Oregon credit Burnett's victory to the balance of power held by the Oregonians voting in the mining centers. These men knew Burnett and his good record in Oregon.

In August, 1845, the Oregon House of Representatives elected Burnett Judge of the Supreme Court. He remained on the bench until January 1, 1847, when he resigned to re-enter the legal profession. In 1846, after much reading and thought, Burnett joined the Roman Catholic Church. He noted in his recollections that early in life he was a deist, but in 1840 he had joined the Disciples of Campbellites. In 1860 he explained his faith in a book, *The Path Which Led a Protestant Lawyer to the Catholic Church.* In 1884 he wrote *Reasons Why We Should Believe in God, Love God, and Obey God.*

Burnett won election to the 1848 Oregon territorial legislature, but he resigned in September to captain a wagon train to California, which pioneered the first wagon route from Oregon to California. Burnett arrived at Long's Bar on the Yuba River November 5, 1848. Word reached him that President Polk had appointed him Justice of the Supreme Court of Oregon, but he declined the office because of additional financial losses he would have incurred. He remained at the mines until mid-December, selling his wagons and teams and accumulating enough gold to sustain him six months.

Burnett planned to move to San Francisco to establish his

law practice, but he stopped over at Sutter's Fort where he was retained as attorney and agent by John Sutter, Jr., to handle his legal affairs and to sell lots in Sacramento. For these services he received one-fourth of the gross proceeds.

Not long after his arrival in Sacramento, the question arose regarding the organization of a civil government for California. The major problem was that no one knew much, or could gain information, about the existing Mexican legal code. Public opinion held that a *de facto* government was in order. At a meeting held at Sacramento in January, 1849, to lay plans for such a government, Burnett was elected president. Later in 1849 he moved to San Francisco where he became a member of that city's Legislative Committee. This committee demanded in June local self-government but General Bennett Riley, the military governor, denied the validity of its views. He did, however, issue at the same time his "Proclamation to the People of California" calling for a special election to select local officials.

In July, 1849, Burnett returned briefly to Sacramento to close his affairs with Sutter. He sold a half-interest in some of his Sacramento lots for $50,000 while retaining title to other choice ones for his own use. He discovered that during his absence from San Francisco he had been nominated and elected to be one of the four members of the Superior Tribunal, established by Riley.

He went to Monterey from his new residence of San Jose in mid-September to sit as one of the tribunal judges. The court had little business to transact and Burnett followed closely the proceedings of the constitutional convention. Believing that there was no doubt about the outcome of the convention's work, Burnett announced himself as a candidate for governor. He made a successful swing through the gold fields, Sacramento, and San Francisco, winning the election. He far outstripped his nearest competitor, W. Scott Sherwood, receiving 6,716 votes to Sherwood's 3,188. John W. Geary, John A. Sutter, and William M. Steuart together received 4,295 votes. Burnett also received 157 votes for lieutenant governor.

As governor, Burnett tried to offend no one. His attempt to avoid commitment on certain political questions brought criticism from the legislature and the state press. According to Hubert Howe Bancroft, Burnett had polished manners and conducted himself in such fashion that the general public was impressed with his opinions and his personality. Elisha O. Crosby, while a state senator, felt that the governor lacked the backbone to handle issues and vacillated in the face of political pressures. Crosby wrote that Burnett lacked self-confidence and thus was timid in meeting the problems of the day. In particular, Burnett was too conservative in fiscal matters at a time when bold leadership in state finance was needed.

On December 20, 1849, Peter H. Burnett took his oath of office as governor. The next day he sent his first message to the pioneer legislature. Burnett pointed out the many organizational tasks facing the new state government, counties, and towns. The governor felt that even though California had not yet been admitted to statehood the legislature had every right to proceed with its business, holding that the federal government had only limited powers over the states.

The legislature proceeded with implementation of constitutional provisions. County governments were organized; legislative districts, district courts, and a supreme court were established. Plans were laid for a state library at San Jose and a marine hospital at San Francisco.

Burnett felt that California had an opportunity to adopt the best legal code in the nation, covering civil and criminal law. He suggested that the legislature study certain codes and from these derive an outstanding civil and criminal code. His proposal was rejected and English common law was established as the basis of the California codes, except where the United States constitution, the state constitution and state law made other provisions. Burnett accepted this legislative decision without public comment.

Burnett estimated that the cost of state government for 1850 would be in excess of $500,000 which had to be raised either by taxation or loans. Burnett, an advocate of "pay as you go" financing, opposed state borrowing through issuance of bonds inasmuch as this passed on the tax burden to future generations. He demanded direct taxation based on a poll tax and real and personal property. There were many in California, he reasoned, who were there only to extract gold and then planned to leave the state. These people would not be anxious to pay any tax. To circumvent non-payment, Burnett suggested that those who evaded payment be deprived use of the state courts for one year or until they had paid in full any delinquent taxes. He believed the honest individual would not feel the impact of such a restriction.

The first legislature was equally aware of the revenue problem for there were no funds with which to meet expenses. At first individuals were approached to lend money to the state secured by the credit and good name of the state but this method failed. Despite the governor's recommendations, the legislature provided for a bond issue of $300,000 with a 3 percent interest rate per month. This issuance plagued the next two administrations because of multiplying interest on outstanding bonds. A poll tax of $5.00 was levied on men between the ages of twenty-one and fifty. A 30 cent tax on every $100 of real and personal property was also enacted during the first session. No action was taken on Burnett's proposal to deny court privileges to evaders. The governor accepted this revenue program although state finances were to haunt him and his successors.

His first message took up the matter of free Negroes in California. He claimed that while the state constitution had wisely prohibited slavery it had overlooked the question of residence for colored free people. He believed the first legislature had one of two alternatives. It could give free Negroes equal status or it could exclude them from the state. Since free Negroes were deprived of all rights of citizenship within the state, it was only fair, he thought, that they be excluded to avoid their further degradation. The Assembly considered a bill preventing the immigration of colored people in California. After being amended, it was tabled by the action of David Broderick, bringing Burnett's proposals for Negro exclusion to an end.

For the most part harmony existed between Burnett and the first legislature. The governor used his veto power sparingly. He differed with the lawmakers over the method of incorporation of cities, holding that there should be one general act covering the procedure rather than a succession of individual acts for each city. After his veto of the incorporation of Sacramento was overridden, he and the legislature settled their differences in a friendly manner.

The selling of city lots in San Jose and San Francisco brought trouble to the governor. After interceding in the sales in both cities, Burnett found himself in the middle of a controversy between the San Francisco Ayuntamiento, the town council, and the Prefect of San Francisco, Horace Hawes. On the recommendation of the Ayuntamiento, Burnett removed Hawes. Hawes denied Burnett's authority to do so. As a result of the governor's action, Hawes wrote to Speaker pro-tem John Bigler that he wished impeachment charges brought against Burnett. Bigler's motion to table the communication was accepted.

One unique function or duty charged to the legislature and the governor was the approval of all changes of names for individuals. This obligation lasted through the administration of Frederick F. Low. Another function of the governor, judicial in nature, was the pardoning power. Burnett exercised this power but once.

Following the adjournment of the legislature, Governor Burnett and the other executive officers had the major responsibility for conducting the state's affairs. His own private business matters also caused Burnett great concern. He and others worried about squatters on their land in Sacramento and when the squatter riots broke out in August, 1850, he called out the militia to suppress the rioters. In addition to his Sacramento real estate, Burnett invested in land at Alviso for it was his hope that this town would become the port for the capital, San Jose.

The governor called out the militia on two other occasions to quell Indian uprisings in El Dorado County and along the Colorado River. In his second message to the legislature in 1851, he stated that he had received repeated calls for military aid to suppress the Indians, but it was impossible to heed every request because of the great size of the state. With these two exceptions only, he let each locality protect itself. He indicated his opinion of the Indians when he said, "A war of extermination will continue to be waged between the races until the Indian races become extinct."

Governor Burnett in 1850 acquired the wrath of many citizens and the ridicule of others when he proclaimed a Saturday in November to be Thanksgiving rather than the traditional Thursday. The *California Courier* claimed that the day such a governor left office would be a more likely day of thanksgiving.

Burnett's second message, delivered January 7, 1851, was coldly received by both houses. The legislature initiated the custom of having the reading of the message stopped and ordering its printing. Such a custom endured until the administration of J. Neely Johnson. The correspondent of the *California Courier* was greatly shocked by such treatment of the governor at the hands of the legislature. He reported that no one cared for the governor or respected his office. He had been, said the writer, "unpopular with the last Legislature, and has gained no special favor from the present one."

Burnett claimed that the state government had behaved properly during 1850 in its struggle for statehood. He once more urged the exclusion of Negroes and again the legislature did not accept his suggestion. He proposed amending the criminal law to provide better enforcement and quicker transaction of justice. In light of existing conditions, he believed that stiffer punishments were needed. To counter the increasing crime rate, he proposed the death penalty for grand larceny and robbery until permanent county and state prisons could be erected. Such an extreme proposal was typical of Burnett who made many such unusual suggestions. This one, like most, was not considered by the legislature.

Turning to the problem of state finance, Burnett focused attention on an argument, which was to bother his successors, between the state and the federal government over California's claim for the return of taxes collected in the state by the United States between December, 1849 and September, 1850, the period that the state government operated without federal authorization. Burnett maintained that this fund rightfully belonged to the state. Most importantly, this money would help solve California's immediate financial embarrassment. He still opposed the incurring of great debt. To rectify the situation, he called for cutting expenditures, including reduction of official state salaries and eliminating the Spanish translation of legislative proceedings. Since the treasury was empty, he proposed that current rates on real and personal property continue although there should be a reasonable reduction of the poll tax. In this message he called for the establishment of the office of superintendent of public instruction, his only reference to building a public school system.

On January 9, 1851, Governor Burnett sent his resignation to the legislature which accepted it without comment. Burnett stated that he was forced to return to a full time consideration of his personal affairs. The reasons for his resignation are difficult to explain. It was true that resignation was not a new experience for him; in fact, he had a long record of resignations and business failures behind him. Elisha O. Crosby has suggested that the governor did not possess leadership qualities. The press noted that he had not been a popular governor and had been subjected to considerable criticism from the legislature. Above all else was the imposing problem of his indebtedness. Some believed he sought the governorship because the $10,000 a year salary might prove a means of freeing himself from debt. The salary, paid in depreciated state scrip, did not meet the high cost of living in California or reduce his debts. Satisfying his personal debts and managing his real estate ventures made great demands upon his time. It would appear that the financial burdens and an unpopular image caused him to resign. It seemed to be in keeping with his past career—when conditions became too difficult, one simply resigned.

Burnett then re-entered the legal profession in San Jose with his two sons-in-law. By early 1852, having paid off his Missouri debts, he accepted a temporary appointment to the state Supreme Court. In December, 1852, he moved to Sacramento to manage his real estate affairs where for a time he was a member of the city council.

In January, 1857, after returning from a visit to eastern states, he was appointed to the Supreme Court by Governor J. Neely Johnson. In September, he was elected a justice for a short term, serving until October 2, 1858. In 1863, he succeeded Sam Brannan as president of the Pacific Bank of San Francisco. He moved from San Jose to San Francisco where he resided for the remainder of his life. He remained president of the bank until the death of his wife in 1880. After retirement he lived with his son until his death on May 17, 1895, at the age of eighty-eight.

Peter H. Burnett was California's pioneer civil governor. He had to solve all the problems confronting an executive without the benefit of precedent to serve as a guide. Governor Burnett and the first legislature successfully launched a stable state government in the face of tremendous fiscal difficulties. While it was true that the governor proposed some startling innovations, it must be remembered that all segments of the state's political life were groping for solutions to immediate and pressing problems. Peter Burnett was a man willing to experiment with the functions of government in order to establish for California a superior instrument to execute the wishes of the people. Burnett's tenure in office was marked by personal respectability and high sense of public morality. He left his mark upon his office and was remembered for more than being the first governor. His abilities in public office measured well in comparison to those who were his immediate successors.

BIBLIOGRAPHY

MANUSCRIPTS

Bowman, J.N., "The Early Governors of California: Archival Records Showing the Kinds of Men They Were," (California State Archives, 1952).

Burnett, Peter H., "Autograph Family Legal Documents, 1849 *seq.* of Peter H. Burnett," (Bancroft Library).

————, "Letters to and from Peter Burnett," (Bancroft Library).

————, "Letters," (California Section, State Library).

————, "Letters and Commissions 1850, Day Book," (California State Archives).

Norris, Thomas W., "Collection," (Bancroft Library).

Ryland, Cassius T., "Papers," (Bancroft Library).

Vesaria, Louis, "Papers," (California Historical Society).

CONTEMPORARY ACCOUNTS

Assembly Journal, 1st-2nd Sess., 1849-51.

Senate Journal, 1st-2nd Sess., 1849-51.

Barker, Charles A., ed., *Memoirs of Elisha Oscar Crosby* (San Marino, 1945).

Buffum, E. Gould, *Six Months in the Gold Mines* (Philadelphia, 1850).

Burnett, Peter H., *Address to the inhabitants of New Mexico and California on the omission by Congress to provide them with territorial governments, and on the social and political evils of slavery* (New York, 1849).

————, *The Path Which Led a Protestant Lawyer to the Catholic Church* (New York, 1860).

————, *Reasons Why We Should Believe in God, Love God and Obey God* (New York, 1884).

————, *Recollections and Opinions of an Old Pioneer* (New York, 1880).

————, "Letters of Peter H. Burnett," *The Quarterly of the Oregon Historical Society,* III (1902), 398-426.

Lennox, Edward H., *Overland to Oregon* (Oakland, 1904).

SECONDARY SOURCES
Arbuckle, Clyde, "The Governor Resigned," *Grizzly Bear*, LXXII (May, 1944), 7.
Bancroft, Hubert Howe, *Chronicles of the Builders of the Commonwealth* (8 vols., San Francisco, 1891-92).
———, *History of California* (7 vols., San Francisco, 1886-90).
Davis, Winfield J., *History of Political Conventions in California, 1849-1892* (Sacramento, 1893).
Ellison, Joseph, "The Struggle for Civil Government in California, 1846-1850," *California Historical Society Quarterly*, X (1931), 3-26, 129-164, 220-244.
Ellison, William H., *A Self-governing Dominion: California 1849-1860* (Berkeley, 1950).
Franklin, William E., "A Forgotten Chapter in California History: Peter H. Burnett and John A. Sutter's Fortune," *CHSQ*, XLI (1962), 319-324.
———, "Peter Burnett and the Provisional Government Movement," *CHSQ*, XL (1961), 123-136.
Frazer, Robert W., "The Ochoa Bond Negotiations of 1865-1867," *Pacific Historical Review*, XI (1942), 397-414.
Hall, Frederic, *The History of San Jose* (San Francisco, 1871).
Hittell, T.H., *History of California*.
Morse, John F., *The First History of Sacramento City Written in 1853* (Sacramento, 1945).
Shuck, Oscar T., *History of the Bench and Bar of California* (Los Angeles, 1901).
Stewart, Frank M. "Early California Impeachment Proceedings," *PHR*, XXIV (1955), 261-274.
Wyman, Walker D., "California Emigrant Letters," *CHSQ*, XXIV (1945), 17-46, 117-138.

NEWSPAPERS
Daily Alta California, Dec. 29, 1849, carries account of Burnett's first message; Jan. 12, 1851, comments on his resignation; Nov. 23, 1852, gives an estimate of his career.
San Francisco Call, May 18, 1895, carries Burnett's obituary.
San Francisco Herald, Jan. 13, 1851, comments on governor's resignation.

THESES
Basher, Eli, "Early Evidence of Political Parties in California" (M.A., Stanford University, 1926).
Cain, Estill V., "The Career of Peter Hardeman Burnett" (M.A., University of Washington, 1930).
Franklin, William E., "The Governorship of Peter Hardeman Burnett, First Governor of the State of California" (M.A., Stanford University, 1948).
———, "The Political Career of Peter H. Burnett" (Ph.D., Stanford University, 1954).

Capitol at Monterey, 1849. The building in which the first Constitutional Convention met from September 1 to October 15, 1849. Named Colton Hall, on account of its having been built by Walter Colton, the Alcalde. The 48 delegates met on the upper floor which ran the length of the building. It was leased by the state in 1903, and is preserved today as a California Historical Landmark.

Calendar of Events

1818	McDougal born in Ross County, Ohio.
February 28, 1849	McDougal arrived in San Francisco on the *California*.
1849	McDougal went to mines and managed his brother's store at Sutterville.
April, 1849	McDougal elected by Sacramento District voters to a commission to frame laws for that area.
September, 1849	McDougal served as a delegate from Sacramento to the Constitutional Convention at Monterey.
November 13, 1849	McDougal elected first Lieutenant Governor.
December 20, 1849	McDougal became first President of the California Senate.
January 9, 1851	McDougal succeeded Peter Burnett as Governor.
May 19, 1851	McDougal sought unsucessfully Democratic nomination as Governor.
August 24, 1851	McDougal clashed with First Vigilance Committee of San Francisco.
January 8, 1852	State capital moved to Vallejo.
January 12, 1852	McDougal fought duel with A. C. Russell.
July 19, 1854	McDougal presided at convention of the southern wing of the state Democratic party.
October, 1856	McDougal arrested, but acquitted of election fraud.
March 30, 1866	McDougal died in San Francisco.

John McDougal

2ND GOVERNOR—INDEPENDENT DEMOCRAT
BORN: 1818   DIED: MARCH 30, 1866
TERM OF OFFICE: JANUARY 9, 1851—JANUARY 7, 1852

JOHN MCDOUGAL WAS BORN in early 1818 into a destitute family in Ross County, Ohio. At a young age he had left home to work in a dry goods store; later he accompanied his family in a move to Indianapolis. He saw service in the Black Hawk War while but fourteen. In 1841 he was appointed a superintendent of the Indiana state prison at Jeffersonville. The year, 1846, was an eventful one for McDougal. He married, and following the outbreak of the Mexican War, he was elected first lieutenant of an Indiana volunteer company. He later advanced to rank of captain and served throughout the war. McDougal's regiment, attached to General Winfield Scott's command, saw action from Vera Cruz to Mexico City. Following the war, he returned to Indianapolis where he learned that his brother, George, had become a successful merchant in the Sacramento area. Determined to take his family to California, he secured passage from New Orleans for Panama, leaving December 18, 1848. While in New Orleans, the McDougals and their fellow passengers learned of the California gold discovery. From Panama the McDougals were able to secure passage on the *California* which brought the first gold seekers from the east to San Francisco, arriving February 28, 1849.

Upon arrival, McDougal, like most men, headed for the gold fields but was not successful as a gold-seeker. For a brief period he transported supplies to the miners. Willing to extend credit, he made many friends who later supported him in his campaign for lieutenant governor. He returned to Sutterville to manage his brother's store while George McDougal returned to the east coast. Attempting to corner the miners' trade, John

McDougal advertised that he would sell merchandise at cost. The Sacramento merchants joined together to meet this threat and by underselling forced the closing of the McDougal store.

In April, 1849, John McDougal was elected by the voters of the Sacramento District to a board of fourteen commissioners which framed a code of laws and suggested proper officials to govern the district. In the summer of 1849, he was elected a delegate from the Sacramento District to the constitutional convention meeting at Monterey. McDougal was then thirty-two years old.

At first his right to a seat was disputed, but on September 8, 1849, he was sworn in as a delegate. McDougal took part in two major arguments—the state boundary and the admission of Negroes to the state. As chairman of the boundary committee, he first proposed that the eastern boundary of California be the 105th meridian. For some unexplained reason, he quickly changed his mind, however, and announced that the proper boundary seemed to be the Sierra Nevada. He suggested that annexing the entire Mexican Cession would lead Congress to reject California's statehood request. He assumed that convention delegates with southern sympathies wanted a larger California so as to leave the question of slavery in abeyance.

Although the constitution in its final form prohibited slavery, some delegates demanded further assurances. Many wanted the Negro race excluded completely from California. This view was later advanced by Burnett while he was governor. John McDougal was cautious at the convention concerning the slavery question. He expressed fear that slaveholders might free their slaves in the South, binding them to a contract to come to California to work in the mines for their former owners. He proposed that the first legislature should create laws prohibiting the introduction of any Negro or mulatto who had been a slave, under bonds of indenture. Although his amendment was rejected by the convention, McDougal still felt that many slaveholders would be pleased to emancipate their slaves in order to receive free labor in the gold fields. He had no apparent concern, as did other delegates, about the influx of free Negroes into the state.

Based on his recent experience in the Mexican War, McDougal made some observations regarding state militias. He thought it regrettable that field officers could be elected by the men since officers incapable of performing their duties were often selected. He suggested that while company officers should be elected by the men, the higher ranks of the militia should receive appointments from the governor or the head of the corps. With tongue in cheek, he suggested the convention might well examine New York's constitution on this subject, as he said, "I think it certainly the best and the most complete— particularly as my great grandfather was born in New York."

McDougal opposed the constitutional proposal that dueling would lead to the loss of the right to vote and to hold office. As a result of a duel he later fought, his thoughts on the subject at the convention proved interesting. He observed that those men who chose to stand face to face and shoot it out were doing mankind a great benefit by eliminating themselves from society and the world. He stated, "Such a class of men are not wanted here. Let them take their own course and we will get rid of them sooner."

McDougal irritated some delegates with his sense of humor and on several occasions received sharp rebukes. He in return made some rather pointed jabs at his fellow delegates. As the convention was closing, he expressed the hope that "this House has originality enough about it to form a message of its own, without referring to New York, or any other state. I desire to see in this Constitution a few lines at least of our own manufacture." He had reference to the fact that other state constitutions were being used as models for the California constitution.

While he did introduce many resolutions, subsequently rejected, one important one was passed. It stated that the money collected as duty on foreign goods, which constituted the Civil Fund, be returned to the state. This resolution led to a long standing controversy between the state and the federal government.

Although not a dominant personality at the convention, McDougal contributed significant ideas. His freely stated opinions had an impact on the final phrasing of various sections of the constitution. The *Daily Alta California* related that he was the "author and framer of many of the most important provisions." Elisha O. Crosby, a fellow delegate, agreed that he was something of a working member, but that his effectiveness was weakened by excessive drinking.

Following the conclusion of the convention, John McDougal successfully ran for lieutenant governor. He received a vote of 7,374 which was the largest number of votes cast for any candidate running for state office in the first election.

John McDougal gained friends easily. This trait was reflected in part by his success at the 1849 polls. Those who knew him described him as having superior natural talents and an extremely sociable and companionable disposition.

Coming to the office of lieutenant governor at the age of thirty-two, he had behind him already an active and varied career. As presiding officer of the Senate at San Jose he demonstrated good judgment, fine conversational powers and a cultivated mind. He rode a wave of high popularity during 1850 and the first few months of 1851.

The key blow to his political life came in 1851, when the Democrats chose Bigler over McDougal to be the standard-bearer. He contributed to his eventual downfall by standing firm against various vigilance committees of 1851. He also impaired his effectiveness through constant use of alcohol. His contemporaries frequently remarked that his drinking destroyed his political career.

Inaugurated lieutenant governor on December 20, 1849, he thanked the voters for their support and promised to try to merit their confidence. There were no great demands upon his time during the first session. In fact, on April 15, he notified the Senate that he would be absent for the rest of the session and complimented it on its work. The Senate responded in kind, unlike its treatment of Governor Burnett. The *Daily Alta California* commented that McDougal had been an able presiding officer.

With Burnett's resignation in January, 1851, John McDougal became the second governor. Several important gains were made during his year as the state's chief executive. The legislature enacted laws regulating proceedings in both criminal and civil cases which endured some twenty years without amendment. An important law, the homestead act, advocated first by Burnett, exempted from forced sale the homestead and other properties in settlement of a judgment. One act, resulting in considerable controversy during John Bigler's administration, granted tidal water lots to the city of San Francisco for ninety-nine years.

During McDougal's tenure, state institutions were created to care for the sick and the criminals. In San Francisco the State Marine Hospital, created by legislative action in April, 1851, opened its doors on July 1. The hospital treated not only marine patients but also served as the city hospital for San Francisco. State hospitals were also erected at Stockton and Sacramento for the dual purpose of caring for the sick and the mentally ill. The two inland institutions were designed to care for the people in the mining areas while the one in San Francisco ministered to those arriving by ship.

In April, 1851, the legislature enacted the granting of a ten year contract to Mariano G. Vallejo and James M. Estell to provide a prison for the state's criminals. A board of state prison inspectors was created to oversee terms of the contract. Governor McDougal during his one year in office proved more generous than Burnett as he granted eighteen pardons and commuted one sentence.

One pressing problem facing all early governors was recurring Indian wars. Although the state militia was available to protect the state's citizens, the early governors held that protection from Indian raids should be furnished by federal troops. McDougal in special messages to the legislature lamented the lack of federal assistance in the matter. He noted that the first legislature had made no provisions for protecting citizens other than calling out the militia. However, no plans had been made to pay, arm, and supply those citizen soldiers called to duty, and in four campaigns the cost had been borne by the fighters. The second legislature agreed with the governor and enacted a measure authorizing him to call out troops to defend the state's frontiers and providing for compensation for militia duty.

On April 25, 1851, the governor reported an irregularity in the office of Quartermaster-General. General Joseph C. Morehead had sold 400 muskets and 90,000 cartridges without authority and had pocketed the money. McDougal requested legislation empowering the state to pursue and arrest Morehead or to establish a reward for his capture. Morehead had planned to use the proceeds and some of the weapons to equip a filibustering raid to Mexico. He barely escaped arrest in San Diego on his way to an ill-fated venture. Morehead had the dubious distinction of being the first state official known to misuse the trust placed in him.

Governor McDougal and the legislature had only minor difficulties over his use of the veto power. He vetoed five bills and was sustained twice. Of these two, one measure, reworked, gained his signature. In general, there were only differences of opinion concerning interpretation of the intended acts and the legislature considered McDougal's views as incorrect.

During the 1851 session, the *Daily Alta California,* assessing McDougal's ability as governor, felt that he had been both able and popular. The San Jose correspondent referred to him as a Jeffersonian Democrat with the ability to make friends and keep them. The reporter stated, "I presume that at this moment there is no man in the state who possesses more personal friends than John McDougal." The same journal wrote in April that McDougal had a good chance for renomination. However, in May, the Democratic convention nominated John Bigler on the sixth ballot.

In the spring of 1851, McDougal began to lose popularity as he utilized his power to grant reprieves. He did so at a time when local citizen groups were either on the verge of taking the law into their own hands or actually doing so. When he granted a reprieve to a man who had killed a prominent Napa citizen in order that a hearing could be held before the California State Supreme Court, the Napa citizens hanged the governor in effigy. In May, when the governor commuted the sentence from death to life imprisonment, the prisoner was removed from jail by a mob and hanged.

His reputation was further damaged by his stand against the First Vigilance Committee of 1851, organized in San Francisco in June of that year. On July 23, McDougal issued a proclamation deploring the formation of such a committee, and asked for cooperation between the vigilantes and the elected authorities. When the Vigilance Committee condemned Robert McKenzie and Samuel Whittaker, two criminals, to die on August 20, open conflict between the committee and the regularly constituted authorities developed. McDougal learned of the planned execution on August 19, and hastened to San Francisco where he and the mayor secured a warrant for the immediate release of the prisoners. Together with the sheriff, the two went to the hall of the committee and seized the prisoners. McDougal issued a proclamation condemning the actions of the vigilantes in defiance of the constitution and for assumption of the power of the courts. On August 20, he called upon the citizens to resist such activities and to place full confidence in the elected authorities. The *Daily Alta California* commented that it was too late for the governor to make such a statement and that in doing so he appeared only in a ridiculous and indefensible position. The committee, on August 24, openly defied the governor by recapturing and hanging the two men. McDougal was powerless to retaliate.

As the governor lost control in San Francisco, the Sacramento citizens unlashed their wrath against him. McDougal had reprieved a man tried, convicted, and sentenced for highway robbery. When word of the reprieve reached Sacramento, "the people took the man and hung him up between Heaven and Earth," according to the *Daily Alta California*. A letter, sent from a mass protest meeting, called upon McDougal to resign. The letter noted that "the mantle of office cannot fall on one less worthy."

The third session of the legislature met in 1852 at the new state capital, Vallejo. Governor McDougal's protest that San Jose was still the permanent seat of government was tabled. McDougal sent his only annual message to this legislature. He called particular attention to the unfair tax burden placed upon the southern agricultural counties. These counties, with 4 percent of the population, paid 66 percent of the state taxes. He called for a convention to revise the constitution and to discuss the governmental inadequacies that had come to light. While the Assembly concurred with his views, the Senate did not. Out of this controversy grew a movement to divide the state.

He suggested that the legislature adopt practical ways of disposing of public lands. Speaking of swamp lands, he felt that these could be well utilized by the Chinese who were "one of the most worthy classes of our newly adopted citizens—to whom the climate and character of these lands are peculiarly suited." Regarding immigration he declared that some surveillance should be established at the ports of entry to exclude foreign criminals, the cause of much of the lawlessness in San Francisco. The third legislature, following Governor Bigler's lead, rejected any friendly attitude toward the Chinese. Legislation was enacted controlling incoming passengers who might be criminals.

McDougal adhered to the popular contemporary notion regarding California's Indian problem. Claiming that Andrew Jackson had been right in removing the Indians from the eastern states, the governor suggested that the 200,000 Indians in California be removed.

McDougal contended, too, that a federal mint should be established in California to coin gold dust to offset the great flow of gold from the state. He urged establishment of a public school system and stressed the necessity for a state university. Although Vallejo and Estell had a contract to manage state convicts, McDougal found need to construct a state prison. In discussing finances, he demanded that the 3 percent bonds be redeemed at an early date and that the legislature find means to defray current expenses and overcome past indebtedness. Acts providing for a system of common schools and a state prison were passed in 1852. Both Bigler and the legislature agreed with McDougal on the 3 percent bonds.

While the legislature was considering the 1851 election returns, it received from Governor McDougal a message stating, *"Gentlemen,* I hereby tender my resignation as Governor of California. John McDougal." He offered no reason for this unusual action. It was not accepted and later the message was ordered struck from the journal. McDougal always maintained that this resignation had made Senator David Broderick governor for one day.

Following his term as governor, McDougal returned to San Francisco where he challenged Andrew C. Russell, editor of the *Picayune,* to a duel for a newspaper account heaping abuse upon him and his abilities as governor. Russell accepted the challenge and the duel took place on the San Jose Road in Santa Clara County early in the morning. McDougal's shot glanced off the butt of Russell's pistol into the editor's chest, wounding him slightly. Russell felt that satisfaction had been gained and the affair ended. Later in 1851, McDougal challenged Edward C. Kemble, editor of the *Daily Alta California,* to a duel for his treatment of the governor. As the two men faced each other on the field, authorities arrested them and the affair ended.

McDougal became a party hack in Democratic circles. He was one of two men nominated for president of the state Democratic convention of 1854, and in the resulting chaos and party split, presided over the southern, or chivalry, wing of the party. In 1856, he was arrested for alleged election frauds in San Mateo County. He was accused of double voting, but was quickly acquitted of the charge by a jury.

McDougal in later life became an addicted alcoholic. Governor Frederick Low said that McDougal was a drunkard whose talents had been drowned in whiskey. Heavy drinking finally affected his mind and during the last two years of his life he was apparently mentally ill. In October, 1865, he attempted suicide because he thought he was dying of an incurable disease. He was suffering from a kidney ailment from which he seemed to be recovering when he died of apoplexy in San Francisco on March 30, 1866. He was forty-eight years of age.

Opinions regarding his ability as governor have been influenced and perhaps prejudiced by his addiction. The *San Francisco Chronicle* in 1898 has given perhaps the fairest estimate when it stated that he was not a bad governor nor was he particularly a good one.

John McDougal introduced some important ideas to the legislature. He stood firm on the principle of legally constituted authority and as a result became involved in difficulties with vigilance committees throughout the state. McDougal had only a brief career as the state's chief executive. He left office with no certain career in sight while having gained the enmity of many of his contemporaries for standing firm in face of opposition. McDougal has been underestimated to a degree because he was overshadowed by Gwin, Broderick, and Bigler. Finally, he has not been treated fairly by defenders of the vigilantes and by historians who have confused his career and life with that of Senator James A. McDougall.

BIBLIOGRAPHY

MANUSCRIPTS

Bigger, Samuel, "Governor's Papers," (Archives Division, Indiana State Library).

Bowman, J.N., "The Early Governors of California. . ."

Crosby, Elisha O., "Statement of Events in California," (Bancroft Library).

McDougal, John, "Letters from the Governor," (California State

Archives).
Norris, T.W., "Collection," (Bancroft Library).
Reading, Pearson B., "Letters," (California Section, State Library).

CONTEMPORARY ACCOUNTS
Assembly Journal, 2nd-3rd Sess., 1851-52.
Senate Journal, 1st-3rd Sess., 1849-52.
Ayers, James J., *Gold and Sunshine: Reminiscences of Early California* (Boston, 1922).
Barker, Charles A., *Memoirs of Elisha Oscar Crosby.*
Browne, J. Ross, *Report of the Debates in the Convention of California.*
First Steamship Pioneers (San Francisco, 1874).

SECONDARY SOURCES
Bancroft, H.H., *Chronicles of the Builders. . .*
————, *History of California.*
————, *Popular Tribunals* (2 vols., San Francisco, 1887).
Davis, W.J., *History of Political Conventions. . .*
Ellison, W.H., *A Self-governing Dominion. . .*
Goodwin, C., *The Establishment of State Government in California . . .*
Hittell, T.H., *History of California.*
Melendy, H. Brett, "Who Was John McDougal?" *Pacific Historical Review*, XXIX (1960), 231-243.
Morse, John F., *The First History of Sacramento. . .*
Pickett, Barbara, "The Life of John McDougal, the second Governor of California," (Typescript, California Section, State Library, 1939).
Shuck, Oscar T., *Historical Abstract of San Francisco* (3 vols., San Francisco, 1897).
Stewart, George R., *Committee of Vigilance: Revolution in San Francisco, 1851* (Boston, 1964).
Williams, Mary Floyd, *History of the San Francisco Committee of Vigilance of 1851* (Berkeley, 1921).
———— ed., *Papers of the San Francisco Committee of Vigilance of 1851* (Berkeley, 1919).

NEWSPAPERS
Daily Alta California, March 3, 1851, has sketch of McDougal's life; April 24, 1851, gives estimate of McDougal as governor; July 23, 1851, criticizes his proclamation against vigilantes; March 31, 1866, has his obituary.
Sacramento Union, Oct. 1, 1856, McDougal arrested for election fraud, but acquitted, Oct. 19, 1856; March 31, 1866, reported his death.
San Francisco Bulletin, March 31, 1866, has his obituary.
San Francisco Call, Sept. 4, 1886, has history of McDougal family.

OTHER SOURCES
Hayes, Benjamin I., "Scrapbooks, California Politics," Vol. I (Bancroft Library).
————, "Scrapbooks, California Notes," Vols. III & V (Bancroft Library).

Capitol at San Jose, 1849-1851. Standing on what is today marked as an historical landmark in the 100 block in South Market Street in San Jose, was the "State House," or what is generally considered the first capitol in California. It was a large adobe structure, originally built as a hotel. The upper story was occupied by the Assembly, and the largest of four rooms in the lower story by the Senate. The building was destroyed by fire on April 29, 1853.

Calendar of Events

January 8, 1805	Bigler born near Carlisle, Pennsylvania.
August 31, 1849	Bigler arrived in Sacramento.
November 13, 1849	Bigler ran for seat in the Assembly.
December 20, 1849	Bigler seated in Assembly after contesting the election.
January 10, 1850	Bigler elected Speaker pro-tem.
January 8, 1852	Bigler inaugurated Governor.
January 16, 1852	State government moved to Sacramento for the legislative session.
April, 1852	Bigler launched anti-Chinese agitation.
January 11, 1853	State government moved from Vallejo to Benicia for legislative session.
September 7, 1853	Bigler won second term, defeating William Waldo.
February 25, 1854	Legislature named Sacramento to be permanent capital.
June 29, 1855	Democrats nominated Bigler for a third term.
September 5, 1855	J. Neely Johnson defeated Bigler in the general election.
April 21, 1857	President Buchanan appointed Bigler Minister to Chile.
September, 1863	Bigler, Democratic nominee for a seat in the House of Representatives, defeated in general election.
October, 1866	President Johnson appointed Bigler Federal Assessor of Internal Revenue for the Sacramento District.
January, 1867	U.S. Senate refused to confirm Bigler's appointment.
October, 1867	President Johnson appointed Bigler as a railroad commissioner to inspect the Central Pacific railroad.
November 29, 1871	Bigler died in Sacramento.

John Bigler

3RD GOVERNOR—DEMOCRAT
BORN: JANUARY 8, 1805   DIED: NOVEMBER 29, 1871
TERM OF OFFICE: JANUARY 8, 1852—JANUARY 9, 1856

JOHN BIGLER, CALIFORNIA'S FIRST two-term governor, was born near Carlisle, Pennsylvania, January 8, 1805, where he grew up on a farm. He entered Dickinson College but was compelled to leave before graduating when the family moved to Mercer County north of Pittsburgh. Bigler was apprenticed to a Pittsburgh printer and upon expiration of his term in 1827, he moved to Bellefonte, Centre County to edit the *Centre County Democrat* until 1832. He next studied law and was admitted to the bar in 1840, practicing first in Pennsylvania and then in Mount Sterling, Illinois. On April 2, 1849, he left Mount Sterling with his wife and daughter, traveling overland to Sacramento and arriving there August 31. Finding no opportunity for a lawyer, he turned to odd jobs, serving as assistant to an auctioneer, cutting wood, making calico bed comforters, and working as a stevedore on the Sacramento docks.

In the first state election of 1849, John Bigler was a candidate for the Assembly for the Sacramento District. When the legislature convened, he contested the election of his opponent, W. B. Dickenson, and a special committee on contested elections found that two precincts, sending in late returns, had not been included in the totals. The recount showed Bigler the winner by fifty-six votes. The Assembly accepted the findings and Bigler took his seat. Early in the session, he was elected Speaker pro-tem. At the second session of the Assembly, 1851, Bigler, elected Speaker, proved to be an able legislative leader and one of the bright lights in the emerging state Democratic party.

In May, 1851, at Benicia, Bigler won his party's nomination for governor at its first state convention as he defeated incumbent John McDougal and five other candidates on the sixth ballot. In the September general election he polled 22,613 votes while Pearson B. Reading, the Whig candidate, received 21,531. This margin of only 1,082 votes led to the charges of election fraud. The Whigs contended that county returns had not been properly sent to the Speaker of the Assembly. The legislature, after investigation, declared Bigler elected.

Bigler was renominated in April, 1853, for a second term and in the September general election he polled 38,090 votes to William Waldo's 37,454. Bigler's margin this time was only 636 over his Whig opponent. Again charges of election irregularity were leveled since thirteen counties had not sent official returns to the Speaker. A legislative committee visited the secretary of state for a check of the informal county returns. Although Waldo had a lead in these counties, Bigler still received a majority and was declared re-elected. Thus he became the only man in the nineteenth century to be returned for a second term.

Since this election was also disputed, a legislative joint committee in 1854, dominated by Democrats, investigated the two elections of 1851 and 1853. Its report indicated that there was not sufficient evidence to show fraud in 1851 and that the 1853 returns in the files of the secretary of state showed no alterations.

John Bigler took his oath of office as governor at Vallejo on January 8, 1852. In his first inaugural address, he intimated that "the fewer and plainer the laws by which a people are governed, the better." Calling attention to the Compromise of 1850, he asserted that the federal constitution must be upheld. Joining the national debate on the structure of the union, he said, "In union consists our national being; with it we must stand or fall, and the day which writes its epitaph will sound the dirge of American glory and renown."

The governor sent three special messages to the 1852 legislature which reflected the major policies of his two administrations: the plight of state finances, help for agriculture, extension of the San Francisco water front under state control, and the restriction of Chinese immigration. The 1852 session saw considerable unanimity between the executive and the legislature.

Perhaps the greatest problem facing Governor Bigler, as with Burnett and McDougal, was state finance. That the governor was worried about the solvency of California was seen in his first special message to the legislature in January, 1852. The state had, he claimed, to solve the matter of raising revenue, of meeting its obligations, and establishing its credit on a permanent and sure basis. He felt that the existing system of issuing bonds was detrimental and advised issuance of comptroller's warrants to be receivable for debts incurred by the state. He advised careful and complete revision of the revenue system and the enactment of more stringent provisions to secure greater tax collections, noting that some counties had yet to pay one cent of tax money into the state treasury.

Taxes, he maintained, should not become burdensome and should be levied only to meet minimum governmental expenses. The legislature enacted laws granting the comptroller the right to sue county treasurers who failed to collect and turn in tax money and funding the 1851 and 1852 state debt. It also enacted legislation for the redemption of all outstanding 3 percent bonds, a major continual drain on state financial resources.

Bigler's first annual message in 1853 advocated constitutional reform to decrease the cost of state government, curtailment of institutional services, and the selling of waterfront lots to help solve the fiscal emergency. He took up McDougal's burden, demanding that the legislature petition Congress to settle the matter of the Civil Fund, amounting to about $250,000, as one important way to reduce the state debt.

Bigler's second inaugural message of 1854 reiterated the principles which had guided him in his first term. He urged the legislature to liquidate the state debt by "devising a thorough system of retrenchment and reform."

His 1855 annual message indicated great improvement as he reported that only six other states were in better financial condition. California's debt had been reduced some $1,700,000 since December, 1853. Bigler hoped that expenditures could be adjusted to income, thus ending the tax of 30 cents on the dollar. Recognizing that the failure of the state to pay cash on demand was an unhappy situation for all in the state's

employment while additional delays in payment of state warrants would cause further depreciation, he suggested during the
sixth session in 1855 that the legislature fund all outstanding
civil warrants and that these be numbered to be paid in order
of registry. The legislature, in agreement, funded this debt
for the years 1853 through 1855.

Throughout his two terms, Bigler advocated economy in
government and yet costs steadily increased. His political opponents made much of this fact, overlooking the expansion of
state services. Bigler remained sincerely concerned about the
problem of indebtedness and did what he could to reduce it.

During his second administration, the governor devoted much
attention to escheated estates as a revenue source for education as decreed by the constitution. In March, 1854, he asked
the legislature to take the necessary steps to gain possession of
the Leidesdorff estate. In 1855, he again called for action in
this case and two others, noting that their total valuation was
about three million dollars. The legislature followed his lead,
enacting regulations for such estates.

Bigler in 1853 attempted to tie reduction of the state debt
with the extension of beach and water lot property in San
Francisco which brought charges of corruption and favoritism
against him. Although an act of 1851 had released this property to the city, Bigler felt that the city had not lived up to its
obligations. He proposed that the city limits be extended into
the bay and additional lots be provided under state control with
proceeds from sales to go to the state treasury. He thought such
sales would reduce the state debt by about two million dollars.
During the fourth session in 1853, Bigler stressed in a special
message the right of eminent domain and the need to provide
for an expanding waterfront to keep pace with growing commerce. Many San Franciscans violently opposed the extension
idea claiming that street grades would have to be re-established
and that the harbor would be destroyed.

In his 1854 annual message, Bigler maintained that the
state had to dispose of its remaining beach and water lots as
previous titles had not been properly confirmed and the state
had received but little income. He demanded that back payments be made and again urged his extension plan as the
means of wiping out the debt and providing a surplus. Responding to his request, the Assembly passed an extension bill

but the Senate adjourned without considering it. In 1855, he tried to revive his plan but the legislature refused to act.

John Bigler considered himself a champion of small farmers, and while governor, offered several recommendations on their behalf. While his own political career seemed influenced by Democrats of the Tammany wing, Bigler expressed many views consistent with Jeffersonian Democracy. His first inaugural address and his first special message urged promotion of agricultural interests by opening up state lands. He believed that the Spanish and Mexican land grants had retarded preemption and donation to actual settlers. Bigler, in these messages, became the first governor to advocate irrigation as one solution to the development of the arid regions.

Defending land preemptors in his 1854 annual message, Bigler said that honest settlers had made errors in locating preemption claims and that in such cases where honest mistakes had occurred, some compensation should be made for the improvements. He also urged the legislature to demand free land from the federal government for farmers instead of the existing price of $1.25 an acre and he insisted that the state quickly qualify for swamp and reclaimed lands. Reviewing the condition of agriculture in 1854, he noted that California possessed flourishing vineyards and he hoped some day that it would be famous for fine wines.

In Bigler's first term, public education was established although he objected to the superintendent of public instruction being an elected official. During the fourth and fifth legislative sessions, he called attention to the need of a seminary for teachers and suggested that the lands of Mission San Luis Rey be designated the location of a southern branch of such an institution. Much to his astonishment, the 1854 legislature defeated bills relating to school lands acquisitions and seminary lands.

The governor, having made the overland trek to California himself, long had expressed interest in the well being of emigrants and the need for better means of transportation. In 1852, in a special message to the third session, he requested that help be advanced to aid emigrants despite the strain it would place on state finances. He asked for an immediate allocation of $15,000 and added that, while the state could not afford this expense, those aided would, in time, help solve the tax burden as taxpayers. Always the specter of the state debt loomed before Bigler as he attempted to solve immediate pressing problems. The legislature granted the allocation, but a controversy developed in the 1853 session over the handling of these funds and over the requests for reimbursement of those who had used their own money. The equipment and records had been burned in a Sacramento fire leaving only the verbal testimony of the governor and the commissioners. Earlier, in July, 1852, Edward Gilbert, editor of the *Daily Alta California,* charged that Bigler had used the relief train, which carried aid to the emigrants, for personal political gain. James W. Denver and the nine other agents of the train objected to the tenor of Gilbert's articles. In a series of letters, Gilbert demanded that Denver retract his offensive statements and Denver demanded that the articles defaming Bigler be retracted. On August 1, Gilbert challenged Denver to a duel outside of Sacramento. The fight took place the next day and the editor was killed.

Bigler wanted a wagon road built through the Sierra Nevada for both freight and emigrant purposes. He requested in 1855 that the legislature petition Congress to build a series of forts for the protection of emigrants and for an eventual stage route. From his first year as governor, Bigler also showed keen interest in a transcontinental railroad.

Although Bigler favored emigration from eastern states, he was the first governor to attack Chinese immigration. In April, 1852, in a special message he declared that wholesale immigration of coolie or contract labor was a danger to the prosperity and tranquility of the state. Anti-Chinese sentiment was then sweeping over the state. Bigler held that immigration must be limited to the Caucasian race. He believed the Chinese were incapable of becoming good citizens. To stop the human flood from China, he advocated that the legislature exercise taxing power to check unlimited immigration and petition Congress for a law prohibiting the shipping of Chinese to the gold mines. He held that his advocacy of restriction was one of the most important duties he would perform as governor. Although a Senate committee reported agreement with the governor, nothing was done to exclude the Chinese during his first term. However, a foreign miners' tax was enacted.

In 1855, he again took up the problem, insisting that the state had a right to regulate immigration. He asked for a head tax on Asiatic immigration to serve both as a check against the Chinese and as revenue for the state treasury. The legislature took the first step toward restriction by enacting a $50 tax on all immigrants who could not become citizens.

Governor Bigler shared Burnett's and McDougal's views regarding the California Indians. He presented a two-fold program to the legislature demanding that the Indians be removed from the state and that the federal government bear the expense of equipping the state militia for Indian wars. In his first 1852 special message Bigler objected to the federal policy of settling Indians on reservations, claiming it deprived settlers of good farm land. In his 1854 annual message he reiterated McDougal's views about Indian removal and lamented that the federal idea of keeping Indians in the state led to conflict between whites and the Indians. At that moment, Indians were on the warpath in the northern counties. During the fifth session he approved an act prohibiting sale of arms and ammunition to Indians and chastised the legislature for its lack of action on the whole problem.

The Indian war debt, first reported by Governor McDougal, developed because of the federal government's inability to supply sufficient troops to check Indian resistance. Time after time the state had to absorb the cost of calling out the militia. By 1855, the federal government agreed to pay $924,259.65 of the debt if the state would furnish proper statements of expenditures. After a lengthy correspondence with the Secretary of War, John C. Calhoun, Bigler refused to forward archival materials, and the federal government withheld payment.

California's third governor was faced with certain administrative problems such as the location of the state capital, a prison, hospitals, and constitutional revision. The location of the capital caused considerable furor during Bigler's tenure. Soon after his inauguration in Vallejo, it was apparent that this site was inadequate for the needs of state government. The legislature with Bigler's concurrence adjourned to meet in Sacramento for the third session in 1852. The fourth session met again in Vallejo but shortly adjourned to Benicia. During the fifth session, 1854, held at Benicia, Bigler approved the act making Sacramento the permanent seat of government. His 1855 annual message urged the erection of permanent buildings at the new capital.

The proper policy of the state regarding convicts and the state prison developed into a raging controversy that lasted through Bigler's administration and beyond. The legislature had approved an act in May, 1852, to construct a prison but in the final enrollment of that act the upper limit on expenditures had been left out. Bigler signed this open ended bill and thus made himself liable to the charge of corruption by his opposition. The governor responded that his sole duty had been to see that the contract went to the lowest bidder and it had. An act prepared the way in May, 1853, for actual construction at an estimated cost of $100,000. This guess fell short by $53,000.

Bigler announced in 1854 that the building was ready for immediate use. General James Estell still had his ten year contract to care for prisoners in exchange for their labor. Estell found that he was losing money and asked the legislature in 1855 to release him from the contract. The lawmakers agreed but Bigler vetoed the measure. Estell had posted a $100,000 bond guaranteeing performance of the contract of 1851. The legislature had approved instead paying to Estell $100,000 in state bonds at 7 percent interest and an additional $50,000 for improvements made at San Quentin. The governor held that Estell had not abided by the terms of the contract and should forfeit the bond instead of being paid. He noted that additional fiscal burden would be placed upon already inadequate state resources. His veto of this measure was upheld.

Estell protested the veto. He announced the prison was full and that he would not accept additional prisoners and certify their safekeeping. He stated that he could not continue with the contract for, with publication of the veto message, his creditors had attached his property. On the last day of the 1855 legislative session, Bigler relented and signed a measure providing for state operation of the prison.

As chief executive, Governor Bigler used his pardoning power seventy-one times, granting reprieves and commuting sentences. In April, 1852, he wrote a letter to the Monterey County District Attorney which showed Bigler's concern for the ordinary people of the state. A Mexican woman, Rosa Avila, was to have a fine remitted by a Justice of the Peace as ordered by an 1852 executive order. It was not done and Bigler wrote, "Rosa Avila, though a humble member of the community, is entitled to the protection of the laws of the state; and as the officer named has refused to obey an Executive order. . . ." he hoped that the district attorney would take appropriate action.

During Bigler's tenure, the state hospital system was reorganized, primarily for economy but also to differentiate the functions of the existing institutions at San Francisco, Sacramento, and Stockton. Prior to 1852, all institutions admitted the mentally ill, but in May, 1852, the legislature converted the Stockton State Hospital into an insane asylum with all mental patients, totaling 124, transferred there. In 1853, the existing state general hospital system was abolished and the county hospital plan was established. The State Marine Hospital at San Francisco was continued but the Sacramento hospital was closed. Bigler noted in 1854 that while the Marine Hospital was a state agency, 62 percent of the patients were wards of San Francisco, and that city reaped financial benefits since the amount paid per patient did not cover expenses. By the close of the 1854 session, he commented that the state hospitals cost too much. In 1855, he approved bills bringing to an end the State Marine Hospital, leaving the state with one insane asylum and transferring the care of the sick to the counties.

Throughout his two terms, Bigler reiterated his view that the governor could only recommend needed reforms, but that it was the responsibility of the legislature to act. He repeatedly claimed that it was the legislature's duty to reduce public expenditure and taxation. One important way that this could be done, he felt, was by amending the constitution. In his 1853 annual message, he advocated some specific revisions. He asked for biennial, instead of annual, legislative sessions lasting not more than ninety days. He asked that the constitutional demand for a state census be repealed. He opposed the required census of 1855 as a luxury that the state could not afford. He wanted the office of superintendent of public instruction eliminated and the office of surveyor-general changed from an elective to an appointive position. He suggested elimination of the printing of revisions of acts or sections of laws prior to actual passage. He finally suggested that the fiscal year begin December 15 instead of July 1 so that when the legislature met there would be a clearer picture of the current financial situation. In addition to these revisions, Bigler thought the legislature should abolish the office of superintendent of public buildings, reduce the number of judicial districts, eliminate state prison directors, and reduce salaries of state officials while paying on a cash basis. He held that these recommendations would save the state about $512,700 annually.

An Assembly select committee agreed with the governor on biennial sessions, reduction of judicial districts, elimination of certain state officials, and abandonment of the 1855 census. Although the committee agreed the basic problem was one of state debt, its solution advocated a measure calling for voters to decide whether there should be a second constitutional convention—but this measure never worked its way through the legislative mill. A Senate select committee returned a majority report and two minority reports on constitutional revision. All three rejected the governor's views as well as disagreeing with each other.

Bigler in his 1854 message again asked for constitutional reform, adding two more ideas to his earlier proposals. He thought that any proposal for constitutional change should be submitted to the vote of the people for which there was no proviso in the existing constitution. He also stated that he saw no need for Spanish translations of the legislative journals.

Actual administrative changes made during his tenure were few. The offices of state prison directors and the superintendent of public buildings were abolished. There was no change in salaries with Bigler receiving—as had his predecessors—$10,000 annually as governor.

His fourth annual message of 1856, delivered after his defeat for a third term, gave an estimate of his success. He reviewed the fiscal difficulties under which the state administration had commenced in 1849 and the tremendous problem of securing adequate funds while abolishing the scrip system. The hope had been for six years that state finances would soon be on a cash basis. While there had been severe drains on the treasury, Bigler stated that California had done well in comparison with other states—only three had a smaller indebtedness.

California's debt had increased $50,728.10 from January, 1852, to December, 1855. But he claimed the unpaid $924,-259.65 due from Congress on the Indian war debt would create a good working balance, yet the federal government was still holding up payment awaiting validation from the California archives. Bigler still refused to send the documents.

California's economy had prospered even though the state government faced financial handicaps. Mining remained the major economic support while agriculture had become a second important enterprise. He repeated his concern for the need of protecting the settler who might be ejected from the land without financial satisfaction for his effort. To entice settlers into the state, he again asked for a chain of forts and a transcontinental railroad. Reflecting Democratic orthodoxy, he advocated that such a railroad be constructed through organized federal territories.

With reference to state services and institutions, he claimed that when he became governor a school system had been authorized but no money had existed in the school fund. During his two terms 221 schools had been established and there was over $500,000 in the school fund, resulting from the sale of school lands. He added that the asylum at Stockton was performing its function and he noted that the state prison with enlarged facilities was now operated for the first time by the state. However, management of these two institutions was greatly criticized by the next gubernatorial administration.

Bigler also commented on his constitutional recommendation had been adopted by the previous legislative session. providing for a direct vote by the people on any new constitution had been adopted by the previous leigslative session. Bigler still urged abolition of certain state offices as being unnecessary. In conclusion, he said that although he had been castigated for many of his actions, he believed that everything he had done had been for the benefit of the state and he was content to let his record as governor speak for itself.

Following the close of his second term, John Bigler returned to the eastern states for his first visit since coming to California. During his absence, his administration was greatly abused by the Whig newspapers and he was accused of being a party hack and a leading figure in schemes of fraud and plunder.

While in the east visiting his brother, William, who had been governor of Pennsylvania, John Bigler campaigned actively for the nomination of James Buchanan for president. (It has been reported that the two Biglers have been the only brothers to hold governorships at the same time.) When Bigler returned to California, he brought with him a commission as Collector of the San Francisco Custom House. In April, 1857, Buchanan appointed him Minister to Chile. Many Californians were happy to see him leave. The *Daily Alta California*, a bitter opponent, wrote its opinion in an article entitled, "Good-by John":

> We understand that John Bigler, who unfortunately for California was Governor of this state for four years, will leave today for Valparaiso. We are exceedingly obliged to Mr. Buchanan for having done us the favor to appoint John Bigler to a foreign mission. May swift winds waft him to the place of his destination and may they always blow him away from these shores. California could spare a great many better men than John Bigler.

Bigler was the first Californian assigned a major position in the United States diplomatic corps. Buchanan paid his political debt to Bigler in this fashion. As Minister to Chile, the former governor performed ably for the United States. While in that country, he also met Henry Meiggs, who had fled from San Francisco for forging city warrants. Bigler helped Meiggs get a second start in life. In time Meiggs became an important railroad builder in the Andes. Years later when Meiggs had become successful, he sent a check to Bigler, acknowledging his debt of gratitude. This check enabled Bigler to build his Sacramento home. With the election of Lincoln to the presidency, Bigler was replaced as minister and he returned to California.

During the sixties, he was active in Democratic political circles. He was one of three Democrats nominated for Congress in 1863, but was soundly defeated. In 1864, he was a state delegate to the national Democratic convention which nominated General George McClellan for the presidency. He was also a delegate to the 1868 national convention.

In October, 1866, President Johnson appointed Bigler to the office of federal assessor of internal revenue for the Sacramento district. The incumbent, however, refused to give up the office and Bigler employed a deputy marshal to take possession. In January, 1867, Bigler was forced to vacate when the United States Senate refused to confirm his appointment. In October, 1867, Johnson appointed him one of the railroad commissioners to examine and pass upon the construction work of the Central Pacific.

In January, 1868, he helped found the *State Capital Reporter*, a newspaper which became the Democratic party's voice in Sacramento. He served as editor until his death at the age of sixty-six on November 29, 1871. He had been ill several months preceding. The cause of death was stated to be dropsy. The third governor was buried in the Sacramento City Cemetery.

Bigler during his life in California championed the cause of people struggling to make a new start in the golden state. He was the particular friend of the settler seeking free farm lands. It was from these groups that Bigler drew his political strength. Both in his private and public life, the governor worked to ameliorate their living conditions. He was one of the early leaders in the movement to establish emigrant stations east of the Sierra Nevada to aid impoverished travelers. During the 1850 Sacramento cholera epidemic which killed many people, Bigler endeared himself to the citizens as he did yeoman service in fighting the disease without regard for his own health. He went everywhere in the city to administer relief to the destitute and suffering people. He carried with him a lump of camphor wrapped in a handkerchief which he pressed to his nostrils in the belief that this would protect him. Dr. John F. Morse in his early history of the city of Sacramento singled out Bigler as the one individual who deserved special mention for his heroic work. During this epidemic, John McDougal almost died from cholera.

Bigler was forty-seven years old when he became governor. Born of Pennsylvania Dutch stock, he was short of stature and tended to be rotund. He had an oval face which reflected an easy going sense of humor. One peculiarity of dress set him apart. He topped off his short physique with a high silk hat which he wore on the back of his head. During his life in California, he proved to be energetic in public office as well as a leader in the Democratic party. Many people remembered him as a devoted party man who was a shrewd politician and a keen judge of men. As a key figure in his party and as governor, Bigler made many enemies but in his personal life he attracted life-long friends from all walks of life.

Governor Bigler was the target of great abuse by the opposition press and has been charged by nineteenth century historians of being a party to great frauds—but none of these claims have

ever been proven. Bigler was the first California governor to
be elected by an organized political party and to face an
organized opposition. Well schooled in the practices of every-
day political maneuvering, he did play politics on some important issues with short-view goals in mind, such as the Chinese
question. He appeared sincere in his effort to make the state
financially solvent, but like his predecessors, he found this
difficult to do. He worked diligently as governor and did his
duty as he saw it. He appeared to be forthright in his ideas and
he made his influence felt. In some instances he was steadfast
to the point of obstinancy which lessened his effectiveness as a
leader. His many proposals to solve the debt problem created
powerful political enemies and many of his suggestions were
consequently sidetracked. Bigler, however, having served a
term in the Assembly, came to the office of governor with a good
understanding of the state's problems.

An estimate of his esteem among fellow Democrats can be
seen by the action of the 1854 legislature when it named the
large lake of the Sierra Nevada, Lake Bigler. The 1870 legislature, when asked to reaffirm this name, rejected it in favor of
Lake Tahoe.

BIBLIOGRAPHY

MANUSCRIPTS
Bigler, John, "Letters," (California Section, State Library).
———, "Letters from the Governor," (California State Archives).
Bowman, J.N., "The Early Governors of California. . ."
Gwin, William, "Memoirs," (Bancroft Library).
Norris, T.W., "Collection," (Bancroft Library).

CONTEMPORARY ACCOUNTS
Assembly Journal, 1st-7th Sess., 1849-1856.
Senate Journal, 3rd-7th Sess., 1852-1856.
Bigler, John, "Address of Gov. Bigler at a public meeting of the
    citizens of Santa Clara" (c.1855).
———, "The Vetoes Vetoed. An Address to the People of California, on
    the Approaching Gubernatorial Election, including a review of the
    Veto Messages of 1855 by Brutus."
"Remarks of the Chinese merchants of San Francisco upon Gov.
    Bigler's message, and some common objections" (San Francisco,
    1855).

SECONDARY SOURCES
Bancroft, H.H., *Chronicles of the Builders. . .*
————, *History of California.*
Davis, W.J., *History of Political Conventions. . .*
Hittell, T.H., *History of California.*
Morse, John F., *The First History of Sacramento. . .*
Sandmeyer, Elmer C., *The Anti-Chinese Movement in California* (Urbana, 1939).
Sherman, William R., *The Diplomatic and Commercial Relations of the United States and Chile, 1820-1914* (Boston, 1926).
Carl Schurz Memorial Foundation Bulletin, II (Oct., 1943), 3.
Shuck, Oscar T., *Representative and Leading Men of the Pacific* (San Francisco, 1870).
Stewart, Watt, *Henry Meiggs, Yankee Pizarro* (Durham, 1946).

NEWSPAPERS
Daily Alta California, Sept. 15, 1853, opposes Bigler's second campaign; Jan. 6, 1854, has editorial comment about his annual message; June 30, 1855, reports Bigler's nomination for third term; July 27, 1857, carries sarcastic article about his appointment as Minister to Chile; Nov. 30, 1871, has his obituary.
Daily California Chronicle, Jan. 5, 1855, reports his annual message.
Northern Independent (Eureka), Feb. 16, 1870, discusses controversy over renaming Lake Bigler as Lake Tahoe.
Sacramento Union, Nov. 30, 1871, has his obituary.
San Francisco Bulletin, Dec. 1, 1871, has his obituary.
San Francisco Call, Sept. 7, 1890, gives estimate of his career.
San Francisco Chronicle, Feb. 6, 1898, gives estimate of Bigler's contribution as governor and all other governors to 1898.
San Francisco Examiner, Dec. 1, 1871, reports death of Bigler.

OTHER SOURCES
Bancroft Scraps, "Educated Men of California: Biographies," (Bancroft Library).
Hayes, Benjamin I., "Scrapbooks, California Notes," Vol. V (Bancroft Library).
————, "Scrapbooks, California Politics," Vol. I (Bancroft Library).
The Pioneer (San Jose), I (Nov. 10, 1877), 2.
"Scrapbook of newspaper clippings, 1856-1860" (California Section, State Library).
Themis, I (Sept. 21, 1889), 1-2.

Calendar of Events

August 2, 1825	Johnson born in Johnson Township, Gibson County, Indiana.
July, 1849	Johnson arrived in Sacramento.
February, 1850	Johnson elected Sacramento City Attorney.
August, 1850	President Fillmore appointed Johnson as special census agent.
June 7, 1852	Johnson served as presiding officer at the California Whig State Convention.
November, 1852	Johnson elected to Assembly from Sacramento.
August 8, 1855	Johnson nominated by the American Party for Governor.
January 9, 1856	Johnson inaugurated Governor.
May-June, 1856	Johnson involved with the Second Vigilance Committee of San Francisco.
1857	Impeachment proceedings were held against State Treasurer Henry Bates and State Comptroller George W. Whitman.
July 29, 1857	Johnson made an unsuccessful bid for renomination by the American Party.
1863	Johnson served as a delegate to first Nevada State Constitutional Convention.
1864	Johnson served as president of second Nevada State Constitutional Convention.
May, 1867	Johnson appointed to Nevada Supreme Court.
August 31, 1872	Johnson died in Salt Lake City.

J. Neely Johnson

4TH GOVERNOR — AMERICAN (KNOW-NOTHING)
BORN: AUGUST 2, 1825   DIED: AUGUST 31, 1872
TERM OF OFFICE: JANUARY 9, 1856—JANUARY 8, 1858

BY 1855, AN ORGANIZED STATE Whig Party had ended and opposition to the incumbent Democratic party was carried on by the American party. Better known as the Know-Nothings, it held its first state convention at Sacramento in 1855, to select candidates for the state offices with J. Neely Johnson, just thirty years old, receiving the gubernatorial nomination.

The campaign of 1855 was particularly hard fought for Democrats had occupied the governor's chair since 1849. The American party's campaign was best presented in the *Southern Californian* of August 29, 1855:

> Our candidate for governor, J. Neely Johnson of Sacramento, is a man every way worthy to lead the ticket in the van of the contest against the dynasty of mis-rule and corruption that is sought to be again fixed upon the people for another gubernatorial term. "Biglerism" which has become a by-word and a synonym of official prostitution and vacillating weakness, will never be "tried on" again, now that the American people who *work* and *pray* are aroused to a sense of their duty.

The American party had overwhelming success, electing its entire ticket of administrative officers. Johnson received 49,078 votes to Bigler's 44,370, giving the Know-Nothing candidate a sizeable margin of 4,708 votes over the Democrat in the latter's third term attempt.

John Neely Johnson was born in Johnson Township, Gibson County, Indiana, August 2, 1825. His father had been a member of General William Henry Harrison's staff and after Indiana's admission as a state, had been state adjutant general and a prominent politician. J. Neely Johnson, as a youth, read law in Evansville, Indiana. At the age of twenty-one he was admitted to the bar at Keokuk, Iowa. He came overland to California in 1849, arriving in Sacramento in July. As Bigler had also discovered, there were no opportunities for lawyers so Johnson drove a mule train between Sacramento and Stockton. After a brief period of mining at Cook's Bar on the Consumnes River, he returned to Sacramento to start a law practice with Ferris Forman.

Johnson's political career was launched in 1850 when he was elected as Sacramento city attorney, and re-elected the following year. In the fall of 1850, he was appointed state agent to lead the relief expedition to meet incoming emigrant trains on the eastern flanks of the Sierra Nevada.

That he had early become a man of political prominence in California was demonstrated by his appointment in August by President Millard Fillmore as special agent to conduct the 1850 census of the Territory of California. Johnson was active in the Whig ranks during that party's existence in California. By 1851, he was one of the prominent Whigs in the state; in that year he presented the resolutions at the state convention. In 1852 and 1854, Johnson was state convention president. In 1853, he was a losing contender for the Whig nomination as attorney-general.

In June, 1851, Johnson married Mary Zabriskie, the daughter of a leading Sacramento family. From this marriage two children were born.

While Johnson was still Sacramento city attorney, Governor McDougal in 1851 appointed him to his own militia staff with the rank of lieutenant colonel. McDougal sent Johnson to accompany Sheriff James Birney in quelling the Indian uprisings in Mariposa County. One inadvertent result of this disturbance was the discovery of Yosemite Valley.

In 1851, Johnson also served as one of the three trustees for the Sacramento State Hospital. During this year, he became involved in a unique fight on the streets of Sacramento that nearly cost him his life. He approached J. E. Lawrence, editor of the *Sacramento Times and Transcript,* demanding whether he had been responsible for a defaming article about Johnson. When Lawrence refused several times to answer, Johnson snatched the editor's nose and severely wrung it. Lawrence stepped back, drawing his pistol, but before he could fire, some bystanders seized him.

In 1852, the Whig Party nominated and elected Johnson as an Assemblyman from Sacramento County. The Whigs chose him as their candidate for Speaker of the Assembly, but since they comprised the minority party, he was not elected. Johnson's contemporaries remembered him as one of the strong fighters against Bigler's waterfront extension program and as playing an influential role in having the capital moved from Vallejo to Benicia. His active participation on the Assembly floor was, however, slight as he was granted eleven leaves of absences ranging from one day to one week in duration during the 1853 session.

There can be no doubt that J. Neely Johnson in 1855 showed to his contemporaries the prospect of an outstanding political future. A man, still in his twenties, he had held many responsible offices, and in each instance, had acquitted himself well.

Johnson took his oath of office as the fourth governor on January 9, 1856. In his inaugural address he agreed with Bigler that state credit had to be restored and obligations honored. He added that previous legislatures had violated the constitution by providing for special expenditures, beyond normal governmental operations, in excess of $300,000. The constitution held that except for war there could be no debt larger than $300,000 unless the legislative act establishing such a debt was approved by vote of the people.

The constitution also clearly indicated, both Bigler and Johnson stated, that no corporation could be formed by special legislative act—previous sessions had insisted on asking gubernatorial approval of corporations which did not have municipal functions. The new governor demanded cessation of this practice.

Claiming that the people of California demanded rigid economy, Johnson advocated enactment of certain of Bigler's ideas. He called for abolition of all needless offices, reduction in fees, amendments to legal codes to insure speedy and impartial dispensing of justice, fair election laws, and settlement by law, not by emotion, of the thorny Mexican land claims. Johnson, too, called for the adoption of biennial legislative sessions.

Johnson's message, alluding to the developing national crisis, stated his position, which was the stand of the American party. He believed that California had become part of the union under difficult circumstances and although slighted by the national government in the formative years, there had never been any thought of secession. Johnson held that California stood for preserving the union in 1856.

Lastly he turned to the use of the veto power. He held that the veto, an executive prerogative, must not be used rashly or without due consideration. Johnson felt, as did many Californians, that Governor Bigler had misused his veto power in a headstrong manner and, on some occasions for selfish ends. Johnson claimed that the purpose of a veto was to keep intact the constitution and to restrain any unconstitutional extension of legislative power. He stated that if necessary he would use his veto but only to protect the constitution. In spite of these views, Johnson sent fourteen veto messages to the seventh legislative session of 1856. Half of these concerned bills whereby cities and counties attempted to solve their financial problems or bills which failed to restrict properly municipal and county indebtedness. He regretfully vetoed legislative appropriations for the San Francisco and San Rafael orphan asylums—not being state institutions, they were not entitled to state aid. An unusual bill granting state money to heirs of an estate in recompense for funds stolen in a robbery received his veto. A judge, holding these funds as public administrator, had been robbed and Johnson held that the legislature could not assign public money from the state treasury except to specific state agencies.

The 1856 session received one veto message regarding corporations. The legislature had granted telegraph companies the right to appropriate trees for their use, but Johnson claimed this was an invasion of private property without due compensation since the bill made no distinction between public trees and private trees. He also vetoed two bills which appeared to circumvent the regular order of payment to state bondholders. The legislature seemed not to object to Johnson's vigorous use of the veto for he was not overridden in any of his objections. In some instances, bills were rewritten to conform to the governor's views.

Some important acts were approved by the governor in 1856. Mechanics liens were legalized; inspectors of pork, beef, and salt provisions were authorized for appointment. The state debt was funded with approval granted to issue comptroller's warrants to be drawn against the General Fund. The debt was amalgamated into one fund and paid off as reserves accumulated. The hope was that a system of warrant payments could be established with those issued earliest receiving first priority. This procedure had first been advocated by Bigler. To supervise payment of claims, the state board of examiners was created. Governor Johnson also approved the act providing for actual construction of the capitol building.

Johnson's administration had its difficulties too in managing the state prison. Following state assumption of the prison's operation in July, 1855, the maintenance cost had been excessive. In fact the monthly average cost from July through December, 1855, had been $54,603.83. To counter this, a board of state prison directors was created in 1856. Under this board's direction the cost had averaged $25,486 per month. The directors leased out prison labor so that the inmates were not a complete financial burden to the state. However, investigations in 1856 found that state control was not working satisfactorily and a return to the former leasing system was advised. Legislators believed that the San Quentin installation was in a poor location and a second site should be soon acquired.

Also created in 1856 was the state board of prison commissioners, consisting of the lieutenant governor, comptroller, and treasurer who were empowered to lease the prison grounds. The significant part of the act was the return to leasing of convict labor with the state paying $10,000 a month to the lessee. James Estell again received the contract—for five years. He was to guard, clothe, feed, and provide medical care for the prisoners. In 1857 Estell once more was in financial difficulties for the attorney-general claimed the 1856 contract to be unconstitutional. The state board of examiners as a consequence refused to pay Estell, who appealed to the legislature for relief. His plea was heeded and an act was passed to tide him over his difficulties.

Johnson broke the deadlock on the Indian war debt problem in 1856 by sending all the archival materials demanded by the federal government. Congress agreed to pay $924,259.65, leaving a balance of some $200,000 to be settled. Johnson asked the legislature to divert this money to New York City to pay off eastern bonds. The governor stated that Indian troubles still persisted—there were outbreaks of fighting in the

Crescent City and Klamath areas of the state.

The most momentous event during Johnson's term was his conflict with the Second Vigilance Committee of San Francisco. The committee had been created following the shooting of James King of William, editor of the *San Francisco Bulletin*. Governor Johnson, at the request of Mayor James Van Ness, went to the city on May 16, to meet with the chairman of the committee, William T. Coleman. Just what was decided at this meeting became the subject of controversy on the two sides, but it was apparent that the vigilance leader had outmaneuvered the governor. With the growth of the power of the Vigilance Committee, Governor Johnson on June 3 ordered Major General William T. Sherman to call out the militia to suppress the committee's activities. Bolstered by the support of the law and order group, which opposed the vigilantes, the governor on June 4 issued a proclamation declaring San Francisco to be in a state of insurrection and placed it under martial law. He demanded that those who opposed the legally constituted authorities disband and submit to the laws of the state. Johnson had assumed, based on a prior conversation with General John E. Wool at Benicia, that the state could draw arms from the arsenal to quell the committee's efforts. At the crucial moment, Wool stated that he could not do so without authorization from the president. The state militia then deserted to the Vigilance Committee, which seized the arms of the state. Johnson's appeal to President Pierce for help was refused. His proclamation remained in force until November 3, when he revoked it after assurances that the committee would return the arms and disband.

This clash between the governor and the Vigilance Committee cost him his political leadership. Because of his firm stand, almost alone against the great popularity of the committee, Johnson became ineffective as chief executive. The Know-Nothing party was a tenuous political party at best and Johnson's unpopular position destroyed him and his party's force. In the midst of the controversy, William T. Sherman wrote:

> Governor Johnson is a young man elected by the Know-Nothing Party, and of a very high personal character. When, however, this storm burst upon him his old friends left him, and he was found to ally himself with men who had private griefs to avenge, or who acted from extreme notions. . . . He is now powerless; for the

militia, his only reliance to coerce obedience to his orders, have deserted him in mass, leaving him the naked, unsupported position of governor.

Johnson's first annual message to the eighth legislative session of 1857 devoted considerable attention to the Vigilance Committee and his part in the controversy. He claimed that he acted as he did in the face of threats and jeers to uphold the highest law of the land, the United States Constitution.

He announced that at present there were no Indian outbreaks. He felt that the federal government's plan, while most humane in its concept of treating the Indians of California, had not worked. Agreeing with his predecessors that the reservation system could only bring destruction to the Indians and continue the conflict, he supported Indian removal beyond the Sierra Nevada.

His message commented at length on financial conditions. Claiming that the state faced bankruptcy in the face of growing expenditures, he said that a solution must be found. He suggested legalizing all outstanding indebtedness and having the comptroller issue warrants which would not come due until July 1, 1857. He felt that both principal and interest had to be paid in full to restore state credit. He called for doubling personal and real property taxes, and demanded that existing sources of income—miners' taxes, poll taxes, and licenses— be collected in a more vigorous manner. The governor then additionally proposed an income tax with a $1,000 exemption and a stamp tax on all bonds, bills of exchange, and notes. The legislature enacted the stamp tax as a means of receiving additional revenue. Johnson also noted that the custom duties, the Civil Fund, still had to be settled and he agreed with his predecessors that this money belonged to California.

The governor next called attention to the fact that the banking firm, Palmer, Cook & Company, had not delivered funds in New York City to cover the state's interest payments. An investigation had been started to recover the money from the company. The state treasurer had paid out the necessary funds, but his activities, as well as those of the state comptroller, were also being investigated.

Johnson observed with satisfaction the settlement of the war debt claims for the years 1850-1853. However, he charged the legislature to press for federal payment for the Indian wars of

1854-1856. Settlement of these claims would, he added, reduce the state debt by about $218,000.

Johnson asked for a legislative definition of overflowed and swamp lands to protect land titles for buyers. He said that there was an immediate need to set apart the school lands before all valuable land was claimed, leaving only inferior lands upon which to base support of public schools.

This 1857 message commented on two state institutions. He felt the state library, created in 1850, had made a good start with its book collection. The building program of the Stockton insane asylum had been well conceived and the institution had become an outstanding facility for the mentally ill, but he called attention to serious charges levied against the former resident physician and the need for an investigation to ascertain the truth.

Believing there were certain weaknesses in the state constitution, Johnson asked the legislature to refer to the people the calling of a convention to rectify these. The legislature concurred in this request, but the voters rejected the proposal. He also called for new legislation. He counseled that divorce cases be heard in open court to make divorce more difficult. Following Governor Burnett's earlier suggestion, Johnson called for one general incorporation act for all towns and cities, ending the need for special acts for each town. He sought to shift the onerous burden of appointing notary publics from his office to the people by asking that such officers be elected. He became the first governor to call for a special house of refuge for the punishment of youthful offenders instead of placing them in San Quentin. He thought a register of deaths was in order to help clear up estates and show, or at least compare, the healthfulness of California's climate with the rest of the country. He noted that the existence of the state prison commissioners made needless the board of prison directors and suggested its abolition. This was subsequently done.

His message speculated on the future need of the Pacific railroad and the immediate need for a national wagon road. He then called upon the legislature either to accept his solutions on the immediate problems or to propose proper alternatives.

The *Daily Alta California*, which had opposed Johnson's position against the Vigilance Committee, proclaimed his message the "ablest state paper that has emanated from the Executive Department of California." The eighth session passed several important measures which Johnson asked for while others were sidetracked because of the heat of partisanship and because his political prestige had already been shattered.

The governor continued to use his veto power during the 1857 session. He vetoed an Assembly measure creating Del Norte County because of bad spelling, improper punctuation, and numerous erasures in the bill which made it impossible to determine the bill's intent. He reprimanded the enrollment committee for not paying more heed to correct form. His veto was upheld. While approving a bill to incorporate Marysville, he again noted "flagrant and inexcusable errors which so frequently occur in the Assembly enrolled bills," and asked the Assembly to re-examine the bill to determine its precise meaning. As Bigler had done, Johnson vetoed bills of a special nature which violated the constitution. In these he was upheld.

A significant veto message sent by the governor to the Senate objected to an appropriation bill defraying the civil expenses of the government from February 1 to June 30, 1857. He admitted that the legislature had the right to enact such a measure, but the proposal would have created a $300,000 deficit by July 1. He chastised the two houses for reverting to practices of previous legislatures by approving expenditures without providing increased revenue. He admonished that "it is now time that we should stop and reflect upon the condition of affairs, and instead of making appropriations, first devise ways and means to meet these expenditures." He hoped that legislative action would soon place the state on a cash and carry basis, bringing the use of scrip to an end. The veto message was tabled and no further legislative action taken.

During the 1857 session, impeachment proceedings were started against State Treasurer Henry Bates and State Comptroller George W. Whitman. The Assembly, investigating Bates' case, found fourteen causes for impeachment stemming from the delivery of money for interest payments to an agent of Palmer, Cook & Company without receiving proper security. He was additionally charged with contriving to use state funds for personal gain and of manipulating state warrants in return for gold and money. In the midst of the impeachment proceedings, Bates resigned and Johnson appointed, with Senate approval, James L. English as new state treasurer. Bates became the first elected official to be impeached and found guilty. His resignation negated further action but the Senate forbade him from holding any office of trust, honor, or profit in the state of California.

The Assembly, in finding articles of impeachment against Whitman, held that he had been guilty of protecting the state treasurer by willfully denying information to the board of examiners. He had also drawn warrants in favor of James Estell without approval of the examiners, making him guilty of a misdemeanor. Governor Johnson's appointment of Edward F. Burton as a replacement received Senate confirmation. Whitman was, however, cleared by the Senate of all charges and in time he was returned to office. In both cases, Johnson as governor and a member of the board of examiners was called upon to testify.

In April, 1857, Governor Johnson appointed George W. Ryder as gauger of wines and liquors and brought down upon himself a charge of corruption by the displaced gauger, Lansing B. Mizner. Mizner charged that the governor had tried to force him to appoint R. N. Berry as an assistant to repay a political debt for Johnson. After an investigation and examination of all witnesses including the governor, a select legislative committee held that Ryder should be confirmed in his position and that there had not been "any official corruption on the part of the Executive."

J. Neely Johnson, repudiated by his party as a candidate for renomination, sent in his annual message to the ninth session of 1858 just prior to leaving office. Reviewing gains made under his administration, he called attention to problems still unsolved.

State finances had never been better, he claimed. In fact, 1857 was the first year the state treasury had been able to meet demands for payment on a current basis. Johnson called attention to the existence of a reserve to meet present and future obligations. Governmental expenditures had been reduced and adjusted to anticipated income; a fund to provide bond payments and a sinking fund to retire the public debt had been created. One economy instituted had been the reduction of salaries of elected officials. The governor's salary had been reduced from $10,000 to $8,000 a year with other officials experiencing a similar $2,000 decrease. Johnson suggested that the new

legislature might consider a tax reduction in light of an anticipated $4,000 treasury surplus.

Tax collection, with the exception of the poll tax, he stated,
had been most efficient. Johnson believed that the stamp act
had been one of the most useful measures enacted by the last
legislature for it had netted the state almost $49,000. With
some disgust he observed that the Civil Fund question was
still unsettled.

He asked the legislature to move ahead with a building program for the state capitol. However, he urged caution in the
supervision of construction and asked that the capitol commissioners be given this power.

Johnson reviewed at length the condition of the state prison
and its administration. He recommended ending the lessee
system, making each county assume the responsibility of keeping prisoners. In the continuing war against crime he called
a second time for a house of refuge for young criminals.
He also felt the need of a law establishing an apprentice
system to take charge of wayward boys who were foot-loose in
the larger communities of the state. Such a program, he urged,
would provide the essential training to make useful adult
citizens.

In conclusion, Johnson suggested that the constitution had
been violated by the submission of bills to the governor during
the last two days of the legislative session. The constitution
provided that the governor would have time to consider important bills and render a decision prior to the legislature's adjournment. Governor Weller, Johnson's successor, made the
same observation in his inaugural address.

Following his term as governor, Johnson retired from California politics. In 1858, he engaged in large scale mining
activities in Trinity County but suffered heavy losses. Early
in 1860, he moved to Washoe, Nevada, where for a time he
managed the Bowers mine. He also practiced law in Carson
City, gaining some measure of financial security. In 1863,
he was a delegate from Ormsby County to the first Nevada
state constitutional convention. He played a prominent role,
serving as chairman of the judiciary committee. The second
constitutional convention of 1864 elected him president.

In 1867, Johnson was appointed by the governor of Nevada
to fill a vacancy on the state supreme court and at the next

general election was elected to a full term on the bench. In January, 1871, his term having expired, Johnson resumed his law practice. In the spring of that year, President Grant appointed Johnson as a member of the board of examiners to visit West Point. Following this inspection, Johnson went to Salt Lake City to open a law practice. On July 26, 1872, he suffered a sunstroke followed by delirium and physical prostration. He died August 31, 1872, at the age of forty-seven and was buried at Camp Douglas Cemetery, Salt Lake City.

J. Neely Johnson's political career showed him to be a tireless and energetic young man. Held in high esteem, he had been a popular lawyer and elected official in Sacramento. The Whig party counted him as one of its favorite orators. Johnson was the first California governor whose political affiliation was other than Democratic. He and the American party made a sincere effort to run the state government more efficiently than had the Democrats. During Johnson's tenure some economies were enacted and some reforms were undertaken in an effort to reduce the crushing weight of the state debt. Johnson's major handicaps were his youthfulness which led him to some impetuous decisions, and his leadership of an ephemeral party which could not maintain its state or national strength. Johnson's determined decision to stand against the vigilantes of 1856 was the proper course, but a man with more political experience might well have solved the problem with tact and moved on to carry out his own governmental program with more success.

Bibliography

MANUSCRIPTS

Johnson, J. Neely, "Daily Journal for 1857," (California State Archives).

————, "Record of the Official Acts of J. Neely Johnson, Governor of California Commencing January 1856 and ending————," (State Archives).

Norris, T.W., "Collection," (Bancroft Library).

CONTEMPORARY ACCOUNTS

Assembly Journal, 4th & 7th-9th Sess., 1853 & 1856-58.

Senate Journal, 2nd-3rd & 6th-9th Sess., 1851-52 & 1855-58.

Coleman, William T., "San Francisco Vigilance Committees," *Century Illustrated Monthly Magazine*, XLIII (1891-92), 133-150.

Sherman, William T., "Sherman and the San Francisco Vigilantes," *Century Illustrated Monthly Magazine*, XLIII (1891-92), 296-309.

SECONDARY SOURCES

Bancroft, H.H., *History of California.*

Davis, Sam P., ed., *The History of Nevada* (Reno, 1913).

Davis, W.J., *History of Political Conventions. . .*

Ellison, W.H., *A Self-governing Dominion. . .*

Florcken, Herbert G., "The Law and Order View of the San Francisco Vigilance Committee of 1856," *California Historical Society Quarterly*, XIV (1935), 350-74; XV (1936) 70-87.

Hittell, T.H., *History of California.*

Hurt, Peyton, "The Rise and Fall of the Know-Nothings in California," *CHSQ*, IX (1930), 16-49, 99-128.

Morse, John F., *The First History of Sacramento. . .*

NEWSPAPERS

Daily Alta California, July 19, 1851, reports Johnson in Sacramento street fight; June 20, 1856, editorializes on Johnson and the Vigilance Committee; Jan. 9, 1857, carries favorable editorial on his annual message.

Daily California Chronicle, Jan. 10, 1857, comments favorably on annual message; Jan. 9, 1858, reports on last annual message.

Sacramento Transcript, Aug. 14, 1850, has account of Johnson's role with Sierra relief train.

San Francisco Bulletin, Aug. 31, 1872, has his obituary.

San Francisco Chronicle, Feb. 6, 1898, has estimate of Johnson as governor.

OTHER SOURCES

Hayes, Benjamin I., "Scrapbooks, California Politics," Vol. I (Bancroft Library).

Calendar of Events

February 22, 1812	Weller born in Montgomery, Ohio.
1825-1829	Weller attended Miami University in Oxford, Ohio.
1832	Weller admitted to Ohio bar.
1833	Weller elected District Attorney of Butler County, Ohio.
1836-1846	Weller served as a Trustee of Miami University.
1838-1844	Weller represented Ohio's Second District in Congress.
1846-1848	Weller participated in Mexican War.
1848	Weller defeated as Democratic candidate for Governor of Ohio.
January 16, 1849	President Polk appointed Weller to International Boundary Commission.
June 1, 1849	Weller arrived in California.
January 30, 1852	Weller elected United States Senator.
January 8, 1858	Weller installed as Governor.
April 19, 1859	Governor Weller signed act permitting six southern California counties to form a separate territory.
September 12, 1860	Weller elected chairman of the Breckenridge State Convention.
November 17, 1860	President Polk appointed Weller as Minister to Mexico.
September 2, 1863	Weller defeated as a candidate for Congress.
May 10, 1864	Weller elected a delegate to the Democratic National Convention.
August 17, 1875	Weller died in New Orleans.

John B. Weller

5TH GOVERNOR — DEMOCRAT
BORN: FEBRUARY 22, 1812   DIED: AUGUST 17, 1875
TERM OF OFFICE: JANUARY 8, 1858—JANUARY 9, 1860

JOHN B. WELLER WAS BORN in the village of Montgomery, Hamilton County, Ohio, on February 22, 1812. His parents, who were natives of New York State, had moved to Ohio about two years earlier. In 1825, the family settled in Oxford, Ohio, where young Weller attended Miami University for four years, but did not graduate. He then studied law in Hamilton and was admitted to the Ohio bar just prior to his twenty-first birthday. Shortly thereafter the Butler County Democratic convention nominated him for district attorney and he defeated his former law tutor, the Whig candidate, by a sizeable majority. After completing his term as district attorney in 1836, he served as a trustee of the University of Miami for the next ten years.

In 1838, Weller was elected representative from Ohio's second congressional district. He was re-elected twice and at the end of his third term he declined nomination to resume his law practice. In Congress he gained a reputation as an effective orator, participating in numerous debates such as the famous New Jersey contested election dispute. He served on the commerce, Indian affairs, and ways and means committees.

Weller was married four times. Early in his congressional career he married the daughter of a prominent merchant of Hamilton. After a few years, his first wife died. Then he married the daughter of the state auditor of Ohio. She also died, and in 1845, he married Susan McDowell Taylor, daughter of a Virginia Congressman and a niece of Senator Thomas Hart Benton of Missouri. Within three years Weller was a widower for the third time. In 1854, he married his fourth

81

wife, Mrs. G. W. Staunton. They had one son, Charles L.
Weller. Weller's first son, John B., Jr., was by his second wife.

Upon the outbreak of the Mexican War he volunteered as a
private. He raised a company of volunteers in his county,
the Butler Guards, and was elected its captain. His company
became a part of the Second Ohio Regiment of Volunteers
with Weller being elected lieutenant colonel. His regiment
participated in numerous campaigns and Weller heroically
led them in Battle of Monterrey, later being distinguished for
gallantry.

After the war, he returned to his law practice in Hamilton.
In the election of 1848, Ohio Democrats nominated him for
governor. In a fierce campaign, in which he canvassed seventy-
five counties, he was defeated by the Whig candidate, Seabury
Ford, by 345 votes out of a total vote of approximately 300,000.
In fact the election was so close that its outcome remained in
doubt for several weeks.

On January 16, 1849, President Polk appointed Weller as
United States Commissioner on the International Boundary
Commission to determine the boundary between the United
States and Mexico. Weller then left Washington, D.C., for
Hamilton, Ohio. After attending to private business there,
he boarded a river boat at nearby Cincinnati and arrived at
New Orleans on February 25. He waited several days for
other commissioners, and when they failed to arrive, he sailed
aboard the *Alabama* for Chagres on March 12. At the Isthmus
he was delayed several months before embarking aboard the
side-wheeler *Panama* for San Diego. This vessel sailed on
May 17, and reached San Diego on June 1.

After Weller had been in California a while, rumors began
to circulate that he had been on "a bender" in New Orleans
and that he had brought a prostitute to the Isthmus. Whig
newspapers on the Atlantic seaboard contended that Weller's
dilatory actions were endangering the success of any boundary
settlement and some accounts claimed that he had returned to
New Orleans without reaching California.

While mystery clouded Weller's journey to California, the
publicity became worse once he was on the scene. He was
charged with provoking Andrew B. Gray, a United States sur-
veyor with the boundary commission, into a gun fight. He was
accused of wasting the boundary appropriation and his conduct

was portrayed as a disservice to the United States.

When the Whig administration under President Taylor came to power, Weller was recalled. On August 26, 1849, Weller wrote a letter from San Francisco which stated as follows:

> It is rumored that I am suspended. As far as personal interests are concerned, I have no regret if the rumor is true. The commission will be broken up and the boundary survey delayed indefinitely. I can readily find professional employment here. Many lawyers are here, but business will be very extensive.

After his official removal, Weller did practice law in San Francisco and became involved in cases arising out of the activities of the 1851 Vigilance Committee. He quickly entered the California political arena. At the first Democratic state convention meeting at Benicia, Weller was one of several unsuccessful gubernatorial nominees.

On January 30, 1852, Weller was elected by the legislature as United States Senator to succeed John C. Frémont. Weller's main opponent in the contest had been the aggressive and ex-Tammany Hall politician, David C. Broderick. Although Weller probably was not the equal of Broderick, he had the important backing of the Gwin or pro-Southern machine. In the Senate he served as chairman of the committee on military affairs and as a member of the committee on foreign affairs. Perhaps his greatest single contribution as Senator was his role in securing passage of the overland mail bill. While in the Senate, Weller attended the national Democratic convention of 1852 at Baltimore where he received as a courtesy the vote of the California delegation for president and then the vote of the California and Ohio delegations for vice president.

In the senatorial contest of January, 1857, Broderick replaced Weller as United States Senator. Still Weller possessed strong political power and at the Democratic state convention meeting on July 14, he was nominated for governor on the first ballot. A fellow Ohioan, Joseph Walkup, was Democratic candidate for lieutenant governor. In an overwhelming victory Weller polled 53,122 votes to 21,040 for the Republican candidate, Edward Stanly, and 19,481 votes for the American party candidate, George W. Bowie.

On January 8, 1858, Chief Justice David S. Terry administered the oath of office to Weller. Tall and stout in appearance, Governor Weller had an easy command of language and an agreeable voice. In his inaugural address he expressed his opposition to mob rule and corrupt elections. He complained about "ballot-box stuffers" and proposed that elections laws be extended to "primary meetings." Weller solemnly pledged that he would use the whole power of the state, when necessary, to safeguard organized tribunals and to maintain supremacy of the law. These sentiments were in accord with his earlier stand and that of J. Neely Johnson in opposing the vigilantes.

In a discussion of the vexing problem of land titles, Weller blamed the congressional land-commission act of March 3, 1851. He asserted that this measure had hindered settlements and that the claimants holding perfect titles under Mexican grants had suffered in numerous cases. He agreed with his predecessors that many landholders had been impoverished by litigation with the federal government.

Weller, like Bigler, favored the squatters. He charged that the best farm lands of California were held by a few because of the confirmation of Mexican grants. He claimed that many farmers, who had improved what they had supposed to be public lands, were endangered by the prospect of losing their improvements.

In discussing financial matters he stressed the need for rigid economy, complaining that each year since statehood, expenditures had exceeded receipts and that the state debt had risen to about four million dollars. He pointed out that this deficit had occurred despite the constitutional limit of a maximum debt of $300,000. As a remedy he proposed reducing expenditures for the state prison and for state printing. He protested that Californians were taxed $120,000 per year to provide for prisoners while other states made prisoners self-supporting.

Turning to transportation he predicted that the overland mail route would benefit California, but urged, as had Bigler and Johnson, that Congress should also extend wagon roads across the Rockies. With adequate roads, provided with proper military protection, Weller visualized that thousands of unemployed from the East could seek relief from the Panic of 1857 and migrate to the bountiful mines and agricultural valleys of California. Weller also urged a railroad which he viewed as essential for military and political purposes. To substantiate his argument he stated: "A war with any respectable maritime power would cut us off effectually from our sister states, and leave our trade, our commerce, our material wealth, if not our lives, at the mercy of the public enemy."

Weller devoted a large part of his inaugural address to the slavery issue and expressed his pro-southern sympathies. In defending the right of the slave states to maintain their own institutions he charged that the agitation of the slavery question in the North threatened the Union. He declared that the states could not be held together by force and he favored extending slavery into the territories. These views were probably acquired by Weller from his southern Ohio environment.

One of Weller's more difficult problems was concerned with the state prison at San Quentin. As a result of accumulated grievances the legislature enacted a measure on February 27, 1858, which authorized Governor Weller "to possess" the prison and to assume custody of the convicts. On March 1, Weller, Lieutenant Governor Joseph Walkup, and Secretary of State Ferris Forman personally took possession of the prison over the objection of John F. McCauley's agents. McCauley had obtained a sub-lease from James M. Estell. The gubernatorial party had to break open some office doors in order to obtain the prison keys. Three days later Weller reported to the Assembly that he had been compelled to use a "little force."

While making his inspection Weller ordered that a large hall housing over 200 prisoners be converted into six rooms. He appointed C. W. Robinson as superintendent of the prison. Weller found that the convicts were "wholly unemployed." In his report to the legislature he pointed out the need for a branch prison. In considerable detail he objected to the practice of the courts in sending men to prison for long terms. He noted that a number of first offenders for grand larcency had been sentenced to ten-year and fifteen-year terms. Then he warned that because of the severity of many sentences made by the courts of sessions, he might pardon several prisoners given long sentences. At this point Weller offered the following commentary on executive clemency:

> The pardoning power is vested in the Executive for wise purposes, and will be used by me whenever, in my opinion, justice demands it. I shall not stop to count the number or take the opinion of the community on the subject. I will guard as faithfully as I can the public weal, but if I err, I prefer erring on the side of mercy.

Weller used his pardoning power more than any of the

other two-year governors. He granted seventy-seven pardons, six commutations, and sixty restorations. As a result of his visit to San Quentin, Weller also recommended changes in the criminal code. In particular he opposed the placement of juvenile offenders at San Quentin and referred to the prison as "the most efficient school of villainy that can be found in any country." After Governor Weller and the other state officials had occupied the prison, McCauley brought suit against them. The prison question was litigated for two years and it haunted Weller during his entire term. After he left office, the issue was resolved in April, 1860, when a monetary settlement was made to Estell and McCauley.

During his term Weller signed and vetoed important bills relating to San Francisco. To his credit he approved the Van Ness ordinance which settled many land titles, particularly in the Western Addition. Also he approved a bill for bringing more water into the city by the Spring Valley Water Company. On April 26, 1858, he vetoed a bill designed to divide the city and county into townships. Weller disapproved it since the measure was exclusively local in character and because the San Francisco delegation to the legislature had unanimously protested its passage.

After a year in office, Governor Weller in his first annual message to the legislature on January 5, 1859, reported that finances were in the best condition since statehood. He praised the steady progress in agriculture and mining and recommended, as had Bigler, that San Francisco be made a whaling fleet depot. In discussing purely legislative matters he criticized special legislation and blasted the lobbyists. Moreover, he again recommended laws to control primary elections. He repeated his criticism of the state prison and explained that the large number of patients in the state insane asylum was caused by two factors. First, a shortage of county poor houses caused many unfortunates to seek refuge in the asylum; and secondly, many newcomers to California actually became demented when they failed to obtain easy wealth from the mines.

On March 7, 1859, in a special message to the legislature, Weller announced that during the past year he had devoted two months of his time exclusively to duties as director of the state prison. He suggested removing the office of governor from the board of prison directors and said in part: "I venture the assertion, that in no other State are the duties of the Governor so varied and arduous as in California."

In addition to the prison problem Weller had to concern himself with Indian disturbances in Humboldt County in the fall of 1856. In the following spring, he was compelled to send arms to Sheriff H. C. Stockton of Shasta County to suppress an anti-Chinese riot being threatened by some 300 armed men. In a letter to the sheriff, Governor Weller advised: "This spirit of mobocracy must be crushed out, no matter what blood it may cost." In quelling this riot Weller was not motivated by any sympathy toward the Chinese, for he had signed an act the previous year to prevent further immigration of Chinese or Mongolians into California. The explanation for his action was that Weller was a law and order man.

During Weller's term the six southern counties of Los Angeles, San Bernardino, San Diego, Santa Barbara, San Luis Obispo, and Tulare voted to separate from California and form the territory of Colorado. This attempt to divide the state was narrowly supported by the legislature and signed by Governor Weller on April 19, 1859. However, any state division would require approval by Congress. The national legislators were unwilling to take action because of more pressing sectional issues. As it will be seen, Weller's successor also had to consider the matter of state division.

In his final message to the legislature before leaving office in January, 1860, Weller reviewed the entire prison question and recommended a branch at Folsom or elsewhere. He related that the prohibition of dueling was ineffectual and warned against a revival of vigilantism. He reiterated the need for reforms of "primary elections," stating: "By double voting and false returns, the active and unscrupulous minority select candidates for the people." Weller also recommended calling a constitutional convention to correct political abuses, to reorganize the courts, and to revamp the revenue system.

With reference to the growing sectionalism on the national scene, Weller commented that California had wisely refused to tolerate slavery, but had no desire to interfere with the domestic institutions of other communities. After saying that California would defend the institutions of both the North and the South, he stated: "But after all, if the wild spirit of fanaticism which now pervades the land should destroy this magnificent Confed-

eracy, (which God forbid) she will not go with the South or
the North, but here upon the shores of the Pacific found a
mighty republic which may in the end prove the greatest of
all.''

In conclusion Weller conceded that he had committed some
errors, but felt that these would not adversely affect the state.
The outgoing governor expressed the following views upon
his office:

> He who expects to find the Executive chair an easy one will be
> sadly mistaken. It is difficult, indeed, in a community like ours,
> where so many duties are imposed upon the Governor, and where
> there are so many conflicting elements at work, to administer
> public affairs satisfactorily to the people. His efforts to promote
> the general good will not always be properly appreciated, and his
> motives will sometimes be misunderstood or misrepresented by the
> designing.

Weller was not considered for re-election in 1859—his popularity in California Democratic circles was waning. In the
presidential campaign of 1860, he supported the southern or
Breckenridge ticket and was elected chairman of the Breckenridge state convention. Once he was shelved on the California
political scene, he returned to Washington and was able to
obtain an appointment from President Buchanan as Minister
to Mexico. He served at this post from November 17, 1860
until May 14, 1861. He was recalled by the Lincoln administration which appointed Thomas Corwin in his place.

Weller returned to California and engaged in farming. For
two years he remained politically inactive, but in 1863, along
with former Governor John Bigler and N. E. Whiteside, he
was an unsuccessful candidate for Congress. Just prior to his
nomination by the Fusion Democratic convention he delivered
a speech on June 6, before the Democratic Club of Petaluma
in which he condemned the Lincoln administration for planning
to subjugate the South and to abolish slavery. Weller asserted
that Lincoln had erred when he stated that the Republican
party merely opposed slavery extension. As evidence that
abolition was an objective of Republican leaders, Weller cited
their endorsement of Hinton R. Helper's book, *The Impending
Crisis of the South*. In violent words the former governor
opposed what he termed a "military slaughter" designed to
give freedom to millions of the African race.

As governor, Weller did not make any startling contributions, but he possessed a good awareness of the state problems. His recommendations for political reforms and for reductions of expenditures were largely ignored by the legislature. To his credit several recommendations were later acted upon by successors. For example, in cases involving capital offenses he recommended full testimony be recorded and transmitted to the governor.

In his exercise of the power of executive clemency, Weller never permitted personal or party feelings to influence his decisions. However, frequent charges were made that he abused his pardoning power. He vetoed many special and private legislative bills which caused much criticism.

Weller was not a dynamic politician and he lost popularity during the secession crisis. In the war years disgrace was associated with his name because of his pro-southern attitude. However, as a former governor he had been considered by his party for the gubernatorial nomination in 1863, before obtaining his congressional nomination in that year.

During the statewide political campaign of 1863 the Union military authorities in California became deeply concerned with the extreme utterances of ex-Governor Weller first in his Petaluma speech and later in Visalia, considered a stronghold of Confederate sympathy. Weller's last political activity in California occurred during the presidential campaign of 1864, when he was elected a delegate to the Democratic national convention.

After the election, Weller made an extended prospecting trip in Oregon, Idaho, and Utah. Then for brief periods he resided in Salt Lake City and in Washington, D.C. Late in 1867, he moved to New Orleans where he practiced law. Commenting upon his arrival there the *Daily Alta California* of February 18, 1868, stated in part: "A Southerner of at least six weeks standing, he is taking an active part in everything that concerns that section." In New Orleans, Weller participated prominently in one political campaign of the Reconstruction era, but during his last years he confined his attention to his practice. On August 17, 1875, he died at New Orleans from small pox and was survived by his two children and a brother. His remains were interred at the Lone Mountain Cemetery in San Francisco.

BIBLIOGRAPHY

CONTEMPORARY ACCOUNTS
Assembly Journal, 9th-11th Sess., 1858-60.
Speech of Ex-Governor John B. Weller, Delivered before the Democratic Club at Petaluma (San Francisco, 1863).

SECONDARY SOURCES
Bancroft, H.H., *History of California.*
————, *Popular Tribunals.*
Davis, W.J., *History of Political Conventions.* . .
Ellison, W.H., *A Self-governing Dominion, California.* . .
Goetzmann, William H., *Army Exploration in the American West, 1803-1863* (New Haven, 1959).
Hittell, T.H., *History of California.*
Ray, P. Orman, "John B. Weller," *Dictionary of American Biography,* Johnson, Allen and Malone, Dumas, eds., (22 vols., New York, 1928-44), XIX, 628-29.
Shuck, O. T., ed., *Representative and Leading Men of the Pacific.*
A History and Biographical Cyclopedia of Butler County, Ohio (Cincinnati, 1882).

NEWSPAPERS
Daily Alta California, Aug. 4, 1857, has a biographical account of Weller; Jan. 9, 1858, has an editorial on "Governor Weller's Inaugural"; Feb. 18, 1868, has data on Weller's arrival in New Orleans; and Aug. 20, 1875, has an obituary of Weller.
New Orleans Times, Aug. 18, 1875, has an obituary of Weller.
New York Daily Tribune has accounts of Weller while he was in charge of the International Boundary Commission in the following issues: June 27, July 7, 12, Sept. 5, Oct. 1, Nov. 2, and Dec. 18, 1849; March 15 and April 6, 1850.

Capitol at Vallejo, 1852-1853. Vallejo was the capitol of California from February 4, 1851, to February 4, 1853. However, it was not until the third session of the legislature in January, 1852, that the above wooden building was occupied. It was used again for the 1853 session. Later it was destroyed by fire, and the site is marked today as a State Historical Landmark at 219 York Street, Vallejo.

Calendar of Events

May 23, 1827	Latham born in Columbus, Ohio.
1845	Latham graduated from Jefferson College, Pennsylvania.
April 15, 1850	Latham arrived in San Francisco.
1850	Latham appointed court clerk in San Francisco.
1851	Latham elected District Attorney of the Sacramento Judicial District.
November 2, 1852	Latham elected to Congress.
1855	President Pierce appointed Latham Collector of the Port of San Francisco.
September 7, 1859	Latham elected Governor.
March 5, 1860	Latham took seat in United States Senate.
1865	Latham appointed Manager of the London and San Francisco Bank.
1867	Latham headed the California Pacific Railroad.
1879	Latham moved from San Francisco to New York.
1880	Latham elected President of the New York Mining and Stock Exchange.
March 4, 1882	Latham died in New York City.

Milton S. Latham

6TH GOVERNOR — LECOMPTON DEMOCRAT
BORN: MAY 23, 1827   DIED: MARCH 4, 1882
TERM OF OFFICE: JANUARY 9—14, 1860

CALIFORNIA'S SHORTEST TERM GOVERNOR, Milton S. Latham, held the office for only five days. He was born on May 23, 1827, in Columbus, Ohio, the son of an attorney, Bela Latham. He attended various schools in Ohio and graduated from Jefferson College, in Pennsylvania, in 1845. Shortly thereafter, he moved to Russell County, Alabama, where he taught school for a brief period, served as a court clerk, and became a lawyer.

On April 5, 1850, he arrived in San Francisco where he served as a court clerk. Then he moved to Sacramento where he was elected district attorney for the area's judicial district. On November 2, 1852, he won election as a congressman on the Democratic ticket from the northern district. During his single term in the House of Representatives he urged better overland mail service, advocated the establishment of a mail steamship service to the Orient, and generally favored legislation benefiting California. While in Congress, Latham married Sophie Birdsall of San Francisco. After her death in 1867, he was married to Mary McMullen and they had one son.

In the election of 1854, Latham received a split nomination in the congressional race, but to provide unity in his party he withdrew. Yet he polled 1,843 votes. In 1855, President Pierce appointed him collector of the port of San Francisco. Latham occupied this office for almost two years. His duties as revealed by his letter book were concerned with the revenue service, smuggling cases, the United States marine hospital, and the lighthouse at the Farallon Islands.

Within the faction-torn Democratic party of California, Latham steered independently of the rival political leaders, Broderick and Gwin. In fact Latham became a faction in his own right and acquired ambitions of also winning a United States senatorship. In the bitter senatorial controversy of January, 1857, Latham mustered the patronage of the custom house to contest Gwin for the short term, but an agreement between Gwin and Broderick frustrated his effort. Later that year he resigned his collectorship to resume private law practice.

Despite minor controversies over his conduct as collector, Latham evolved into a dignified and popular leader. His native abilities combined with his ambition caused him to be elected California's governor when only thirty-two years of age. In 1859, the Lecompton or Southern Democrats nominated Latham over his rivals, John B. Weller, John Nugent, and James W. Denver. In the election Latham defeated the anti-Lecompton Democratic candidate, John Curry, and the Republican candidate, Leland Stanford. Latham polled 44,023 votes to Curry's 24,180, while Stanford only received 8,466 votes.

Before a joint convention of the legislature, meeting on January 9, 1860, Chief Justice Stephen J. Field administered the oaths of office to Latham and to John G. Downey as lieutenant governor. In his inaugural address Latham hesitated to promise any achievements, for he claimed that it was better for an official to enumerate his accomplishments upon terminating his office. He then advocated no interference with general laws unless absolutely required. He condemned "experiments" which had burdened California with a debt of $3,885,000, pointing out that the state had only one adequate public building—its insane asylum—to show for this vast expenditure. Latham related that the state would eventually need buildings for the blind, deaf and dumb, reform schools, and other institutions. Moreover, he recommended that the current legislature appropriate a small sum to commence construction of a state capitol building.

Governor Latham believed the most important issue demanding legislative attention was proper disposition of the state prison, and like Weller he urged that state control should replace the lessee system. In reference to the pardoning power he criticized its liberal use by his three immediate predecessors who had granted executive clemency to 167 convicts, or to 9 percent of the total number of inmates during the past eight years.

In a discussion of the bulkhead or sea-wall project planned for the San Francisco embarcadero, Latham alluded to the powerful opposition to the scheme and to the dangers of a monopoly, suggesting that the legislature carefully consider this issue. He decried the recent lawlessness prevalent in California and mentioned the evils of patronage. To eliminate patronage he proposed making all offices elective whenever possible. Latham also urged a daily overland mail as well as a transcontinental railroad.

During his brief tenure Governor Latham communicated with the legislature about the proposed separation of six southern counties and their formation into a territory. The voters of these counties had been allowed to vote on the question during Weller's administration had returned an affirmative answer. In a message to President Buchanan, Latham deemed the act valid even though California voters as a whole had not been consulted. He held that the United States constitution provided for state division and that it did not prevent the people in a portion of a state from organizing a territory. Despite some disagreement with Latham's opinion, the legislature sanctioned his view. However, Congress never considered the matter because of its preoccupation with more serious issues accompanying the secessionist crisis. Nonetheless, at a later date Latham's detractors falsely asserted that he had favored state separation as a device to create a new southern state. This erroneous contention was to be repeated by several later historians, but actually Latham had pointed out that Californians as a whole had opposed separation and that it was an issue for Congress to decide.

The inaugural address and his message to Buchanan comprised the primary features of Latham's administration, but his daily journal indicated that he attended to several routine matters while governor. He suspended a sentence; approved commissions for a few notaries, and appointed two port wardens and several pilot commissioners at San Francisco. Also he approved three Senate and two Assembly bills.

Two days after his inauguration, the legislature agreed to

elect a United States Senator to fill the vacancy left by the death of David C. Broderick in his duel with Judge David S. Terry the previous September. Latham preferred the senatorship over the governorship and he defeated in party caucus his closest rival and Senator Gwin's choice, former Governor Weller. In the legislative joint convention he won over Edmund Randolph, the anti-Lecompton candidate, and Republican Oscar L. Shafter. Despite the fact that he was chiefly interested in Washington and had sought the office, Latham's election as Senator came as a surprise to many Californians. Some believed that he had erred in accepting the federal office, but others considered as did the editor of the *Sacramento Union* that the "defeat of Gwin was adequate compensation for losing a governor." The *Daily Evening Bulletin,* a leading San Francisco newspaper, in its issue of January 11, 1860, remarked:

> We regret that the exigencies of political ambition—honorable as it is high—should take the new governor from so wide and promising a field of usefulness; but we find some consolation in the conviction that in his future sphere of action at Washington, he will be able to do much to advance the interests of California and the entire Pacific coast.

On March 5, 1860, Latham took his seat in the United States Senate as its youngest member. In his initial speech he expressed pro-Southern sympathies and alluded to the possibility of an independent California in the event of a collapse of the Union. During the presidential election campaign he supported the Breckenridge ticket. However, on December 10, he repudiated the idea of a Pacific Republic on the Senate floor. As civil war came nearer he opposed secession. Upon the outbreak of war he supported its prosecution, but criticized the Lincoln administration.

Latham was not re-elected by the Republican legislature and his term ended on March 3, 1863. He then traveled in Europe for two years. While there he completed arrangements to act as manager of the newly established London and San Francisco Bank upon his return to San Francisco. By 1867, he headed the California Pacific Railroad which had built a line from Vallejo to Marysville with a branch to Sacramento—but the Central Pacific directors prevented it from being successful. Latham also invested in other railroads and for a time he controlled Sacramento River and San Francisco Bay steamers.

The London and San Francisco Bank, popularly referred to as "Latham's Bank," enjoyed prosperous times. It specialized in real estate and mining investments and in the selling of California securities in Europe. The bank proved itself one of the city's financial bulwarks during the panic of 1875.

During his banking career, Latham built a splendid and ornate residence in San Francisco which he converted into a veritable mecca of culture. He imported expensive statues and paintings and accumulated a sizeable private library of about 5,000 volumes. In 1872, he purchased an estate at Menlo Park, also embellishing it with books and art collections.

In 1875 and 1876, Latham invested quite heavily in extending the North Pacific Coast Railroad from Tomales to Moscow on the Russian River. He had hoped to tap the opulent timber resources of that area, but a sudden drop in the price of lumber brought disaster. Latham lost his wealth and moved to New York where he was compelled to sell his oil paintings. In 1880, he became the president of the New York Mining and Stock Exchange. On March 4, 1882, he died in New York City at the age of fifty-five. He was buried in the old Lone Mountain Cemetery at San Francisco.

Latham's governorship was most noted for its brevity. Yet a great deal transpired in those five days. His stand on state division was probably the most significant aspect of his term. Latham is also remembered for being the first California governor to relinquish the office in order to be elevated to the United States Senate.

Although Latham probably lacked the political acumen of such kingpins as Broderick and Gwin, he was superior to them in intellect. Slender and above average in height, he had long, darkish hair and deep set eyes. Genial and affable in his relations with others, he appeared as a determined young man who could command respect. As a public office-holder he was noted for his honesty, integrity, and administrative excellence. When Latham resigned the collectorship of the port of San Francisco in 1857, James Guthrie, the secretary of the treasury, stated that he alone had discharged the duties correctly and promptly.

In actuality Latham only wanted the governorship to win a seat in the United States Senate. Soon after his nomination as a candidate for governor, the *Daily Evening Bulletin* of June 29, 1859, prophesied:

> It is well known that the Gubernatorial chair has no special charm for Mr. Latham, except as a means to an end. The goal of his ambition is the seat in the United States Senate occupied by Wm. M. Gwin; and he played for and won the Gubernatorial nomination only that he might be inside the ring of politicians, and insist upon his right to a hand in their games. It is very rare that a man of character, practical common sense judgment and unalterable fixedness of purpose fails to attain any such position in the United States, if he presses steadily towards the mark. Mr. Latham, we believe, will do this; and as Governor, if elected, he will seek to make his administration popular as possible, and to thus establish his claims to the Senatorship.

Whereas Latham expected to replace Gwin, Broderick's untimely death brought his dream to reality. In his letter of resignation to the legislature Latham said: "I accept the new position so honorable in its character and vacate the Executive Chair without hesitation at the bidding of the State, firmly believing that I can serve her more effectually in the National Council than elsewhere."

BIBLIOGRAPHY

MANUSCRIPTS
"The Day Journal of Milton S. Latham, January 1 to May 6, 1860,"
(Bender Room, Stanford University Library). Also edited by Edgar
E. Robinson in *California Historical Society Quarterly*, XI (1932),
3-28.
"Latham Letters," (Bender Room, Stanford University Library).
"Latham Papers," (California Historical Society).
"Letter Book of Milton S. Latham, 1855-1857," (Huntington Library).

CONTEMPORARY ACCOUNTS
Assembly Journal, 11th Sess., 1860.

SECONDARY SOURCES
Apponyi, Flora H., *The Libraries of California* (San Francisco, 1878).
Cross, Ira B., *Financing An Empire, History of Banking in California*
(4 vols., Chicago, 1927).
Davis, W.J., *History of Political Conventions. . .*
Hall, Gaven D., "Milton S. Latham," in O.T. Shuck, ed., *Representative
and Leading Men of the Pacific.*
Kneiss, Gilbert H., *Redwood Railways* (Berkeley, 1956).
Phelps, Alonzo, *Contemporary Biography of California's Representative
Men* (2 vols., San Francisco, 1881-82).
Robinson, Edgar E., "Milton Slocum Latham," *Dictionary of American
Biography*, XI, 13.
Shuck, O.T., ed., *History of the Bench and Bar of California.*
Thompson, William F., Jr., "M.S. Latham and the Senatorial Con-
troversy of 1857," *California Historical Society Quarterly*, XXXII
(1953), 145-59.

NEWSPAPERS
New York Herald, March 5, 1882, has an obituary of Latham.
San Francisco Chronicle, March 24, 1878, describes Latham's collection
of paintings.

THESES
Colton, Virginia G., "The Political Career of Milton Slocum Latham"
(M.A., Stanford University, 1931).
Thompson, William F., Jr., "The Political Career of Milton Slocum
Latham of California" (M.A., Stanford University, 1952).

Calendar of Events

June 24, 1827	Downey born in Roscommon County, Ireland.
1849	Downey sailed from New Orleans to California.
1851	Downey acquired United States citizenship.
September 5, 1855	Downey elected to the Assembly.
September 7, 1859	Downey elected Lieutenant Governor.
January 14, 1860	Downey became Governor, when Latham resigned.
March 2, 1860	Downey signed bill for capitol site in Sacramento.
April 16, 1860	Governor Downey vetoed bulkhead bill.
May 11, 1861	Downey refused to attend the Union Mass Meeting in San Francisco.
May 15, 1861	Cornerstone of capitol building laid.
July 8, 1861	John Conness, instead of Downey, nominated as Union Democratic gubernatorial candidate.
April 24, 1863	Board of State Harbor Commissioners created.
September 2, 1863	Downey defeated by Low.
1868	Downey and James A. Hayward opened a bank in Los Angeles.
April 10, 1871	Downey and Isaias W. Hellman opened the Farmers and Merchants Bank in Los Angeles.
1873	Downey helped to found the Los Angeles Board of Trade.
1880	Downey elected to first board of trustees of the University of Southern California.
1883	Downey elected a vice-president of the Historical Society of Southern California.
March 1, 1894	Downey died in Los Angeles.

John G. Downey

7TH GOVERNOR — LECOMPTON DEMOCRAT
BORN: JUNE 24, 1827   DIED: MARCH 1, 1894
TERM OF OFFICE: JANUARY 14, 1860—JANUARY 10, 1862

JOHN GATELY DOWNEY, the first of California's three Civil War governors, was born on June 24, 1827, in Roscommon County, Ireland. His parents, Dennis and Bridget Gately Downey, were rural people who endowed their son with a love of the soil. Some writers contend that Downey was born in a castle while others say his birthplace was a mud house. Downey in his dictated autobiography adhered to the castle theory. Whatever his origins were—noble or humble—he came to America as a boy of fifteen. After attending a Latin school in Maryland, he served as an apprentice pharmacist in Washington, D.C. Then he moved to Vicksburg, Mississippi, where he was employed in the drug and stationery firm owned by Oliver O. Woodman. In 1846, Downey operated his own pharmacy in Cincinnati in partnership with John Darling.

Joining the gold rush he took passage from New Orleans for California via the Isthmus in 1849. After a brief mining experience in the Grass Valley District, Downey worked for Henry Johnson & Co., a wholesale drug firm, in San Francisco. In partnership with James P. McFarland, Downey opened a drug store in Los Angeles in December, 1850. "Doctors" McFarland and Downey enjoyed a thriving business in this only drug store then functioning between San Diego and San Francisco. In 1851, Downey acquired United States citizenship and the next year he married Maria Guirado, a native of Los Angeles.

From the start Downey participated actively in Los Angeles civic affairs. He was elected to two terms on the common

101

council. With profits from his drug firm he began to raise
livestock and to dabble in real estate. In November, 1854,
Downey along with Phineas Banning, Don Benito Wilson, and
William Sanford purchased a large part of Rancho de San
Pedro bordering the bay to the rear of Rattlesnake Island with
the objective of converting San Pedro into a harbor. However,
it was not until after his governorship that Downey took a
direct interest in his landholdings. At the time of his election
to the Assembly on the Democratic ticket in 1855, he left the
drug business. He was not active in the legislature during his
one-year term because of sickness. For a time he served as
collector of the port of San Pedro during the Buchanan administration.

In 1859, Downey was nominated as lieutenant governor on
the Lecompton Democratic ticket, becoming the running mate
of Milton S. Latham. In the election Downey easily defeated
John Conness, the Anti-Lecompton candidate, and James F.
Kennedy, the Republican candidate. When Latham resigned,
Downey became the second California lieutenant governor to
become governor.

Downey probably could not have been elected directly as
governor because he resided in the then less populous section
of California. In part he was selected as Latham's running
mate to balance the ticket, not only on a statewide geographical
basis, but also on a national sectional basis with the expectation
that Latham would attract Northern Democrats and that Downey
would attract Southern Democrats. The *Sacramento Bee* explained Downey's selection as follows:

> He was nominated as we judge from the appearance of things
> because of certain trades effected—because he had money, and for
> the purpose it may be, of offsetting among the Irish voters the
> selection of Conness upon the other side.

The Irish-Catholic governor was square built and of medium
stature which gave him a rotund appearance. His auburn hair
was slightly dulled with some gray and he wore full whiskers
that were trimmed short. His deep set hazel eyes gave him a
keen look. In the Los Angeles area Downey was a prominent
figure at public meetings over which he frequently presided.
His manners were courtly and polished, and he seemed to
possess an innate admiration for public applause. A forceful

and concise speaker, he was quick to express his opinions.

In his brief inaugural message of January 14, 1860, he promised a rigid and just economy and simply announced that he would pursue the general policies of Latham. When Downey succeeded Latham, Isaac N. Quinn of Tuolumne County became presiding officer of the Senate and in effect lieutenant governor. The next year when Quinn's term expired, Pablo De La Guerra of Santa Barbara was elected lieutenant governor.

Shortly after he was in office, Governor Downey condemned the methods Governor Weller had used in quelling Indian hostilities. In a special message of January 18 to the Assembly he indicated that $69,468 had been expended for this purpose in Tehama and adjoining counties. Downey urged a "rigid scrutiny" of such large expenditures and this practice was adopted. In fact a policy was soon implemented whereby the United States Army instead of the state assumed responsibility for controlling Indian hostilities thereby ending a point of friction between California and the federal government.

Several important political issues were considered by the 1860 legislature. Again a proposal for territorial government of the six southern counties was adopted, but the movement ended with the outbreak of war the next year. The question of the location of the state capitol was revived, and Sacramento, San Jose, San Francisco, Oakland, and other cities again contended for the building. On March 2, 1860, Governor Downey signed the bill which allowed the city of Sacramento to acquire four blocks of land and grant it to the state as the capitol site. A construction fund of $500,000 was appropriated and the act also provided for a board of capitol commissioners. Later in the year ground was broken for the foundations of the capitol, and on May 15, 1861, the cornerstone was laid.

Downey, the first California governor from Los Angeles, already enjoyed considerable popularity in southern California. As a candidate for lieutenant governor he had not been well known in northern California, but an opportunity to gain fame as governor occurred a few months after he took office. On April 4, 1860, the Senate passed the notorious bulkhead bill designed to create a gigantic monopoly of the San Francisco waterfront. Eight days later the bill passed the Assembly. In fact the bulkhead lobby had been active for some time. The

bulkheaders had played a role in elevating Latham to the
United States Senate in an effort to forestall gubernatorial
opposition. Levi Parsons and John B. Felton lobbied the bill
through the legislature. Then Parsons applied pressure to
Downey and according to some reports even attempted to bribe
the governor.

The bulkhead bill, if signed, would grant to the San Francisco Dock and Wharf Company the right to build a bulkhead,
or sea wall, with piers, wharves, and docks upon the water
line of 1851 with the right to collect dockage and wharfage
tolls. Moreover, the company could appropriate and possess
any franchise, lands, or wharves belonging to either the city
or to private parties. San Franciscans resented this nefarious
scheme and in protest a Citizens' Anti-Bulkhead Committee was
formed. Henry E. Highton, Sacramento correspondent of the
San Francisco Bulletin, led the opposition, drafting a memorial
to the legislature and contributing articles to the local press on
the subject.

Governor Downey, though not a man of great intellectual
gifts, was honest and just. He carefully studied the bill. He
reviewed all testimony recorded at committee hearings and
studied the engineers' plans. Despite approval of the bill by
majorities in both legislative houses, Downey ascertained that
only a minority of the San Francisco wharf owners favored
it. On April 16, Downey vetoed the bill, stating that: "after
giving this bill the most careful consideration in all its details,
I am led to the irresistible conclusion that its provisions are
not only in conflict with the Constitution and the principles of
natural justice, but that the measure, as a whole, is calculated
to work irreparable injury to our commerce, internal and ex-
ternal, of which San Francisco is, and must ever remain, the
metropolis."

Suddenly, Downey was a hero in San Francisco. The *Bulletin* hailed him as the "Andrew Jackson of California." In an
editorial entitled, "A Great Power Gone," the journal commented that: "He has vetoed the most gigantic scheme ever
presented to a Governor in America. A great and growing
power, built up and organized by the cohesion of corruption, is
stricken down today." In gratitude the citizenry of San Francisco persuaded Governor Downey to visit the city and he was
greeted at the Sacramento boat dock by elated throngs. A

torchlight procession and bands escorted the gubernatorial party from the waterfront to the Old American Theater on Sansome Street where leaders of the Citizens' Anti-Bulkhead Committee and other prominent persons praised Downey. Meanwhile, Parsons and Felton made an effort to persuade the legislature to override the veto. Fortunately, the Senate failed to do so by a 15 to 15 vote.

One July day, a year after his famous veto, Governor Downey again visited San Francisco. While strolling down Montgomery Street, he met two businessmen known to him, General Henry A. Cobb and John Middleton. They began to converse and soon turned to the subject of politics. In an argument over the recent Democratic slate, Downey called Middleton a "bulkheader." The accused retorted that the governor was "either asleep or tight," whereupon Downey struck Middleton a sharp blow on his forehead. Almost immediately General Cobb separated the two men and a crowd gathered, shoving Middleton back. Myles D. Sweeney, a liquor importer, grabbed Middleton and yelled: "You shan't strike the governor, damn you." Middleton then punched Sweeney in the eye just before the police arrived on the scene. The two combatants, Middleton and Sweeney, were hauled off to police court where they were charged with misdemeanors and then released after paying court costs. The seriousness of the fracas was exaggerated and a rumor even circulated that Governor Downey had pulled a derringer. For a few days San Franciscans were agog that the governor had engaged in a street fight, but the incident was soon forgotten.

In the presidential campaign of 1860, Downey declared himself for Stephen A. Douglas despite the fact that a majority of the Democratic state committee had been for John Breckenridge. This fact indicated that Downey was not strictly a Lecompton Democrat.

In his first annual message to the legislature, dated January 7, 1861, Downey referred to the "unexampled prosperity" of the past year, but criticized the extravagance, dishonesty, and poor administration of the previous years which had created an indebtedness of over four million dollars. He complained that despite heavy expenditures California had only an uncompleted prison and an inadequate asylum while lacking railroads, canals, a capitol, and a seminary of learning. He related that the increased revenue of 1860 had to be used to pay for the ruinous prison contract and for expensive Indian wars. Also he noted that the preliminary construction of the capitol, state reform school at Marysville, and the deaf, dumb, and blind asylum at San Francisco had made demands on the treasury. Furthermore, he expressed concern over the ten million dollar indebtedness accumulated by cities and counties since 1850, and said: "Like the State, they have but little to show for this vast expenditure."

On the positive side Governor Downey announced that the prison problem had been solved when the assignees were paid $275,000 on August 11, 1860. He related that the prison was now operated economically by the state with expectation that taxpayers would be relieved of a "terrible incubus."

Governor Downey devoted considerable space in his message to the Washoe mines which had been developed since 1859. Although he did not refer to Nevada as a colony of California, he stressed the eastward migration of thousands of Californians to the silver area. He asserted that the original settlers of Utah Territory lived in the Salt Lake region and were willing to allow separation of the silver region. Hence Downey recommended that the legislature memorialize Congress for permission to extend the eastern boundary of California. The governor concluded these sentiments by saying: "This would embrace the silver region of Utah, add to our material wealth, and bring within the jurisdiction of our own State thousands of citizens whose interests, sympathy, and attachments, are purely Californian."

The last part of his message dealt with federal relations. Here he discussed the danger of a disruption of the Union and condemned the personal liberty laws of the northern states. Yet Downey asserted that the people of California were loyal to the Union and disapproved sectionalism.

During the second year of his term Governor Downey was faced with the serious problem of squatters in San Jose during the so-called "Settlers' War" of 1861. It occurred at a time when the United States Land Commission was settling the long-standing disputes over Santa Clara Valley's land titles. In April the title to Yerba Buena Rancho, located southeast of San Jose, was confirmed to Antonio Chabolla. For several years William D. Ryan and other settlers had occupied this land. When the Third Judicial District court ordered the squatters ejected, Sheriff John M. Murphy summoned a posse of six hundred men to enforce the court order. Upon assembling at the courthouse, the citizens refused to assist the sheriff and were dismissed. Armed settlers then paraded in the streets of San Jose and settlers' leagues from nearby communities hurried in reinforcements and mustered a small cannon.

The settlers drafted a "Declaration of Rights," appealing to a "higher law" to resist the court order. They informed Governor Downey that they were defending themselves and their homes against a grasping monopoly of land speculators. The squatters claimed that they held rights to the Chabolla grant since it was "public" land under the pueblo title of San Jose. When Sheriff Murphy asked Governor Downey for aid, he urged the legislature to appropriate $100,000 to enforce the court decree. Downey said: "The State must assert its majesty and power to enforce the laws, or anarchy and confusion will ensue." Downey's threat to intervene crushed the spirit of armed resistance. On the local scene Judge Samuel B. McKee's refusal to hold court until the people observed the laws also helped to restore peace.

With the outbreak of the Civil War, Downey continued to uphold the majesty of the law. Although he opposed the policies of the federal government, he felt bound by the constitution to support the Union. Nonetheless, Downey was unfairly labeled as disloyal. In part, this charge had been made because Downey refused to attend a Union mass meeting at San Francisco on May 11, 1861. The governor explained in a letter to the Union demonstration committee that the pressure of business prevented his presence. He also expressed his attitude as follows:

> I believe the only means of preserving the American union is honorable compromise and respect for the constitutional rights of every section. I believe in the government using all its constitutional powers to preserve itself and resist aggression. I did not believe, nor do I now, that an aggressive war should be waged upon any section of the confederacy, nor do I believe that this union can be preserved by a coercive policy.

Among the speakers at the meeting was Senator Milton S. Latham, who now condemned Southern leaders and asserted that "California takes her post, with ready and willing heart to do her duty, whatever it may be, to preserve the Constitution inviolate and the union intact." The other speakers adhered to the same theme. At the meeting Downey's letter was read. His "anti-coercion" doctrine was vehemently denounced. The San Francisco press generally viewed his attitude as one fostering disunion. The *Marysville Democrat*, a Douglas journal, considered his letter as "an approval of the battle cry which is to rally the Secession Pacific Republic party of California in the coming campaign." The *Marysville Appeal*, a Republican newspaper, commented: "Governor Downey greatly mistakes the temper of the people of this State, if he supposes that any considerable portion of them will sustain him in the position which he has taken."

As a result of the journalistic attacks upon his loyalty Downey explained his sentiments further in a letter appearing in the *Sacramento Union* on May 17. In part the governor said:

> I did not intend that anything emanating from me should breathe aught but patriotism and devotion to the country and its Government. I have no sympathy with secession or those who brought it about, as I have always believed that all evils or grievances growing out of our system and diversity of interests peculiar to each section of the Union could find their remedy within that Union itself and under the broad aegis of the Constitution.

Downey further explained that as chief magistrate he felt obligated to support the United States constitution and the California constitution, under all circumstances and at every sacrifice. He assured his readers that he would obey all laws and authority whether or not the laws coincided with his particular views and even if he politically opposed those in authority. However, he reserved the right as a free citizen to express his personal opinions "as to the policy of any and every law of the Federal Government." Then Downey related that he opposed an invasion of the South by an army having in view its subjugation as conquered provinces and the incitement of servile insurrections. Instead, he believed in merely defending the national capital, federal forts, and arsenals and in collecting federal revenues.

This "anti-coercion" doctrine caused Downey's popularity to wane. Many Unionists considered him pro-Confederate and the politically cunning Republicans exaggerated Confederate threats in order to weaken the Democratic party.

Despite charges of his critics, Downey remained loyal to the letter of the law in discharging his duties as governor. On July 24, 1861, Secretary of War Simon Cameron called upon Downey for troops to guard the overland mail route. Downey met this call and other requisitions for various purposes as they were made. After completing the second requisition, Governor Downey wrote on August 28, to General Edwin V. Sumner, commanding the Department of the Pacific, and stated in part: "Enlisting is going on rapidly, and the fife and drum are heard in every village. I have repeatedly assured you that none other than those loyal to the General Government would be offered bearing 'commissions' of the State."

On September 2, 1861, Governor Downey informed President Lincoln as follows:

> The first requisition made upon this State for 1,500 volunteers has been filled and the command given to Colonel [James H.] Carleton. It having been intimated by the War Department that it was your desire that this officer should have the command, I cheerfully complied, as I had every confidence in his experience, patriotism and gallantry.

The First California Infantry and Cavalry were mustered in at the San Francisco Presidio and trained in Oakland at Camp Downey and Camp Merchant. Instead of guarding the overland mail route, the regiment was assigned to southern California because of rumored Confederate threats to that area. Then the regiment became the nucleus of the famed California Column that marched into Arizona and New Mexico to repel a Confederate army commanded by General Henry H. Sibley. Another regiment under Colonel Patrick E. Connor, also requisitioned by Downey, assumed responsibility for guarding the overland route.

Meanwhile, in July, 1861, the Union Democratic convention meeting at Sacramento nominated John Conness over Downey on the fourteenth ballot. Despite his failure to obtain renomination and his personal opposition to the Lincoln administration, Downey continued to perform his duties faithfully during his remaining months in office. For example, when Secretary of State William H. Seward urged Downey on October 14, to present the matter of coastal defense to the legislature, the governor complied.

In his second and final annual message to the legislature on January 8, 1862, Downey related that: "the record of the past year is replete with the most gratifying evidence of prosperity and of social and material progress." The outgoing governor devoted considerable space to economic affairs. He favored continuing the small appropriations to the State Agricultural Society and to local farm societies and urged the legislature to offer bounties for cultivating flax, coffee, tea, and sugar.

Downey visualized the United States as a great commercial power in the Pacific and claimed that the time was ripe to have a large navy upon its waters "both for the protection of our maritime and commercial interests, and for the peaceful conquest by a wise policy of the nations that from their natural position must sooner or later become commercial tributaries of California."

Downey detailed his concept of manifest destiny with considerable fervor. He warned California to exploit her natural advantages before Great Britain and France could gain the trade of the Orient forever once those two nations completed the Suez Canal. To circumvent British and French competition he pointed out the need for a transcontinental railroad and the need for steam communication with Japan, China, Australia, and the Pacific islands. To strengthen his argument for this geopolitical blueprint Downey claimed that the railroad was essential to preserve California with the Union.

Downey was sincere, direct, and independent as governor. He impartially guarded the interests of the public. His judicious veto of the bulkhead bill was the most significant achievement of his administration. Although state control of the port of San Francisco was delayed until Stanford's administration, Downey's veto prepared the way for this action. On April 24, 1863, the board of state harbor commissioners was created and gradually the San Francisco waterfront improved.

Despite his misgivings as to Lincoln's policies, Downey as California's first Civil War governor remained loyal to the federal government. He met the various calls for troops and was responsible for the appointment of reliable and loyal military leaders. The state prospered during his administration and he succeeded in reducing the public debt. A saner policy regarding Indian hostilities was adopted and prison management improved. The state library was reorganized and appropriations were made for the important geological survey under the direction of Josiah Dwight Whitney. In the fields of agriculture and viticulture considerable progress was made. Downey appointed Colonel Agoston Haraszthy of Sonoma, J. A. Ramirez of Marysville, and Colonel Juan José Warner of Los Angeles as viticultural commissioners to improve grape culture and wine-making. Downey approved Haraszthy's European trip which enabled him to collect choice vines and cuttings and to instruct California grape growers and wine makers on the latest progress of continental viticulture.

Although no important political reforms occurred under Downey, he unsuccessfully proposed a biennial legislative session. The decision to make Sacramento the permanent state capital was reached. While Downey saw the need for a state university and for a Pacific railroad, these were but dreams for the future.

In 1863, the Democratic state convention nominated Downey for a second time as its gubernatorial candidate, but he was defeated by Frederick F. Low. The next year he was elected as a delegate to the national convention of the Union party. He was nominated from the first district as a congressional candidate by the Democratic state convention of 1864, but declined to accept. In the later sixties and in the seventies Downey remained active in the California Democratic party, but he never held office again. In 1879, he was a member of the executive committee of the New Constitution party and in the same year declined to become gubernatorial candidate of the Workingmen's party.

After his service as governor ended, Downey returned to his home in Los Angeles. He became primarily interested in banking and real estate. In 1865, he subdivided Rancho Santa Gertrudis into fifty acre tracts purchasable on a ten year installment plan. Under his sponsorship the town of Downey began its development. In 1868, Downey and James A. Hayward of San Francisco opened the first bank in Los Angeles. It only lasted a few months and in 1871, Downey consolidated his banking interests with Isaias W. Hellman, when they established the Farmers and Merchants Bank. This bank prospered and survived the panic of 1875, which paralleled the collapse of the Nevada silver boom. Downey also founded the second horse railway in Los Angeles and became a director of the Los Angeles and San Pedro Railroad with Phineas Banning and Benito Wilson. Downey along with these two men and Harris Newmark were also instrumental in persuading the Southern Pacific Railroad to enter Los Angeles.

From 1868 to 1876, Downey in several ways aided the first land boom in Los Angeles. In August, 1868, he and some partners bought land near Compton and drilled the first artesian wells in southern California. He helped to develop retail trade by constructing the Downey block at Main and Temple Streets and in 1873, he was a founder of the Board of Trade, forerunner of the Chamber of Commerce. Downey was also active in the Pioneer Oil Company and in the Los Angeles Water Company.

While assisting in transforming Los Angeles into an enterprising American city, Downey recognized the need for cultural institutions. In 1872, he was instrumental in establishing the library association. In 1879, Downey, Isaias W. Hellman, and Ozro W. Childs donated 308 acres of land in western Los Angeles for establishing the University of Southern California. The next year Downey was elected as a member of the university's first board of directors. In 1883, Downey was a founder and a vice-president of the Historical Society of Southern California.

Downey's final political activity of importance took place in 1880, when he was a member of the executive committee urging state division. He republished the original act for state division of 1859, claiming that it was still valid. As an argument Downey stated: "From the morning of our existence as a commonwealth the southern counties of this state have been uneasy and restless under the lash of unequal taxation and the unequal distribution of the benefits derivable therefrom."

On January 20, 1883, Downey and his wife were involved in a railroad accident near the summit of Tehachapi Pass. When the engine was refueled, it was detached from the coaches which were derailed on a down-hill grade. Twenty passengers, including Mrs. Downey, were killed. After this tragedy Downey suffered poor health and was forced to neglect his business properties. For several years he traveled in Europe and then stayed with relatives in San Francisco. Upon returning to Los Angeles he resumed control of his business activities and married Rose V. Kelley in 1888. His second wife died in 1892.

There were no children by either of Downey's marriages. Following a slight attack of pneumonia, Downey died on March 1, 1894, in Los Angeles.

Thus closed the career of California's first Civil War governor. His loyalty, although questioned by some contemporaries, remained true as the threat to the Union became more grave. As a private citizen of Los Angeles his activities were locally prominent and of enduring success. He earned a fortune while improving the agriculture and commerce of southern California. His political career faded away early in life leaving him the opportunity to serve as an enterprising business man and philanthropist at the height of his maturity.

BIBLIOGRAPHY

MANUSCRIPTS
Bancroft, Hubert H., "History of the Life of John G. Downey and Material for Its Preparation, 1886-1889," (Bancroft Library). Contains a typed transcript of an article by Oscar T. Shuck in the *San Francisco Star*, Feb. 6, 1886, Downey's dictated autobiography, and letters to the History Company and N. J. Stone from Edwin W. Fowler with notes and instructions concerning the biographical sketch of Downey.

CONTEMPORARY ACCOUNTS
Assembly Journal, 11th-13th Sess., 1860-62.
Bartlett, Lanier, ed., *On the Old West Coast, Being Further Reminiscences of a Ranger* by Horace Bell (New York, 1930).
Newmark, Maurice H. and Marco R., eds., *Sixty Years in Southern California, 1853-1913* (Boston, 2nd ed., 1926).

SECONDARY SOURCES
Bancroft, H. H., *Chronicles of the Builders of the Commonwealth.*
Camp, William M., *San Francisco, Port of Gold* (Garden City, 1947).
Davis, W.J., *History of Political Conventions. . .*
Hittell, T.H., *History of California.*
Macleod, Julia H., "John G. Downey as One of the 'Kings,' " *California Historical Society Quarterly*, XXXVI (1957), 327-31.

NEWSPAPERS
San Francisco Call, March 2, 1894, has an obituary of Downey.

THESES
Bergstrom, Elizabeth, "The Life and Activities of John G. Downey, with a Short sketch of the City of Downey" (M.A., University of Southern California, 1930).
Purdy, Mary, "The Governorship of John Gately Downey of California, 1860-1862" (M.A., Stanford University, 1933).

Calendar of Events

March 9, 1824	Stanford born in Watervliet, New York.
1845	Stanford studied law in Albany, New York.
1850	Stanford ran for District Attorney of Washington County, Wisconsin.
July 12, 1852	Stanford arrived in San Francisco and later opened a store at Cold Springs.
1853	Stanford moved to Michigan Bluff.
1855	Stanford settled in Sacramento.
September 2, 1857	Stanford defeated as Republican candidate for State Treasurer.
September 7, 1859	Stanford defeated as Republican candidate for Governor.
1860	Stanford stumped for Lincoln.
September 4, 1861	Stanford elected Governor.
January, 1862	San Francisco became temporary capital.
July 18, 1862	California State Normal School opened at San Francisco.
1862	State offices extended to four-year terms and legislative sessions made biennial.
September 3, 1862	Union party elected John Swett as Superintendent of Public Instruction.
May 10, 1869	Transcontinental railroad completed.
January 28, 1885	Stanford elected to United States Senate.
January 14, 1891	Stanford re-elected to United States Senate.
October 1, 1891	Stanford University opened.
June 21, 1893	Stanford died at Palo Alto.

Leland Stanford

8TH GOVERNOR — REPUBLICAN
BORN: MARCH 9, 1824   DIED: JUNE 21, 1893
TERM OF OFFICE: JANUARY 10, 1862—DECEMBER 10, 1863

THE VARIED CAREER OF LELAND STANFORD, first Republican and second Civil War governor of California, has been the subject of considerable historical writing, particularly with respect to his role as railroad builder, United States Senator, and university founder. The primary emphasis in this study is with his governorship. The fourth of eight children of Josiah and Elizabeth Phillips Stanford, he was born in Watervliet township, New York, on March 9, 1824, being reared on the family farm in the Mohawk Valley between Albany and Schenectady. His full name was Amasa Leland Stanford, but he never used the entire name after reaching young manhood. He obtained his early education in public schools and at home. For a few years he worked for his father, although it has been stated that he first earned money by selling lumber to the New York Central Railroad. At the age of seventeen Stanford attended the Clinton Liberal Institute near Utica, and later attended the Cazenovia Seminary near Syracuse.

In 1845, Stanford was an apprentice in the law firm of Wheaton, Doolittle, and Hadley in Albany. After admittance to the bar, he moved to Port Washington, Wisconsin, in 1848, where he practiced in partnership with Wesley Pierce. Stanford also participated in local politics, joined a literary and debating society, and wrote on occasion for a Milwaukee newspaper. In 1850, he was candidate of the Whig party for district attorney of Washington County, but was defeated by Eugene S. Turner, a Democrat, of longer residence and more experience. In the summer of 1850, Stanford returned briefly to Albany

115

and married Jane Elizabeth Lathrop, the daughter of an Albany merchant. The newly-weds resided in Port Washington less than two years. On March 16, 1852, a fire enveloped the town, destroying Stanford's law office and library valued at $3,000. Because of the fire and since he was in financial straits after four years' unrewarding practice in Wisconsin, the young lawyer decided to join his brothers in California. Stanford sailed from New York in June, via the Nicaragua route, reaching San Francisco aboard the steamer, *Independence*, on July 12, 1852. His wife, who remained at the family home in Albany, later joined him in California.

For a brief period Stanford stayed with his brothers. He later opened a store in partnership with Nicholas T. Smith at Cold Springs, a mining camp located as a way station between Placerville and Coloma. In the spring of 1853, after this camp declined, the partners opened a merchandise store at Michigan Bluff on the American River. Here Stanford served as a justice of peace, holding his only public office prior to his governorship.

In the spring of 1855, when his father-in-law died, Stanford and his wife went back to Albany. In the fall they returned to California, settling in Sacramento, where he operated a general store. He later took in David Meeker as a partner.

In the capital, Stanford, a former Whig, was a founder of the Republican party of California along with Cornelius Cole, Collis P. Huntington, Mark Hopkins, and Charles and Edwin B. Crocker. He actively participated in the Frémont campaign of 1856. He assisted in organizing the Sacramento Library Association and served as a member of its first board of trustees. In April, 1857, Stanford was an unsuccessful candidate for alderman. In July, he received the Republican nomination as state treasurer, but was defeated.

On June 9, 1859, the Republican state convention unanimously nominated Stanford as governor after the withdrawal of such notable candidates as Edward D. Baker, Timothy G. Phelps, and Frank M. Pixley. In his acceptance address he expressed his preference for free white citizens to any other race, his belief that the federal government should benefit all sections alike, and his support of a transcontinental railroad. Then he said: "I am in favor of a Railroad, and it is the policy of this State to favor that party which is likely to advance their interests."

Although Stanford called himself, "not much of a talker," he campaigned vigorously. After delivering addresses in San Francisco and Sacramento, Stanford toured the then populous Mother Lode country in company with Judge Frederick P. Tracy and spoke to attentive and sometimes enthusiastic audiences in Placerville, Coloma, Georgetown, Michigan Bar, Nevada City, Downieville, and other mining towns. While generally making a good impression, Stanford again received the least number of votes in his second bid for a state office.

In 1860, Stanford was elected as a delegate to the Republican national convention at Chicago, but did not attend, being replaced by an alternate. In the campaign of 1860, he stumped for Lincoln, who carried California. After the victory, Stanford left for Washington to discuss the California patronage problem with President Lincoln.

With the outbreak of war Stanford's chances for nomination and election improved and at the Republican state convention, meeting at Sacramento on June 18, 1861, he asked for the gubernatorial nomination in the upcoming election which he described as a struggle of democracy against aristocracy. Stanford won on the first ballot obtaining 197 votes to 104 for Timothy G. Phelps and 24 votes for David Jackson Staples. For lieutenant governor the Republicans nominated John F. Chellis. Stanford was probably acceptable in 1861 because of his willingness to run in 1859 in view of almost certain defeat at that time.

The Breckenridge Democratic convention nominated John R. McConnell for governor and Jasper O'Farrell for lieutenant governor, while the Union Democratic convention nominated John Conness for governor and Richard Irwin for lieutenant governor. From June 29 to September 2, Stanford campaigned in northern California in company with Cornelius Cole. They canvassed extensively in the mining regions from Weaverville in the north to Sonora in the south. The Republican party swept the election. Stanford ran ahead of his ticket, winning 55,935 votes. His two opponents together polled 63,816. Hence Stanford—like Lincoln—was a minority executive.

The primary reason for the Republican victory in California was that Stanford was considered a Union man and many Northern Democrats voted for him. For example, a group of

San Francisco business men, which included Henry W. Halleck, James Phelan, Henry M. Naglee, and Levi Strauss, supported Stanford despite their opposition to the Republican party. Actually Stanford's election was assured, for the vast majority of Californians had migrated from the North and were loyal to the Union.

When the legislature convened at Sacramento on January 6, 1862, the Republicans and Union Democrats held strong majorities in both houses. On inauguration day, four days later, Sacramento's most disastrous flood inundated the capital necessitating Governor-elect Stanford and his party to row from his home to the temporary capitol in small boats. Before a joint convention Judge Edward Norton administered the oaths of office to Leland Stanford and John F. Chellis.

In opening his address Stanford presented a brief statement of general policy because of the change to a Republican administration. First he pledged his cooperation in encouraging intellectual, scientific, moral, and agricultural improvements. He reiterated Bigler's anti-Chinese policy which most California governors of the nineteenth century followed, when he stated:

> There can be no doubt but that the presence of numbers among us of a degraded and distinct people must exercise a deleterious influence upon the superior race, and, to a certain extent, repel desirable immigration. It will afford me great pleasure to concur with the Legislature in any constitutional action, having for its object the repression of the immigration of the Asiatic races.

Partly to point out the need for encouraging immigration from the Eastern states, Stanford emphasized the importance of the projected overland railroad. He indicated that trade with Asia depended upon a railroad and he also stressed the importance of steam transportation between California and the Orient. Then he discussed the vast undeveloped wealth of Nevada and stated that the most difficult link of the transcontinental railroad which must pass through that territory was within the boundary of California. After alluding to the railroad as a military necessity, he expressed the belief that the most arduous aspect of its building could be achieved without direct financial aid from the federal government. But then he asked the legislators the following question: "May we not, therefore, with the utmost propriety, even at this time, ask the National Government to donate lands and loan its credit in aid of this portion of that communication, which is of the very first importance, not alone to the States and Territories west of the Rocky Mountains, but to the whole Nation, and is the great work of the age?"

Stanford was the first California governor to ask for state control of the forests. He suggested petitioning the federal government to cede forest lands in California to the state and proposed that any profits from their sale should be used to foster education, charitable works, and internal improvements. With regard to the existing mining laws and regulations, he stated that these should not be disturbed and he opposed any attempt by the federal government to restrict or interfere with mining. Stanford requested a "retrenchment" in public expenditures, but asked that aid for charitable and educational purposes be "munificent."

In a letter of January 17, 1862, Governor Stanford answered an inquiry of Secretary of Treasury Salmon P. Chase, asking whether California would assume its share of the national tax as enacted by Congress on August 6, 1861. On January 30, Stanford was able to inform Secretary Chase that California would pay its direct tax of $254,538. Meanwhile, the legislature had adjourned because of flood conditions and eventually it was compelled to convene in the Merchants' Exchange Building in San Francisco for the remainder of the session.

While the legislature agreed with Stanford on issues to support the Union, the Senate rejected some of his appointments. Stanford first vetoed a Senate bill transferring $100,000 from the swamp land fund to the General Fund in order to pay the legislators and their employees. The governor's primary doubt was whether the money, to which the swamp land fund had exclusive rights, could be repaid from the General Fund since the latter was already heavily in debt. However, the legislators wanted their salaries promptly and passed the measure over the veto. Stanford's four other vetoes were sustained. One of these was an Assembly bill to incorporate Sacramento. He vetoed it on grounds that the measure was local in character and was opposed by most of the citizens of the city.

There were several important measures enacted by the 1862 legislature. One authorized the establishment of savings and loan associations. Another provided for military training in colleges and academies. The militia system was reorganized.

Several new agricultural and industrial products were subsidized. A township system was developed to simplify local
government.

At the same session several significant amendments to the
state constitution were proposed and subsequently approved by
the voters. These established biennial legislative sessions;
lengthened the term of governor and other state officers from
two years to four years; lengthened the term of assemblymen
from one year to two years and of senators from two to four
years; and revamped the judicial system.

On March 25, in accordance with a concurrent resolution of
the legislature, Governor Stanford telegraphed Secretary of
State William H. Seward to ascertain whether the condition
of foreign relations necessitated any measures to improve San
Francisco harbor defenses. Seward replied that affairs were
peaceful, but that in Lincoln's opinion, as long as civil war
continued, there existed the danger of foreign aggression. The
national administration suggested that one or two iron-clad
steamers at San Francisco would insure adequate defense. The
problem of San Francisco harbor defense haunted the entire
Stanford term and the first part of his successor's term.

Meanwhile, the three political parties of California—Republican, Union Democratic, and Breckinridge Democratic—prepared for the election of 1862, which only involved one statewide office, that of superintendent of public instruction. Many
prominent Republicans and Union Democrats favored a fusion
of their forces in support of Lincoln. At first Stanford advised
calling a Republican convention but he was criticized by some
newspapers for differing with the majority of the Republicans.
Later at a meeting, Republican and Union Democratic legislators decided to call a Union state convention. As a result some
Union Democrats joined with the Republicans in the Union
party while others refused to disband their party. Hence there
remained three parties, but in the election John Swett easily
won on the Union ticket. Moreover, all state Senators and most
of the Assemblymen elected were Unionists. On September 4,
1862, Stanford telegraphed Lincoln as follows: "Our general
election was held yesterday. The result is a triumphant and
overwhelming victory in favor of the Union and the National
Administration."

All three of California's war governors cooperated with the

War Department in meeting the call for troops. Most of the California volunteers fought in Indian skirmishes, guarded the overland mail, or engaged the Confederate forces in the Southwest. Toward the end of 1862, some young San Franciscans, who were anxious to fight on the Atlantic coast, volunteered their services to Governor John A. Andrew of Massachusetts. When he approved their enlistment in the Massachusetts contingent, Governor Stanford protested in a letter, dated January 24, 1863, to General George Wright, commanding the Department of the Pacific, in these words:

> The proceedings under by force of which these troops are to be raised are clearly irregular and in violations of the rights of this State. I know of no authority by which the Governor of Massachusetts can raise volunteers in California, either through the orders of the War Department, or the inconsiderate and officious action of citizens of this State.

Stanford explained that he would not interfere at present because of the sacrifices of sister states and because of the comparative exemption of California in previous calls for troops. He protested against the practice being considered as a precedent. In other words he did not want to deny a single soldier to the federal government; yet he did not care to permit an invasion of the rights of his own state.

For its 1863 session the legislature had returned to Sacramento and on January 7, Stanford presented his first annual message. He mentioned that a succession of floods had devastated the state during the previous legislature, but now the process of physical reconstruction had been completed. Despite flood damages, California had enjoyed an unparalleled prosperity. However, Stanford related that state indebtedness had totaled $5,569,284 on the previous December 1. After asserting that his administration had inherited a large debt, he recommended higher property taxes to reduce the debt and proposed the *"pay as you go system"* to put the treasury on a strict cash basis. Stanford recommended a special tax to create a fund for improving the militia and he urged "an increased exhibition of military ardor among our people, and a more rapid organization of companies throughout the State."

Stanford warned of the danger of a federal tax on mining claims. He believed that the issue had been revived and opposed it as unjust. He recommended a continuation of the payment of subsidies for certain agricultural goods and expressed his gratitude that construction of the Pacific railroad had been approved.

The legislature of 1863 was primarily concerned with war measures. Funds were appropriated to equip the volunteer soldiers and to create a soldiers' relief fund. Legislation was enacted to insure loyalty and patriotism. For example, one law made it a misdemeanor to display Confederate flags. Loyalty oaths were required for attorneys and public school teachers. On April 25, 1863, an act was passed to prevent the arming and equipping of privateers or piratical vessels. This measure resulted from the unsuccessful attempt by Asbury Harpending and Ridgely Greathouse to sail the *J. M. Chapman* from San Francisco as a Confederate privateer.

In his final message to the legislature on December 9, 1863, Stanford indicated that despite higher state taxes and larger assessments, California's budget remained unbalanced largely because of military appropriations. In reference to the Pacific railroad he said: "To this great work the last Legislature made an appropriation creditable to its sagacity and the enterprise of the State." After discussing the disposition of the California volunteers and praising their services, he explained that because of the distance from the theater of war California had not placed many volunteers in the field. Yet he could proudly note that California was the "foremost State" in sustaining the Sanitary Commission, the Red Cross of the Civil War.

Stanford defended the action of Congress in issuing legal tender notes and urged Californians not to embarrass the federal government by refusing to accept them. He closed his message with a few remarks about political reconstruction of the South, suggesting that it might be beneficial to disregard old state boundaries.

The leading candidates for nomination as governor by the Union party in 1863 were Stanford, Aaron A. Sargent, and Frederick F. Low. At first the prospect of Stanford's renomination appeared likely, but Low's supporters were very active and Senator John Conness, a successful organizer of Union Leagues, opposed Stanford. As the Low forces gained additional strength, Stanford withdrew from the contest and returned to private life.

In "The Great Prize Fight," appearing in the *Golden Era*

of October 11, 1863, Mark Twain wrote a story satirizing both California politics and prize fighting as depicted by contemporary sportswriters. An imaginary prize fight was held at Seal Rock Point near the Cliff House between Governor Stanford and Governor-elect Ferdinand F. Low for "a purse of a hundred thousand dollars." Seconds for Stanford and Low were respectively, William M. Stewart, soon to be a Nevada Senator, and Justice Stephen J. Field of the United States Supreme Court. General George Wright, commanding the Department of the Pacific, acted as the referee in Twain's story.

When Stanford was governor, he enjoyed robust health and was quite energetic. Physically a large man, he stood almost six feet tall and weighed about 250 pounds. He was deliberate in thought and a slow speaker. His speeches, written in advance, were delivered in an uninspired manner. On social occasions he was always cordial and hospitable. He appeared to revel in occasions such as the State Fairs and ground-breaking ceremonies when he could mingle among the people. At the tenth annual State Fair in Sacramento on September 26, 1863, he gave the opening address and began by saying: "The State Fair is a great holiday. It is a time of physical relaxation and of general social enjoyment." Stanford possessed considerable personal vanity and often exhibited a love of display.

Stanford had come to California with small means. Through his business sagacity he created a small fortune before his election as governor. Once in power he did not hesitate to use his office to benefit his railroad interests. As a private citizen Governor Stanford was president and director of the Central Pacific Railroad. While Mark Hopkins, Collis P. Huntington, and Charles Crocker attended to other functions, Stanford attended to political and financial affairs in California and Nevada. The legislature passed several subsidy acts aiding the Central Pacific Railroad which Stanford approved. The prevailing attitude was that Stanford's actions were justified in view of the benefits California would gain by the railroad's completion. On January 8, 1863, near the foot of K Street in Sacramento, ground was broken to start the building of the railroad. Before a large crowd, including state officers and legislators, Governor-elect Stanford turned the first earth with a spade of silver. Although he would not be inaugurated for two days, Stanford stated that it was proper that the "Governor of the State should be present and perform the first act of labor. . . . " He also said: "The blessings which are to follow the completion of the work which we this day inaugurate can not be fully estimated. Agriculture, commerce, manufactures, wealth, and population, will feel its influence, and will commence with it a new era in progress." The Big Four—Stanford, Huntington, Hopkins, and Crocker—risked their own fortunes in building the railroad and in making larger fortunes. At the time few questioned that Governor Stanford had a conflict of interest. In later years many viewed Stanford as a shrewd and mighty magnate and "political wire-puller."

Stanford sponsored minor administrative and legislative reforms. He was the first governor to propose a codification of laws to simplify legislation in an effort to shorten legislative sessions. He also attempted to transfer law-making of a local nature from the legislature to the county boards of supervisors. During his term new agricultural and manufacturing projects were subsidized and savings and loan associations were authorized. His program of military training for college students was the forerunner of military education in California. Stanford was aware of the need for conservation and he approved two forest laws. As previously noted, major constitutional changes occurred in 1862.

Indian depredations, particularly in Humboldt, Trinity, and Butte Counties, hampered his administration. By proclamation Stanford enlisted a Mountain Battalion of volunteers to replace regular troops and it soon controlled the situation. As a war governor Stanford felt that treason should be swiftly punished. While realizing that Californians came from all parts of the Union, he insisted on supremacy of the national government and demanded that California not forget that it was one of the United States. Stanford was the uncompromising Union man that the voters wanted, and he was faithful to the Lincoln administration in all respects. He even justified legal tender notes despite the fact that gold was the accepted medium of exchange in California. When the war shut off the import of cotton, tobacco, and naval stores from the Southern states, Stanford encouraged local production. Hence the production of turpentine, pitch, and tar temporarily increased. When his term closed, Stanford jubilantly said: "And while the trade and staples of North Carolina are languishing under the blighting influence of secession, the mountains of California may snatch from her grasp the distinction of being the chief tar State."

During Stanford's tenure California farmers produced more wheat and barley to meet greater demands in the East and Great Britain. In addition to contributing gold to the national economy, California also increased her production of lesser metallic minerals. The New Almaden Mine in Santa Clara County produced a large percentage of the quicksilver utilized in California and Nevada for extracting gold and silver. Considerable copper excitement developed in 1862 and 1863, when hundreds of copper mining companies were organized. The more important mines were in the vicinity of Copperopolis, Camp Seco, and Lancha Plana in Calaveras County. By the spring of 1863 the shipment of copper ore from California assumed sizeable proportions.

California prospered during Stanford's administration, largely because of the Civil War. As a result, the indebtedness of the state was reduced in half. Moreover, Stanford helped to settle land titles by a firm enforcement of the law in a movement to stop squatterism.

While Stanford has been criticized for using his office to further his own interests and for his narrow stand on the rights of minorities, he did have the ability to grasp large and visionary projects, of which many were forged into reality. While he is remembered more for other works, his governorship was successful. As an administrator he was always able to meet emergency conditions, whether it be a flood, an Indian raid, or an attempted Confederate conspiracy.

After driving the golden spike in 1869, Stanford devoted the remainder of his life to the railroad and to a new political career. On January 28, 1885, he was elected to the United States Senate and re-elected in 1891, serving until his death two years later. Stanford was not conspicuous on the Senate floor despite his previous experience as a governor. He fought the Interstate Commerce Act designed to regulate railroads, favored the Blair Educational Bill, and served on minor committees.

Besides his political and railroad careers Stanford's name is remembered in the fields of photography and education. He sponsored publication of *The Horse in Motion* based upon studies made at his Palo Alto farm by Eadweard A. Muybridge. As governor, Stanford signed the act of May 2, 1862, establishing California State Normal School, a successor of the earlier Minns' Evening Normal School, and later San Jose State College. Governor Stanford was an ex officio member of its first board of trustees. After the institution's removal to San Jose from San Francisco, Stanford maintained an active interest in its welfare. In 1885, as a memorial to their only son, Leland Stanford, Jr., who had died at fifteen, Stanford and his wife founded the famous university which opened rather precariously in 1891. On June 21, 1893, Stanford died at his Palo Alto home, closing the career of California's best known nineteenth century governor. He was interred on the grounds of the Stanford campus.

BIBLIOGRAPHY

MANUSCRIPTS

Bowman, J.N., "The Early Governors of California. . ."

"Daily Journal, Leland Stanford, 1862," (State Archives).

"Letters and research notes from Judge Charles L. Larson, Port Washington, Wisconsin to B.F. Gilbert, Dec. 22, 1959 and Jan. 7, 1960."

"Letters from Leland Stanford, Jan. 17 and 30, March 18, 1862 to Salmon P. Chase; Jan. 24 and June 27, 1862 to General George Wright; and March 25, 1862, to William H. Seward," (State Archives).

CONTEMPORARY ACCOUNTS

Assembly Journal, 13th-14th Sess., 1862-63.

Clark, George T., ed., "Letters of Leland Stanford to Mark Hopkins," *California Historical Society Quarterly*, V (1926), 178-83.

War of the Rebellion: A Compilation of the Official Records of the Union and Confederate Armies (128 vols., Washington, D.C., 1880-1901), Ser. I, Vol. L, Pt. II.

SECONDARY SOURCES

Bancroft, H.H., *History of California.*

———, *History of the Life of Leland Stanford* (Oakland, 1952).

Brown, W.E., "Leland Stanford," in O.T. Shuck, ed., *Representative and Leading Men of the Pacific.*

Clark, George T., *Leland Stanford, War Governor of California, Railroad Builder, and Founder of Stanford University* (Stanford University Press, 1931).

Daggett, Stuart, *Chapters on the History of the Southern Pacific* (New York, 1922).

———, "Leland Stanford," *Dictionary of American Biography*, XVII, 501-506.

Davis, W.J., *History of Political Conventions. . .*

Dunlap, Boutwell, "Some Facts Concerning Leland Stanford and His Contemporaries in Placer County," *CHSQ*, II (1923), 203-210.

Elliott, Orrin L., *Stanford University* (Stanford University Press, 1937).

Gilbert, Benjamin F., *Pioneers for One Hundred Years: San Jose State College, 1857-1957* (San Jose, 1957).

Hittell, T.H., *History of California.*

Lewis, Oscar, *The Big Four* (New York, 1938).

Myers, Gustavus, *History of the Great American Fortunes* (New York, 1936).

Sabin, Edwin L., *Building the Pacific Railway* (Philadelphia, 1919).

NEWSPAPERS

Milwaukee Journal, Dec. 21, 1959, has data about Stanford's Wisconsin career.

San Francisco Examiner, June 21, 1893, has a lengthy obituary of Stanford.

Calendar of Events

June 30, 1828	Low born near Frankfort, Maine.
June 14, 1849	Low arrived in San Francisco.
1850	Low Brothers Company established at Marysville.
1854	California Steam Navigation Company incorporated.
June, 1861	Low defeated in bid for Republican nomination as State Controller.
June 2, 1862	Low seated in House of Representatives.
1863	Low appointed Collector of the Port of San Francisco.
December 10, 1863	Low inaugurated as Governor.
1865	Thirteenth Amendment ratified by California.
1866	First appropriation made for administration of Yosemite grant.
1867	Low declined renomination.
December, 1869	President Grant appointed Low as Minister to China.
1870	Low-Rodgers Mission sailed to Korea.
1874	Low resigned as Minister to China.
1874	Low appointed manager of Anglo-California Bank.
1884	Low served as president of the San Francisco Clearing House Association.
July 21, 1894	Low died in San Francisco.

Frederick F. Low

9TH GOVERNOR — UNIONIST
BORN: JANUARY 30, 1828   DIED: JULY 21, 1894
TERM OF OFFICE: DECEMBER 10, 1863—DECEMBER 5, 1867

COMPARABLE IN STATURE to Leland Stanford, but generally less known, was Frederick F. Low, another Civil War governor. Also a Republican or Unionist, Low assumed the gubernatorial post at a crucial time in the state's history when the nation was still locked in its great struggle for survival in 1863. Moreover, the office at this time acquired additional responsibility and prestige, for in accordance with the 1862 constitutional amendment the tenure had been extended from two to four years. Another amendment lengthened the legislative session from an annual to a biennial one which placed upon the new governor the authority for sponsoring two-year legislative and fiscal programs.

California's first four-year governor was born near Frankfort, Maine, on June 30, 1828, where his parents worked a small farm. Low attended local common schools and an academy. Despite his lack of the advantages of wealth and higher education, he was to develop into a successful businessman, politician, and diplomat.

At the age of fifteen Low became apprenticed to the East India firm, Russell, Sturgis, and Company of Boston. For five years he worked in the counting room of this mercantile house and here first interested himself in California and the Far East. In his spare hours he acquired considerable self-education by attending lectures at Faneuil Hall and the Lowell Institute.

When the news of the California gold discovery reached the East, Low decided to join the rush. On March 1, 1849, he boarded a ship at New York, which sailed only as far as Colón. At the Isthmus he was delayed sixty-three days waiting transportation to San Francisco. Finally he succeeded in obtaining passage aboard the Pacific Mail Steamship Company vessel, *Panama*. Among a few of the other illustrious passengers of this over-crowded steamer bound for the land of gold were William M. Gwin, Jessie Frémont, John B. Weller, Darius O. Mills, and Lieutenant George H. Derby. On June 14, the *Panama* stood into San Francisco. Low pitched a tent on the line of California Street, but soon embarked on a river boat to Sacramento, whence he journeyed on foot to the mines at Horseshoe Bar on the north fork of the American River. During the summer he earned over $1,500 in gold and returned to San Francisco at the beginning of the winter rains.

In that booming frontier city he formed a partnership with Henry Lambert, opening a merchandise store on Sacramento Street near the intersection of Kearny Street. The fire of June, 1850, destroyed their store and its entire stock. The partners reopened in a new brick building, but Low soon dissolved the partnership. In the fall, he moved to Marysville, supply center for the northern mines. Here he married Mollie Creed and the next year Low with his two older brothers, Joseph W. and Charles L., established a mercantile and shipping business under the name of Low Brothers Company. In 1854, the two older brothers retired and Frederick Low continued in business by himself. Meanwhile, he had gained an interest in river steamers plying the waterways between Marysville, Sacramento, and San Francisco. In partnership with five associates he organized the California Steam Navigation Company in 1854 and consolidated nearly all inland water transportation to the northern mines.

In 1855, a financial panic struck northern California, causing several bank failures in San Francisco. When Adams and Company—an express and banking firm—failed, Frederick and Charles Low took over the Marysville branch and operated it successfully as Low Brothers and Company until 1861, when they sold out. Frederick Low then moved to San Francisco where he operated as a capitalist and investor.

Low made his debut as a political candidate when he was considered but defeated for state controller at the Republican state convention in June, 1861. However, two months later he was nominated by the Republican state committee as a congressman-at-large, when it was believed that California was entitled to an additional—or third representative—based upon apportionment of the 1860 census. In the September election, Timothy G. Phelps, Aaron A. Sargent, and Low were the winning congressional candidates. Low polled 39,060 votes or the least of the three. When he offered his credentials to the thirty-seventh Congress as a Republican member-elect, the act granting California three congressmen had not yet been passed. Thus Low had to present arguments to win his seat until Congress admitted him by special act on June 2, 1862. As a representative Low was not particularly active, but he did concern himself with revenue and banking bills and the problems of California land titles.

In the next election Low was not a candidate for renomination. After his term expired, President Lincoln appointed him, in 1863, collector of the port of San Francisco, succeeding Ira P. Rankin. Although this federal office did not carry a lucrative salary, the administration of the custom house was a significant position during the Civil War, when revenues were vital to the government. Moreover, the collector was partly concerned with the problem of San Francisco harbor defense and with the possibility that a Confederate privateer might be outfitted in the port. Low constantly reminded military authorities of the weaknesses of fortifications and of the fear of the local citizenry of a Confederate or foreign attack upon the city. Collector Low also played a significant role in the noted New Almaden Quicksilver Mine crisis of 1863, and assisted President Lincoln in correcting a grave political error.

While Low was gaining valuable political experience in the federal post, his supporters worked diligently among the Union Leagues to win his nomination for governor over the incumbent, Leland Stanford. After Low delegates gained strategic control in the preliminary county conventions of San Francisco and Sacramento, Stanford withdrew from the contest. At the Union state convention, held on June 18, 1863, Low was nominated on the first ballot, receiving 176 votes to 93 for Aaron A. Sargent. Low's Democratic rival in the campaign was former Governor John G. Downey. In the election the Union ticket was victorious with Low polling 68,482 votes to his opponent's 44,632. These figures included the soldier vote which stood 4,159 for the victor and 140 for the vanquished Downey.

A few weeks after Low's election Mark Twain penned a comic description of The Lick House ball for the *Golden Era* of September 27, 1863. He described San Francisco fashions and wrote about the governor's-elect wife in these words:

> Mrs. F.F.L. wore a superb toilette habillée of Chambry gauze; over this a charming Figaro jacket, made of mohair, or horsehair, or something of that kind; over this again, a Raphael blouse of cheveux de la reine, trimmed round the bottom with lozenges formed of insertions, and around the top with bronchial torches; nothing could be more graceful than the contrast between the lozenges and the roches; over the blouse she wore a robe de chambre of regal magnificance, made of Faille silk and ornamented with macaroon (usually spelled "maccaroni") buttons set in black guipure. On the roof of her bonnet was a menagerie of rare and beautiful bugs and reptiles, and under the eaves thereof a counterfeit of the "early bird" whose specialty it hath been to work destruction upon such things since time began. To say that Mrs. L. was never more elaborately dressed in her life, would be to express an opinion within the range of possibility, at least—to say that she did or could look otherwise than charming, would be a deliberate departure from the truth.

When Low was elected governor at the age of forty-five, he was recognized as a successful businessman and political leader. His Boston apprenticeship had served him well, but like so many young Argonauts he began his self-made career as a miner before turning to the more lucrative opportunities offered in merchandising, banking, and transportation. When still in his twenties Low developed into a shrewd and prudent businessman, but he once told historian Hubert Howe Bancroft that the most agreeable time in his life was the three months he had spent mining. In a biographical sketch of Low prepared for the *Chronicles of the Kings*, but never used, Thomas Savage of the Bancroft Library staff wrote: "His career is one of the shining examples of what fertility of brain, versatility, and resolution can accomplish in a country where a young man must rely upon his own merits to carve for himself a position."

Low's business acumen was probably the primary reason that the Union State convention nominated him for governor. As collector of the port of San Francisco, Low had solved many intricate revenue problems and was highly respected by San Francisco merchants. His inaugural and legislative messages as governor were lucid expositions, particularly on economic matters.

Modest and unassuming in character, Governor Low was fearless and honest and had a strong sense of duty. His defense of the Chinese in an age of racial bigotry showed that he had a large measure of moral courage. When he presided over a banquet at San Francisco in January, 1867, held to commemorate the opening of steamship service with China, Low delivered a speech on United States-China relations. In part he said: "We must learn to treat the Chinese who come to live among us decently, and not oppress them by unfriendly legislation, nor allow them to be abused, robbed, and murdered, without extending to them any adequate remedy." When his term as governor ended, Pacific coast businessmen who were interested in China as a market supported Low for the post of Minister to China.

About ten or eleven years following his term as governor Low dictated a memoir for Hubert Howe Bancroft in which he discussed his office as follows:

I was elected and entered upon the duties of the office in December of that year [1863], and served until December, 1867. This covered a portion of the time of the war, and it was perhaps one of the most difficult positions ever held by an Executive in the State, for we had a large secession element here, and it required a great deal of care to watch it, and good judgment to keep ourselves from being mixed in broils here. Every claim and demand made on me by the general government for troops was met promptly, and the expenses that the state was put to in the way of bounties and extra pay to volunteers was liberally provided for, and no debt today exists against the state on that account.

Low's reference to "a large secession element" was probably true in his mind because Confederate sympathizers were vocal in California, but in actual numbers were few. His statements about the California volunteers and their bounties and extra pay were accurate.

In 1883, during an interview Hubert Howe Bancroft questioned Low about other governors who both preceded and succeeded him. Low stated that his successor, Henry H. Haight, was an excellent governor, but he commented: "There is not much chance to display one's ability in the governors office of this state even if you be brilliant." In making this statement Low was probably referring to the governorship as a whole rather than to just himself.

On December 10, 1863, Frederick Low took his oath of

office and delivered his inaugural address before the Assembly and Senate in joint convention. He stressed the fact that the new four-year gubernatorial term and biennial legislative session increased responsibilities of both the executive and the legislature since they were designed to decrease governmental expenses and to make legislation more durable. Because of civil war and the threat of foreign intervention he emphasized the necessity of a well-organized and disciplined militia.

Low promised to use his veto power with caution, but pointed out that he would defeat any act "inconsistent with the fundamental law or with the public welfare." He called special legislation a "crying evil" and complained that in the past the legislature had wasted time with relief bills, measures granting franchises, and other special privileges.

With regard to economic matters, Low wished to see mining production increased because of the federal government's financial difficulties brought about by the war. He espoused the principle of free mining and favored recognition of United States title to mineral lands. Also he praised the current geological survey of California, directed by Josiah Dwight Whitney, and recommended publishing its results. Although Low considered mining the more important economic activity of the state, he encouraged increased agricultural production.

Low concluded his inaugural by looking to the future Reconstruction of the nation. He alluded to the political problem of Reconstruction, but stated that the nature of local governments in the rebellious areas should not be decided until they ceased to be battlefields. However, he felt that "rebels" should not participate in establishing the reconstructed governments in the South.

During the legislative session of 1863-64, Governor Low made extensive use of the veto power. Many of his vetoes were sustained, but others were overridden. One of his first successful vetoes was the disapproval of a bill to transfer money in the state hospital fund to the legislative fund. Another was the veto of a bill granting certain exclusive rights and privileges to the Yreka Drainage Company. Most of Low's vetoes were aimed at eliminating special legislation. For example, he vetoed, as had former governors, several special bills to construct turnpikes and bridges in the belief that they only tended to encumber the statute books whereas general laws provided ample provisions for such measures. Also he vetoed many bills designed to settle and distribute the estates of deceased persons on the grounds that these were judicial matters.

The first legislative session of Low's administration was dignified and succeeded in reducing the state debt despite the extra pay and bounties granted to California volunteer soldiers. The legislature adjourned on April 4, 1864, and did not reconvene until December, 1865. Meanwhile, with the war's end the Union party of California split into two factions: the "shorthairs" and the "long-hairs." United States Senator John Conness, political boss of California and leader of the "shorthairs," wanted Governor Low to be elected as his colleague in the Senate and endeavored to return his backers to the legislature of 1865-66. However, to refute the charge that he alone had split the Union party, Low withdrew as a candidate. At the general election of September 6, 1865, the "long-hairs" won and defeated the Conness faction.

When the legislature convened on December 4, 1865, Governor Low in his first biennial message urged members to reduce state taxes since federal taxes were increasing. He recommended legislation to clarify land titles and to provide a general system of irrigation. Alluding to the drought of 1864, which had caused considerable farm distress, Low favored developing a proper irrigation system to avoid a repetition of the catastrophe. Moreover, he felt that an irrigation system would permit the introduction of rice culture on the low flats of the rivers of California. This in turn would provide employment "to the Asiatic population which is tending to our shores." He also encouraged experiments in cultivating hops, silk, cotton, and tobacco as well as scientific breeding of livestock and improvements in viticulture. In referring to the depressed status of the Nevada mines, he suggested an investigation of California incorporation laws and remedial legislation to prevent deceit by mining corporations in selling stock.

Low strongly recommended that this legislature establish an agriculture college capable of teaching all branches of learning. He said: "It is the individual professors who popularize all renowned institutions of learning, rather than imposing edifices." Also the governor suggested a merger of the proposed agriculture college with the proposed state university.

Five days later the *Daily Alta California* of San Francisco editorialized on "The Governor's Message," and called it ". . . a very extended and, upon the whole, a very satisfactory review of the general condition of the State." The newspaper further commented as follows:

> In it, the Governor devotes himself to figures, facts, and suggestions, rather than to flourishes of rhetoric and flights of the imagination. And very properly, for it is not an essay finished in the highest style of art that the people expected from their Chief Magistrate, but a plain and unvarnished statement of our finances, the condition of the public institutions, and the changes and reforms necessary for the promotion of our prosperity.

During this session Low applied the veto to a number of measures aiding railroads on the grounds of economy. He vetoed a bill granting a board of commissioners in San Francisco excessive power to dispose of public lands. Ultimately this veto accrued to the benefit of San Franciscans by saving the future site of Golden Gate Park from the manipulation of speculators.

In the gubernatorial election of 1867, Low declined renomination. Senator Conness, who had seemed to gain political strength since 1865, selected George C. Gorham as the Union candidate, but Gorham was defeated by a revived Democratic party, which elected Henry H. Haight.

In his second biennial message to the legislature, delivered on December 2, 1867, the outgoing governor reported that state finances were highly satisfactory. He mentioned that good progress was being made in constructing the new capitol building and that the next legislature would convene there. He referred to the success of state prison reforms during his administration and to the remodeled state militia now named the California National Guard.

Governor Low recommended ratification of the fourteenth amendment and praised the Congressional plan of Reconstruction. In retrospect he commended the victory of the American people in the war. He noted advances made in agriculture and industry, the establishment of steam communication with Hawaii, China, and Japan, and asserted that since 1863, the assessed value of property in California had increased about $40,000,000. In concluding, Low summarized his aims and announced that he would retire to private life.

The outstanding achievements of Low's administration were

in the fields of education and political reform. Public school attendance greatly increased and he encouraged a generous endowment of the newly-established California State Normal School. Low favored the establishment of a state university based upon the University of Michigan plan. He initiated steps to take advantage of federal grants-in-aid of land to foster higher education. In a sense Low was a founder of the University of California, for he first suggested a merger of the existing College of California with the proposed state university, which was so chartered in 1868.

To safeguard the franchise from abuse, Low encouraged electoral reforms. During his term the legislature enacted a registry law and the Porter Act which curtailed fraud in primary elections. Low gallantly fought against special legislation and raids on the state treasury. He vetoed several bills granting special subsidies to the railroads. For example, one bill would have empowered the state to pay all interest on bonds to finance the building of the Placerville and Sacramento Valley Railroad and the Western Pacific Railroad. By vetoing this bill, Low saved the taxpayers approximately three million dollars.

Low exercised extensive use of the veto power. An advocate of home rule, he vetoed several measures designed to give the legislature more control over local government. While his important vetoes were usually sustained, some of a minor nature were overridden by large majorities. Although he opposed state support of private charities, he improved public benevolent institutions. During his term the state archives was reorganized.

In a period of mounting racial tension Low took a courageous stand to protect minorities. He believed in proper treatment of the Mission Indians of southern California. He denounced a law excluding Mongolian and Indian testimony from courts in cases where a white person was a litigant. He advocated tolerance of the Chinese in California, for his attitude was that China would develop into a great market for California products.

The decision to make Yosemite and the Mariposa Big Trees Grove a public recreation area occurred during Low's administration. Although Low should not be viewed as a pioneer conservationist, it is significant that he was at least interested in preserving natural beauty and that he urged the legislature to accept the property and to appropriate money for a survey. In 1864 President Lincoln signed the Congressional act granting the lands to California as a public trust. On April 2, 1866, Governor Low signed the legislative act which accepted the area and met the federal terms to care for and to supervise it for public recreation. As a result Yosemite Valley became the first state park in California as well as the first in the nation. Under the terms of the act of 1866 the governor and eight men appointed by him were made "the commissioners to manage the Yosemite Valley and Mariposa Big Trees Grove" and their duties were to manage, to improve, and to preserve the area. The grant was returned to the federal government in 1906 and later became a national park.

Above all Low was loyal to the concept of national sovereignty. He cooperated to the fullest extent with the Lincoln administration in performing his political and military duties. In fact Lincoln confided in him as an adviser on Pacific coast matters. Low also served as president of the California branch of the United States Sanitary Commission. In December, 1865, he approved the joint resolution passed by both houses of the legislature which ratified the thirteenth amendment, abolishing slavery. He later urged ratification by California of the fourteenth amendment, but without success. As a Republican and Unionist he naturally opposed and condemned President Andrew Johnson, but as a Westerner he favored the purchase of Alaska.

Although the achievements of Low's administration were not spectacular, they were quite noteworthy. Low was a popular governor whose consideration for the public good figured prominently in making most of his decisions.

After a brief retirement, Low returned to public life in December, 1869, when President Grant appointed him Minister to China, succeeding J. Ross Browne. Shortly following his arrival in Peking, the Tientsin massacre of 1870 occurred, resulting in the murder of the French consul and nineteen foreigners. Low in his correspondence to the State Department attributed the general anti-foreign feeling in China to the illegal actions of the French Catholic missionaries.

On April 20, 1870, Secretary of State Hamilton Fish authorized Low to negotiate a treaty with Korea, a supposed vassal of China, in order to protect shipwrecked mariners due to the previous loss of an American schooner, *General Sherman,* in Korean waters. Low was provided with an imposing naval force of five warships of 85-guns and 1,230 men, commanded by Admiral John Rodgers. This procedure was in the tradition of the Perry expedition to Japan. However, the Low-Rodgers mission failed miserably when Korean forts fired upon the squadron. In retaliation American sailors and marines participated in a large scale amphibious operation against the Koreans. Thus the United States became involved in its first war in Korea, which was the nation's largest foreign military action between the Civil War and the Spanish-American War.

As Minister to China, Low was an able and competent observer. He wrote voluminously and wisely to the Secretary of State. He participated in the delicate audience question that was finally resolved by western diplomats in 1873. Low stressed the need for trained interpreters and translators in the United States legation in Peking and various consulates throughout China. He encouraged the exchange of students between the United States and China. When the first thirty Chinese students were ready to leave Shanghai for San Francisco in 1872, Low wrote to Secretary Fish: "I shall look with interest to the reception which this modest and humble scheme meets with from our people. If it be generous and cordial, the result will prove of more practical value to our interests here than an increase in the number of our vessels of war."

In the fall of 1873, Low returned to California on a leave of absence and in the following spring he resigned his diplomatic post. For the next eighteen years he was manager of the Anglo-California Bank in San Francisco. Under his management the bank ranked second only to the Bank of California in the amount of business transacted within the state. In 1884, he served as president of the San Francisco Clearing House Association, and for many years he was president of the Sutter Street Railway Company. At times Low was interested directly in Hawaiian sugar plantations and in lumber properties of Humboldt County.

Frederick Low died in San Francisco on July 21, 1894, at the age of sixty-six. He was survived by his wife and an unmarried daughter. Funeral services were held at the family residence and he was buried in the Laurel Hill Cemetery.

BIBLIOGRAPHY

MANUSCRIPTS

Bancroft, Hubert H., "Frederick F. Low: A Biographical Sketch," (Bancroft Library).

Low, Frederick, "Observations on Early California," (Bancroft Library).

———, "Political Affairs in California," (Bancroft Library).

"Government in California: A Biographical Sketch of Frederick F. Low, prepared for *Chronicles of the Kings*," (Bancroft Library).

CONTEMPORARY ACCOUNTS

Assembly Journal, 15th-17th Sess., 1863-68.

Becker, Robert H., ed., *Some Reflections of An Early California Governor Contained in A Short Dictated Memoir by Frederick F. Low, Ninth Governor of California, And Notes from An Interview between Governor Low and Hubert Howe Bancroft in 1883* (Sacramento, 1959).

Schroeder, Seaton, *A Half Century of Naval Service* (New York, 1922).

Sullivan, G. W., *Early Days of California* (San Francisco, 1888).

War of the Rebellion: A Compilation of the Official Records . . . Ser. I, Vol. L, Pt. II.

SECONDARY SOURCES

Bancroft, H.H., *History of California*.

Clyde, Paul H., "Frederick F. Low and the Tientsin Massacre," *Pacific Historical Review*, II (1933), 100-108.

Dennett, Tyler, *Americans in Eastern Asia* (New York, 1941).

Ellison, Joseph, *California and the Nation* (Berkeley, 1927).

Gilbert, Benjamin F., "San Francisco Harbor Defenses during the Civil War," *California Historical Society Quarterly*, XXXIII (1954), 229-40.

Hittell, T.H., *History of California*.

Sheppard, Eli T., "Frederick Ferdinand Low, Ninth Governor of California," reprint from *University of California Chronicle*, XIX (1917).

Treat, Payson, "Frederick Ferdinand Low," *Dictionary of American Biography*, XI, 445-46.

Weil, Samuel C., *Lincoln's Crisis in the Far West* (San Francisco, 1949).

Wells, William V., "Frederick F. Low," in O.T. Shuck, *Representative and Leading Men of the Pacific*.

NEWSPAPERS

Daily Alta California, Dec. 9, 1865, has a commentary on "The Governor's Message."

Daily Evening Bulletin (San Francisco), March 31, 1866, has data on Low's veto of a bill extending state aid to the Placerville Railroad and the Western Pacific Railroad.

Morning Call (San Francisco), July 23-25, 1894, have biographical data about Low.

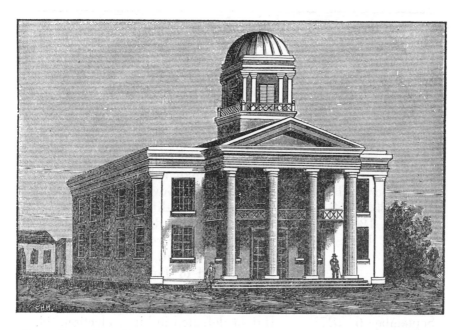

First Capitol at Sacramento, 1853 and 1854. Governor McDougal was
one of those instrumental in having the Capitol moved from Vallejo to
the Sacramento Court House (above) during the 1852 legislative session.
The legislature met again in the building in 1854. The building was
completed as Sacramento's first courthouse, at Seventh and I streets, in
1851. It was destroyed by the great Sacramento fire of July 13, 1854.

Calendar of Events

May 20, 1825	Haight born in Rochester, New York.
1844	Haight graduated from Yale College.
July, 1847	Haight admitted to the Missouri bar.
January 20, 1850	Haight arrived in San Francisco.
1853	Haight ran as candidate for the State Legislature.
1859-60	Haight served as chairman of the Republican State Committee.
1864	Haight campaigned for McClellan.
September 4, 1867	Haight elected Governor.
March 23, 1868	University of California chartered.
May 10, 1869	Transcontinental Railroad completed.
January, 1870	State Legislature refused to ratify the 15th Amendment.
1870	State Board of Equalization created.
June 14, 1871	California State Normal School opened at San Jose.
September 6, 1871	Haight defeated in his re-election bid.
June 19, 1878	Haight elected as a delegate to the Second Constitutional Convention.
September 2, 1878	Haight died in San Francisco.

Henry H. Haight

10TH GOVERNOR — DEMOCRAT
BORN: MAY 20, 1825   DIED: SEPTEMBER 2, 1878
TERM OF OFFICE: DECEMBER 5, 1867—DECEMBER 8, 1871

HENRY H. HAIGHT, born in Rochester, New York, May 20, 1825, was the eldest son of Fletcher M. and Elizabeth S. Mac-Lachlan Haight. At the age of thirteen he entered Rochester Collegiate Institute. Two years later he enrolled at Yale College where he proved himself a scholarly student. After graduating with high honors in 1844, he studied in his father's law office at Rochester. In 1846, the father and son moved to St. Louis and in July, 1847, Henry was admitted to the Missouri bar. He practiced law in St. Louis and for a time edited a Free Soil newspaper. In 1849, he was attracted by the gold rush to California, and left New Orleans on December 11, arriving at San Francisco, via the Isthmus, on January 20, 1850, where he opened a law office.

In a letter to his father dated July 17, he remarked that he did not intend to make San Francisco his permanent home because of its unfavorable climate. Instead he planned to stay two or three years until he became financially independent. He also mentioned that he had been elected a trustee of the First Presbyterian Church of San Francisco.

Haight gradually acquired permanent roots in San Francisco. By 1853, he acquired some property in the city and he had two law partners, Joseph E. Gary and Alexander Wells. Haight first ran for office in the election of 1853 as an independent candidate for the legislature, but in a letter dated September 15, he told his father that he had no chance of election, explaining that he had only "bolted" in an unsuccessful effort to defeat the Democratic gubernatorial candidate, John Bigler. The next

143

year Fletcher Haight joined his son and they practiced law together in San Francisco. In 1861, the father was appointed
district judge for the southern district of California by President Lincoln. According to some sources Henry Haight also
practiced law with James A. McDougall in the fifties. And
just prior to his governorship he practiced with William M.
Pierson.

Henry Haight returned to St. Louis for a short stay and
married Anna E. Bissell on January 24, 1855. They had five
children, one of whom died in infancy. The family moved to
Alameda from San Francisco in 1867, while Haight continued
his law practice in San Francisco.

During the decade of the fifties Haight on occasion changed
his political affiliations, a practice commonplace at the time.
The evidence available suggests that at first he was a Democrat,
then an independent. For a brief period he was a Whig, but
in 1856 he supported Frémont, the Republican presidential
candidate. In 1859 and 1860, Haight served as chairman of
the Republican state committee. In the presidential campaign
of 1860, he actively supported Republican candidates. In fact
he was a Straight Republican, who opposed fusion with the
anti-Lecompton Democrats into a Union party. After Lincoln's
inauguration, Haight soon altered his politics for several reasons. First and foremost he opposed the objectives of the
Radical Republicans, particularly their abolitionist tendencies.
Also he probably felt slighted by the Republican party and
sought more political opportunity within the Democratic party.

On May 3, 1861, the future governor wrote a letter to a relative named George, who was probably George Bissell, in which
he discussed politics. Haight stated that he had voted for
Lincoln in 1860, fearing that the election might otherwise be
decided in the House of Representatives and thereby create
confusion. He further explained that he had supported the
Republican plank for a Pacific railroad. Haight, in his letter,
viewed his vote as an error and indicated that he would first
indict the Republican party and then the Democratic party.
He referred to secession as a "folly" inasmuch as no rights had
been violated by Lincoln. Yet he held that the Republican party
was equally guilty, since it had offered no concessions or
compromises to the South. Haight also objected to the recently
enacted Morrill tariff. He further related that with the out-

break of war the future appeared dismal, and concluded:

> In California at present the cry is to sustain the "administration."
> I will stand by my government in one sense as long as anyone but I
> will never endorse a policy which I utterly detest. Henceforth I
> acknowledge no allegiance to any party.

In 1863, when the objective of the Union party became abolition, Haight returned to the Democratic fold and in the presidential campaign of 1864 he supported George B. McClellan against Lincoln. The Unionists won the election and Lincoln again carried California in 1864 as he had in 1860. With the war's end in 1865, the division within the Union party revived the Democratic party in California. Hence the disorganized Democrats of 1865 were able to dominate the political scene two years later.

In 1867, Senator John Conness supported George C. Gorham for governor. Gorham had experience as a newspaper editor and as superintendent of the state reform school in 1862, and as a clerk of the United States Circuit Court in 1863. In 1864, he served as private secretary for Governor Low.

Meanwhile, in the 1865-66 legislature the Union party enacted the Porter primary election act. The law was optional, but if a political party decided to function under it, it would have to give notice as to the time, place, and manner of holding the primary as well as the qualifications for voting. In San Francisco and Sacramento, Union men opposing the manipulations of Conness refused to adhere to regular county conventions and organized their own primaries. Moreover, they held separate county conventions and sent a separate delegation to the Union state convention. As a result division existed in the Union party prior to the state conventions. Nonetheless, both factions met as one body at the Union convention meeting in Sacramento on June 12, 1867.

Conness was able to assume control and he manipulated the short-hairs or Douglas faction against the long-hairs. Hence the Conness-Gorham faction was able to carry the convention and Gorham won the nomination by a vote of 148 to 132 for John Bidwell. John P. Jones was nominated for lieutenant governor without opposition.

The independent newspapers which had previously supported Union candidates now denounced Conness, and journals such as the *San Francisco Bulletin* and *Sacramento Union* opposed

Gorham. Various elements of the long-hair faction then devised a new political slate which caused a rebirth of the Republican party hitherto absorbed by the Union party. There-
upon the Republican convention nominated Caleb T. Fay, a
former San Francisco Assemblyman, for governor, after John
Bidwell had refused the nomination. The Republicans did not
bother to nominate a candidate for lieutenant governor.

Factionalism within the Union party and the revival of the
Republican party strengthened the Democrats who did not fuse
with any faction of the Union party as they had in 1865. In
the campaign of 1867, the Democrats held their own primaries
and county conventions in preparation for their state convention which met at Turn Verein Hall in San Francisco on June
19, 1867, with Eugene Casserly as chairman. In their platform
the Democrats called for defeat of the Radical Republicans
and condemned Congressional reconstruction as "harsh, illib-
eral, and oppressive." Also they opposed Negro, Chinese, and
Indian suffrage as dangerous to Republican institutions and
called upon Congress to protect the Pacific states and territories
"from an undue influx of Chinese and Mongolians."

Henry H. Haight was nominated unanimously after General
William S. Rosecrans and William M. Lent had withdrawn.
For lieutenant governor the Democrats nominated William
Holden without opposition after William Irwin withdrew. In
a brief acceptance speech Haight pledged loyalty to the state
platform and to the principles of the national Democratic party.

The racial issue was injected into the campaign of 1867.
The Democrats had opposed Negro suffrage in 1865, but in
1867, they were largely concerned with both Chinese suffrage
and immigration. In San Francisco an Anti-Coolie Association
had been formed which sought the views of the Union gubernatorial candidates. Gorham opposed coolieism, but also opposed
the Anti-Coolie Association. The regular Union state convention adopted a resolution endorsing restriction of Chinese immigration, but was silent on the suffrage issue whereas Gorham
opposed Chinese suffrage. The Republican state convention
opposed coolie labor, but favored voluntary immigration and
announced: "That we are in favor of impartial suffrage without distinction of color."

The post-convention campaign of the Democrats began with
a series of rallies in the San Francisco and Sacramento areas.

At a Democratic mass meeting held at Union Hall in San Francisco on July 9, Haight was the featured speaker where he answered charges of his opponents. He denied that he had made "abusive epithets to Mr. Lincoln" in 1864 in Union Hall as described in the *Democratic Press*. He also refuted charges that he had not been sound upon the war and cited his letter of September, 1863, in the *Daily Alta California* in which he had opposed secession as lawlessness. Furthermore, he asserted that the Union party assumed it had a monopoly of patriotism and loyalty. Haight claimed that the Unionists and Republicans were coercing the South and favored indiscriminate suffrage for the Chinese, Indians, and Negroes. He stated that Congress through military force had overridden the rights of the states to regulate suffrage. Referring to California voting, Haight asserted that anyone with the sum of $12,500 could gain political control of the forty or fifty thousand Chinese residents. Then he concluded somewhat fantastically: "The Central Pacific Railroad with ten thousand Chinese laborers, could outvote the entire voting population of the mining counties, through which the road passes."

After his San Francisco speech, Haight spoke at mass meetings in Oakland and Sacramento. Then he began a campaign tour in the northern part of the state. In August, he canvassed in Stockton, Jamestown, Sonora, Mokelumne Hill, and Oroville. Toward the end of the month he spoke again in San Francisco and at San Jose. Apparently he felt it was not necessary to campaign in the less populous area of southern California. At Platt Hall in San Francisco he denied that he had ever been a member of the Know Nothing party, a charge often made by Unionists. Haight delivered his last campaign speech at a mass meeting held on September 3, at the crowded intersection of Market, Post, and Montgomery Streets in San Francisco.

The Democrats had tremendous backing in San Francisco from the large German and Irish elements and also enjoyed the endorsement of the Workingmen's convention. The *San Francisco Bulletin* claimed that at least 3,000 Germans, who had formerly been Unionists, supported the Democratic ticket since the Democrats promised to repeal the "Sunday Laws" which had prohibited "barbarous and noisy amusements" and had kept markets closed on the Sabbath.

The Democratic newspapers faithfully supported Haight and referred to "Saint" Lincoln and George "Coolie" Gorham. The *San Francisco Examiner* stated:

> The love of the Mongrel leaders for the Africans is measured simply by the available capital they can make out of him in their struggle for political ascendancy. Convince them that the negro would cast his vote with their opponents and their love would soon be turned into hate.

Unfortunately for Gorham, the Unionists lacked their previous support from the press. Moreover, the Democrats were more violently anti-Chinese. As a result Gorham's campaign had less impact and the Democrats won all statewide offices in the election of September 4, 1867. The final gubernatorial tally gave Haight 49,905 votes to 40,359 for Gorham and 2,088 for Fay. The Democrats were also victorious in gaining legislative seats, but because of hold-overs the Union majority in the upper house was sustained. The defeat of the Unionists ended their existence as an effective party in California.

Although Haight had never held public office before, he was well versed in California politics. By capitalizing on division in the Union party and by appealing to the racial prejudice of California voters, he came to power. Unfortunately, contemporary records do not reveal much about Haight's personality. A learned lawyer, he was an able but slow speaker. He appears to have had an incisive style of writing. One associate said: "He took broad and comprehensive views of a subject, looking at it in all its relations. His mind was synthetic, rather than analytical. His mental perspective was perfect."

Haight, an ordained Presbyterian elder, was faithful to his creed, but most tolerant of the opinions of others. Of Scotch descent, he collected books relating to Scotland and early Scottish history. He was active in the St. Andrew's Society at San Francisco and had been associated with charities.

Haight was honest, fearless, and independent and as governor he was incorruptible. On an occasion when an office-holder asked him for permission to name his own successor, Haight replied: "If gentlemen who hold public positions can dictate their successors, the obvious result would be corrupt trading in offices and their virtual sale and purchase for a consideration." Haight felt it was his duty in such matters to consult only his own conscience. Haight had high moral standards and once said: "We must refuse to recognize two codes of morals, one for private and a lower one for political affairs."

In view of his New York birth and later association with the Free Soil movement in Missouri, it might seem difficult to explain Haight's prejudice toward the Negro and the Chinese. Haight admittedly believed in white supremacy and it was politically expedient for him to support President Andrew Johnson in his struggle with the Radical Republicans on the national scene and to oppose the Chinese on the local scene.

When the legislature convened in December, 1867, the Democrats had a majority of twenty-two in the Assembly while the Union party had a majority of four in the Senate. In his inaugural address of December 5, Haight emphasized national rather than local issues. He implied that Republican radicalism had been carried to excess and endangered the nation. He condemned what he called the usurpations of the constitution by Congress and the division of the ten Southern states into conquered territory as five military districts. Moreover, he asserted that enough whites had been disfranchised to give political control in the South to Negroes.

Haight claimed that the question of Negro suffrage belonged to each state to resolve for itself. He related that the people of California opposed both Negro and Chinese suffrage and that it was "a question not of inalienable right, but simply of expediency." He stated that some Californians favoring Negro suffrage hesitated to advocate Chinese suffrage. Haight himself felt that the "inferior" races should have civil rights, but should never vote or hold office.

The new governor urged that the influx of Chinese be discouraged by all lawful means. He warned that the people of Europe and of the Eastern states would not migrate to California upon the completion of the Pacific railroad if the labor market was filled by Mongolians. With rank prejudice the governor concluded this portion of his inaugural with these words: "What we desire for the permanent benefit of California is a population of white men, who will make this State their home, bring up families here, and meet the responsibilities and discharge the duties of freemen. We ought not to desire an effete population of Asiatics for a free State like ours."

In a discussion of California matters Haight urged a legal eight hour day for the working class and amendment of the

present registry law to remove discriminations against natural-
ized citizens. He suggested that corporations should not be
subsidized by public funds. He urged general laws rather than
special legislation and indicated that the general statutes needed
revision by a commission. He recommended the appointment
of judges for a period of good behavior rather than for a
specific term. He also pointed out the need for prison reforms
and the organization of the University of California.

In commenting on Haight's inaugural, the *Daily Alta California*, an opposition newspaper, related that the address
sounded more like that of a president than that of a governor.
The newspaper concluded: "Never was there an inaugural in
which more was said that might better be left unsaid, or more
was left unsaid that ought to be said."

The first important matter brought before the legislature of
1867-68 was the election of a United States Senator to succeed
Conness. In a corrupt election Eugene Casserly, a Democrat,
was the victor. The Democratic legislature of California passed
various resolutions siding with President Johnson in his fight
with the Radical Republicans. The most important legislation
of the session consisted of the repeal of an act which had made
fugitives out of incoming slaves (prior to statehood), a measure establishing an eight hour working day, a codification of
the laws of California, and the chartering of the University of
California. Several of these measures had been recommended
by Haight which indicated that he had the cooperation of the
legislature.

As early as February 5, 1868, Senator Casserly informed
Governor Haight that the Democratic state convention would
probably support him for the presidency. Later in the month
the Democratic state central committee adopted a resolution that
Governor Haight stood "pre-eminent among the great of the
nation." The San Francisco County Democratic convention
meeting on April 27, adopted a resolution declaring that Haight
was its unanimous choice as a presidential candidate. But
on April 30, at the Democratic state convention meeting in San
Francisco, a motion to pledge delegates to the Democratic
national convention in New York to support Haight for president was ruled out of order. Yet for several months Haight's
name had appeared in the press as a likely candidate. In a
"private" letter of May 7, to ex-Governor Bigler, one of the

delegates to the national convention, Haight stated that it would be improper for him to permit his name to be considered before the national convention inasmuch as the state convention had not expressed any preference for him. Haight explained to Bigler that he did not feel it justifiable to resign as governor since he had not received "an imperative call to duty." Moreover, he stated that others with more public experience possessed better qualifications and were better known to voters in the East. Thus Haight put an end to any attempt to present his name in New York.

Before the legislature of 1868-69, Haight opposed the fourteenth and fifteenth amendments as designed to centralize the federal government "and to deprive each State of any control over its local affairs." In discussing the fifteenth amendment he asserted that if it were adopted, "the most degraded Digger Indian within our borders becomes at once an elector and, so far, a ruler." Then he warned that by a slight amendment of the naturalization laws the Chinese could qualify as electors.

Governor Haight presented his first biennial message to the legislature on December 9, 1869, in which he remarked upon the general prosperity of California and upon the end of her isolation by the completion of the transcontinental railroad. He related that state indebtedness had been reduced by over a million dollars since he took office and he urged further economy. He was the first to recommend a board of equalization to assess taxes.

In considerable detail he dwelt upon the land system of California which tended to facilitate the acquisition of large areas by corporations. He expressed regret that Congress in granting land to railroads had not allowed the continued preemption by settlers, granting to "the corporation the proceeds at some fixed price." He explained that as a result of this neglect, many farmers, who had bought lands from the state as swamp and overflowed lands, had had their farms claimed under the railroad grants and had become involved in costly litigation. Haight requested that Congress be asked to remedy this situation.

In referring to the newly chartered University of California, Governor Haight announced that a board of regents had been appointed, buildings commenced, and professors selected. With a faculty of ten instructors, the enrollment was about fifty students.

Haight proposed establishing immigration agencies in New York and Baltimore and in Europe to attract farmers to California. To circumvent the immigration of "inferior" races and Chinese prostitutes, the governor requested legislative action. Yet despite his prejudice against the Chinese, Haight favored the removal of all barriers to testimony in court from any class or race.

On January 6, 1870, Governor Haight submitted to the legislature the proposed fifteenth amendment to the constitution of the United States and recommended that it not be ratified. Later in the month, after considering several resolutions, the legislature formally rejected it by a large majority. The legislature also failed to ratify the fourteenth amendment. Another significant highlight of the 1869-70 Democratic legislature was the vindication of Judge James H. Hardy, who had been impeached and removed from office during the Civil War for "seditious and treasonable language."

Among the legislative measures enacted in the 1869-70 session was a bill which permitted the Mercantile Library of San Francisco to pay off its indebtedness by operating lotteries. Another law of importance to San Francisco expedited the settlement of the so-called "outside lands," facilitating the city's development.

During the session Haight vetoed several bills designed to benefit the railroads through county aid. The governor vehemently opposed any measure tending to tax the people beyond the cost of necessary governmental functions. In particular he opposed financial strengthening of the Central Pacific through state funds. After the session closed, Haight continued his own investigation of the constitutionality of legislation authorizing donations to railroads by cities and counties. In two published letters he condemned the practice as illegal claiming that the "forced" donations were invasions of property rights. Moreover, he asserted that the railroads, despite their benefits, had no right to plunder the citizenry.

Early in 1871, the Democrats searched for a candidate to succeed Haight, for he had decided not to seek re-election because of financial sacrifice and poor health. At the time the governor's annual salary was $7,000 and Haight could earn more through his private law practice. However, he changed his mind and sought re-election, as he asserted, to protect the people from private corporations. In June, Haight was renominated and the Democratic lieutenant gubernatorial candidate was E. J. Lewis. However, by 1871, the Republican party had strengthened itself sufficiently to defeat the incumbent gubernatorial candidate.

In his final message to the legislature of December 5, 1871, Haight reported that state finances were in good condition, but he recommended a reconsideration of the equalization of tax assessments. He urged purity in elections and legislation to forestall the growing menace of bribery. At this point Haight condemned the "Mare Island Election Ticket" whereby officers of the navy yard had compelled employees to use a ballot in the recent election which only had Republican candidates printed on it. He also suggested making gambling at elections a misdemeanor as well as a basis for disfranchising guilty parties.

In recommending improvement of the state militia Governor Haight related that a single company of infantry at Los Angeles probably could have suppressed the recent mob action there which had resulted in the "barbarous murder of a number of Chinamen, most of whom were innocent of any offence whatever." Haight recommended relieving the lieutenant governor of his duties as prison warden. In reference to the pardoning power he reminded the legislators that an act of 1868 had infringed upon his power which, according to the constitution, was the governor's sole responsibility. This measure had permitted the board of prison directors to select cases and present them to the legislature which upon its approval could authorize the governor to act. Haight demanded repeal of the act. The governor asserted that railroad rates were excessive and reminded the legislators that both the Republican and Democratic parties had opposed taxation for the benefit of private corporations.

In a brief review of what he considered his accomplishments, Governor Haight mentioned reducing the state debt by about one-third, reducing the tax rate from $1.13 to 86½ cents, reforming the prison system, and revising statutes. He also remarked about the overthrow of the Republican subsidy system which had benefited corporations and the repeal of the bounty system whereby the state had paid premiums for raising silk cocoons, planting mulberry trees, and manufacturing woolen fabrics. He referred to the organization of the state university, the erection of a state normal school at San Jose, and improvement of the state archives.

Despite Haight's views on such matters as race, many features of his administration were real achievements. Indeed, higher education as sponsored by the state had a noble beginning and Haight endeavored to secure its permanent success. The establishment of the board of public health was an important achievement and Haight's prison reforms were commendable. The California Labor exchange, founded in 1867, as the first free employment agency, obtained state support beginning in 1870. The state board of equalization was created in 1870, but became ineffective because of adverse judicial decisions.

During Haight's administration the transcontinental railroad was completed. Two days before the golden spike was driven into a California laurel tie by Leland Stanford at Promontory Point, Governor Haight delivered an address at Sacramento, on May 8, 1869, in which he predicted that a vast population would pour into California. In part he said: "Tourists will be attracted by the most sublime scenery on the Continent, and thousands will come to repair physical constitutions racked by the extremes of climate, the inclement air, and the miasma of the States east of the mountains."

Railroad mileage within California was also extended. Irrigation projects in the uplands of the San Joaquin and Sacramento valleys and the reclamation of swamp and marsh lands were begun. Despite the repeal of the bounty laws, considerable industrial development occurred.

To his credit Haight realized the need for administrative and governmental reforms. Commissioners were appointed to revise the statutes and he saw the need for judicial reforms. Haight felt that nearly every article of the state constitution should be amended and he favored calling a constitutional convention. He believed that his office should have more power and he viewed himself as a mere chairman of committees who could be overruled and then held responsible by public opinion. He considered the pardoning power as a physical, moral, and political strain upon the governor. Haight also viewed the task of dispensing executive patronage as "an ungracious and unpleasant one."

Haight's dissatisfaction with his office may partly explain why he tended to have such a great interest or even too much interest in national politics. An outstanding feature of his administration was its complete reversal of the national political policies of Stanford and Low. In refusing to ratify the fourteenth and fifteenth amendments, California in a sense was rejecting the results of the Civil War. In another sense a majority of the California voters were merely unwilling to accept the Radical Republicans.

Upon leaving office Haight returned to his law practice. When Casserly resigned as United States Senator in 1873, Haight was offered the unexpired term, but refused it. In 1878 he was elected on the Non-Partisan ticket to the constitutional convention from the second congressional district comprising Oakland and Alameda. As a delegate he had planned to reduce taxation, reform county government, and elevate the office of governor. However, before the convention convened Haight died unexpectedly on September 2, 1878, in San Francisco. Two days later his funeral services were held in Oakland.

BIBLIOGRAPHY

MANUSCRIPTS
"Haight Papers," (Huntington Library).

CONTEMPORARY ACCOUNTS
Assembly Journal, 19th Sess., 1871-72.
Senate Journal, 17th-18th Sess., 1867-70.
Buchanan, A. Russell, ed., "H.H. Haight on National Politics, May 1861," *California Historical Society Quarterly,* XXXI (1952), 193-204.
Haight, Henry H., *Speech of . . . , Democratic Candidate for Governor* (San Francisco, 1867).
Letters of Gov. Haight on the Constitutional Power of the Legislature to Authorize Cities and Counties to Donate Bonds to Railroad Corporations (Sacramento, 1870).
Tabor, Rodney L., *In Memoriam of Henry H. Haight* (San Francisco, 1878).

SECONDARY SOURCES
Bancroft, H.H., *History of California.*
Davis, W.J., *History of Political Conventions. . .*
Galpin, Philip G., "Henry H. Haight," *The Californian,* II (1880), 330-332.

NEWSPAPERS
Daily Morning Call, Sept. 3, 1878, has an obituary and biographical sketch of Haight.
Stockton Weekly Independent, Sept. 7, 1878, has a biographical sketch.

Calendar of Events

December 30, 1825	Booth born in Salem, Indiana.
1846	Booth graduated from Asbury College, Greencastle, Indiana.
1849	Booth admitted to Indiana bar.
October 18, 1850	Booth arrived in San Francisco aboard the *Oregon*.
February, 1851	Booth opened a grocery business in Sacramento.
1856	Booth returned to Indiana.
1860	Booth settled in Sacramento again.
September 3, 1862	Booth elected State Senator.
September 6, 1871	Booth elected Governor.
January, 1872	State Senate blocked ratification of 14th and 15th Amendments.
January 1, 1873	Revised California Codes put into effect.
March 4, 1875	Booth became United States Senator.
July 14, 1892	Booth died in Sacramento.

Newton Booth

11TH GOVERNOR — REPUBLICAN
BORN: DECEMBER 30, 1825   DIED: JULY 14, 1892
TERM OF OFFICE: DECEMBER 8, 1871—FEBRUARY 27, 1875

NEWTON BOOTH WAS BORN IN Salem, Indiana, on December 30, 1825. His parents were Quakers. His father, Beebe Booth, was born in Connecticut and his mother, Hannah Pitts, was a native of North Carolina. In 1846, Newton Booth graduated from Asbury College (presently De Pauw University), a Methodist institution, located at Greencastle, Indiana. For two years he worked in one of his father's chain stores at Terre Haute. Then he studied law in W. D. Griswold's office before passing Indiana's rigid bar examination in 1849. The same year he obtained a master of arts degree from Asbury.

In 1850, Booth started out for California via New York and the Panama route, arriving at San Francisco on October 18, aboard the *Oregon,* which vessel carried the long awaited news of California's admission. In San Francisco he found the law profession overstocked, so he went to Sacramento. When the great cholera epidemic broke out, he moved to Amador County where he engaged in business for several months. By February, 1851, he had opened a wholesale grocery business in Sacramento on J Street in partnership with Charles Smith. At first the firm was known as Smith & Booth and it quickly became an important source of supplies for Mother Lode mining camps. Primarily a wholesale house, it handled some retail trade.

In 1852, a fire damaged the store. Then L. A. Booth of a different firm became a partner and the firm assumed the name, Booth & Co. In 1856, Newton Booth returned to Terre Haute and associated with H. D. Scott in the practice of law. Meanwhile, Kleinhans & Co. merged with Booth & Co. After two years in Indiana, Newton Booth toured Europe and then in 1860, he returned to Sacramento to head the grocery firm. When Leland Stanford was elected governor in 1861, he sold his business to Booth & Co. As the oldest business of its kind in Sacramento, Booth & Co. enjoyed profitable trade throughout northern California and Nevada.

At first Booth had been a Democrat, but in 1860, he campaigned for Lincoln. In 1862, the merchant prince of Sacramento won election as a state senator from his county and launched his political career. Despite his busy mercantile and political pursuits, Booth devoted his leisure to a study of history, politics, and literature. He accumulated one of the finest private libraries in California. Also he became noted as a public speaker. With his well-modulated voice Booth frequently spoke on literary subjects. Gradually he began to deliver political orations of high quality and gained a reputation comparable to that of Senator Edward D. Baker of Oregon.

In 1862, Booth was a member of a Sacramento committee canvassing subscriptions to Central Pacific Company stock. In the state senate Booth was a friend of the railroad, considering it necessary to California's development and as an essential war measure. When an effort was made to require the directors of the Central Pacific to let contracts to the lowest bidders, Booth assisted in defeating the bill, hence allowing the company to have its own construction company.

By the close of the Civil War, Booth had reversed his attitude toward the railroad and was defeated for re-election by a few votes. Booth participated in the presidential campaign of 1868 when Ulysses S. Grant carried California by a small majority. As the Central Pacific monopoly grew in power Booth gained a reputation as an anti-railroad man. Since Governor Haight's political strength was largely based upon his anti-railroad attitude, the Republican party realized that it would also have to nominate an anti-railroad candidate.

Early in 1871, the *Sacramento Union* and other Republican journals opposed to railroad subsidies endorsed Booth as a gubernatorial candidate. In the campaign of 1871, the subsidy question became the main issue. Despite his vetoes of railroad subsidy bills, Governor Haight had signed on April 4, 1870, the so-called 5 percent subsidy law which had empowered counties to aid railroads to the degree of 5 percent of their taxable property in the event the voters so approved. On the surface this appeared as an inconsistency, but apparently Haight had felt that a maximum limit and voter approval were justifiable controls. Nonetheless, this probably hurt Haight, for the Republicans now campaigned against railroad subsidies.

In addition to Booth, Charles A. Washburn and Mayor Thomas H. Selby of San Francisco were considered by the Republicans as possible candidates. However, the former gained no strength and the latter was believed to be too friendly toward the railroad. On June 24, 1871, Booth publicly announced his opposition to state, county, or municipal subsidies and declared in favor of repeal of the 5 percent law. Four days later at the Republican state convention at Sacramento, Booth was nominated unanimously and Romualdo Pacheco became his running mate.

Henry Edgerton in his speech nominating Booth referred to him as a merchant of "highest character," "a competent lawyer," "a legislator of extended experience," and as a person "in the front ranks of your scholars." In his acceptance speech Booth stated that the Republican party had saved the government in wartime, but now the enemy was more dangerous— "the corrupting power of money in shaping legislation and controlling political action." He related that the basic controversy was the subsidy question and it meant: "Shall this government be and remain a mighty agency of civilization, the protector of all, or shall it be run as a close corporation to enrich the few?"

In the campaign both the Republicans and Democrats favored repeal of the 5 percent law and both opposed the Chinese. The Republicans charged the Haight administration with abuses of power. They won an almost complete victory in the election on September 6, when Booth and Pacheco defeated Haight and Lewis by approximately a 5,000 majority.

The new governor was a bachelor and remained so until the last year of his life. Above average in height, the slender and angular Booth had dark brown hair, blue eyes, and a high and broad forehead, and wore a full beard. He dressed faultlessly and possessed agreeable and winning manners. He was a modest, dignified, and scholarly man who exhibited high moral values and a sense of justice.

Booth considered both sides of every question that confronted him. Once he reached a decision, he fearlessly declared his convictions. While political friends revered him, his enemies feared him and detractors might label him an agitator, a demagogue, an alarmist, or a communist.

Booth's inaugural address, delivered on December 8, 1871, was one of the most eloquent of any California governor. According to custom he briefly outlined his policies. In expressing his views on legislation, probably with the 5 percent subsidy law in mind, he said: "the wisdom of the legislator is oftener shown in the repeal of old statutes than in the enactment of new." Booth's political philosophy was that the best government confined itself within its sphere of duties and imposed only essential restrictions upon the individual in order to safeguard society.

In a discussion of local government, Booth stated that the state should restrict political subdivisions from accumulating debts and in levying excessive taxes. However, he felt that government should be brought nearer to the people by granting cities self-government.

As expected, Booth warned the legislators of the danger of a railroad monopoly and asked them to protect the public from overcharges. Moreover, he related that corporations exercised undue political and financial influence and that the organization of corporations within corporations should be absolutely prohibited by law.

With regard to education he said: "The doors of our schools should be open to all, with no prejudice of caste without, and no sectarian teaching within, which will prevent any child from freely entering." He next spoke about the codification of laws relating that he and Haight had cooperated in preparing a revision of the compilation made by a commission appointed by the out-going governor.

Booth devoted considerable attention to elections. He protested the practice of holding separate elections for judicial and political offices and urged approval of a proposed amendment to eliminate that practice. Furthermore, he suggested holding the general state election at the time of the presidential election. He also recommended uniform ballots and additional legislation against corrupt elections.

On the matter of Chinese immigration he reiterated apprehensions expressed in both the Democratic and Republican platforms about the cheapening of labor and the problem of assimilation. However, he felt that the issue of Asiatic immigration was exclusively a federal problem and noted that treaties, commercial relations, and tradition opposed any local restrictions on immigration. He stated that it might be difficult to persuade Congress of the need for restriction, but concluded that the Chinese in California must be given protection of the law. In unsparing language he criticized the recent outbreak of mob violence in Los Angeles against the Chinese when he said: "I trust that during my administration the spirit of lawless violence which has sometimes disgraced our past may never be exhibited."

When Booth took office, the Democrats controlled the Senate and the Republicans controlled the Assembly. Many issues were settled by joint conventions and the Republicans usually decided issues because of their numerical superiority in the lower house. However, in January, 1872, when the Republicans endeavored to ratify the fourteenth and fifteenth amendments, the Democrats in the Senate blocked the move. These amendments had also been rejected in the Haight administration. Although the necessary number of states had already made them a part of the United States Constitution, the Republicans felt that it would be proper and fitting for California to ratify them.

In the legislative session of 1871-1872 a major achievement was the adoption of the new California codes. The codes were divided into four parts: penal, civil procedure, political, and civil. They became effective on January 1, 1873, and established the basis for today's system. Few railroad issues were discussed in the session despite the notoriety given to the question in the campaign of 1871. A large portion of the time was devoted to Booth's many vetoes in which he was always sustained.

In the campaign of 1873 for the election of county officers and state legislators a powerful anti-railroad party evolved under Governor Booth's leadership. Although no formal organization existed, Booth had the support of the powerful *Sacramento Union* and of several other newspapers. The previous year various farm clubs had been formed and established the State Farmers' Union which soon evolved into the Granger movement. In 1873, Booth acquired the ambition to become United States Senator as successor to Eugene Casserly, whose term would expire in March, 1875. The Grangers and the anti-railroad faction of the Republican party combined to assist Booth with his new objective. His supporters were a group called the Dolly Varden party. As election day drew nearer the Dolly Vardens gained strength, for many Liberal Republicans who had supported Horace Greeley in the presidential election of 1872, had an opportunity to return to the Republican fold. Hence Booth's anti-railroad party won the election of September 3, 1873, which meant that he would soon become Senator.

The legislature of 1873-1874 organized with Democratic leadership in the Senate and with Morris M. Estee, a Dolly Varden, as Speaker in the Assembly. On December 1, 1873, Governor Booth presented his first and only biennial message in which he noted that California had not experienced the financial reverses of other states during the past two years. He mentioned that the recently organized board of equalization had brought some semblance of uniformity in determining property values and that the assessment rolls were equalized and had been increased.

Booth proudly informed the legislators that the University of California had occupied its first buildings on the Berkeley campus. He felt that the institution of eighteen instructors and 199 students was fortunate in having Daniel Coit Gilman as its president and said: "Instruction of a high order is given in literary and historical studies, and in science, with special reference to the agricultural, the mines, and the engineering works of the State."

In a discussion of the pardoning power Booth stated: "The prerogative involves duties more painful, and graver responsibilities, than any other appertaining to the office of Governor." Then Booth reviewed the issue of capital punishment, relating that whereas executions had been private in the past, they were now reported to every home in the new journalistic age. Hence he recommended abolition of the death penalty and urged devising some type of imprisonment as an alternative.

In protest against special legislation, Booth complained that only 152 of the 637 acts of the last session had been of a general character. Again he asked for election reforms and recommended a new apportionment to make population the basis of representation.

He repeated his previous fears concerning Chinese immigration and warned of the danger of a caste system developing since the Chinese were denied political rights. Booth next recommended a division of the state into irrigation districts and urged that the federal government grant California control of inland waters.

In considering the subsidy issue, Booth related that certain counties were still exempted from the repeal of the "Five Per Cent Act" and he recommended a general repeal. He stressed the viciousness of subsidies and proposed regulation of railroad freight rates and fares. In strong terms Booth expressed his anti-railroad policy and asserted that if the railroads failed to devise a just tariff, the next legislature would strictly control them by forbidding free passes, by scheduling every article of freight, by establishing both minimum and maximum rates, by preventing consolidation of competing lines, by allowing them to own no land except that essential for operation, and by regulating their accounts—all views held by the Grangers.

Booth realized that his message to the legislature was his last one, for he was preparing to become United States Senator. As anticipated, he was criticized because he had made a pledge in 1871 to the Republican party to serve the full four-year term. This in part explained why Booth bolted the Republican party and adhered to Granger principles in the 1873 campaign. Actually Booth had a precedent since Latham had resigned in 1860 to become Senator.

Booth's opportunity came earlier than expected because on November 28, 1873, Senator Eugene Casserly, whose term was to expire on March 3, 1875, resigned because of sickness. On November 16, 1873, the legislature considered candidates for both the unexpired term and the full term. John S. Hager, a Democrat, was elected to the unexpired term. For the full term from March 4, 1875 to March 4, 1881, Booth, the Dolly Varden candidate, won over James T. Farley, a Democrat, and James M. Shafter, a Straight Republican.

After his election to the Senate, Booth retained his office of governor until he was ready to take his seat in Washington. Since Booth would not take his new office for fifteen months, it was believed that he would resign allowing Pacheco to become governor. However, he did not resign until February 27, 1875, five days before becoming Senator.

Meanwhile, in the legislature Senator Philip A. Roach of San Francisco led a group who felt that Booth should resign. He proposed an amendment to the state constitution that the governor should be ineligible to the office of United States Senator or any other elective office during his term. Although the proposed amendment was not adopted at the time, it became a factor in the calling of a constitutional convention in 1878-79, and Roach's amendment became Section 20 of Article V of the new constitution.

During the legislative session of 1873-74 the 5 percent subsidy law was repealed, but nothing was accomplished in the matter of regulating railroad freights and fares. The subject of woman suffrage was discussed, but no action was taken. When Henry Meiggs, who had absconded with funds in San Francisco and then escaped to South America to make a fortune, wanted to revisit California, his friends in the legislature enacted a bill to dismiss indictments against him. Governor Booth vetoed the bill, but the legislature passed it over his veto. Fortunately for all concerned Meiggs finally decided not to return. Booth's vetoes at this session were not as numerous as the previous one and they were usually sustained. For example, he vetoed an Assembly bill which purported to limit the hours of drivers and conductors of street cars to twelve hours of labor when in reality the law already provided for an eight-hour day. Also Booth prevented the division of Solano County against the wishes of its residents by vetoing a Senate bill.

Booth's administration, although not spectacular, was commendable in that he suggested many new laws as well as amendments to existing laws. Many of his recommendations were adopted during his governorship or at later dates. He administered the office with dignity and high standards except for marring his record by acceptance of the political expediency of anti-Orientalism.

Booth believed that government was only the agent of the people for specified purposes and that the law should be the simplest possible expression of the necessities of society. An advocate of purity in elections and of a large measure of municipal home rule, he felt that state laws should confer upon local authorities adequate powers for local government.

Although he used his veto power freely, he approved 1,316 laws. In 1872, he pocket-vetoed a bill creating a state forester and a board of forestry, but he approved damage and trespass laws which afforded some protection to forests. Booth is best remembered for his fight against the railroad monopoly and special legislation. His greatest achievement was probably the adoption of new California codes to interpret the statutes, but this must be shared with Governor Haight. Booth favored various educational reforms, but the legislature failed to support him. While state institutions remained much the same, he at least contributed to some modest improvements.

In the Senate, Booth continued his struggle against railroad monopoly and against Chinese immigration. He participated in the adoption of the silver certificate and in the passage of a bill to settle land titles in California. He served on the committee on public lands, committee on patents, committee on manufactures, and committee on appropriations.

Upon the conclusion of his single term he returned to his home in Sacramento and participated again in the wholesale business. In February, 1892, he married Mrs. Octavine Glover, the widow of a former business partner. Five months later, on July 14, Booth died at Sacramento. Booth himself was a man of literary attainment and it is interesting to note that he left a namesake in his nephew, Newton Booth Tarkington, the novelist, who was better known as Booth Tarkington.

BIBLIOGRAPHY

CONTEMPORARY ACCOUNTS
Assembly Journal, 19th-20th Sess., 1871-74.
Crane, Lauren E., ed., *Newton Booth of California: His Speeches and Addresses* (New York, 1894).
Open Letter of Newton Booth to John B. Felton (Sacramento, 1873).

SECONDARY SOURCES
Bancroft, H.H., *History of California.*
Davis, W.J., *History of Political Conventions. . .*
————, *An Illustrated History of Sacramento County* (Chicago, 1890).
Hittell, T.H., *History of California.*
Young, John P., *San Francisco, A History of the Pacific Coast Metropolis* (2 vols., Chicago, 1912).

NEWSPAPERS
Sacramento Daily Record-Union, Jan. 1, 1883, has a description of Booth & Co.
Sacramento Daily Union, Sept. 26, 1873, has a sketch of Booth.
San Francisco Call, July 15, 1892, has an obituary.

Calendar of Events

October 31, 1831	Pacheco born at Santa Barbara.
1838-1843	Pacheco resided in Hawaii.
1846-1848	Pacheco served as supercargo officer on coastal ships.
1854	Pacheco elected San Luis Obispo County Judge.
September 2, 1857	Pacheco elected as State Senator.
September 2, 1863	Pacheco elected State Treasurer.
September 1, 1869	Pacheco returned to State Senate.
September 6, 1871	Pacheco elected Lieutenant Governor.
February 27, 1875	Pacheco became Governor.
November 7, 1876	Pacheco elected to Congress.
February 7, 1878	Pacheco unseated in Congress by Peter D. Wigginton.
September 7, 1879	Pacheco re-elected to Congress.
November 2, 1881	Pacheco again re-elected to Congress.
December 11, 1890	Pacheco appointed Minister to Central America.
January 23, 1899	Pacheco died in Oakland.

Romualdo Pacheco

12TH GOVERNOR — REPUBLICAN
BORN: OCTOBER 31, 1831   DIED: JANUARY 23, 1899
TERM OF OFFICE: FEBRUARY 27—DECEMBER 9, 1875

ROMUALDO PACHECO HAD THE DISTINCTION of being the first native son of California to serve as governor in the American period as well as having been the only one of Spanish descent to occupy this high office after California became a state. He was born a Mexican citizen at Santa Barbara on October 31, 1831. Although this date appears in most sources, the Santa Barbara Mission records give his birth a month earlier. His parents were Captain Romualdo Pacheco, a Mexican army officer, and Ramona Carrillo, whose beauty was once vividly described by Richard Henry Dana. The father died heroically in a skirmish in 1831, while saving the life of Governor Manuel Victoria. On February 5, 1832, Victoria in a letter to the secretary of war and marine reported that Captain Pacheco had left a helpless widow with two small sons. Captain José Antonio de la Guerra y Noriega served as the protector of Doña Ramona and her children until her remarriage. Her second husband was Captain John Wilson, a native of Dundee, Scotland, who had been master of the English brig, *Ayacucho.* Later Wilson acquired Los Osos Rancho and other lands in San Luis Obispo County.

In 1838, when Romualdo was seven years of age, he and his elder brother, Mariano, were sent to Hawaii for their education. They attended the Oahu Charity School in Honolulu which was directed by their stepfather's missionary friends, Andrew Johnstone and his wife. This was an English language school where Romualdo temporarily forgot his native tongue and learned English and French. After five years' residence in

167

Hawaii the boys returned home. At the age of fifteen Romualdo began service as a supercargo on his stepfather's ships in the California and Mexican coastal trade.

When the conquest of California began during the Mexican War, Pacheco's vessel flying the Mexican flag was captured in San Diego by the sloop-of-war, *U.S.S. Cyane.* He was then permitted to sail to San Francisco under the same flag. Upon his arrival in the northern port the vessel was captured again by an American warship, but Pacheco was released when he took an oath of allegiance to the United States.

Romualdo Pacheco in 1848 engaged in ranching on his parents' large estates. He apparently became skilled in stock-raising. He was noted for his excellent horsemanship and it has been stated that he was the only California governor who had ever lassoed a grizzly bear.

In 1854, Pacheco was elected San Luis Obispo County judge, serving a term of four years. In 1857, he was elected state senator on the Democratic ticket from the district comprising Santa Barbara and San Luis Obispo Counties. The outbreak of the Civil War motivated him to switch his affiliation to the Union party in 1861, when he was re-elected.

In 1863, the state convention of the Union party nominated him for state treasurer without opposition. In the election of September 2, he polled 64,984 votes to 43,768 for Thomas Findley, the Democratic rival. However, he took over the office two months early since State Treasurer Delos R. Ashley had resigned and Governor Stanford appointed Pacheco to fill the unexpired term.

On October 31, 1863, Pacheco married Mary McIntire, a native of Kentucky, at St. Mary's Cathedral in San Francisco. Two days later the *Daily Alta California* wittily commented: "Hon. Romualdo Pacheco, State Treasurer, has found a treasure at the very threshold of his official career." His wife became the writer of several successful plays and a novel. They had two children—a daughter, Maybella Ramona, and a son, Romualdo, Jr.; the latter died in early childhood.

In 1867, Pacheco was renominated on the Union ticket, but was defeated by Antonio F. Coronel by less than 3,000 votes. On September 1, 1869, he was returned to the state senate from Santa Barbara and San Luis Obispo Counties in a contested election. His defeated opponent, Patrick W. Murphy, claimed

that Pacheco was not a duly qualified elector of the third senatorial district, nor of either county. Moreover, he asserted the
vote had been fraudulent. Following an investigation by the
Senate committee on elections, Pacheco was awarded his seat.

At the Republican state convention of 1871, Pacheco was
nominated lieutenant governor on the first ballot, becoming the
running mate of Newton Booth. Pacheco defeated his Democratic rival, E. J. Lewis, by over 5,000 votes.

On February 27, 1875, Pacheco was elevated to the governorship, when Booth was elected by the legislature to the United
States Senate. During his nine-month term Pacheco was concerned with routine matters since the legislature was not in
session. However, he was responsible for some appointments
and considered many applications for pardon. Perhaps the
most noted effort to gain executive clemency was the attempt
by John J. Marks, who had been convicted of embezzlement
while a state harbor commissioner in San Francisco. Marks
was a political power of some influence and he allegedly was
ready to resort to bribery to buy a pardon. Pacheco resisted all
pressure to release Marks who remained in San Quentin prison
until the next administration. Nonetheless, Pacheco granted
seventy-nine pardons, a fairly large number in less than a year.

During one of the last days of his term Pacheco sent his
only biennial message to the legislature. It indicated that the
governor possessed a keen insight into the outstanding economic
and political problems of California. Pacheco was pleased
that the state debt was less than it had been in over two decades
despite two recent financial panics. He pointed out that relations between the state and private corporations needed to be
solved. The primary issue, he contended, was which one held
superior power. And he warned that the impending question
of regulating railroad fares and rates would create new discord.

Pacheco devoted considerable space in his message to the
improvements in taxation that had been implemented by establishing the board of equalization. Previously the revenue provisions of 1861 had been virtually ignored and taxation burdens
had been distributed unevenly. With the creation of the board
in 1870, the former revenue system of false values and gross
inequalities ended. Pacheco recommended a continuation and
strengthening of the board of equalization.

The governor also suggested that the legislature investigate

San Francisco harbor conditions, relating that state operation had been fraudulent primarily as a result of legislative neglect. However, he praised the recently appointed harbor commissioners as a prudent administrative body.

Pacheco complained that only 42 percent of the 1,075 prisoners at San Quentin were employed in worthwhile pursuits. Hence he proposed that a permanent board of control should devise a system to make the prison self-supporting. The governor discussed in detail the problem of state lands and recommended a statewide policy concerning irrigation. He stressed the need for additional buildings and adequate library space at the University of California, and remarked: "Much of the future welfare of California depends on the higher culture of her sons and daughters. There is nothing to prevent our establishing a University that will be peer to any in the world." He described the California State Normal School, recently removed from San Francisco to San Jose, as indispensable for teacher training.

He reported the new state capitol building was nearing completion, and commented that the recently established state printing office should reduce the cost of printing. He recommended an appropriation for the California exhibit at the forthcoming centennial celebration in Philadelphia. In conclusion Governor Pacheco urged the legislators to be judicious in their control of public revenues, warning that as a rule special legislation was a general evil.

Pacheco was anxious to retain the governorship in his own right, but at the Republican state convention meeting in Sacramento on June 10, 1875, Timothy G. Phelps was nominated as the party's gubernatorial candidate. Pacheco was not even considered for lieutenant governor and the Republicans nominated Joseph M. Cavis for that office. Hence Pacheco abandoned his affiliation temporarily with the Republican party and was nominated for the lieutenant governorship by the People's Independent party which represented dissident elements opposed to the contemporary tendency of corporate interests to dominate the major national parties. The Democratic party nominated William Irwin as governor and James A. Johnson as lieutenant governor. In the Democratic sweep of the state election Johnson defeated Pacheco, but interestingly Pacheco polled 2,403 more votes than the Republican candidate for lieutenant governor.

On August 10, 1876, the fourth congressional district Republican convention met at San Francisco and nominated Pacheco as its candidate for Congress. In a rather unique election he defeated the Democratic incumbent, Peter D. Wigginton by 19,104 to 19,103, or one vote! Wigginton contested the returns and Secretary of State Edward H. Hallett refused to grant Pacheco a certificate of election. However, the State Supreme Court intervened and required Hallet to issue the certificate.

Pacheco was sworn in during the first session of the forty-fifth Congress and was appointed to the committee on public lands. He introduced two bills, neither of which became law. In the second session he introduced four bills and one became law. At this time Wigginton contested the seat and Pacheco was unseated on February 7, 1878.

Pacheco returned to California and in the state election of September 7, 1879, he was elected to the same seat unequivocally, defeating Wallace Leach and James J. Ayers, candidates of the Democratic and Workingmen's parties respectively. Pacheco took his oath of office on December 1, 1879, the opening date of the second session of the forty-sixth Congress. He was appointed to the committee on private land claims and to the committee on public expenditures. In the third session Pacheco delivered his first speech in Congress, arguing in favor of an appropriation bill that provided funds for the breakwater at Wilmington harbor; however, this measure failed to pass.

Pacheco was re-elected on November 2, 1881, defeating Wallace Leach by only 191 votes. In the first session of the forty-seventh Congress Pacheco gave his second and last speech on the House floor. He favored the Chinese exclusion bill—which passed—but President Arthur vetoed.

Pacheco was not an aggressive Congressman. His committee work largely related to matters of land claims. He labored for his constituency in support of their personal claims, for public buildings and harbor improvements, and for restriction of Chinese immigration. He introduced a total of fifty bills, all for individual or local benefit, and only two were enacted. Pacheco's term ended in 1883, and he was not a candidate again.

For the next eight years Pacheco remained a private citizen. Then on December 11, 1890, President Harrison appointed him Envoy Extraordinary and Minister Plenipotentiary to Central America. From February until May of the next year he presented his credentials in the various capitals of Guatemala, El Salvador, Honduras, Costa Rica, and Nicaragua. On July 1, 1891, the *San Francisco Morning Call* commented that he was exceptionally qualified for the office because of his cultured manners and knowledge of Spanish. On June 6, 1892, when he sailed aboard the steamer, *San Juan,* on one of his diplomatic missions to Guatemala and Honduras, his brothers of the Alcatraz Parlor of the Native Sons of the Golden West saw him off at the Pacific Mail dock along the San Francisco embarcadero. It is interesting to note that the steamer flew the Bear Flag of California as it stood into each Central American port. It should be mentioned that although the Native Sons originated during his tenure as governor, Pacheco was not at first eligible, for the society's constitution only permitted membership to men born in California on or after July 7, 1846, the day the American flag first flew officially over Monterey. After its constitution was changed, Pacheco qualified as a member.

Toward the end of his diplomatic career, Pacheco managed a cattle ranch in northern Coahuila in Mexico. When the Cleveland administration returned to power, he lost his diplomatic post. Pacheco then settled in San Francisco where he engaged in the brokerage business. After his retirement, he resided in Oakland during his last years. He died on January 23, 1899, being buried in Mountain View Cemetery.

From the romantic viewpoint his life symbolized a link from Mexican rule to the American era, but in reality the connection was weak. His long career of public office was commendable, but not outstanding. As a congressman his interests did not transcend his native state and he accepted local prejudice on the Chinese issue. To appraise critically his governorship would not be warranted inasmuch as few controversial issues arose. The *Daily Alta California* of December 4, 1875, in editorializing on his gubernatorial message to the legislature, stated in part:

> Governor Pacheco has been at the head of the State Government for only nine months, and in that period there has been no session of the Legislature, nor have circumstances otherwise thrown into

his way, opportunities for becoming familiar with the important business that sometimes devolves upon his present office. His Gubernatorial experience has been brief and quiet.

BIBLIOGRAPHY

CONTEMPORARY ACCOUNTS
Journals of Senate and Assembly, 18th Sess., 1869-70; 21st Sess., 1875-76.

SECONDARY SOURCES
Angel, Myron, *History of San Luis Obispo County* (Oakland, 1883).
Bancroft, H.H., *History of California.*
Barrows, David P., "Romualdo Pacheco," *Dictionary of American Biography,* XIV, 124-25; also see Barrows, Albert L., comp., "Governor Romualdo Pacheco of California" (Bancroft Library), which comprises the research notes for this article.
Conmy, Peter T., *Romualdo Pacheco, Distinguished Californian of the Mexican and American Periods* (San Francisco, 1957).
Hittell, T.H., *History of California.*
Mason, Jesse D., *History of Santa Barbara County* (Oakland, 1883).

NEWSPAPERS
Daily Alta California, Dec. 4, 1875, has an editorial on Pacheco's biennial message.
Oakland Tribune, Jan. 24, 1899, has an obituary of Pacheco.
San Francisco Call, Dec. 5, 1890, July 4, 1891, and June 5, 1892, have articles about Pacheco as Minister to Central America; Jan. 24, 1899, has an obituary.
San Francisco Chronicle, Jan. 24, 1899, has an obituary.

Calendar of Events

1827	Irwin born in Butler County, Ohio.
1848	Irwin graduated from Marietta College, Ohio.
1851	Irwin arrived in San Francisco.
September 4, 1861	Irwin elected to Assembly from Siskiyou County.
1866	Irwin became editor of the Yreka *Union*.
September 1, 1869	Irwin elected to Senate from Siskiyou County.
December 1, 1873	Irwin elected President pro tem of the Senate.
February 27, 1875	Irwin named acting Lieutenant Governor and warden of San Quentin.
December 9, 1875	Irwin inaugurated Governor.
September, 1875	Workingmen's Party established.
June 19, 1878	Delegates elected to second Constitutional Convention.
September 28, 1878	Irwin opened Constitutional Convention as temporary chairman.
May 7, 1879	Second California Constitution ratified by voters.
September, 1879	California voters approved statement opposing Chinese immigration.
1883	Irwin appointed chairman of the Board of Harbor Commissioners by Governor Stoneman.
March 15, 1886	Irwin died in San Francisco.

William Irwin

13TH GOVERNOR — DEMOCRAT
BORN: 1827   DIED: MARCH 15, 1886
TERM OF OFFICE: DECEMBER 9, 1875—JANUARY 8, 1880

WILLIAM IRWIN WAS BORN IN Butler County, Ohio, in 1827.
He attended first a country school and then Carey's Academy
near Cincinnati. He graduated from Marietta College in 1848.
He found employment as an assistant teacher at the Port Gibson Academy, Port Gibson, Mississippi, for one year. He returned to Marietta College and taught there for two years. In
the fall of 1851, he planned to study law in Chicago but went
instead to New York and booked passage for California. After
arriving in San Francisco, he went to Oregon where he joined
his uncle in a lumber concern. Returning to San Francisco in
June, 1854, he opened a lumber yard. In the fall of 1854,
Irwin started a lumber mill south of Yreka. In 1855, he and
L. Swan opened a slaughter house near Humbug. Irwin was
associated with Swan until 1860. He also tried his luck at
mining, and was, for a time, owner of a livery stable and a
line of stage coaches. Irwin's early life in California parallels
that of many of the pioneer settlers—striving in a variety of
ways to succeed in life in the face of adversity.

Irwin's political career was launched in Siskiyou County when
he was elected to the 1862 Assembly as a Democrat. He was
re-elected for the 1863 session and was chosen as the Democratic nominee for Speaker. Being of the minority party, he
received but four votes. In 1865, Irwin was defeated for the
office of Siskiyou County Tax Collector. On December 21,
1865, he married Amelia Elizabeth Cassidy at Fort Jones.
From this union one daughter was born. Shortly after his
marriage, Irwin, allying with other Democrats, purchased the

Yreka Union. He became editor and remained as such until his election as governor. During 1865 and 1866, Irwin also served as a town trustee of Yreka.

At the 1867 state Democratic convention, Irwin withdrew his name as a nominee for lieutenant governor, giving William Holden an uncontested nomination. However, Irwin had become known as a prominent figure in the north of the state. During 1867-68, he was president of the Mount Shasta Agricultural Association. In 1869, he was elected to the state Senate for a two year term from Siskiyou County, and was re-elected in 1873.

In 1873 Irwin was elected President pro tem of the Senate. When Lieutenant Governor Romualdo Pacheco became governor, Irwin became acting lieutenant governor and warden of San Quentin prison. An earlier legislature had assigned the duty of warden and resident director of the prison to the office of the lieutenant governor.

In 1875, Irwin received the Democratic nomination for governor on the seventh ballot. The *Daily Alta California*, while opposed to him, agreed that the Democrats had selected one of their best men for the nomination. The editor stated that Irwin had been an honest and useful senator and that it was plainly evident that "he did not become rich by holding office." Earlier, the *Alta* had printed that Irwin had little talent as a speaker, organizer, or writer and had not been a particularly outstanding politician. His main recommendation was his honesty.

The gubernatorial campaign of 1875 saw three strong candidates in the race. The Dolly Vardens cut deeply into Republican ranks giving Irwin the victory by a margin of fifty-nine votes over the combined total of the others. Irwin received 61,509 votes to Phelps' (Republican) 31,322 and Bidwell's (Dolly Varden) 29,752. The Temperance candidate received 356 votes.

William Irwin came into the governor's office at a time of economic disorder in California and the nation. Unemployment was rampant throughout the state and widespread stock market manipulations had disastrous effects. In August, 1875, many banks, over-extended in their resources, began failing and the financial structure of the state remained badly damaged for several years. During Irwin's administration, the Workingmen's party developed as a protest against economic hardships and became a prominent political force which the two major parties were forced to recognize. The new party was formed in San Francisco on October 5, 1877. While the members held divergent opinions, one dominant theme was to wrest control of the state government from the wealthy and place it in the hands of the common people. Opposition was expressed against the accumulation of wealth and the growth of monopoly. The workingmen also opposed the Chinese as dangerous competitors for the jobs of white men. At this time of economic depression, the workingmen sought solutions, some of them desperate, to their dilemma. In 1877, the brutal San Francisco riots against the Chinese saw the forming of another vigilance group under William T. Coleman to oppose the workingmen's efforts. This vigilance committee received the governor's approval.

On December 9, 1875, Irwin took his oath of office as governor. His salary was a basic $7,000 with an additional $1,000 for ex-officio duties. In his inaugural address he held that his election was a mandate to conduct the state's affairs in a prudent, safe, and economical fashion. Irwin, however, showed a lack of understanding of the new issues confronting California as his message dwelt upon problems of the past. He claimed that irrigation was the most important and most difficult matter facing the twenty-first legislative session. He called for establishment of irrigation districts with rights clearly defined to protect all participants. He believed that each district had to bear the complete cost of its irrigation system, for this expense was not a justifiable charge against the state or any county.

Irwin examined the proper relationships that ought to exist between the state and railroad corporations, claiming that the state's duty placed "it under the highest conceivable obligations to compel the corporations to maintain and conduct their roads *primarily* in the public interest, not for the enrichment of the stockholders." At the same time, the state had the obligation to protect the property rights of the railroad; Irwin held that the two positions were not incompatible. He claimed that the constitution gave the legislature the power to fix rates through its right to amend charters. Concluding his views on the railroad question, he asked for the appointment of a railroad commission to serve as a fact finding agency to enable passage of appropriate laws and to enforce this legislation.

The governor reviewed the problem of unequal property assessment in California, noting that the state supreme court had declared unconstitutional a state board of equalization whose job was to equalize the property tax, the state's prime source of income. The governor called for a constitutional amendment creating such a board to establish a common method of assessing and tax collecting in California.

Irwin's monetary views were conservative. He claimed that California had always been a hard money state and only gold and silver should be the medium of exchange. He observed that gold currency notes were being forced into circulation with difficulty and called for resumption of specie payments and a contraction of currency by the federal government at the earliest possible moment.

As the retiring resident director of San Quentin, his remarks regarding that institution were quite enlightening. He claimed that of all state institutions the prison was in the most unsatisfactory condition. He believed it had failed as a reformatory and that costs of operation were excessive. He called for enlargement of the Folsom prison and asked that its experiment of quarrying and dressing granite be continued. He suggested, as a penal reform, that prisoners be paid incentive wages to improve morale and the quality of work. Irwin cited the need for an educated permanent corps of prison officers. Irwin's message concluded with his view of government:

> . . . according to the theory which I have been taught, government is instituted not for the benefit of those who administer it, but for the common good of all; and that that government, which is simplest in its form, and least expensive in its operations, is the best if it accomplish [sic] the purposes for which governments are instituted. In a word, government is the agent of society for the accomplishment of certain specific purposes. And society, like an individual or a corporation, is interested in having its agent perform the work assigned him, in the most efficient and cheapest manner.

The 1875-76 legislature did not accept many of Irwin's suggestions. It did authorize appointment of commissions of transportation. The most notable of the commissioners appointed by Irwin was George Stoneman. Earlier in the twenty-first session, Irwin had appointed another future governor, George C. Perkins, to a two year term as a trustee of the Napa Asylum. Still another famous appointee, in January, 1876, was Henry

George as inspector of gas meters.

The legislature agreed to an expansion of state prison facilities. It also launched the West Side Irrigation District, which served as the prototype for future districts. During this session, acts were passed allowing incorporation of societies for prevention of cruelty to children and for establishing and maintaining free public libraries and reading rooms. The latter act began the city and county library system. Also enacted was a law forbidding changes in state textbooks to prevent unnecessary revisions.

Irwin, for his part, showed no reluctance about using the veto power. As had many of his predecessors, Irwin checked the legislature's desire to enact special measures in behalf of corporations. He vetoed a bill concerning the St. Luke's Hospital Association which revised its charter to allow the receiving and holding of land given through wills. Irwin held to the old view that such special bills were in violation of the constitution which permitted only municipal corporations to have special acts passed. When the legislature passed a bill modifying charters of charitable corporations dedicated to scientific, literary, or educational purposes to receive willed land, Irwin again objected. He believed that this would provide a loophole by which much land would disappear from general use.

Irwin's inaugural message had commented that although a constitutional limit was imposed on the state debt, cities and counties were free from such a restriction. He asked the lawmakers to refrain from legislation that would plunge local governments deeper into debt. When, nevertheless, they approved a bond issue for a Tehama County academy, Irwin vetoed the bill because of the county's existing debt and its inability to pay off the increased bonded indebtedness. Irwin had indicated that he stood firm for reduced expenditures, but he objected when the legislature proposed cutting maintenance costs of the capitol building and grounds as false economy. He held that the state's investment had to be maintained.

At the time of the 1876 presidential election, a special election was conducted to fill the office of state controller, caused by the death of the incumbent in February, 1876. Irwin had appointed William B. C. Brown to the office, but in the election Brown was defeated at the polls by Republican D. M. Kenfield. When Kenfield applied for his commission, Governor Irwin refused to issue it on the grounds that no proclamation had been issued calling for the special election. Kenfield applied for a writ of mandate to compel issuance of the commission. Irwin filed a demurrer. Both a lower court and the state Supreme Court upheld the governor's action and Brown remained in office.

Governor Irwin, in January, 1877, received a communique from the Mexican Consul objecting to the use of California as a base for filibustering raids into Sonora. Irwin replied that the request for a proclamation against such activities was not in order, but as governor he would do all he could to stop the raids.

Irwin's first biennial message, 1877, reflected the view that time and patience would correct any economic maladjustments. He deplored the rise of violence among California workers. Although the message mirrored conservatism, it did present some ideas for improving conditions in the state. Irwin offered the reassurance that for the most part the California economy was doing well. Crops had failed because of inadequate rainfall and the mining industry had gradually diminished in importance. These factors had led, he said, to some unemployment and to a belief that a business depression gripped the state. Irwin blamed the plight of the worker not upon the economic structure but upon the Chinese. Commenting on labor's unrest over the Chinese issue since 1875, he felt that its unhappiness was aimed "rather at the anticipated evils of the future, resulting from the presence of an alien and unassimilative population, than at any they were then suffering." Calling the recent labor riots both violent and unlawful, he noted these were aimed specifically at the Chinese. Irwin detected in these riots a rise of class conflict on the part of the working class against the monied class. He advised the laborers to follow orderly and legal procedures and to refrain from violence.

During Irwin's administration, agitation continued throughout the state for Chinese exclusion. Centered mostly in San Francisco and sponsored by the Workingmen's party, this agitation was soon exploited by politicians of all parties as a popular means of gaining voting strength. Irwin in his 1877 message claimed that "it is unnecessary that I should make an argument to demonstrate the evils of Chinese immigration. In this State, and everywhere on this coast, they are universally, or next to universally conceded." He feared the consequences of immigration as allowed by the Burlingame Treaty of 1868, but commented that the legislature's only alternative was to petition Congress to restrict immigration. The governor professed at length the need of fairness to those Chinese already residing in the state and guaranteeing them full protection of the law. He assured the legislature that he would attempt to secure equal protection for all residents in California; moreover, he said the courts had been impartial in their cases concerning the rights of the Chinese. Treatment of Chinese at the municipal and state level during the 1870's, however, did not bear out Irwin's contention.

Other than his remarks on the Chinese, his biennial message was a factual report without many recommendations for change. His thinking may well have been conditioned by the knowledge that shortly a new constitution would be written which could resolve existing problems. In fact, his message concluded with the idea that since there was to be a new constitution, the twenty-second session ought to enact only laws dealing with immediate matters.

Irwin reported that during his first two years in office the funded debt of the state had been reduced $61,000 and that the debt total was $3,411,000. He felt the framers of the 1849 constitution had been wise in limiting state indebtedness; because of this and through careful management, the state's financial condition remained good. He asked the legislature to continue using care in making appropriations, since increased state services increased expenditures. He also called attention to the declining property values, resulting from the general business depression, and the subsequent tax increase of 13 cents per $100 added to the 1875 rate of 73.5 cents. He hoped the new constitution might include a state board of equalization to bring equity in taxation.

Irwin reiterated his view about prisons serving as reformatories, believing that most prisoners were hardened and could not be rehabilitated. Those, however, who were young should be separated from the confirmed criminal and given a chance for rehabilitation. Irwin spoke strongly against his pardoning power, claiming that not only should it be taken from the governor but completely eliminated.

Irwin called for the establishment of an agricultural department at the university to meet the needs of California. He noted, too, that with the state's assumption of the care of Yosemite Valley and the Mariposa Big Trees the legislature had to provide for the development of these areas. He complimented the superintendent of state printing who, assuming his duties for the first time in 1875 as the head of the newly reconstituted state agency, had reduced printing costs by about 45 percent over the preceding two years.

He believed that the state militia needed to be more efficient and better trained to meet rising emergencies such as had recently plagued the state. He claimed it was the militia's duty rather than the United States Army's to quell uprisings within California's borders.

The transportation commissioners, he stated, had quickly found the Central Pacific Railroad Company obstinate as it refused to file a schedule of rates and fares. The commission, with his permission, had started court action. Irwin held that it was clearly in the right as borne out by the recent national decisions known as the "Granger Cases."

Irwin also recommended amending the registry law for voters after the 1876 election disclosed fraud. Votes cast illegally for persons absent from the state or the polls, and the deceased, indicated the obvious need to scrutinize precinct lists.

He demanded, too, a better protection of depositors at savings banks and of mining stockholders from mismanagement by directors. He added that a tax on stock transactions might be a good source of state income. Irwin began in 1877 to show awareness of the current economic picture of the state as he requested these reforms.

The legislature of 1877-78 enacted many timely proposals. One such act, which received the governor's approval, was to determine by vote the will of the citizens regarding Chinese immigration. At the general election in September, 1879, 154,638 votes were cast against immigration while 883 supported the Chinese. Governor Irwin's conclusion was *"that the citizens of this State are substantially unanimous against the continuance of Chinese immigration."* Other acts created a board of bank commissioners and a single commissioner of transportation replacing the former three man commission. Irwin approved regulation of ballots to eliminate bogus election tickets. An interesting act, protecting the state's dairy interests, prevented the sale of oleomargarine under the name, or as a pretense for, butter.

Irwin, during the course of this session, notified the legislators that Serranus C. Hastings desired to donate $100,000 to found and maintain a college of law. Enabling measures were passed and the Hastings Law College came into existence. Perhaps the most important measure of 1877, however, called for the convention to draft a new constitution.

Irwin vetoed several measures in 1877. Perhaps the most notable was his veto of an act appropriating $25,000 to the Howard Benevolent Association of Sacramento for relief of victims of recent rains and floods. Irwin, reflecting his conservatism, noted his sympathy for the needs of the distressed people, but that unfortunately public funds could not be spent in such a manner. He held that "the State is not a grand insurance company" standing ready to reimburse from taxes any losses suffered by taxpayers. He also stated that the government of California was not a charitable institution whose job was "to distribute gratuities to the needy, or to assist the weak and unfortunate." He referred again to his concept of state government: to promote law and order and to protect the citizenry. In discussing California's proper role in charitable help, Irwin claimed that only those who were completely powerless to aid themselves were proper wards of the state, such as orphans and the mentally ill.

In March, 1878, Irwin followed his predecessors by transmitting to Congress a resolution asking for reimbursement of about $242,000 for the cost of Indian wars within the state. Settlement of this debt had been pending for several years, growing out of Indian troubles in the early 1870's.

Following the close of the twenty-second session, Governor Irwin actively campaigned for the selection of delegates to the constitutional convention. He asserted that those delegates chosen should know the weaknesses and strengths of the existing constitution.

The delegates assembled in Sacramento on September 28, 1878, and were greeted by Irwin who, as temporary chairman, presided over the convention during its preliminary organization and its bitterly contested selection of a president. With the election of Colonel Joseph P. Hoge, Irwin's official capacity was completed. Following the drafting of the second constitution, Governor Irwin became in 1879 one of the prominent spokesmen against its adoption. He related that he had favored constitutional revision, had signed the bill calling the convention, and had been temporary chairman. However, the results were not what he had desired. He admitted that while there were several good points, the bad ones were of such character that the new constitution would do more harm than good. He charged that the alliance of the Workingmen's party and the Granger elements at the convention had injected most of the bad features. The new constitution was, nevertheless, approved by the voters in May, 1879, and Irwin issued a proclamation putting the new document into effect July 4, 1879, with new state officers to assume office in January, 1880. This proclamation made Irwin's term the longest four year term in the history of the office of governor.

On January 8, 1880, Governor Irwin sent his second biennial message, his last official communication, to the legislature. While comparing the state's economic improvement with recent past difficulties, he saw in the economy's upswing an accompanying improvement in social and political conditions. He noted that previous strong differences of opinion over the new constitution were now academic and all citizens should work hard to make the document succeed. For the most part, his message simply related the workings of the various state departments and their requests for funds. With some pride, Irwin pointed out that the state debt had been further reduced during his last two years, if only by $8,000. The retiring governor paid high tribute to the old constitution with its enforced debt limitation and he hoped that the incoming legislature would amend the new constitution to include this provision.

His final state paper expanded upon two topics—one an old theme and the other a new idea. Reporting on the Chinese question, Irwin referred to the 1879 referendum and claimed that there should be no doubt anywhere in the United States that all classes of citizens were opposed to Chinese immigration. Irwin felt that California could do nothing about restricting Chinese immigration; the state could only use its police powers as provided in the new constitution to restrict the influence of the Chinese residing in the state. Introducing the debris question, which was to haunt the Perkins administration, Irwin noted the conflict which had developed between hydraulic mining and agricultural interests. Irwin hoped that legislative action rather than a judicial decision would resolve the controversy.

Irwin concluded by stating the governorship had been an honorable, onerous, and responsible position. He then commended Governor-elect Perkins to the legislators.

William Irwin retired for a time into private life, but in 1883, Governor George Stoneman appointed him to a four year term as chairman of the board of harbor commissioners, the first such appointee under a new 1883 act. Irwin served in this position until his death in San Francisco on March 15, 1886. He died at the age of fifty-nine with the cause of death described as either Bright's disease or diabetes.

Governor Irwin served as chief executive during difficult times. The rise of the Workingmen's party, the Chinese question, and the new state constitution were all major events during his term. Irwin most certainly spoke for the conservatives in the state on all of these questions. The major complaint of his contemporaries was his vacillation on important matters. His messages demonstrated this weakness as he tried to show both sides of issues or merely presented facts without recommendations. He was known as a patient, friendly man. He was not a quick thinker, but his contemporaries reported that he worked diligently to master details and had been a useful member of the Senate and a fairly able governor. Although a partisan Democrat, he did not place party interests above the state's welfare. The administration of Governor William Irwin was conducted honestly and independently from the railroad monopoly interests. While his term was not particularly brilliant, Irwin must receive credit for keeping a firm hand on executive matters during a period of turmoil in California.

BIBLIOGRAPHY

MANUSCRIPTS
Bowman, J.N., "The Early Governors of California . . ."
Irwin, William, "Letters," (California State Archives).
————, Official Record of Executive Department," (State Archives).

CONTEMPORARY ACCOUNTS
Assembly Journal, 21st-22nd Sess., 1875-78.
Senate Journal, 21st-23rd Sess., 1875-80.
Debates and Proceedings of the Constitutional Convention of the State of California (3 vols., Sacramento, 1880).

SECONDARY SOURCES
Bancroft, H.H., *Chronicles of the Builders.* . .
————, *History of California.*
Davis, W.J., *History of Political Conventions.* . .
History of Siskiyou County, California (Oakland, 1881).
Hittell, T.H., *History of California.*
Parkinson, R. R., *Pen Portraits*: *Autobiographies of State Officers, Legislators, Prominent Business and Professional Men of the Capital of the State of California* (San Francisco, 1878).

NEWSPAPERS
Daily Alta California, Sept. 2, 1875, has editorial on Irwin's election as governor; Dec. 10, 1875, has editorial on inaugural message; Jan. 7, 1880, compares Irwin to Perkins; March 16, 1886, has Irwin's obituary.
Sacramento Union, April 25, 1879, and May 2, 1879—Irwin speaks against adoption of the new state constitution.
San Francisco Bulletin, Jan. 8, 1880, discusses Irwin's final message as governor.
San Francisco Call, March 16, 1886, has Irwin's obituary.
San Francisco Chronicle, March 16, 1886, carries an obituary.

OTHER SOURCES
California Blue Book, 1907 (Sacramento, 1907).
"Daggett Scrapbook" (California Section, State Library).
Themis, I (July 7, 1889), 1.

Capitol at Benicia, 1853-1854. The building in which the legislature met at Benicia in 1853 was of brick and two stories in height. The rear end of the lower story constituted the Senate chamber. The Assembly occupied the rear part of the upper story. The building is still standing, at First and G Streets, and is a California Historical Landmark.

Calendar of Events

August 23, 1839	Perkins born at Kennebunkport, Maine.
1855	Perkins arrived in San Francisco.
September 1, 1869	Perkins elected Republican Senator from Butte County.
1872	Perkins joined in organizing the Goodall, Nelson & Perkins Steamship Company.
1873	Perkins re-elected in special election to Senate, representing Butte, Lassen, and Plumas Counties.
1879	Perkins named President of the San Francisco Merchants' Exchange.
January 8, 1880	Perkins inaugurated first Governor under second state Constitution.
1880	Perkins first used newly established item veto against an appropriations bill.
April 4, 1881	First special session of the legislature held.
March 4, 1882	Perkins declared a legal holiday for demonstrations against the Chinese.
1888	Perkins appointed by Governor Waterman as a director of the Deaf and Dumb and Blind asylum.
1889	Perkins appointed by Governor Waterman as a trustee of the Mining Bureau.
July 26, 1893	Perkins appointed by Governor Markham to fill unexpired term in the U.S. Senate, caused by death of Leland Stanford.
March 3, 1915	Perkins retired as U.S. Senator.
February 26, 1923	Perkins died in Oakland.

George C. Perkins

14TH GOVERNOR — REPUBLICAN
BORN: AUGUST 23, 1839   DIED: FEBRUARY 26, 1923
TERM OF OFFICE: JANUARY 8, 1880—JANUARY 10, 1883

GEORGE CLEMENT PERKINS, first chief executive under the state's second constitution and only governor elected for a three year term, was born at Kennebunkport, Maine, on August 23, 1839. Here he lived on the family farm and attended school until he was twelve. He then ran away to sea where for the next four years he sailed on several voyages. In 1855, he arrived in San Francisco where he purchased some mining equipment and headed for the mines. He walked from Sacramento to Butte County where he tried his luck unsuccessfully. He decided to strike out for the Fraser River country in British Columbia, but in San Francisco he had a change of heart and remained in California. He worked his way through Sacramento and Oroville to Ophir where he drove a mule team. In 1856, he was a porter in an Oroville store, bought and sold the ferry at Long's Bar for a $1,000 profit, and then clerked at the same Oroville store for $80 a month. With business at a low ebb, Perkins bought the store and by the time he was twenty, it was grossing about $500,000 a year.

Perkins' life provided another case study of the Horatio Alger "success story." He remained in business at Oroville until 1875, when he moved to San Francisco, leaving his brother in charge. In addition to his Oroville mercantile interests, Perkins had purchased sheep and cattle ranch lands, had engaged in mining and lumbering, and had helped found the Bank of Butte County. He also led in establishing the Ophir Flour Mill. In 1864, he married Ruth Parker. From this marriage were born three sons and four daughters.

Perkins played an active role in Republican politics before running for governor. He was a member of the Republican state central committee by 1867. In 1871 and 1872, Perkins was one of the vice presidents of the Republican conventions' permanent organization. In 1871, he also served on the committee on resolutions.

In 1869, Perkins was elected to a single term in the state Senate from Butte County. This proved a turning point in his life, leading to both a political career and a vastly expanded business career centered in San Francisco rather than in the agricultural Sacramento Valley. As a freshman senator, Perkins, with a marked independence of thought, showed that he was not another senator in the pay of the Central Pacific railroad. His colleagues found him a hard worker, an independent thinker, and an ambitious servant of the people. As a member of the finance committee, he submitted a one man minority report favoring passage of a bill granting state support to the University of California. The Senate adopted his report and for the first time the state provided financial aid to the university.

Perkins gained considerable fame as the only Republican senator who voted to sustain Governor Haight's veto of the bill giving the Central Pacific alternate sections of land for a railroad in the San Joaquin Valley. Perkins later explained this "lapse of orthodoxy," stating that as a businessman he believed that the road would be successful without state aid. In 1870, he again showed his independence of the dominant Republican wing in the Senate by voting against the fifteenth amendment to the constitution. In 1873, after the expiration of his own term, he won a special election filling a Senate vacancy for Butte, Lassen, and Plumas Counties.

It was while senator that the opportunities of new business ventures presented themselves to Perkins—for it was at Sacramento that he met Captain Manor Goodall. From this acquaintance he joined the San Francisco firm of Goodall & Nelson in 1872, forming the Goodall, Nelson & Perkins Steamship Company. Shortly renamed the Pacific Coast Steam Navigation Company, it became quite successful in coastal shipping. In 1881, the company had twenty-one ships operating from Mexico to Sitka. Perkins greatly expanded his business interests by becoming a member of the Oregon Railway and Navigation

Company, president of the Arctic Oil Works, and vice president
of the Pacific Steam Whaling Company, the first concern to send
steam whalers into Arctic areas. He was president of the Pacific
Coast Railway, a road in Santa Barbara and San Luis Obispo
Counties, and a director and large owner in Starr and Company,
which operated the largest flour mill and warehouses on the
coast. He was a vice president of the West Coast Land Company and a director for the Bank of Butte, the California State
Bank of Sacramento, and the First National Bank of San
Francisco. In 1879, the San Francisco business community
recognized Perkins' success by electing him president of the
Merchants' Exchange. At the threshold of his nomination for
governor, George C. Perkins, a run-away sailor lad, had become an accepted spokesman for the conservative well-to-do
circles of the state's business world.

Prior to his nomination, Perkins was one of those Californians firmly opposed to the new constitution, but after its
adoption, he stated that the will of the people must be observed
and allowed that he would do his part to support the new plan
of government. Perkins' selection as the Republican nominee
for governor was not a matter of chance; he was carefully
chosen as a counterbalance against other political forces in
the state.

At the Republican state convention of 1879, Perkins received his party's vote on the first ballot. He was presented as
a man worthy of the support of both labor and capital, having
belonged to both groups. In the campaign, Perkins opposed the
Central Pacific while carefully noting that the power of control
was not in the governor's hands but in those of the board of
railroad commissioners. He denied any connection with the
railroad, stating that as a coastal shipper he had been a direct
competitor. His supporters made much of his famous vote
supporting Governor Haight in the late 1860's. Perkins' campaign reflected a nautical theme based on the Gilbert and Sullivan operetta, *H.M.S. Pinafore,* recently performed in San
Francisco. His backers launched for the duration of the campaign the "Good Ship Geo. C. Perkins." The crew of the good
ship brought its captain safely home in the 1879 election with
Perkins receiving a plurality vote—67,966 ballots. His nearest
opponent, Democrat Hugh J. Glenn, received 47,665 votes.

On January 8, 1880, George C. Perkins took his oath of

office and delivered the first inaugural address under the new constitution. He announced that he and Governor Irwin had earlier appointed a committee to prepare codes and statutes to harmonize with the new constitution. Supervision of this task was Perkins' major contribution to the office of governor. Perkins, like Irwin, expressed the orthodox conservative view about proper relationships between labor and capital. The part of his message long remembered concerned his suggestion that prison labor provide much needed burlap sacks for California grain interests. He advocated growing jute in California and building a jute mill at San Quentin. The reasons for this advocacy, apart from personal interest in wheat, was the fact that contract prison labor was ending as a result of the second constitution and some work had to be found to make the prisons self-supporting. His inaugural address noted the Folsom prison building program was nearing completion. He advocated making the two penal institutions more reformatory in nature.

Perkins commented briefly on two problems confronting the valley farmers—debris and irrigation. He expanded in detail on the problem of railroad rates and fares, charging the new commission to be more harmonious in its work than had been its two predecessors. He also gave his views on revenue and taxation. Since the second constitution provided for an income tax, Perkins suggested that a fair beginning would be to tax those with personal incomes in excess of $5,000. This, he felt, would lead to an equitable sharing of the tax burden among all classes in California. However it was not until 1935, during Merriam's administration, that such a tax was enacted.

Perkins' address contained the traditional anti-Chinese viewpoint. Reviewing the 1879 vote on the Chinese question, he claimed that the entire nation had learned that all of California was opposed to Chinese immigration. While he believed that the federal government would have to solve the matter of immigration, he announced that he would cooperate with the legislature in applying certain state measures to abate the problem.

Perkins reflected the beliefs of the governors of the 1850's in his discussion of the existing land monopoly. The governor's solution was to use time and taxes to break up the large Mexican land grants still in existence to make more land available to productive farmers.

The 1880 session saw considerable legislative delay as a result of the decision that all bills be read three times aloud in their entirety, consuming much valuable time and putting the legislators far behind schedule. Most of the laws enacted dealt with governmental reorganization under the second constitution. The mining bureau and the commission of viticulture were established. Perkins signed a number of bills aimed at controlling the Orientals. One interesting act repealed the protection of seals and sea lions near the San Francisco Cliff House in response to an appeal from fishermen that these animals were destroying the fish in that area.

During this session of 1880, Governor Perkins used for the first time his new power of the item veto on three proposals in a general appropriations bill. He was sustained by the Assembly.

Governor Perkins' first biennial message to the 1881 legislature, while generally appreciative of the state's recovery from the recent depression, devoted particular attention to problems of agriculture. He suggested expanding the state board of agriculture to serve all segments of California. He noted with some dismay that the creation of the viticultural commission had led several groups to demand special boards to develop their own interests. For the benefit of all and in the interest of economy, Perkins requested that one agricultural board do this work. While speaking about state aid to agriculture, he charged that certain district fairs allowed games of chance and gambling on the fair grounds in direct violation of anti-gambling statutes.

Perkins considered the greatest agricultural problem to be irrigation. He held the practice of dry farming was the most certain way to insure the growth of land monopolists since small farmers could not be successful in this technique. The current conflict was between water usage based on the English common law custom of riparian rights and the opposing usage of appropriation for the irrigation needs of dry regions. Since the matter was at an impasse, his view was that the state should plan a system of water diversion to utilize water presently being wasted, while providing compensation to riparian owners. The governor made no headway in this area during his term.

The governor offered no new solution when discussing transportation. He noted that previous legislatures had been un-

successful, showing nothing but failure in the matter of regulation. Perkins refrained from making recommendations as the
new railroad commission had not yet announced its findings.

Reporting on state institutional services, Perkins recommended expansion into new fields while economizing in existing
agencies. He believed that some of the state's financial difficulties stemmed from over-ambitious programs. He called,
however, for a commission of immigration which would produce brochures setting forth advantages of the entire state
to induce settlers to come to California; he believed such a plan
was fair to all, beneficial to the whole state and not the interest
of just one area. It should be recalled that this was the beginning of the land boom of southern California with its at-
tendant promotional schemes. Still another service the state
needed to provide, Perkins added, was a labor bureau to help
resolve some of the differences between capital and labor since
both had to work together. It was the duty of the state, he felt,
to help the many deserving men, currently unemployed, find
work.

He suggested that the state needed to plan armories for the
national guard at San Francisco and Sacramento and supply
equipment rather than money allotments for such an arrangement would save state funds. His report on the insane asylums
asked that the superintendents be empowered to refuse admission to all except those clearly insane or who were admitted
upon proper application. Many counties had been emptying
their hospital wards by sending patients to the asylums where
they had to be admitted, with the state bearing additional transportation costs. He urged that the commissioners of immigration be given sufficient power to protect California from foreign
arrivals who were mentally unfit, for institutional records
showed a large number of foreign born being committed upon
arrival in the state. As a former trustee of the Napa hospital,
he indicated he spoke with some authority on these matters.

He was more concerned with the role of state prisons as
reformatories rather than with the financial aspect of their
operations. He forwarded recommendations of the directors
and wardens, asking for prisoner classification to separate
youthful offenders from hardened criminals. He asked, as had
other governors, for a state boys' reform school. Perkins noted
that he had granted executive clemency to several young boys,

removing them from the prison environment in an effort to restore them to society. Perkins pointed out that great inequality of sentences existed for the same conviction. He believed that there was no rational reason for these unjust judgments and noted that about one-half of the applications for executive clemency were based on excessive sentencing. He had found in most instances these claims were correct.

He asked for legislative scrutiny into administration of orphan asylums to see that charity was not being abused through lax admission standards, holding that many children in these homes were not truly orphans. The surviving parent should be made to assume the obligation of care, not the state.

Governor Perkins demanded continued economies for while the state's debt had been reduced another $6,500, leaving the total indebtedness at $396,000, installation of the revised state government had been expensive. There had been also the necessity of building and rebuilding certain state facilities such as the San Jose Normal School which had been destroyed by fire. He claimed that the boom times of the past were over and that county governments, as they were revised to conform to the new constitution, ought to reflect a more sober approach to county indebtedness. The legislature needed to establish a low tax rate to protect taxpayers and to keep counties within their proper means.

He complimented the citizens on having over 100,000 children in school, but lamented the fact that another 50,000 children were not attending school. Briefly examining the purpose of public education, he concluded that serious consideration be given to providing instruction in trade or mechanical skills to enable those who comprise the greater part of the population in every community to become better qualified to earn a living.

One unusual feature of Perkins' message related to the right of women to vote for all school officers and upon those educational questions not restricted by the constitution to only qualified voters. Perkins thought it was an excellent idea to have women vote for school officers but when it came to voting on other questions, he held that women in their present capacity as the family advisers were able to assert a strong moral force on the male voter that would be negated once the power to vote was granted. While this was a weak argument, it perhaps indicated who held the whip hand on family matters within the Perkins' household.

His message included the usual biennial reference to the Chinese. He noted that opposition was still high and that although those laws passed at the last session had been declared unconstitutional, the federal government had been aroused sufficiently to appoint a commission to arrange a new treaty with China.

On January 14, 1881, Perkins presented a special message on the mining debris question, the problems raised by hydraulic mining and the inundation of Sacramento Valley farmlands. Perkins reviewed point by point the difficulties, indicating that both the farmer and the miner had to be protected for the sake of the state's economy. Beyond stating the facts in the case for both sides and reporting on the attitudes of the engineers retained for the survey, Perkins only called for remedial legislation to restore the streams and farmlands to their normal usefulness while allowing the miners the opportunity to continue operations. In short, he reviewed the existing situation and passed the burden of solution to the legislature, offering no gubernatorial leadership.

In this 1881 session, three readings of pending bills caused a log jam. Perkins sent a sharp message on March 3, rebuking the proposed legislative adjournment without any appropriations being voted for state expenses for the next two years. He suggested that such an appropriations bill fell in the urgency category as indicated in the constitution and could be passed without three readings. He asked that there be no adjournment until an appropriations bill and a corresponding tax levy bill had been passed. The governor's appeal fell on deaf ears. It was apparent that he had no power in directing legislative matters; the assemblymen and senators took directions from legislative leaders who did not work closely with the governor.

George Perkins gained a gubernatorial first by calling the legislature into its first special session. Setting the time limit for this April, 1881, session at twenty days, he asked consideration of six subjects: a general appropriations bill, determination of the tax rate for the next two years, provisions to pay existing deficiencies, division of the state into legislative districts based on the 1880 census, a general road law to replace the one declared unconstitutional, and consideration of gubernatorial appointments by the Senate.

In his message to the special session, Perkins tried to placate the lawmakers by commenting on their difficult task of passing all necessary laws in the regular session limited to sixty days. He suggested that a future study be made to solve the existing legislative impasse.

Perkins received his general appropriations bill, although he item vetoed the building of the prison wall at Folsom as being an unconstitutional inclusion in the bill. He wrote that items in the general appropriations bill had to refer to measures already enacted by the legislature. The Folsom wall was mentioned for the first time in this particular bill. He also vetoed the general roads bill because supervisors were to be given the right of unlimited property taxation for road construction and because city and county roads were not separately defined. He was upheld in these views.

A very interesting conflict developed between the governor and the legislature during the special session. On April 20, 1881, he signed an act appropriating $42,000 for legislative expenses and salaries which had been one of the first bills rushed through both houses. The lawmakers, procrastinating on the governor's request for legislation, went beyond the twenty day limit. Governor Perkins vetoed their proposal for an additional allocation for salaries, claiming that twenty days should have been ample. Although the requested bills had been introduced, no one could explain to him why these had not passed. Both houses overrode his veto.

Perkins exceeded his predecessors in issuing pardons and commutations. In three years, he granted eighty-four pardons to state prison inmates, 129 pardons to county jail prisoners, fifty commutations and two reprieves. Perkins never intervened until he had personally interviewed the prisoner and learned his story. If convinced that the man was a good risk, executive clemency followed. It has been stated that only one such person was returned to prison in violation of his parole.

Perkins spelled out his attitude regarding pardons in a letter written in 1880 to Martha A. Ruggles of Hanford. He stated that her letter along with about 100 other applications for pardons had been studied. He said that he had examined all petitions and looked at both sides. He wrote, "I believe it the duty of the Governor not to be *influenced* by *sympathy* or *prejudice* but to act *justly* doing only that *which he honestly believes* to be *right.*" Perkins then added that he had investigated the case and had decided that if some member of the family would go to San Quentin and take the boy into the home as if nothing had happened, the pardon would be granted.

In September, 1881, while accepting the resignation of Wallace Everson as a state prison director, Perkins unburdened himself of his feeling regarding the office of governor:

> I fully appreciate your feeling at the adverse criticism of the public press. It would appear that one has but to be a candidate for, or accept a public position, to at once be a target for unfriendly criticism.
>
> It has been my earnest endeavor to honestly, conscientiously, and faithfully do my whole duty in the discharge of every official trust, and I doubt not that you can say with me if you have erred it has been an error of the head and not of the heart.

In 1882, Governor Perkins became an active leader in the Chinese question. On March 2, he issued a proclamation declaring that, because the immigration bill pending before Congress was so important to California, March 4, 1882, was to be a legal holiday in order that Californians might demonstrate their sentiments to Congress. He called for one universal demonstration against immigration. On March 3, he wrote his regrets to Mayor Maurice C. Blake of San Francisco, who was president of the Great Anti-Chinese Meeting in that city, that he could not be present to join in the demonstration. His letter expressed the orthodox California view:

> . . . that we believe it is the duty of Congress to *immediately restrict Chinese immigration to our country,* that *free* American *labor* may not be *overwhelmed* and *degraded* by *contract-slavery* and *coolie competition!*
>
> The voice of our people rising above party and partizan creed unite today upon the broad platform of human rights; and ask that our representatives declare *this menace* to *Republican Institutions* shall *cease!*

Perkins held deep seated convictions about Oriental labor both as governor and later as United States senator. In April, 1882, he wrote a member of the San Francisco board of health suggesting that any means of eliminating the Chinese was fair. He held that those ships with "invaders" on board who had small pox, cholera, yellow fever, or other contagious diseases ought to be quarantined by the board of health for such a long time that any profit that the ship owner hoped to realize would be lost. He added, "The result will be that they will cease to bring them in large numbers as passengers." The letter ended with "the thought is worthy of your consideration and I trust you will take such action . . . as will protect the interest of the people of our state."

In August, the 1882 Republican state convention brought Perkins' gubernatorial career to an end. An afterthought, introduced from the convention floor, inserted a plank that "the republican party points with pride to the conduct of the affairs of the state under its present faithful executive. . . ." Nevertheless, Perkins was not considered for renomination.

Perkins' 1883 biennial message, his farewell to the legislature, primarily reviewed the state's activities under his leadership. After noting that California was in the midst of prosperity, Perkins turned with pride to the state's financial condition. Indicating that the bonded indebtedness had continued to decrease, he stated that ordinary operating expenses had increased only slightly although there had been an unusual outlay of capital investment in a long range building program and in establishing new state agencies. One such example was the erection of the Branch State Normal School at Los Angeles.

In agreement with some of his predecessors, Governor Perkins thought that the cost of collecting state revenue was too expensive and that there needed to be a general law governing county tax collectors. He criticized the 1881 legislature for not providing an adequate tax rate to underwrite enacted appropriations.

In this second biennial message, as in the first, Perkins made no comments on the efforts of the railroad commission whose report had been sent in late. Perkins at no time officially commented on its apparent failure to solve the state's transportation difficulties nor did he touch upon the issues of the 1882 gubernatorial campaign. The governor also complained of the railroad companies' refusal to pay their delinquent taxes. Perkins, while governor, always vacillated on railroad controversies in official communiques. This last message claimed that since the United States Supreme Court had the railroad tax case on its present docket, it was not right for him to make any other comment.

Perkins was enthusiastic about the progress of the state prisons. The San Quentin jute mill was successful in its opera-

tion and had freed the state grain growers from the "sack
monopoly." The governor claimed that San Quentin was on the
threshold of becoming self-sufficient. He reported that the
Folsom quarry was producing excellent granite for the capitol
building. He again stressed the need of a reform school for
young offenders. He felt such an institution was of utmost
importance because the "peculiar curse of this State" was
"juvenile criminality and the rampant hoodlumism."

The governor appeared pleased with the new state mining
bureau for gaining national recognition at such an early stage
in its development. Two other agencies, the board of viticultural commissioners and the horticultural department, were
also highly praised. Perkins reported that the state engineer's
work on the irrigation problem was completed and soon many
more settlers could be attracted to newly opened lands. He
reported that there was a move to establish a veterans' home in
Napa County and that state aid was to be asked by the founders
to finance a refuge for veterans of the Mexican and Civil Wars.

In conclusion he commented on the recent Congressional
passage of the Pendleton Act leading to federal civil service
reform. He observed that while it was true that he had not been
particularly outstanding in making appointments through a
merit system, he had greatly enlarged the idea of bipartisan
appointments to certain of the state boards. He suggested that
the state might well consider making appointments based on
business principles.

After his term as governor, Perkins returned to his business
interests; however, he was soon called to serve his state again.
In 1888, he was appointed one of the directors of the deaf and
dumb and blind asylum at Berkeley, and was reappointed in
1891. In 1889, he was also appointed a trustee of the state
mining bureau. Perkins was also quite prominent in fraternal
circles, serving as Grand Master of the Grand Lodge, Free &
Accepted Masons of California and as Grand Commander of
the Knights Templar of California. He was prominent in other
societies and clubs.

In 1893, with the death of Senator Leland Stanford, George
C. Perkins was appointed by Governor Markham to fill out the
unexpired term. He was re-elected three times in his own right
by the legislature to the United States Senate, retiring in 1915.
As a senator, he became an authority on maritime affairs and

an advocate for a strong Pacific fleet. He became vehemently anti-Japanese in military and immigration matters. He served on the committees of commerce and appropriations and during his last term was chairman of the naval affairs committee.

Following his third term as senator, he retired because of failing health. He returned to his Oakland home. He died of heart failure on February 26, 1923, at the age of eighty-four.

Perkins had an excellent physical figure. He held himself erect on a well knit frame. Although of large body he was not bulky. He was just under six feet in height. At the time of his nomination for governor, sympathetic newspapers characterized him as a person of industry, integrity and a high fidelity to trust. The *San Diego Union* found his private life pure and his public record useful and incorruptible. The press had publicized his rags to riches role in making the transition from a common laborer to an enterprising California capitalist. Well respected in and out of Republican circles, he had made friends throughout the state through his fraternal, business, and political associations.

In his later life, Perkins became a well known patron of art and literature. He served two years as president of the San Francisco Art Association and was a member of the Bohemian Club. By the time he became United States Senator in his own right, the Southern Pacific Political Bureau had gained a stranglehold on California politics and Perkins became known as a servant of the company.

George C. Perkins never denied that he was the spokesman for the conservatives while he was governor or senator. As governor, he was representative of the group which viewed with apprehension the activities of the Workingmen's party. Governor Perkins was in office during a crucial time in the history of the governorship. His major weakness as governor was his willingness to postpone long standing critical problems and his refusal to take open sides or to offer executive leadership. On the other hand, his handling of the office did not precipitate any new crisis in the state, and the second constitution, so much opposed by people who shared his political convictions, was successfully launched and the new state government firmly installed.

BIBLIOGRAPHY

MANUSCRIPTS
"Biography of men important in the building of the West," (Bancroft Library).
Bowman, J.N., "The Early Governors of California . . ."
Perkins, George, "Executive Records, State of California," (California State Archives).

CONTEMPORARY ACCOUNTS
Assembly Journal, 23rd-25th Sess., 1880-83.
Senate Journal, 23rd-25th Sess., 1880-83.
Congressional Directory, 63rd Cong., 2nd Sess., 1914-15.
Downie, William, *Hunting for Gold: Reminiscences of Personal Experience and Research in the Early Days of the Pacific Coast from Alaska to Panama* (San Francisco, 1893).

SECONDARY SOURCES
Baker, Joseph E., ed., *Past and Present of Alameda County* (2 vols., Chicago, 1914).
Bancroft, H.H., *Chronicles of the Builders. . .*
———, *History of California.*
Davis, W.J., *History of Political Conventions. . .*
Guinn, James Miller, *History of the State of California and Biographical Record of Oakland and Environs* (2 vols., Los Angeles, 1907).
Hittell, T.H., *History of California.*
Mansfield, George C., *History of Butte County California with Biographical Sketches* (Los Angeles, 1918).
Mowry, George E., *The California Progressives* (Berkeley, 1951).
Sacramento Union, Makers of Northern California (Sacramento, 1917).
Sherman, Edwin Allen, *Fifty Years of Masonry in California* (2 vols., San Francisco, 1898).
Whitsell, Leon O., comp., *One Hundred Years of Freemasonry in California* (4 vols., San Francisco, 1950).

NEWSPAPERS
Daily Alta California, Jan. 5 1881, has editorial on Perkins' first biennial message while his second message is presented on Jan. 10, 1883.
Sacramento Union, June 19, 1879, gives an estimate of Perkins as the Republican candidate and on Sept. 5, 1879, comments on his election as governor. Feb. 27, 1923, carries his obituary.
San Francisco Bulletin, Jan. 8, 1880, discusses his inauguration message.
San Francisco Call, Jan. 10, 1880, reports on his first biennial; July 23, 1893, reports on Perkins' appointment to the U.S. Senate.
San Francisco Chronicle, Feb. 27, 1923, reports his obituary.
San Francisco Examiner, Feb. 27, 1923, carries the obituary notice.

Second Capitol at Sacramento, 1855-1869. Erected at a cost of $240,000, after fire destroyed the first Sacramento Capitol, the above building, at 7th and I streets, was finished January 1, 1855. It was also Sacramento's second court house, and county prison, and was rented by the state for an annual rental of $12,000, until the completion of the present capitol in 1869. The building continued to be used as a court house into the 1900's.

Calendar of Events

August 8, 1822	Stoneman born at Busti, New York.
1846	Stoneman graduated from West Point.
1847	Stoneman assigned to the Mormon Battalion and came to California.
1865	Stoneman during the Civil War gained the ranks of major general of volunteers and colonel in the United States Army.
1870	President Grant placed Stoneman in charge of the Arizona Department.
1871	Stoneman relieved of his command and retired from the army.
1876	Stoneman appointed by Governor Irwin as a member of the Transportation Commission.
September, 1879	Stoneman elected as Railroad Commissioner for third district.
January 10, 1883	Stoneman inaugurated Governor.
March 24, 1884	Special legislative session called by Stoneman to consider the railroad problem.
July 20, 1886	Stoneman called another special session to attempt solution of the irrigation question.
1891	Stoneman moved to Buffalo, New York.
September 5, 1894	Stoneman died in Buffalo.

George Stoneman

15TH GOVERNOR — DEMOCRAT
BORN: AUGUST 8, 1822   DIED: SEPTEMBER 5, 1894
TERM OF OFFICE: JANUARY 10, 1883—JANUARY 8, 1887

GEORGE STONEMAN, ONE OF THE FEW PERSONS who had acquired a national reputation prior to gaining prominence in California politics, was born on August 8, 1822, at Busti, Chautauqua County, New York. He attended Jamestown Academy and in 1842, was appointed to the Military Academy at West Point. He graduated with high honors in 1846, just in time to serve in the Mexican War. Assigned first to Fort Leavenworth, he accompanied the Mormon Battalion to California as assistant quartermaster in 1847.

In 1848 and 1849, he was briefly in command at the San Francisco Presidio. Until 1852, Stoneman fought in Indian wars in California and Oregon. From May, 1853 to May, 1854, he commanded the military escort accompanying the railroad survey from Benicia to San Antonio, Texas. In 1855, he was promoted to captain and assigned to frontier duty at Camp Cooper, Texas, but took an eighteen month leave of absence to tour Europe. Upon his return he went to Texas for border patrol duty. With the outbreak of the Civil War, he seized a steamer and removed his command from Texas to the national capital. Stoneman served in various capacities in both the Eastern and Western theaters of the war, gaining a reputation for leading Union cavalry raids. Generals U. S. Grant and W. T. Sherman held different views of Stoneman's ability as a field commander. Grant thought very highly of Stoneman while Sherman admonished him for being captured in a raid on Macon and Andersonville, Georgia.

At the war's conclusion, Stoneman, with the rank of major

general of the volunteers and the regular army rank of colonel, was given command first of the military department of Tennessee and then of Virginia. After the war, Stoneman married Mary Oliver Hardisty of Baltimore. From this marriage came four children.

In 1870, President Grant transferred Stoneman to the Department of Arizona where he launched a retrenchment program to keep the expenses of his command within the allotted $1,000,000. Previously the Arizona budget had been $3,000,-000. This cut-back of expenditures made Stoneman unpopular as many civilians lost jobs and government contracts were sharply curtailed. Apparently he also ran counter to the wishes of the "Quaker policies" of the national administration as he pursued a relentless aggression against the Indians. General Stoneman was relieved of his command in 1871, and General George Crook took charge of the Arizona department. Some citizens of Arizona in asking for his removal charged that Stoneman had been living near Los Angeles rather than attending to his duties.

An element of truth pervaded all these charges, for he had acquired a 400 acre San Gabriel Valley ranch of orange trees and grape vines. He did spend considerable time there with his staff and it was at his Los Robles ranch that he turned over his command to Crook.

That Stoneman had transgressed in the matter of federal policy might well have been the reason that he encountered difficulty when retiring from the army. He was retired with the rank of major general, but President Grant shortly revoked this special order and Stoneman received his regular rank of colonel with a reduction in benefits. The reason given for this change was that the original order had been issued with the understanding that Stoneman had been wounded in battle. The second order said this had not been the case.

For the next few years, Stoneman devoted himself to ranching. In 1873, he became president of the Los Angeles branch of the Veterans of the Mexican War. In 1876, with the establishment of the state commissioners of transportation, Governor Irwin appointed Stoneman as one of the three commissioners, with an annual salary of $3,000. He remained a commissioner until 1878, when the three were combined into the office of commissioner of transportation. President Rutherford B.

Hayes, in keeping with his independent appointment program, named Stoneman in 1878 as an Indian commissioner.

George Stoneman ran for his first elective office in 1879, as a candidate for railroad commissioner of the third district. The new commission had been created as a result of the second state constitution. He received nominations from the Workingmen's party, the New Constitution party, and the Democratic party. He defeated the Republican nominee decisively, receiving 35,518 votes to 19,410. His new position paid $4,000 a year. He accomplished little, for the other two commissioners were pawns of the railroad. Stoneman's stand against the railroad, however, won him wide fame in the state, particularly with the California farmer, and set the stage for the Democratic state convention of 1882.

In the contest with George Hearst for the Democratic gubernatorial nomination, Stoneman received the bid on the fourteenth ballot. The railroad and its hold on the state's economy was the major issue in the general campaign that followed. The name of Stoneman had popular appeal. Many opposed him for the office as did the editor of the *Daily Alta* who claimed that Stoneman, a recent arrival in California, did not understand the state's real problems and that he lacked executive ability. The editor claimed that Stoneman was a poor speaker—that "his heart is all right, but his mouth is as a scatter gun." His record as commissioner was both attacked and defended. Making an appeal for the anti-Chinese vote, the *San Francisco Daily Examiner* wrote:

> He hires principally native Californians. Having always recognized the fact that Mongolian immigration would ultimately bring the State to ruin, he puts precept into practice and rigidly abstains from employing Chinese, even in the lowest menial work about him.

When the political opposition raised the technical question as to whether a retired army officer could hold a state elective office, Stoneman resigned from the retired list giving up his annual retirement pay of $3,300. Significantly, no such charge had been leveled by the opposition in 1879, when he was elected to the railroad commission.

George Stoneman defeated Republican Morris M. Estee for the governorship, garnering 67,175 of the 164,661 votes cast for four candidates. As a plurality governor, he received 40 percent of the votes.

Stoneman, a Jeffersonian Democrat, made his inauguration simple. He delivered his inaugural address on January 10, 1883, expressing his philosophy of government: "The people are the sovereigns and we are the servants." The major theme of his address revolved around the power of the railroad. He noted that while farmers had harvested bumper crops, the railroad charges on these producers were unreasonable. In the recent election, the people had spoken out, Stoneman contended, against special interest groups.

Stoneman paid attention to the continuing impotence of the state board of equalization, asking legislative help in restoring the board's power primarily because several corporations had refused to pay their state taxes. Demanding immediate steps be taken, Stoneman added that permitting nonpayment "to continue is to admit that the State had fostered a servant who has grown into an insolent and tyrannical master."

The governor's previous tenure as a railroad commissioner qualified him to speak with authority on the commission's activities, something his predecessor, George Perkins, had been unwilling, or unable to do. Stoneman regretted that the 1880-82 commission, of which he had usually been the minority member on matters of policy, had completely refused to take any positive steps in regulating rates. He hoped the new commission would be more aggressive in facing "the great living issue of the day . . . regulation of fares and freights." Stoneman said his office stood ready to help the commission resolve the problem.

The incoming governor asked for specific legislation on items requested by some of his predecessors. As had Perkins, Stoneman called for a general road law; as had Burnett and Johnson, he wanted a general law to govern the incorporation of cities; and he asked for a common system of county government.

Governor Stoneman agreed with Irwin and Perkins that state penal institutions should be reformatory in nature, returning useful men to society. He believed that San Quentin should receive all prisoners for classification and for distribution to other institutions. While he thought that a policy of isolation and solitary confinement was the best procedure to separate the most vicious criminal from those men who could be rehabilitated, he appeared to feel this was not practicable and advocated instead his idea of distribution based on the men's prior records.

Stoneman's inaugural concluded with the claim that his administration, while maintaining established public institutions, would cut unnecessary governmental expenses to the bone. His audience listened quietly, but gave loud applause to his plan of payment of railroad taxes.

During the 1883 legislative session, most bills enacted were routine measures for operating the state government. Stoneman's suggestions, made in his inaugural, were not seriously considered. One important measure, which received his approval, created the bureau of labor statistics, the beginning of the department of industrial relations.

On January 20, 1883, Stoneman, in a special message to the Assembly, deplored the alleged conduct of Charles D. Bunker, commissioner of immigration. The governor noted that the only available record concerning this official had been his 1880 appointment by Perkins. Bunker had made no reports, had not established a lazaretto for the confinement of lepers, and had paid no receipts of fees into the state treasury—all of which had been required. Stoneman concluded that the commissioner had withheld excessive funds from the state. The Assembly did not pursue the matter and in March, Stoneman made his own appointment.

In November, 1883, Stoneman wrote to the head of the State Grange setting forth his views on the railroad question. At that time he had considered but rejected the idea of a special legislative session. He was disappointed that the railroad commission had delayed on the rate and fare question. The only basis for a special session would be if inadequate state revenue could be predicted as a consequence of the commission's inactivity. He lamented to the Grange leader that certain elected officials were not upholding their public pledges. He added that the legislature had basically failed by not providing a system of penalties against the railroads for not obeying rates established by the commission. He announced that the federal circuit court had decided against the state regarding payment of delinquent taxes by the railroads and the matter was then pending in the United States Supreme Court. The governor thought that the state would be victorious in recovering the taxes.

Stoneman's anticipated victory in the courts did not materialize, for the state attorney general agreed to an out of court settlement with the railroads whereby only part of the total tax bill would be paid and without heavy penalty. The governor immediately, and for the remainder of his term, refused to accept the settlement or payment of any tax money under the terms of the compromise. He steadfastly maintained that the railroads were obliged as any other citizen to make full payment. In March, 1884, Stoneman called a special legislative session to consider the entire railroad question. In his call he reiterated that the railroads had not paid their taxes for the past four years and that the compromise advanced was unsatisfactory. He also claimed that the board of railroad commissioners had proven a complete failure. Stoneman then submitted a twelve point program to remedy the existing stalemate.

During the special session, the Assembly enacted most of his program, but it failed to pass the Senate. The only measure passing both houses covered the expenses of the extra session. The Speaker of the Assembly, Hugh M. LaRue, delivered a valedictory message complimenting the Assembly for representing so well the wishes of the people. He concluded that all this had been in vain because of lack of cooperation in the Senate. Stoneman and California did not solve the railroad problem in his administration.

Governor Stoneman sent his first biennial message to the twenty-sixth session in January, 1885. Perhaps the message's most important aspect was what he did *not* say regarding the failure of his railroad program in the 1884 extra session. Stoneman's message first concerned itself with state finances. Although he did not say so, the fact was that state income had dropped because of delinquent railroad taxes. He announced a $380,230 revenue loss for his first two years in office. Offsetting this, however, was an even greater decrease of expenditures, exceeding the three year Perkins' administration by $1,212,244. This was accomplished even while carrying out normal affairs of state and a modest building program. Stoneman also reported that in 1884, the state tax rate had reached its lowest point to date in the state's history—45.2 cents.

Stoneman's message advanced new ideas concerning California agriculture. He believed that cereal crop production had reached its limit and that grape and fruit cultivation should now be encouraged. He asked for expansion of the viticultural and horticultural commissioners' powers to protect growers. Adequate pest controls needed to be established and laws were needed to prevent adulterating wines and other agricultural products. Stoneman suggested a protest against proposed reciprocity treaties with Spain and Mexico in the best interests of California's wine and citrus producers.

Stoneman's 1885 message emphasized the irrigation issue and he held the same view as Perkins. He claimed that "the prosperity of our people is largely dependent upon the results of the artificial union of waters and soils." Stoneman agreed with Perkins that the crux of the issue was riparian rights. The courts had continued upholding the rights of those living on the river bank. Stoneman urged changing the law to meet the needs of all people. He offered no solution but merely restated the long standing stalemate. He did suggest that those with riparian rights had to be compensated for the loss of water which they had no right to deny to those who lived inland away from the source of supply. He advocated a clear definition of water rights before attempting any settlement. He advised that the state streams should be administered by the state engineer in developing a state water program.

With regard to the pardoning power, Governor Stoneman intimated that he had initiated a new policy of referring all appeals to prison directors, since they were more qualified to decide such cases. He asserted that the prison board had been of great assistance in helping him do his duty to both the prisoners and the state. In keeping with a spirit of nonpartisanship, he had appointed a new board of prison directors from members of the two major political parties.

At the close of his biennial message, he mentioned the railroad controversy. Stoneman first touched on the 1864 act whereby California agreed to pay the 7 percent per annum interest on some of the Central Pacific's $1,000 bonds for twenty years. In return for this financial assistance, the railroad had agreed to carry free of charge public messengers, convicts to prison, construction materials for the state capitol building, articles for state fairs, and troops and supplies in time of war.

Stoneman observed that, while the state had kept its part of the agreement to the amount of $2,100,000, the railroad had done nothing. The Central Pacific Company claimed that there had been no method of implementation in the 1864 act binding the company. The railroad further argued that the obligations of the act bound the road to performance only on the line from Sacramento to the eastern state boundary. The governor demanded an amendment to the 1864 act to allow the state to recover at least a portion of the amount paid out in interest on the bonds. This attempt was but one in the long running fight that Stoneman unsuccessfully waged against railroad interests.

Commenting on the railroad taxation problem, he reasserted that he had attempted to compel "certain railroad corporations . . . to assist in the support of a Government which enforces their rights and protects their property just as it enforces the rights and protects the property of all its other citizens and corporations." He observed that the situation was as unsettled in 1885 as it had been two years earlier. With reference to the pending appeal—the test case—before the United States Supreme Court he reported this case had not advanced on the trial docket, and that the delinquent railroad taxes as of December, 1884, amounted to $1,041,229.74.

Governor Stoneman appeared frustrated as he tried to pinpoint the fault in the governmental structure that had allowed corporations to remain delinquent in non-payment of taxes. He called for laws providing for the sale of delinquent railroad property. In a moment of pique, he concluded that corporations must be made to pay their taxes or not be taxed at all.

In 1885, several new state institutions and agencies were created with the governor's approval. To prevent overcrowding of the insane asylums, two new hospitals—the California Home for the Care and Training of Feeble-Minded Children and the California Hospital for the Chronic Insane—were established. Also created during this session was the Industrial Home for Mechanical Trades for the Adult Blind of the State of California. In 1887, its name was changed to the Industrial Home for the Adult Blind. California saw established for the first time in 1885 a board of forestry and a mining bureau board of trustees.

Stoneman's 1885 biennial message, and the legislative action that followed, proved a major milestone in California political history. Stoneman ably stated the feeling of California citizens regarding the railroad. He introduced new social legislation, such as regulation of food and drugs, and extension of state care to additional mental patients and the adult blind.

On July 17, 1885, fire destroyed the Stoneman Los Robles ranch home. The family was not in residence at the time, but its personal effects and the governor's papers were all destroyed.

Governor Stoneman, one year later, called the legislature into another extra session in an attempt to break the deadlock on riparian rights. His July, 1886 message reviewed the historical development of water usage in the state and the dependence of southern California and the central valley upon irrigation. The state supreme court decision upholding riparian rights and giving stream bank owners the opportunity to obtain an injunction against water diversion caused serious damage to those dependent upon irrigation. Stoneman asked for water rights for all people, based on a free use of flowing waters.

While the lawmakers were still in session, Stoneman sent a message on August 20, pointing out that those eighty-nine members who had petitioned for this extra session had led him to believe that they would support the doctrine of free use of flowing water. However, no progress had been made and he adjourned the session until September 7 to allow holding of political nominating conventions. When the legislature reconvened, Stoneman met with defeat as he had during the railroad tax session.

George Stoneman was not considered for renomination as governor by the Democrats. Consequently his second biennial message of 1887 was his last official statement as chief executive. In it he reviewed progress as well as problems related to his four years in office.

Although state finances were excellent, Stoneman observed that the cost of government had increased largely because of additional expenditures for state institutions and services. As a result the tax rate in 1886 had increased 10.8 cents above the 1884 rate to the new level of 56 cents. He forwarded the controller's warning that state expenditures had exceeded income by some $374,000, a practice not condoned in private business.

In reviewing the railroad tax affair, he lamented that the supreme court decision against the state had not really decided the question, for the railroad attorneys had turned the case on a technical point. He confessed that he had not been successful in his fight against the railroad. He still maintained that all taxes levied should be paid, with no exceptions allowed.

Stoneman called attention to the continuing difficulties encountered by the state board of equalization in convincing county assessors and supervisors of the counties' role in state taxation. The assessors were not uniform in their appraisal of property which caused unfair tax burdens for some citizens and also deprived the state of needed tax revenues.

Apparently pleased with the prosperous condition of agriculture—the state's major industry—Stoneman expressed hope that horticultural and viticultural successes might soon be complemented by a bountiful sericulture. He visualized California developing into a center of the silk industry as he recounted the work of the state board of silk culture. He held that, while the extra session on irrigation had not seen any immediate progress, much had been accomplished by a thorough airing of the topic. He still believed his opinions were correct and asked that another special session be held to settle this important problem.

He reported a controversy had developed in 1886 regarding competition between prison labor and free labor in the state. After receiving many petitions from labor unions for an investigation, he discerned that such competition by prison labor was against the spirit of the constitution and he ordered a cessation. Believing that the manufacture of jute did not compete, he advocated an enlargement of the mill which would in large measure take care of the San Quentin labor problem. He recommended that the Folsom prisoners continue cutting rough stone for the San Francisco sea wall and for other public works.

The governor endorsed the findings of the penological commission, particularly the parole system as the best way to reform the prisoner. He also asked for a study of the problem of financial aid to discharged prisoners as one means of rehabilitation. He concurred with the commission and with the majority of his predecessors in calling for a reform school for boys to separate youths from state prison inmates.

The Home for Feeble-Minded Children, located in Santa Clara County, had lived up to expectations, he reported, although its facilities needed enlarging to include those children classified as idiots. The new asylum for the chronic insane, under construction at Agnew, would go far, he believed, in solving overcrowded conditions at Stockton and Napa.

General Stoneman had much to say about the national guard. In all cases the guard's equipment was in poor condition and needed replacement. Most of the uniforms, purchased by the soldiers, were threadbare. Stoneman asked for an appropriation to purchase uniforms as one means to attract young men who could not otherwise afford such an expense. After reviewing other state agencies, he thanked the people of California for the kind regard they had shown him while he was governor.

During his four years as governor, Stoneman, working in conjunction with the state prison directors, exercised liberally his pardoning power, granting 260 pardons and 146 commutations of sentence. Many of these were granted during the last weeks of his administration for which the press sharply rebuked him.

At the end of his term, Stoneman returned to his San Gabriel Valley ranch where he resided until about 1891, when he moved to Buffalo, New York, to live with his sister. In 1891, Congress restored him to the retired list with the rank of colonel. In April, 1894, he suffered a stroke from which he never recovered, dying September 5, 1894, at his sister's home. His body, moved under military escort, lay in state in Jamestown, New York. He was buried at Lakewood, close to his birthplace. Seventy-two years old at the time of his death, he was survived by two sons and two daughters.

Contemporary newspapers held that Stoneman was an inadequate executive and an inept politician. The *San Francisco Chronicle* found him apathetic, weak, and vacillating. James J. Ayers, appointed superintendent of state printing by Stoneman, claimed, however, that California had been served by many governors of high integrity who had been conscientious in discharging their duties, and Stoneman ranked outstanding in these qualities. Ayers inferred that the newspapers were perhaps correct in some of their judgments about the governor as Ayers noted that Stoneman was not a "keen sharp man" but "a man of noble purposes." Ayers further claimed that Stoneman with a loyal and unsuspicious nature was frequently trapped by the intrigues of those around him. The petition presented to the governor requesting the extra session on irrigation was a good case in point. The people of California held Stoneman in high regard because of his Civil War record and they had faith in his integrity. Stoneman personally was genial and pleasant with friends from all walks of life.

In comparing the Stoneman administration with others of the same era, it must be concluded that it was one of the most vigorous and in some ways more successful in making its position known. Governor Stoneman showed courage in meeting outright the difficult problems of the railroad and irrigation. In fact, it was to be a long time before another governor fought the railroad corporations. That he did not make any progress was not his fault, for he was fighting against superior and well-entrenched forces. During his term, many advances were made in creating state agencies for the welfare and protection of the average citizen. Insofar as he was able to do so, he carried out his creed of a government for all the people. Governor Stoneman's administration was the brightest period in the history of the office of governor during the last three decades of the nineteenth century.

BIBLIOGRAPHY

MANUSCRIPTS
Gregg, David McM., "Letter Book—Operations of the 2nd Division, Cavalry Corps, Army Potomac, 1863 and 1864," (Recent Manuscripts Division, Library of Congress).
Stoneman, George, "Letters," (California Section, State Library).
————, "Official Record, Executive Department," (California State Archives).

CONTEMPORARY ACCOUNTS
Assembly Journal, 25th-27th Sess., 1883-87.
Senate Journal, 25th-27th Sess., 1883-87.
Ayers, James J., *Gold and Sunshine.*
Barker, C. A., *Memoirs of Elisha Oscar Crosby.*
Grant, U.S., *Personal Memoirs of U.S. Grant* (2 Vols., New York, 1886).
Schmitt, Martin F., ed., *General Crook His Autobiography* (Norman, 1946).
Sherman, W.T., *Personal Memoirs of Gen. W.T. Sherman* (2 vols., New York, 1891).

SECONDARY SOURCES
Bancroft, H.H., *History of California.*
Davis, W.J., *History of Political Conventions. . .*
Hittell, T.H., *History of California.*
McGroarty, John S., *History of Los Angeles County* (3 vols., Chicago 1923).
Storke, Thomas M., *California Editor* (Los Angeles, 1958).
Swasey, W.F., *The Early Days and Men of California* (Oakland, 1891).

NEWSPAPERS
Daily Alta California, May 20 & 22, 1871, reported that Stoneman was relieved of command of Arizona Military Dept.; June 24, 1882, editorialized about his nomination for governor; Jan. 18, 1885, gave editorial comment about his first biennial message.
Sacramento Union, Jan. 11, 1883, reported his inaugural message while his first biennial message was covered on Jan. 18, 1885.
San Francisco Bulletin, Jan. 10, 1883, and Jan. 17, 1885, reported same events as did the *Union.*
San Francisco Call, Jan. 11, 1883, and Jan. 18, 1885, carried editorials on inauguration and first biennial message; July 7, 1885, Stoneman's house and personal papers burned; Sept. 6, 1894, carried account of Stoneman's death.
San Francisco Chronicle, Sept. 6, 1894, printed obituary.

OTHER SOURCES
The California Mail Bag, I (1871), 17.
"The Records of Stoneman and Estee. Read and decide! Whom the anti-monopolist should support" (California pamphlets, Vol. VIII, California Section, State Library).

Calendar of Events

February 29, 1824	Bartlett born in Augusta, Georgia.
November 13, 1849	Bartlett arrived in San Francisco.
May, 1856	Bartlett became a member of Second Vigilance Committee.
1857	Bartlett appointed deputy county clerk for San Francisco County.
1859	Bartlett elected San Francisco County Clerk.
1861	Bartlett re-elected county clerk.
1863	Bartlett admitted to the bar.
1866	Bartlett defeated as Democratic candidate for county auditor.
1867	Bartlett re-elected county clerk.
1870	Bartlett appointed by Governor Haight to fill vacancy on state Harbor Commission.
September 3, 1873	Bartlett elected to Senate.
November, 1882	Bartlett elected Mayor of San Francisco.
November, 1884	Bartlett re-elected Mayor.
January 8, 1887	Bartlett inaugurated Governor.
1887	Legislation enacted and signed creating irrigation districts.
September 12, 1887	Bartlett died in Oakland.

Washington Bartlett

16TH GOVERNOR — DEMOCRAT
BORN: FEBRUARY 29, 1824   DIED: SEPTEMBER 12, 1887
TERM OF OFFICE: JANUARY 8—SEPTEMBER 12, 1887

GOVERNOR WASHINGTON BARTLETT'S ADMINISTRATION lasted only eight months for he was the first governor to die in office. This brief tenure did not allow for many accomplishments. Any discussion of Washington Bartlett must be prefaced by the fact that the two Washington Bartletts in the early days of California statehood has confused some scholars. The one, Washington Bartlett, became governor of the state after long careers in journalism and politics. The other, Washington Allon Bartlett, first American alcalde of San Francisco, was credited with changing that city's name from Yerba Buena.

Washington Bartlett, in a dictated interview with one of Hubert Howe Bancroft's staff members, stated that he was born in Augusta, Georgia, on February 29, 1824. This is the only reference to his birthplace being Augusta; all other contemporary accounts indicate that Bartlett was born in Savannah, Georgia on the same day.

His family moved in 1837, to Tallahassee, Florida, where he grew to manhood. There he learned the printer's trade in his father's newspaper establishment. He sailed from Charleston, South Carolina, in January, 1849, around Cape Horn, and arrived in San Francisco in November. Bartlett refrained from going to the gold fields and immediately set up his print shop. In a short time, he had received a share of the public printing. In January, 1850, with John S. Robb as his partner, Bartlett started the *Daily Journal of Commerce*. This venture came to an end with the great San Francisco fire of 1851. Bartlett had earlier, shortly after his 1849 arrival, published the first English language book printed in California—*California As It Is and As It May Be or A Guide to the Gold Country.*

His brother, Columbus, arrived in the fall of 1852, and the two started a new job printing concern. In 1853, they started publication of the *Daily Evening News;* in February, 1854, another brother, Cosam, joined the enterprise. Washington Bartlett served as editor. In the latter part of 1856, with Edward Connor and William H. Rhodes, he bought out his two brothers and changed the paper to the morning *True Californian.* The enterprise was poorly managed, leaving by 1857 an indebtedness of over $12,000 for Bartlett to face alone which he succeeded in repaying within ten years.

In 1856, Bartlett joined the Vigilance Committee and was appointed captain of one of the military companies. After the committee had disbanded, some of its members established the People's party to protect the citizens of San Francisco and to gain some degree of good government. In 1857, because of his prominence with the vigilantes, Bartlett was appointed a deputy county clerk for San Francisco County. In 1859, as a People's party candidate, he won election as county clerk and was re-elected in 1861. Following his second term, he was admitted to the bar in 1863 and practiced law with his brother, Columbus, until 1867. In 1866, he received the Democratic nomination for county auditor and came within 800 votes of being elected. In 1867, he was again elected county clerk.

In 1870, Governor Haight appointed him to fill a one and one-half year vacancy as a state harbor commissioner. At the same time, he was secretary of the San Francisco Chamber of Commerce. In 1873, he was nominated by the Citizen's Independent party and the People's Union party as one of the state senators from San Francisco. Successful in his bid, he served one four year term. By the second half of his term, he had realigned himself with the Democratic party. Bartlett adopted for his political view, the slogan, "Honesty in Politics."

In addition to his political career, Bartlett helped organize the San Francisco Homestead Union in 1861 and helped found the San Francisco Savings Union in 1862. A member of the Society of California Pioneers, he served as a director in 1873-74, and as president in 1882-83. Fraternally, he was a charter member of the old Parker Lodge No. 124, I.O.O.F. and a director of the Odd Fellows' Association. From 1872 to 1876, he was a partner with Daniel L. Randolph in San Francisco real estate. Throughout his life, Bartlett remained a bachelor.

Following his term in the Senate, Bartlett toured Europe. Upon his return, he was elected to the board of free-holders which drew up the San Francisco city charter. In 1882, running as a Democrat, he was elected mayor of San Francisco and re-elected in 1884.

Bartlett greatly enhanced his political reputation by his forthright handling of the mayor's office and by 1886, he had become a leading figure in the Democratic party. At the state Democratic convention held in San Francisco, August 31, 1886, Bartlett received the gubernatorial nomination on the second ballot. The press conceded that the Democrats had indeed selected their strongest candidate.

In the general election, Washington Bartlett received 84,970 votes to 84,311 for his nearest rival, Republican John F. Swift —a plurality of only 654 votes. Bartlett was a minority governor with 100,653 votes cast against him.

At the moment of his election, California held Washington Bartlett in high esteem. He was quite distinguished looking with hair and beard silvery white. His face was highlighted by bright, penetrating eyes. Those who met him were impressed with his manners, referring to him as a gentleman of the old school. He had a retiring disposition, finding it difficult to make friends easily and yet he impressed people as a man of great capacity and high intellect. He appeared to be more concerned about the public as a whole rather than specific individuals.

He was noted for his energy and respected for having moved from the lower rungs of life to a successful political career. His contemporaries found him faithful to the public trust and competent in the offices entrusted to him. Bartlett—not a dynamic speaker—was able when occasion demanded to express his ideas clearly and forcibly.

Bartlett arrived in Sacramento to be inducted into office on January 6, 1887, but the Speaker of the Assembly revealed that not all county returns had been received to allow an official canvass. Inaugural ceremonies were delayed until January 8.

After taking his oath of office, Governor Bartlett delivered his only formal address of general policy to the legislature.

In two sentences he dismissed California's complex irrigation problem. He noted that the issue needed settlement and that it devolved upon the legislature to arrive at a just solution. However, no gubernatorial advice was forthcoming as to how this might be accomplished. The incoming governor reiterated the traditional anti-Chinese view as he demanded abrogation of the Burlingame Treaty as necessary for the welfare of white laboring classes.

Bartlett expressed high concern, as had Stoneman, over the rising cost of ordinary expenses of the state government for the previous two years. He showed a conservative view regarding state finances when he stated that, "jealous of the State's honor and credit," he was quite opposed to a system of living off future revenues. He urged a strict economy program by the legislature with a view to reform and retrenchment, instead of resorting to increased taxation as the means of keeping the budget in balance.

A highly interesting aspect of this address dealt with public education in California. Bartlett called attention to the national development of industrial training. He criticized what he called the "old scholastic system of learning," which emphasized a love of learning. In reality, he held the majority of public school children were obliged to go to work upon leaving grammar school. The governor therefore called for instruction at the state normal schools aimed at training all the faculties of the child and not just the mind. There needed, he suggested, to be a thorough education encompassing mechanical and artistic talents as well as intellectual pursuits to provide trained people for the various occupations of California.

He also called for correction of abuses in the management of corporations and the selling of stocks on margin, hoping to eliminate the unhealthy atmosphere of gambling that again characterized mining stocks transactions. Bartlett asked for general laws to regulate the stringing of electric wires, the laying of steam and heat conduits, and the selling of these commodities. The previous system of allowing each company to erect its poles or dig its own trenches had resulted in chaos.

The new governor concluded his address by reminding the lawmakers that the sixty day session was a brief time and that they would have to work diligently. He stated that he would not call a special session to help the legislature out of any

situation brought on by idle debate or needless adjournments.
If the legislature could not enact its program, it would have to
answer to its constituents for negligence of duty.

He added that since he and his party had been elected on a
platform of honesty and pledged to an economical administration, he planned to carry out a business-like program. Bartlett
claimed lastly that it was indeed a happy omen that he had been
inaugurated on January 8, the anniversary of Andrew Jackson's
victory at New Orleans and his own inauguration as mayor of
San Francisco.

During the twenty-seventh session of 1887, the legislature
enacted a general irrigation district organization law which Bartlett approved. Contrary to the views of some nineteenth century historians, this measure really did nothing new. For the
most part, the language of the Westside Irrigation District Act
of 1875 was the basis of the 1887 law with added sections only
to bring the statute into line with recent court decisions. The
credit for the basic irrigation law still remained with the legislators of Governor Irwin's era. Bartlett used his veto twice
during the session. However, many more bills later received a
pocket veto.

By the close of the session, Bartlett was seriously ill with
Bright's disease, making it difficult for him to carry out official
duties. In June, he went to Highland Springs in a vain attempt
to regain his health. While there, he stated that "I would like
my administration to be so managed as to influence the young
men of California to depend on honest work and not on political
office." Realizing that he was seriously ill, Governor Bartlett
said, "If I had known the work I had to do would kill me, I
should have kept on just the same, for I could not shirk it. I
think it has finished me!"

During one of the last days of his life, Governor Bartlett
stated his views on his pardoning power:

> It may seem strange that I, who trust so entirely to the mercy of
> God, should refuse to pardon those who are suing for mercy in the
> State prisons; but I believe it to be my duty to consider the best
> interests of the whole state, of the law-abiding citizens of the state;
> and though I pity the poor inmates of the prison, I do not think it
> right to set them free. It has been proved to be bad policy by the
> many pardons that have been given hitherto. Personally if my own
> feelings alone were to be considered, I would set every prisoner free,

and I have not doubt, if I had the strength to look over the papers in their cases, I would find some I could pardon.

He granted six pardons during his tenure. He did not, however, have the strength to do more. He moved from Highland Springs to the Santa Cruz mountains and finally to the home of his sister in Oakland.

On August 22, 1887, he was stricken with paralysis. After lingering twenty-one days, he died on September 12, 1887. He was sixty-three years old. His body was interred at the Mountain View Cemetery, Oakland.

The death of Governor Bartlett was the occasion of great mourning in the state and the writing of many eulogies. All paid tribute to his greatest characteristic in office—his honesty. Apart from his desire to occupy the governor's chair for the benefit of all Californians and not just a few, Bartlett, handicapped by ill health, was incapable of exerting any executive leadership. He might have been a strong and forceful governor if circumstances had been different, but his administration ended on an inconclusive note with his untimely death.

BIBLIOGRAPHY

MANUSCRIPTS
"Biographical sketches of Washington Bartlett," prepared by H.H. Bancroft's staff, 1886-1890. (Bancroft Library).

Bartlett, Washington, "Diary of Washington Bartlett, 1887," (California State Archives).

————,"Executive Records, State of California," (California State Archives).

————, "Statement of Washington Bartlett, A Pioneer of 1849," (Bancroft Library).

CONTEMPORARY ACCOUNTS
Assembly Journal, 27th Sess., 1887.

Senate Journal, 27th Sess., 1887.

Society of California Pioneers, *Memorial of the life and services of Washington Bartlett, late governor of the state of California* (San Francisco, 1888).

————, *Memorial Services in memory of the late Washington Bartlett February 6, 1889 by Senate and Assembly in joint convention* (San Francisco, 1889).

SECONDARY SOURCES
Bancroft, H.H., *Chronicles of the Builders*. . .

————, *History of California*.

Davis, W.J., *History of Political Conventions*. . .

Hittell, T.H., *History of California*.

Melendy, H. Brett, "California's Washington Bartletts" *Pacific Historical Review*, XXXI (1962), 139-142.

Righter, Robert W., "Washington Bartlett: Mayor of San Francisco, 1883-1887," *Journal of the West*, III (1964), 102-114.

Shuck, O.T., *Historical Abstract of San Francisco*.

Works Progress Administration, "History of Journalism in San Francisco" (7 vols., San Francisco, 1939).

NEWSPAPERS
Daily Alta California, Jan. 7, 1887, reported his inauguration; Sept. 13, 1887, has editorial following his death.

Sacramento Union, Sept. 4, 1886, gave estimate of his candidacy; Jan. 10, 1887, reported his inauguration; Sept. 13, 1887, reported his obituary.

San Francisco Call, Sept. 4, 1886, commented on his nomination; Jan. 9, 1887, presented the inauguration; Sept. 13-14, 1887, wrote of his death; Sept. 16, 1887, presented an eulogy.

THESES
Righter, Robert W., "The Life and Public Career of Washington Bartlett" (M.A., San Jose State College, 1963).

Wheaton, Donald W., "Political History of California 1887-1898" (Ph.D., University of California, [1924]).

Calendar of Events

December 15, 1826	Waterman born in Fairfield, New York.
1846	Waterman opened a general store at Belvidere, Illinois.
1849-50	Waterman served as postmaster at Geneva, Illinois.
1850	Waterman traveled to California.
1852-60	Waterman published the *Independent* at Wilmington, Illinois.
1873	Waterman settled at Redwood City.
1880	Waterman located a silver mine in the Calico District.
1886	Waterman Junction renamed Barstow.
1886	Waterman purchased the Stonewall Mine in San Diego County.
November 2, 1886	Waterman elected Lt. Governor.
September 13, 1887	Waterman became Governor.
April 12, 1891	Waterman died at San Diego.

Robert W. Waterman

17TH GOVERNOR — REPUBLICAN
BORN: DECEMBER 15, 1826   DIED: APRIL 12, 1891
TERM OF OFFICE: SEPTEMBER 13, 1887—JANUARY 8, 1891

ROBERT WHITNEY WATERMAN, a descendent of early pioneers of New York State, was born in Fairfield, New York, on December 15, 1826. His father was John D. Waterman and his mother's maiden name was Mary Graves Waldo. The father died in 1837, and a few years later Robert moved west to join two older brothers who were engaged in merchandising at Newburg, Illinois. At fifteen he became a clerk in a store in Belvidere, Illinois, and in 1846, he opened his own general store there. The next year he married Jane Gardner of Belvidere. Waterman served as postmaster at Geneva, Illinois, in 1849 and 1850. The 1850 census listed him as a Belvidere merchant with a wife and two children.

Waterman's brother, Theodore, came to California in 1849, and persuaded Robert to follow him. Waterman drove an ox team across the Plains in 1850, suffering many hardships en route. For a while he mined gold along the Feather and Yuba rivers until he opened a store in the area.

In 1852, Waterman returned to Illinois, settling in Wilmington where he published the *Independent* from 1852 to 1860. Here five additional children were born. Waterman participated in establishing the Republican party of Illinois and in 1856, he supported the Frémont and Dayton campaign. Later he became an earnest and devoted supporter of Abraham Lincoln.

After the completion of the transcontinental railroad, Waterman moved his family to California in 1873, first settling in Redwood City and then moving to San Bernardino the next year. The area in which he settled became known as Waterman Canyon. This remained his home until he became governor. In June, 1880, Waterman and John C. Porter, a mining engineer, started on a prospecting trip into the Calico District. They traveled to Grapevine Station about eighty miles northeast from San Bernardino. A few miles north of Grapevine, they located a rich silver strike in a group of volcanic hills. Between 1881 and 1887, the mine yielded about $1,000,000 net profits; it closed down when the price of silver fell. When the Southern Pacific Railroad surveyed its Mojave-Needles line near the mine, Waterman constructed a mill close to the right-of-way by the Mojave River. The town of Waterman Junction developed and was renamed Barstow in 1886. In a letter dated January 8, 1886, it is interesting to note that Waterman complained to Congressman Henry H. Markham of his district that the railroad was changing the name of his station from Waterman to Barstow.

In 1886, Waterman purchased the Stonewall Mine in San Diego County located ten miles south of Julian at the foot of the Cuyamaca Mountains for $45,000. This rich gold mine had been discovered in 1870, but had been idle for several years. Waterman later bought the entire Cuyamaca grant on which the mine was located. He aided in financing the San Diego, Cuyamaca and Eastern Railroad, a narrow gauge. Also he bought a cattle ranch, which later became the Cuyamaca State Park. Waterman operated the Stonewall Mine until his death and from 1888 until 1891, it yielded over $900,000.

The first notice of Waterman's active participation in California politics occurred at the Republican state convention on July 23, 1884, when he and Ira P. Rankin, the former collector of the port of San Francisco, were elected as alternate presidential electors at large. When the Republican convention assembled at Armory Hall in Los Angeles in August, 1886, George A. Knight, holding a proxy from Mendocino County, nominated Waterman for lieutenant governor. Two hundred and twenty-nine votes were necessary for a choice and Waterman received 239½ votes on the first ballot. At the American party convention of an anti-foreign group meeting at Fresno, Waterman also received the nomination for lieutenant governor after Frank M. Pixley had declined the candidacy.

Waterman won election as lieutenant governor while the

Peter H. Burnett

John McDougal

John Bigler

J. Neely Johnson

—California State Library

John B. Weller

—California State Library

Milton S. Latham

—California State Library

John G. Downey

—California Governor's Office

Leland Stanford

—California State Library

Frederick F. Low

—California State Library

Henry H. Haight

—California State Library

Newton Booth

—Security First National Bank

Romualdo Pacheco

—Bancroft Library

William Irwin

—Bancroft Library

George C. Perkins

—California State Library

George Stoneman

—Bancroft Library

Washington Bartlett

—California State Library

Robert W. Waterman

—Security First National Bank

Henry H. Markham

—California State Library

James H. Budd

—California State Library

Henry T. Gage

George C. Pardee

James N. Gillett

Hiram W. Johnson

William D. Stephens

—California State Library

Friend W. Richardson

—California State Library

Clement C. Young

—*California Blue Book*, 1932

James Rolph, Jr.

—California State Library

Frank F. Merriam

Culbert L. Olson

Earl Warren

Goodwin J. Knight

Edmund G. Brown

Republican gubernatorial candidate, John F. Swift, was defeated by Washington Bartlett. Waterman polled 94,969 votes to 92,476 votes for M. F. Tarpey. For the first time in its history, California had a Democratic governor and a Republican lieutenant governor. As presiding officer of the Senate, Waterman commanded respect and inspired confidence even among his severest Democratic critics.

Waterman served as lieutenant governor for eight months until the death of Governor Bartlett. Then he became the fourth lieutenant governor to be elevated to the governorship, but the first one as a result of a governor's death. The office of lieutenant governor now devolved upon Stephen M. White, president pro tempore of the Senate.

On September 13, 1887, Judge Thomas B. McFarland administered the oath of office to Waterman in a ceremony at the Occidental Hotel in San Francisco. Present at the occasion were distinguished state and federal officials including former Governor Frederick F. Low. The new governor then read his inaugural address and after praising Bartlett, he said in part:

> Called suddenly and unexpectedly from the field and the mine to this responsible position, I may be pardoned if with misgivings I enter upon the discharge of its duties.
>
> If an earnest desire to do right, if a firm determination to carry out the obligations of the solemn oath which I have just taken avail to that end, I hope to discharge the duties of the high office in a manner to merit your approval.
>
> In the administration of the office I shall always be willing to receive—indeed, shall seek—counsel and advice, and at all times, with patience and with pleasure, will hear any of my fellow citizens whose rights may be affected by official acts of mine. With the American doctrine, that governments are instituted to secure "life, liberty and the pursuit of happiness," I am in full accord. With the imported heresies of the Communist and Socialist I have no sympathy. Their doctrines are subversive of our free institutions, and those who promulgate them should be held as enemies of mankind.
>
> With these views I can give you the assurance that my administration of the Executive Department will be within conservative lines.

Waterman also promised strict accountability on the part of public officers and an economical administration of finances. After the governor had finished speaking, his private secretary, Marcus D. Boruck, read a proclamation declaring an official holiday on the occasion of Bartlett's funeral.

On the day of the inaugural a reporter of the *Daily Alta California* inquired about Waterman's intended appointments. The governor replied that it was not the proper time to discuss the matter. However, since the newspapers had speculated on the subject—and to stop rumors—he stated that he would not make any appointments for thirty or forty days except to fill a vacancy on the bench of the Superior Court of San Diego. He further related that most of Bartlett's appointments had been made for specific terms and that the appointees would continue to serve until their terms expired. Then Waterman said: "I intend to run the office of Governor as I would my private business. There are two things I will never tolerate, dishonesty and drunkeness."

Some contemporary observers expected Waterman to be a weak governor because of his lack of experience. The *Daily Alta California* stated that the people would compare his actions with the achievements of Bartlett. The *Sacramento Union* described Waterman as a "lover of fair play" and felt that he would not be subservient to bosses or cliques. The *San Francisco Call* asserted that the test of Waterman's ability would be his appointments.

One of Waterman's first acts as governor was to send some of Bartlett's appointments to the Senate for confirmation. Eventually, however, he did remove some Democrats and replaced them with Republicans. In 1889, a quarrel took place between Waterman and the legislature over the power of appointment. When the legislature appointed employees to the State Library, Waterman refused to issue their commissions claiming that the appointive power rested with the governor. At a later date the State Supreme Court settled the issue in favor of Waterman.

The new executive worked diligently on the routine matters of his office. He personally visited all state institutions. He assumed a special interest in making San Quentin prison self-supporting. Waterman was noted for his detailed consideration of measures. For example, on an insurance bill he sought advice from leading attorneys and astutely studied the proposed act before vetoing it. He set aside a regular day for his judicial function of hearing applications for pardons. He even had notices published so objections could be made. Before making a decision he would consult the judge who had heard the case and the district attorney who had prosecuted it as well as prison officers acquainted with the applicant.

In his first biennial message delivered on January 7, 1889, Waterman recommended, as had Irwin, a constitutional amendment setting a limit on the state debt. He mentioned that the first constitution of 1849 had wisely set a maximum, but that the second constitution of 1879 had no limitation. In his discussion of finances, he indicated that while the state was relatively free from debt, the counties continued to increase their indebtedness as Governor Perkins also had noted in 1881. He proposed an amendment to restrict the counties in this regard to prevent a mortgaging of the state's future.

Waterman recommended a new board of examiners to replace the existing ex officio board comprising the governor, secretary of state, and attorney-general. These constitutional officers were already burdened with tedious duties. Besides approving the state's debts, Waterman wanted the new board to have the power to introduce a modern accounting system. In reference to his own office Waterman said: "The Governor, besides the duties that demand his attention at the Capitol, is the President of the State Board of Education, the President of the Regents of the State University, the President of the three Boards of Normal School Trustees, the Chairman of the Yosemite Commissioners, and the Chairman of the State Board of Capitol Commissioners, and it is further made obligatory upon him as Chief Executive to visit, as often as possible, the different prisons, asylums, and other institutions of the State."

Waterman suggested an increase of state salaries saying: "There is not a State Officer from the Chief Executive down to the last one on the list that is requited as he should be for what he gives in return." At the time the governor's salary was $6,000 per year. He also wanted a governor's mansion where "the Chief Executive may reside and maintain the dignity of his office and meet the many personal demands upon him, without impoverishing himself in the process."

Waterman denounced a recent move to divide the state—which public opinion had opposed—and commented in part as follows:

> There is and can be but one California; and its manifest destiny is as clear to the eye of the thoughtful and loyal, as that the sunlight succeeds darkness. As California she took her place in the sisterhood of States, and as such, though the frosts and snows of

ages may rest upon her brow, she will retain to the end the beauty and loveliness of her maidenhood.

Waterman claimed that he was the first governor to put California upon a cash-paying basis. The state owed money dating back to 1871. In selling to the state, contractors had previously added to the price of the article requisitioned to compensate for the delay expected in payment. Waterman ended the day of the warrant depreciator. At the end of his administration the total funded indebtedness still amounted to $2,642,000, and he recommended a refunding of this debt.

Waterman in his final message of January 5, 1891, questioned the wisdom of retaining the limit of 50 cents on each $100 of taxable property. He was the first governor to suggest that state funds be placed in carefully selected private banks instead of being held by state and county treasurers.

In strong terms Governor Waterman condemned legislative extravagance. He related that according to law the Assembly was entitled to nineteen clerical assistants and the Senate to sixteen, but the last legislature had employed a total of 228. The excess over the thirty-five clerks permitted by statute had been accomplished by legislative resolutions. Waterman suggested consolidating committees in both branches and said: "It was common rumor in and around the Capitol during the last session that a number of clerks enjoying $5 per diem *never* put in an appearance during the entire session, their stipend being carefully drawn, and as carefully forwarded to their places of residence."

The governor favored retaining state ownership and control of the San Francisco waterfront. He indicated that the board of state harbor commissioners planned to erect a passenger depot at the foot of Market Street in a building three stories high in its center with a dome and clock tower. Upon completion of this ferry building he recommended setting aside space for exhibits of the state board of trade and the mining bureau. Waterman urged a bond issue to make improvements on the waterfront and to complete the projected state belt railroad around the entire embarcadero.

In a discussion of the constitution of 1879, Waterman related that many of its expected advantages had not materialized. He claimed that many of the clauses lacked clarity in meaning and nullified some of the most beneficial provisions. For example, he explained that the constitution conferred the power of adopting charters upon cities with a certain stipulated population, but that another provision made such charters subject to general laws. Hence he concluded that a charter which was uncertain in the first place could be changed by a subsequent general law.

As another example, he mentioned that the constitution enumerated many instances in which special laws could not be passed, thus making many obsolete special laws unchangeable. Waterman sympathized with protests by the railroad companies that they were subjected to unjust discrimination under the new constitution since they were not permitted to deduct indebtedness as were other debtors. As a result of all these "defects" Waterman felt that the legislature should formulate amendments or call another constitutional convention.

In a review of prison affairs he noted that the jute mill at San Quentin had enabled farmers to purchase inexpensive grain bags which had aided the harvest of 1889. He recommended new cell buildings at both San Quentin and Folsom and said:

> It must be borne in mind that the prison at San Quentin is located on the edge of a largely populated district where, between the hours of seven o'clock A.M. and five o'clock P.M., women and children in great numbers are in an unprotected state, and it would not be a very advantageous occurrence to have an *emeute* at San Quentin caused by crumbling and decaying walls, thus permitting hundreds of desperate and hardened convicts to sweep down without warning upon the timid and defenseless.

During Waterman's administration the erection of the dam and canal at Folsom Prison designed to utilize the water power of the American River was virtually completed, when the legislature of 1889-90 had provided for a power house. Furthermore, the reformatories at Whittier and Ione had been established in his term. Additional insane asylums were located at San Bernardino and at Ukiah and the site of a home for feeble-minded children was selected at Glen Ellen.

Although Waterman's administration was not characterized by any extraordinary features, he was generally considered a satisfactory governor despite claims by some writers that he was a weak governor. His greatest achievements were probably in finance and in administrative reforms. Moreover, he was vastly interested in solving the problem of juvenile delinquency.

He also devoted attention to the problems of irrigation districts and some progress was made in implementing the Wright Act of 1887 which had been approved by Governor Bartlett. In the field of education Waterman supported the University of California and once said that it was the "only absolutely free University in the world in its academic departments." During Waterman's term the Chico State Normal School opened, but the basic legislation had been enacted in the previous administration. When the legislature of 1889 passed a county high school bill, which provided for schools to prepare pupils for entrance into the university, Governor Waterman pocket-vetoed it for unexplainable reasons. Toward the close of his administration Waterman made a generous use of his pardoning power causing him to lose considerable support. The *San Francisco Examiner*, a Democratic newspaper at that time, editorialized in favor of an amendment prohibiting the governor from granting pardons or commutations during the last six months of his tenure. Actually there had been eighteen commutations and nineteen pardons from December 10, 1890, to January 3, 1891.

As Waterman's term came to an end he was considered for renomination, but did not receive it. Slightly over three months after he left office he became afflicted with pneumonia at his residence in San Diego where he died on April 12, 1891. At the time of his death the *Pasadena Evening Star* probably epitomized correctly his gubernatorial career, when it remarked: "He disappointed many of his political friends, but he always maintained with great firmness that he had sound and conclusive reasons for his acts, and his determined sturdiness removed him from the suspicion of being guided by craft and cunning."

Governor Waterman's strongest trait was integrity and he was nicknamed "Old Honesty." He never took advantage of any man and he was generous almost to a fault. Although a majority of other state officers were not of his political faith, he united with them to give the people of California a prudent government.

BIBLIOGRAPHY

MANUSCRIPTS

"Robert Whitney Waterman's Diary," (California State Archives, Sacramento).

Waterman, Robert Waldo, "Robert Whitney Waterman, Governor of California, 1887-1891," (In possession of Robert Waldo Waterman, Barstow, California).

Letters from Robert Waldo Waterman, grandson of Governor Waterman, to B.F. Gilbert, Dec. 11 and 19, 1959, Jan. 7, 1960.

CONTEMPORARY ACCOUNT

"Second Biennial Message of Governor R.W. Waterman to the Legislature, 29th Sess.," in *California Governors' Messages, Biennial,* 1891-1903 (California State Library).

SECONDARY SOURCES

Boies, H.L., *History of DeKalb County* (N.p., 1860).

Bancroft, H.H., *Chronicles of the Builders. . .*

Davis, W.J., *History of Political Conventions. . .*

————, *An Illustrated History of Sacramento County* (Chicago, 1890).

Hittell, T.H., *History of California.*

Van Dyke, Theodore S., *The City and County of San Diego* (San Diego, 1888).

Waterman, Edgar F., *The Waterman Family* (3 vols., New Haven, c. 1939).

NEWSPAPERS

Daily Alta California, Sept. 13 and 14, 1887, have data on Waterman's inaugural.

Pasadena Daily Evening Star, April 13, 1891, has biographical data and an appraisal of Waterman's governorship.

San Bernardino Sun Telegram, June 29, 1952, has an article by L. Burr Belden, "Waterman Mine Big Producer in Silver Bullion."

San Francisco Call, Sept. 14, 1887, has data on Waterman's inaugural.

INTERVIEW

Robert Waldo Waterman by B.F. Gilbert, Jan. 27, 1960.

Calendar of Events

November 16, 1840	Markham born in Wilmington, New York.
1862	Markham graduated from Wheeler's Academy in Vermont.
November 12, 1863	Markham enlisted in the Wisconsin Volunteer Infantry.
February 2, 1864	Markham promoted from private to second lieutenant.
June 12, 1865	Markham mustered out of service.
1867	Markham admitted to the Wisconsin bar.
1879	Markham moved to Pasadena.
November 4, 1884	Markham elected to Congress.
1886	Markham declined renomination.
March 16, 1889	Markham appointed to Board of Managers for the National Home of Disabled Volunteer Soldiers.
January 8, 1891	Markham became Governor.
1894	Mid-Winter Exposition held at San Francisco.
1904	Markham reappointed to Board of Managers for Disabled Volunteer Soldiers.
October 9, 1923	Markham died at Pasadena.

Henry H. Markham

18TH GOVERNOR — REPUBLICAN
BORN: NOVEMBER 16, 1840   DIED: OCTOBER 9, 1923
TERM OF OFFICE: JANUARY 8, 1891—JANUARY 11, 1895

HENRY HARRISON MARKHAM, the son of Nathan B. and Susan Mcleod Markham, was born in Wilmington, New York, December 16, 1840. In this small farming community he received his elementary education in the public schools and then attended Wheeler's Academy in Vermont where he graduated in 1862. Shortly after completing his education, he and his brothers moved to Manitowoc, Wisconsin. Here he enlisted on November 12, 1863, as a private in Company G of the 32nd Regiment of the Wisconsin Volunteer Infantry, receiving a bounty of $60. His Civil War service record listed his occupation as school teacher and described him as twenty-three with hazel eyes, brown hair, and a light complexion. He stood six feet and two inches in height.

Markham saw action in Tennessee where he was hospitalized for sickness in Nashville. On February 2, 1864, he was promoted from private to second lieutenant. The next year he participated in Sherman's march to the sea. In the Battle of Rivers Bridges in South Carolina he was wounded on February 3, 1865, and sent to the rear. Two months later he was wounded again and was finally mustered out in Washington, D.C., on June 12.

Markham returned to Wisconsin and studied law at the firm of Waldo, Ode & Van in Milwaukee. In 1867, he was admitted to the bar and formed a successful partnership with his brother, George C. Markham, specializing in admiralty cases.

On May 17, 1876, Henry Markham married Mary Adams Dana and they had five daughters. After the war Markham's

237

health was never good and he suffered from persistent attacks resulting from his wounds. As a health seeker he joined the rush to southern California in the seventies. A chance advertisement in a Wisconsin newspaper about a twenty-three acre ranch for sale in Pasadena seemed to answer his problem. He and his wife and their small child moved there in 1879.

During this decade Pasadena, the "Crown of the Valley," was a community of distinctive homes with blooming gardens of roses and fragrant orange orchards. Distinguished and wealthy citizens resided in the city and Markham seemed to blend naturally into this picture. He continued his law practice and dealt with local problems concerning water, transportation, and property boundaries.

Markham also invested in real estate and became a part owner in the Calico Union Mining Company located in the Calico Hills near Death Valley. He became a director of the Los Angeles National Bank, the San Gabriel Valley Bank, and the Oil Supply Company of Southern California. In Pasadena he served on the school board and contributed to the founding of the local public library. In August, 1884, in partnership with General E. P. Johnson and C. H. Bradley, he purchased the earlier firm of Cotter & Bradley and established the Los Angeles Furniture Company.

As a result of his varied interests in southern California it was natural that the Republican party's sixth district convention meeting in Sacramento on July 23, 1884, should nominate him for Congress without opposition. The sixth district comprised fourteen southern counties. However, the Republican central committee refused to aid Markham in his campaign, considering his district hopeless. Yet Markham carried on a vigorous campaign and defeated his nearest rival, Reginaldo F. Del Valle, the Democratic candidate, by 407 votes, as well as Will D. Gould and Isaac Kinley, the Prohibition and Greenback candidates respectively.

Congressman Markham served his constituents well, particularly on the rivers and harbors committee, obtaining large appropriations for improving Wilmington harbor. He also succeeded in having army headquarters for the Department of Arizona, New Mexico, and Southern California established in Los Angeles and he acquired a new post office building for the city. Since the eastern climate had aggravated his old wounds and as his private affairs needed attention, Markham refused renomination in 1886. On March 16, 1889, he was appointed a member of the board of managers for the National Home of Disabled Volunteer Soldiers, serving in this capacity without compensation.

The boom of the eighties in southern California lifted that section into greater political prominence. In a "confidential" letter of December 14, 1885, Harrison Gray Otis of the *Los Angeles Times* informed Congressman Markham that Major George H. Bonebrake, president of the National Bank of Los Angeles and a Republican leader, was anxious to make him governor. Otis, who supported the plan, warned Markham that renomination for Congress would be likely, but that his prospects for the gubernatorial nomination were slim. In fact he believed it would be an unwise move.

Despite Stoneman's and Waterman's residence in the south, Otis was still probably apprehensive about northern political dominance, which had been proved once again in the campaign of 1886, when Bartlett, a San Franciscan and a pioneer, was elected governor. Actually Markham had two disadvantages for any gubernatorial bid in that he represented southern California and he was a "late comer." At least Otis was concerned about a southerner's chances in the Republican party. Yet the Los Angeles area Republicans were hopeful when their party's convention assembled at Sacramento on August 12, 1890, with 667 delegates in attendance. Los Angeles presented Markham and San Francisco supported Congressman William M. Morrow. On the first ballot Markham received 299 votes to 281 for Morrow, but prior to an announcement of the results many delegates switched to Markham. Then a motion passed to make his nomination unanimous. This was the first victory in Republican ranks for southern California and the results were at once telegraphed to Los Angeles and Pasadena where spontaneous celebrations took place. For lieutenant governor the Republicans nominated John B. Reddick of Calaveras County by acclamation. Outside of southern California the Markham victory seemed to displease Republicans and to many it dampened their hopes for the coming election.

The Democratic convention met at Agricultural Hall in San Jose on August 19, with blind Boss Chris Buckley in control. The Democrats nominated Mayor Edward B. Pond of San

Francisco on the fourth ballot. The enthusiastic delegates then carried Pond on their shoulders to a reception at the nearby Auzerais House attended by 2,000 loyal party members. For lieutenant governor the Democrats nominated Reginaldo F. Del Valle of Los Angeles whom Markham had defeated in his Congressional race of 1884. The Prohibition and the American parties both nominated John Bidwell of Chico as their gubernatorial candidate.

In a rather colorful campaign the Democrats adopted the pond lily for their emblem and the Republicans adopted the red rose, calling it the Markham rose. Colonel Markham, as he was now called, campaigned on a platform pledging a "free" ballot, a permanent restriction of Chinese immigration, Sacramento and San Joaquin river improvements at federal expense, anti-monopoly legislation, and a 50 cent tax limit per $100 assessed valuation. The Democratic platform promised a 45 cent tax limit and also favored Chinese exclusion. Among its other planks was one favoring the direct election of United States Senators and one condemning Republican management of San Quentin prison.

During the campaign Republican managers referred to Markham as the "Dashing Colonel from Pasadena" and he made strong appeals to the veteran vote by telling Civil War battle stories. The Republicans accused Mayor Pond of being a tool of Boss Buckley. The *Pasadena Daily Evening Star* of September 1, under the caption of "Buckley's Dividend," asserted that the political boss gave each of his "heelers" at the Democratic convention twenty dollars plus a free round-trip ticket to San Jose. Others accused Pond of representing liquor interests and of participating in a land fraud in Oregon.

In Pasadena the Markham Marching Club and the Young Men's Markham Club were organized. At a Republican mass meeting in Haymarket Square on the evening of September 20, the new Pasadena band played and the Markham Glee Club sang.

The Democrats retaliated to the charge of Buckleyism by accusing Markham of using Chinese labor in his mines. Markham was also condemned for his "old pard" letter in which he allegedly wrote to a friend saying: "that one dollar a day was enough for an Irishman." Prior to his nomination the Republican press of northern and central California in an effort to check his growing popularity, had accused Markham of favoring state division. Now the Democrats repeated the charge and were criticized by the Republicans for so doing.

Markham overcame his handicaps and conducted a magnetic campaign whereas Pond was cold and formal in manner and seemed stigmatized by Buckleyism. Markham had the support of influential journalists such as Harrison Gray Otis of the *Los Angeles Times* and Chester Rowell of the *Fresno Republican.* He had the backing of Charles Crocker and Leland Stanford. In fact Senator Stanford and his wife canvassed the entire state from the northern mountains to San Diego, for he was anxious to be re-elected as Senator and wanted a Republican legislature.

At the polls the Republicans won a resounding victory and all their candidates for state office, except one member of the board of equalization, were elected. Moreover, they elected four out of six Congressmen and gained an overwhelming majority in the legislature. The California Republican victory was a reversal of the national trend east of the Rockies. Markham amassed 125,129 votes while Pond polled 117,184 and Bidwell had 10,073. The Pasadena returns were Markham, 759; Pond, 189; and Bidwell, 113. In the north Markham carried Alameda County by over 3,000 votes. Although the Pond and Bidwell votes made Markham a minority governor, he became the first Republican to be elected to the high office from southern California.

In his inaugural address of January 8, 1891, Markham promised "rigid economy" and criticized excessive appropriations of the previous Democratic legislature. Moreover, he implied that he would exercise his veto power to circumvent local demands for appropriations which were usually obtained by a series of trades that left the taxpayers with excessive burdens. He stated that the Republican pledge of limiting the tax rate should be implemented. He urged a plan whereby labor disputes could be arbitrated, and related that unions were complaining about evasions of the eight-hour day law.

Markham indicated that he was neither for nor against the Australian ballot system but that he would approve a law designed to initiate ballot reform. He recommended, as had Waterman, a legislative reapportionment because of the increase in population in several sections of the state.

The new executive complained that the federal Chinese exclusion act was constantly violated and that Congress should be
urged to correct the law and extend the suspension of immigration beyond 1892. Furthermore, he recommended that Congress
be requested to return insane Chinese to their homeland.

In a discussion of irrigation and forestry he viewed the
Wright Act of 1887 as a practical solution to the irrigation
problem, and he pointed out the need for conserving timber
resources. Markham described hydraulic mining as an inactive industry which would remain so unless the federal
government assisted in reviving it.

During the first part of Markham's administration the Australian ballot was adopted. The board of arbitration was established to settle labor disputes, but the law was ineffectual. In
another matter the legislature passed a law requiring the state
printer to fill only such orders as were approved by the state
board of examiners. Also the board was empowered to edit all
reports and to determine the number to be printed. This measure saved the state several thousand dollars.

After the legislature adjourned, Governor Markham inspected the various state agencies, but he apparently found
some time for social relaxation. For example, the *Pasadena
Evening Star* of April 20, 1891, reported that Governor Markham and his wife had recently been entertained elegantly one
evening by the Union League of San Francisco. This newspaper presented one of the few nineteenth century descriptions
of a governor's lady as follows:

> Mrs. Governor Markham, who is a tall, graceful lady of the
> brunette type, made a fine appearance in a magnificent robe of
> pinkish green, or sea foam brocaded satin en train; the bodice
> and train of brocade, with a front of plain satin of the same shade,
> ornamented with a broad stripe of silver and crystal trimmings,
> ending with a large bow of the satin. The pointed bodice, with
> sleeves of plain satin, was made V-shape in front, pointed, and
> trimmed with silver passementerie and pink mousseline de soie.
> On the bodice and skirt of the robe were graceful groups of light
> blue feather tips; gloves the shade of the dress; hair dressed high,
> and adorned with a feather tip. She wore handsome diamonds
> and carried a white feather fan.

In his first biennial message of January 3, 1893, Markham
reported on the prosperous conditions of California, but revealed that numerous imported articles and staples could be

produced within California. As evidence he stated that over 40,000,000 eggs and probably over 750,000 poultry were shipped into California each year.

The governor related that he had visited every state institution during the past year and recommended that a uniform system of accounts and reports should be required for all institutions. He pointed out that the large percentage of prisoners in California was caused by excessive sentences imposed by judges. Markham devoted considerable space in his message to the problem of capital punishment. In fact he compiled a history of executions in the state and suggested that people no longer favored capital punishment.

During the second half of Markham's term a depression, which followed the national Panic of 1893, hit California. Moreover, the lack of winter rains caused partial crop failures in several sections of the state. As a result of the depression and labor unrest from 1893 to 1895, Governor Markham found it necessary to call out the national guard to assist civil authorities in maintaining order. Although there were few strikes, a serious one occurred against the Southern Pacific.

After the outbreak of the Pullman strike in Illinois, Eugene V. Debs called the American Railway Union to engage in a sympathetic strike which had repercussions in California, particularly in Sacramento. In the summer of 1894, chaotic disturbances broke out in the capital and in Oakland and Los Angeles. In Oakland the strikers raided the roundhouse and shops, obstructing all trains. Markham intervened by ordering in the state militia. Although the strike was of short duration, some bloodshed occurred when the militia became involved in clashes with strikers. Both agriculture and industry suffered while over 10,000 laborers lost about $1,000,000 in wages.

Despite the depression California prepared to participate in the Columbian Exposition at Chicago in 1893, for it had been Markham's hope that the display of her products would increase markets and stimulate immigration. On June 14, 1894, in a letter to Irving M. Scott, president of the California World's Fair Commission, Markham stated that hundreds of visitors had been attracted to California and that many had stayed as permanent residents. As a counterpart to the Chicago fair, San Francisco held its famous Mid-Winter Exposition in Golden Gate Park in 1894, and many of the foreign exhibits at Chicago were moved to San Francisco. The exposition had 1,315,022 admissions and proved a great financial success.

In his final message to the legislature on January 7, 1895, Markham mentioned that five ex-governors—Stanford, Low, Booth, Stoneman, and Waterman—had died within the past four years, but he was pleased to report that Peter H. Burnett still lived. He announced the opening of the Preston School of Industry and recommended that San Quentin prison should be rebuilt if it were to be continued in use. He related that a parole law had been in operation for a year and seemed to be beneficial. He proposed that approximately 150 Chinese prisoners be released upon condition that they be deported to China at their own expense. He also urged the building of better roads to improve immigration and to permit settlement of rural areas. On the question of taxation he noted that taxes were high because of the tendency of the people to look to the state for aid and that 22,000 unfortunates received support.

During his term Markham kept his pledge of keeping the tax rate under 50 cents per $100 valuation. In 1891, the tax was 44.6 cents; two years later it rose to 57.6 cents. Yet by his numerous vetoes of appropriation items an average rate of 48.7 cents was maintained for his four-year term. In total he had vetoed $1,700,000 in appropriations—a sum, he asserted, exceeding that of all previous California governors for a single term. This factor alone was an accomplishment in that many of the proposed appropriations were useless and to Markham's credit he tried to reduce the practice of legislators trading votes on their projects.

Markham was not renominated for a second term in 1894. Even before his term was half completed, he met considerable opposition. He had the misfortune of being governor during a time of depression and labor violence. Markham was criticized for being at the Chicago fair during the Panic of 1893 and for visiting Pasadena on the eve of the railroad strike. Some opponents were dissatisfied with his economy program and others charged him with being lenient toward criminals. Moreover, critics blamed him for the increase in crime during the depression and opposed his stand against capital punishment.

Despite his physical handicap, Markham was a conscientious and energetic governor. Toward the end of legislative sessions he often worked in his office until after midnight. Although he was a shrewd businessman, he was neither able nor expected to implement a comprehensive economic program to combat the depression.

In 1904, Markham was again appointed to the National Board of Managers for Disabled Volunteer Soldiers and he served in that capacity until 1923. As a wounded soldier he took a personal interest in the problems of veterans and was partly responsible for the establishment of the veterans' home at Santa Monica. Markham died in his Pasadena home following a brief sickness at the age of eighty-two on October 9, 1923. His memory has been commemorated by the naming of Mount Markham in Angeles National Forest of southern California.

BIBLIOGRAPHY

MANUSCRIPTS
"Markham Papers," (Huntington Library).
"Compiled Record of Military Service, Henry H. Markham, 32nd Wisconsin Infantry," (National Archives, Washington, D.C.).
Letter from Hildreth Markham West of Pasadena, daughter of Governor Markham, to B.F. Gilbert, April 29, 1959.
"Records, Executive Department: Administration of Governor Markham," (California State Archives).

CONTEMPORARY ACCOUNTS
Assembly Journal, 30th Sess., 1893.
Senate Journal, 30th Sess., 1893.
Inaugural Address and Messages of Governor H.H. Markham to the Legislature of California (Sacramento, 1895).

SECONDARY SOURCES
Bancroft, H.H., *History of California.*
Davis, W.J., *History of Political Conventions. . .*
Newmark, H. and R., eds., *Sixty Years in Southern California. . .*
Page, Henry Markham, *Pasadena: Its Early Years* (Los Angeles, 1964).
Tinkham, George H., *California Men and Events* (Stockton, 1915).
Biographical Directory of the American Congress, 1774-1949 (Washington, D.C., 1950).
The "City Guard," A History of Company "B," First Regiment Infantry, N.G.C., during the Sacramento Campaign, July 3 to 26, 1894 (San Francisco, 1895).

NEWSPAPERS
Pasadena Evening Star, Sept. 1 - Nov. 5, 1890, has data on Markham's gubernatorial campaign.
San Francisco Call, Aug. 14, 1890, has a biographical sketch.

Calendar of Events

May 18, 1851	Budd born in Janesville, Wisconsin.
1858	Budd arrived in California.
1861	Budd settled in Stockton.
1871	Budd served on the Democratic State Central Committee.
1873	Budd graduated from the University of California.
1874	Budd admitted to the California bar.
November 7, 1882	Budd elected to Congress.
1883-89	Budd served as a trustee of the Stockton Public Library.
1889	Budd appointed a member of the Board of Police and Fire Commissioners of Stockton.
January 11, 1895	Budd inaugurated as Governor.
1895	Bureau of Highways established.
April 25, 1898	Spanish-American War began.
January, 1899	Budd appointed attorney for the Board of State Harbor Commissioners
1900	Budd appointed to Board of Regents of the University of California.
July 30, 1908	Budd died at Stockton.

James H. Budd

19TH GOVERNOR — DEMOCRAT
BORN: MAY 18, 1851   DIED: JULY 30, 1908
TERM OF OFFICE: JANUARY 11, 1895—JANUARY 4, 1899

JAMES HERBERT BUDD WAS BORN May 18, 1851, in Janesville, Wisconsin. His parents were Joseph H. and Lucinda Ash Budd, both natives of New York. The father was a graduate of Williams College in Massachusetts and obtained training in law. The Budd family journeyed to California in 1858, first settling in Old Liberty, San Joaquin County. They then moved to Woodbridge, where the father practiced law. In 1861, the family settled in Stockton.

James Budd attended Stockton's public schools where he was greatly influenced by his teacher, Ambrose H. Randall, later principal of California State Normal School at San Jose. After attending Brayton College School, a private preparatory school in Oakland, Budd matriculated with the first class at the University of California, graduating in 1873. The same year Budd married a widow, Inez A. Merrill.

Budd then studied law in his father's office and was admitted to the bar in 1874. After serving as deputy district attorney in Stockton under A. W. Roysdon, Budd was associated in practice with his father and later with Judge J. G. Swinnerton. Budd had acquired a keen interest in politics from his father. While still a student at the university, he was a member of the Democratic state central committee. In 1876, his party nominated him for assemblyman from his district, but he refused to accept. Six years later, he took the Democratic nomination as congressman from his district, comprising Alameda, Sacramento, and San Joaquin Counties, in an election race that was considered hopeless by his party. Running against the Republican incumbent Horace F. Page, the scrappy and artful Jim Budd conducted a whirlwind campaign on buckboard from house to house and defeated his opponent by a vote of 20,229 to 19,246.

In Congress he served on the committee on education and on the committee on invalid pensions. He was primarily interested in fortification measures, Chinese exclusion, and appropriations for the rivers and harbors in his district. He was able to secure a sizeable appropriation for dredging the Stockton channel. After completing one term in Congress, he declined renomination, for he preferred his lucrative law practice as well as the local politics of Stockton. He actively participated as chairman of his party's city and county central committees and carried his county for the Democrats in the election of 1888. From 1883 to 1889, he served as a trustee of the Stockton Library and then became a member of the local police and fire commission.

As a cadet at the University of California he had been associated with the national guard. At graduation he was commissioned first lieutenant and was advanced through the ranks to lieutenant colonel on Governor Irwin's staff, and eventually served as a brigadier general during his term as governor.

In August, 1894, the Democrats met in convention at the Baldwin Theater in San Francisco. Four major candidates were considered for the gubernatorial nomination. In addition to Budd, these were Bernard D. Murphy of San Jose, Congressman James G. Maguire of San Francisco, and Dennis Spencer of Napa. On the convention floor Charles A. Storke opposed Budd arguing that he would be dominated by the Southern Pacific machine. Nonetheless, Budd won on the third ballot.

The Republican party nominated Morris M. Estee, a former Speaker of the Assembly. Two minor parties also nominated candidates. These were the Populist nominee, Jonathan V. Webster, a former Republican, and the Prohibition nominee, Henry French of San Jose.

After setting up campaign headquarters in San Francisco, Budd returned to Stockton where he was given an enthusiastic ovation. The front page of the *Stockton Evening Mail* proudly blared: "Budd Is The Boy." One issue proclaimed: "As a criminal lawyer he has few if any equals in California, for he is sharp, quick, keen in foretelling the effect of any particular piece of evidence, and always ready with a smart retort or humorous sally." Shortly after Budd's nomination the *Riverside Enterprise* in its estimate of the various candidates assessed him in this manner: "Mr. Budd has elements of strength which few, if any, of the other candidates possess to an equal extent. He is a man of strong personal magnetism—one who wins friends by the score whether it be from the stump or in the ordinary walks of life." Indeed, this editorial appraisal was quite accurate.

Budd officially opened his campaign in Sacramento on September 8. Special trains from San Francisco, Stockton, and Folsom transported his supporters to the capital for the occasion. Crowds gathered at the local depot waiting Budd's arrival from Port Costa where he had been speaking. From the depot a thousand backers wearing Budd badges paraded to Armory Hall. Enroute the gay throngs cheered and shot Roman candles. At the meeting place W. D. Lawton, president of the city trustees of Sacramento, presided. A *San Francisco Examiner* reporter wrote that: "Mr. Budd's appearance upon the platform was the signal for a hurricane of cheers."

In his opening remarks Budd alluded to the fact that he had arrived in California as a boy of six. Then he prophesied: "From that time to this I have lived all my life within a radius of fifty miles of the capital of the State, where I shall reside for four years as its Governor." He reminded his audience that he had assisted in obtaining the appropriation for the Sacramento post office. Then he claimed that both he and his running mate, William T. Jeter, had been nominated by an independent convention representative of the people. Budd noted that for the first time in his memory San Francisco was not controlled by a boss. He promised that bossism would not permeate his administration, after asserting that the Republican state convention had been controlled by Boss Daniel M. Burns.

Budd next referred his listeners to that evening's *San Francisco Bulletin*, an independent Republican journal, which reported about Republican boss methods in San Francisco where police had been used to reject dissenters from its district convention. Budd contended that a primary issue in the campaign would be whether citizens could assemble in convention and vote for men unpledged by bosses. Then he said: "One man only had a voice in that convention, and it Burns into their marrow now." This reference to Daniel Burns brought an uproar from the crowd. Budd warned that the same tactics might be used by the Republicans on election day and he stated in part: "One of the issues of this campaign is going to be whether or not a man who happens to be one of the Police Department of San Francisco and can swing 154 solid votes can dictate what candidates he wants."

In discussing issues specified by his opponent, Budd stated that Estee wanted to debate the tariff question. He said he was willing, but believed that it was not a state issue. Instead, Budd preferred to debate extravagance in state government. He charged that the people's money was wasted on unnecessary institutions. He lamented that California now had five insane asylums and "more reform schools than we have political bosses." Budd then promised a reduction in taxes.

With regard to the railroad Budd said: "There is another thing that I want to hold up by the throat, and that is the gigantic Southern Pacific corporation. Not even that can pull me down when I am Governor of the State of California." He proceeded with his anti-railroad tirade protesting the incorporation of the Southern Pacific in Kentucky where it did not own a single mile of track. Then he claimed: "They slipped over there for the purpose of avoiding the laws of the State of California and of forcing us to sue them in the Federal courts." He further objected to the high railroad fares and persistent refusal to pay taxes. As a remedy Budd favored partial government ownership of the transcontinental railroads and objected to Estee's adoption of this plank of the Democratic party which the Republicans had repudiated. He explained that he did not favor complete ownership of all railroads, but only a few trunk lines so that the government could regulate any company using them.

Near the end of his speech Budd denied rumors that he had consulted Boss Chris Buckley, declaring he was a free and independent candidate. He further disclaimed charges of belonging to any order and said: "I only belong to the order of Jim Budd." He concluded that he stood on the Democratic platform and promised that every corporation would have its just rights as would every man.

In San Francisco, Budd possessed the backing of influential newspapers such as the *Examiner* and the *Bulletin*. In one issue the *Examiner* editorialized:

> The election of Estee means the continuation of Burns as the real
> ruler of the state. For the last four years he has been the real Gov-
> ernor of California, using Markham as his tool. It seems unthink-
> able that the electorate will give him another term in office.

Throughout northern California "Jim Budd Clubs" were
organized which participated in torchlight processions and mam-
moth demonstrations. These Democratic clubs also sponsored
"Jim Budd Excursions." For example, early in September an
excursion was made by the Stockton group to the state fair at
Sacramento and enroute the train stopped at Lodi, Galt, Acam-
po, and Elk Grove to pick up supporters.

In comparison to the Budd campaign the Estee canvass was
colorless. Estee accused Democrats of favoring free trade
while Republicans were for the protective tariff which allegedly
aided labor. Moreover, the Republican candidate charged that
Democrats and Populists acted in unison. As the campaign
approached its climax, Republican orators accused Budd of
wronging a girl in his younger days. Also he was accused of
influencing the girl to will him her property. These smears
failed to hinder Budd's cause.

In the Republican sweep of 1894, Budd was the only Democrat to win state office. In this close gubernatorial contest he defeated Estee by about a 2,000 vote margin. As a result of
his whirlwind campaign Budd ran ahead of his party by
33,000 votes and overcame a large Republican majority. While
Estee had traveled by train, Budd had covered a large portion
of the state by buckboard accompanied by his wife. On two
occasions Budd became a hero. At the town hall of a village
he put out a fire and at an open air meeting in a rural district
he saved a girl from a kicking horse. These deeds of valor—
publicized by the press—seemed to assist his candidacy. Budd's
genial personality and ability to win friends undoubtedly contributed to his election. In particular he made strong showings
in San Francisco and in his home area.

In the election both Republicans and Democrats allegedly
hired toughs to stuff ballot boxes and to misuse registry files.
When the legislature convened on January 7, 1895, the Repub-
licans claimed that fraudulent tactics in San Francisco caused
Budd to be elected. These charges were investigated by an
Assembly committee which found them to be groundless.

For the second time in California history the governor and lieutenant governor were of different political parties. Spencer G. Maillard, a Republican, was elected lieutenant governor, but he died after being in office only ten months. Then Budd appointed his running mate, William T. Jeter of Santa Cruz, as lieutenant governor.

James Budd was inaugurated on January 11, 1895. He was forceful, pugnacious, and epigrammatic. As a brilliant trial lawyer he was a lucid and quick thinker who could draw sound conclusions. A man with a large circle of close friends, his geniality was not to be diminished by political success. Budd had that rare ability of combining scholarly attributes with a warm personal touch. Although he became an industrious chief executive, he always maintained a gregarious and homey manner.

The inaugural procession was formed with the Second Sacramento Infantry and a military band in the lead. The principal streets of the city were decorated for the occasion. The Iroquois Club traveled from San Francisco with its brass band. Justice Frederick W. Henshaw administered the oath of office in the Assembly chamber. Then a cannon on the capitol grounds roared forth the gubernatorial salute of nineteen guns and Budd delivered his address. He announced his intention to inspect state institutions and to reduce their expenses, charging that extravagance had deterred both immigration and the influx of capital needed to develop California's latent resources. Despite the recent decline in wages and profits, he believed that tax burdens had increased. He claimed that California ranked fourth among the states in total expenditures, but only twenty-second in population. As a main source of extravagance he pointed to the lunatic asylums. He agreed with Waterman in criticizing the practice of legislators doling out local benefits and noted the presence of inmates in the asylums who were not entitled to admittance. In order to rectify the situation he recommended abolishing the existing asylum boards and replacing them with one nonpartisan board which would be empowered to hire an expert as director.

Budd also proposed single boards for other institutions. He favored consolidating San Quentin prison with Folsom and managing Preston Reform School with that of Whittier. He suggested uniform bookkeeping and uniform reports by state officials. Moreover, he recommended a merger of commissions dealing with horticulture, viticulture, forestry, and similar pursuits into a department of the University of California. As further economy measures Governor Budd urged local support of the dependent poor without state assistance and a repeal of the law of 1891 granting bounties on coyote scalps. Under the caption of "Two Large Leaks" his inaugural message read as follows:

> The evil consequence of permitting the State Treasury to become a grab-bag, into which capacious hands may be thrust with impunity for the benefit of certain sections or interests, is forcibly illustrated in the operation of the law by which counties obtain a bonus on the maintenance of each aged person in indigent circumstances supported at public expense. It is a fit companion of the statute awarding a bounty on coyote scalps.

In his remarks upon the subject of local government Budd stressed the absurdity of having fifty-three classifications of counties in a state which had "fifty-six" counties. He related that the population differential between the thirty-first class and the thirty-second class was only sixteen people. He referred to the system of county government as "a species of the most unjust and unequal legislation imaginable. . . ." Then he recommended granting cities a more liberal self-government by giving each a charter based upon its own peculiar needs. Under the existing law each city with a charter had to maintain a vigilant guard at Sacramento during a legislative session to forestall adverse changes under the guise of general laws that might accord another city special benefit. Hence Budd urged a constitutional amendment granting city charters free from the dictates of the legislature.

The new governor proposed two constitutional amendments to improve the railroad commission. One would require special qualifications for its membership and the other would abolish the clause making its findings conclusive. Budd also criticized the banking system as too lax in that it did not protect depositors nor make bank officials liable for violations. With reference to appointments Budd related that the governor could not remove appointees except by the tedious process of court action. Thus he recommended either a civil service system or a granting of the power of removal to the governor.

In editorializing upon Budd's inaugural, his home town newspaper, the *Stockton Independent*, stated:

> The inauguration of James H. Budd as Governor of California makes history in this State that will be long remembered by the people of the present generation. The introduction into State methods of the reforms and economy promised by the new Governor may not be favored by politicians, but the people, who bear the burdens, will. . .
>
> The times are ripe for a reformer in State affairs and the opportunity presented will hardly be missed by the wide-awake young Executive.

Three months after his inauguration, Governor Budd complained to the Assembly that local boards of trades were lobbying against his proposed economy measure of establishing a single asylum board. This particular reform was delayed for two years, but the board of state viticultural commissioners was transferred to the University of California in 1895. The Republican legislature also acted on a few of Budd's other recommendations by stopping state aid to aged indigents and by repealing the law granting coyote scalp payments.

In his first biennial message of January 4, 1897, Governor Budd pointed out his partial success in economy, but recommended placing state agencies under one financial and supervisory system. Again he recommended improvements in tax collection. He also urged state licensing of saloons and additional control of insurance companies. He proposed the sale of San Quentin prison and favored a merger of the two prisons at Folsom. He mentioned that the previous legislature had established a bureau of highways and indicated that he had made nonpartisan appointments to that body.

He suggested several important changes in the court system and an extension of legislative terms. He recommended that the governor's term should begin on the first Monday in July instead of January. Budd protested that during the previous session, of the 317 bills sent to him, 207 or about two-thirds, came to his desk in the final ten days. He proposed allowing the governor thirty days, instead of ten days after adjournment, to consider bills.

After being in office two years, Budd proposed a civil service system for asylums and "other similar institutions" in stronger language than his inaugural address, stating:

> Unfortunately, however, we find that our five Insane Asylums, our three Normal Schools, our two Reform Schools, our Deaf,

Dumb, and Blind Asylum, and our Home for Feeble-Minded Children, all have heads of one political faith, and occasionally this evident discrimination did not stop with the heads, but, with a few exceptions, ran down the list of pay offices. Whether the employé be of one political faith or the other, such a needless, one-sided political complexion in the management is pernicious and improper.

During the second legislative session of Budd's administration a few more of his recommendations were enacted. For example, in 1897, a state commission of lunacy was created to manage the five state hospitals and to care for the insane. As a result a uniform system of management for all the asylums and standard record forms were adopted.

In his final message to the legislature on January 3, 1899, Governor Budd emphasized improvements in state finances. With reference to the General Fund, which was largely derived from a property tax fixed by a tax levy at each legislative session, he related that the balance had been so small when he first took office that it soon became exhausted. He related that by the end of 1896, the fund was in good condition and had a balance of $665,538 by December 1, 1898. He asserted that this was accomplished by his numerous vetoes of appropriation bills, which allowed the state to pay past claims. Budd took credit for putting the state on a cash basis and for ending the continuous exhaustion of the General Fund.

To circumvent heavy tax burdens on property owners, Budd recommended a graduated income tax on corporate profits. Also he proposed a central state board to attend to purchasing of supplies, construction of buildings, and regulation and equalization of the salaries of state employees.

In summing up his administration Budd claimed that he had implemented his inaugural pledge of improving state institutions. He boasted that he had been one of the few full-time California governors and that most of his predecessors had not relinquished the occupations they held in private life. Budd alluded to his sickness at the end of the 1897 legislative session and then said:

> I have devoted my strength to the welfare of the State, and although, on account of illness, granted a leave of absence, I remained to discharge my duties, in answering the call of the President of these United States for volunteers.
> I lay down the office without health or practice. I hope my suc-

cessor may not be compelled to hew each step of his four years through adverse Legislatures to maintain his pledges to the people.

The *Sacramento Union* criticized "Governor Budd's Farewell" as grotesque and amusing for its attempt to insist upon high virtues for his administration. The newspaper refuted his pretentious claim of economy and charged that seven-tenths of the gubernatorial business had been transacted outside the capital. Yet the journal credited him with decreasing the tax levy and with reducing the per capita cost of maintaining inmates. However, the *Union* concluded: "Its literary merits will not place it among the 'Curiosities' and it will probably find place in the politico-literary junk pile."

Despite Republican dominance of the legislature, Budd gained support for many of his measures. Several of his recommendations were realized and others were enacted at later dates. As the Spanish-American War governor, Budd capably performed his military duties in organizing troops and home defenses as California became the nation's supply and mobilization center for the campaign in the Philippines.

Besides his major accomplishments in finance and governmental reorganization Budd had aided higher education, pure food and dairy legislation, and road building. The University of California was favored when $250,000 was appropriated in 1895 to start construction of the Affiliated College buildings in San Francisco atop Parnassus Heights on property donated by millionnaire Adolph Sutro. The normal schools were reorganized and San Diego State Normal School opened in 1897. A permanent dairy bureau was established in the same year and in 1895 the activities of the board of state viticultural commissioners were transferred to the University of California. The legislature in 1895 created the position of Lake Tahoe Road commissioner and a bureau of highways. The 1897 session appropriated funds to make the Placerville-Lake Tahoe road an excellent mountain thoroughfare and changed the name of the bureau to department of highways. As a result the state highway system was launched with roads that were to run north and south along the coast and throughout the great interior valley and were to touch every county seat.

Because of poor health and probably since he was one of only two Democrats holding statewide office in a Republican era, Budd did not seek re-election. At the end of his term he opened a law office in San Francisco and remained active in Democratic circles as an esteemed former governor. In January, 1899, he was appointed attorney for the board of state harbor commissioners. The next year Governor Henry T. Gage appointed Budd to the board of regents of the University of California.

Gradually Budd's health worsened and he toured Europe in an unsuccessful effort to regain strength. In the spring of 1908, he attempted to resume his law practice, but his health continued to fail. On July 30, 1908, he died at the age of fifty-seven in his Stockton home, survived by his wife, mother, and brother, John. He was buried at the Rural Cemetery. Republican Governor James Gillett, while attending Budd's funeral, paid him the following tribute: "He made an excellent executive officer and endeavored to curtail the expenses of government, which he succeeded very well in doing. In my opinion he was one of California's best Governors and was always fearless and independent in the discharge of his duties."

BIBLIOGRAPHY

MANUSCRIPTS
"Records, Executive Department: Administration of Governor Budd," (California State Archives).

CONTEMPORARY ACCOUNTS
Assembly Journal, 31st-33rd Sess., 1895-99.
Senate Journal, 31st-33rd Sess., 1895-99.
First Biennial Message of Governor James H. Budd (Sacramento, 1897).

SECONDARY SOURCES
Guinn, James M., *History of the State of California and Biographical Record of San Joaquin County* (2 vols., Los Angeles, 1909).
Irvine, Leigh H., ed., *A History of the New California* (2 vols., Chicago, 1905).
Shuck, O.T., ed., *History of the Bench and Bar of California.*
Tinkham, George H., *History of San Joaquin County* (Los Angeles, 1923).

NEWSPAPERS
Sacramento Daily Union, Jan. 4, 1899, has an analytical editorial on "Governor Budd's Farewell."
San Francisco Examiner, July 31, 1908, has an obituary of Budd.
Stockton Evening Mail, Aug. 21- Nov. 13, 1894, covers the gubernatorial campaign.
Stockton Independent, Jan. 12, 1895, gives details and an editorial about Budd's inaugural; July 31, 1908, has an obituary.

Calendar of Events

December 25, 1852	Gage born in Geneva, New York.
1873	Gage admitted to the Michigan bar.
1874	Gage arrived in California.
1877	Gage opened a law office in Los Angeles.
1881	Gage elected City Attorney of Los Angeles.
1888	Gage elected a delegate to the Republican National Convention.
1891	Gage involved in *Itata* incident.
January 5, 1899	Gage took office as Governor.
February 23, 1899	Gage signed "anti-cartoon bill."
March 22, 1899	Gage signed "signature bill."
January 23, 1900	Gage called special session to fill vacancy in United States Senate.
March, 1900	Bubonic plague broke out in San Francisco Chinatown.
October 2, 1901	Teamster-waterfront strike settled at San Francisco.
1909	Gage appointed Minister to Portugal.
1911	Gage resigned his diplomatic post.
August 28, 1924	Gage died in Los Angeles.

Henry T. Gage

20TH GOVERNOR—REPUBLICAN
BORN: DECEMBER 25, 1852   DIED: AUGUST 28, 1924
TERM OF OFFICE: JANUARY 5, 1899—JANUARY 7, 1903

HENRY TIFFT GAGE WAS BORN December 25, 1852, in Geneva, New York. His parents were Dewitt C. and Catherine Glover Gage. When he was a young boy the family moved to East Saginaw, Michigan, where the father entered law practice and became a judge. Gage obtained his education in both public schools and from private tutors. Upon graduation from high school, he studied in his father's law office. At the age of twenty-one he was admitted to the Michigan bar.

In 1874, Gage came to California and for a while he was a sheep dealer. In 1877, he opened a law office in Los Angeles. He quickly developed a successful practice and had several large corporations, including the Southern Pacific Railroad, among his clientele. He participated in local politics and was elected city attorney of Los Angeles in 1881. He was elected a delegate to the Republican national convention at Chicago in 1888, where he seconded the nomination of Levi P. Morton for vice president.

In 1890, Gage married Frances V. Rains, a descendent of José Maria Antonio Lugo, an illustrious Spanish land baron. They had five children and their home near Downey was a show-place of southern California. Here he raised livestock and cultivated oranges, grapes, and walnuts. Gage also became an owner in the Red Rover mines near Acton.

In 1891, President Harrison appointed Gage as attorney to prosecute the crew of the Chilean steamer, *Itata*, which had sailed into San Diego to obtain arms for rebels after the outbreak of civil war in Chile. United States authorities had de-

259

tained the ship, but after his investigation Gage refused to prosecute the case because of his belief that the federal government had erred. Gage's attitude in the *Itata* incident typified his dealings in the law, for he often refused to take cases when his opinions conflicted with prospective clients.

As the 1898 election approached, several leading Republican contenders looked optimistically at the gubernatorial office. Perhaps Budd's poor health and the fact that he was the only Democrat in statewide office prompted the campaign to start somewhat sooner than usual. As early as October 8, 1897, Dr. George C. Pardee, former Oakland mayor, announced that he would be a candidate. About the same time the Columbia Club of Los Angeles brought out Gage as a prospect. By January, 1898, Attorney General William F. Fitzgerald and Secretary of State Louis N. Brown were in the running and by April, they were joined by State Controller E. P. Colgan, ex-Mayor Levi R. Ellert of San Francisco, and others.

The 1898 gubernatorial campaign was related closely to the 1899 contest for a United States Senator. On May 31, 1898, the first biennial convention of the state Republican league clubs met at the Baldwin Hotel in San Francisco to insure unity in Republican ranks. A combination of southern and northern Republicans proposed to renew an agreement of almost four years' standing which had pledged that the next United States Senator should be chosen from the South. They then added a new pledge that the next governor should be chosen from the North. However, the Southern Pacific machine opposed this pledge and supported Gage.

According to the *Argonaut* magazine of June 6, 1898, Michael H. De Young, proprietor of the *San Francisco Chronicle*, persuaded Gage to relinquish a bid for the Senate and to seek the governorship. In return for De Young's aid, Gage was to assist him in becoming Senator. An editorial in the *San Francisco Examiner* of September 16, seemed to confirm this contention by stating that De Young and William F. Herrin, head of the political bureau of the Southern Pacific, had: "invented Gage, because the selection of a southern candidate would open the way to the Senate for De Young. . . ."

Prior to the convention Gage won support of the Republican press, but he kept his machine connections secret. In the August primaries Gage won a plurality of the pledges of delegates to the Republican state convention which opened at Sacramento on August 23.

Henry T. Gage, George Pardee, and the political boss, Daniel M. Burns, established their headquarters at the Golden Eagle Hotel. From the start it was evident that the San Francisco delegation with 156 delegates would be in control. Political bosses controlled the San Francisco delegation and the railroad sought their cooperation. Pardee and Louis N. Brown attempted to organize a solid North, but failed. Gage already had the support of the southern California delegation; then he won over the San Francisco delegation as well as some rural groups. To assure his victory he prevailed upon Jacob H. Neff, a former Senator from Placer County and a favorite of the miners, to become his running mate. When nominations were opened, Timothy G. Phelps of San Mateo nominated Pardee, and Judge Frank Davis of Los Angeles nominated Gage. After much manuevering, Pardee withdrew and asked for a solid vote for Gage which was unanimous on the first ballot.

The Republican platform stressed national issues and endorsed the principles of the national convention of 1896. It favored a program of commercial expansion and approved the recent overseas expansion. Also it favored construction of the proposed Nicaraguan canal, an amendment to immigration laws to protect labor, and an international monetary agreement. With regard to local issues the platform favored a reduction of freight rates and fares and it commended the San Pedro harbor project.

Meanwhile, the Democratic state convention had convened at Sacramento on August 18. The delegates nominated popular Congressman James G. Maguire, a former San Francisco judge and single tax advocate, on a fusion ticket of Democrats, Silver Republicans, and Populists. For lieutenant governor the fusionists nominated Edward L. Hutchinson, a Los Angeles councilman and Populist leader. The state conventions of these parties adopted this fusion ticket over the opposition of anti-fusionist conservatives.

The platform of the fusionists endorsed the war policies, but opposed retaining lands liberated from Spain. It condemned the railroad debt refunding bill and opposed railroad, land, and water monopolies. The platform also favored the direct election of United States Senators and direct legislation. The fusionist ticket had the support of such Democratic leaders as Senator Stephen M. White, William H. Alvord, Democratic state chairman, and Gavin McNab, the reform Democratic boss of San Francisco who had freed the San Francisco party organization from Chris Buckley.

In addition to Gage and Maguire, a third gubernatorial candidate, Job Harriman, was in the contest. He had been nominated by the Socialist Labor party the previous May. During the campaign a series of debates were held between Harriman and Maguire in their respective efforts to appeal to the labor vote.

After the Republican convention adjourned, Gage visited Oakland. At a reception in the Macdonough Theater he received the blessing of Pardee and the Republicans condemned the "peculiar trinity" of the Democrats, Silver Republicans, and Populists. On September 3, Gage gave his first campaign speech in Los Angeles in which he urged annexation of all territory won by the war and the building of a Nicaraguan canal. Such a program, he claimed, would expand trade with the Orient and benefit Los Angeles, San Diego, and San Francisco. Gage denied charges made by Maguire that the Republican convention had been controlled by the railroad and he blasted his opponent's earlier advocacy of the single tax. During the course of his campaign Gage visited most of the counties and promised the people an honest and business-like administration unhampered by any corporate influence.

To compensate for his political weakness in the South, Maguire tried to win as many votes as possible in the San Francisco area. Whereas Gage benefited by shrewd campaign managers, Maguire conducted his own vigorous campaign, making the railroad monopoly his main target. The *San Francisco Call, San Francisco Chronicle, Sacramento Union,* and southern California newspapers endorsed Gage while Maguire had the support of the *San Francisco Examiner.* Students of the University of California and of Stanford University took a keen interest in the campaign and on both campuses Democratic and Republican clubs were formed. On two occasions the Democratic clubs of both institutions held joint meetings in San Francisco where they were addressed by Budd, Maguire, and other Democratic leaders.

On election day Gage received 148,334 votes to 129,255 for Maguire; the Socialist candidate, Job Harriman, polled 5,101 votes while another minor party candidate, J. E. McComas, polled 4,297 votes. The Republicans gained all state executive offices and majorities in both legislative branches. Gage carried thirty-seven of the then fifty-seven counties, including several in the interior which usually went Democratic. He also carried the three most populous counties of San Francisco, Los Angeles, and Alameda.

The Republicans owed their victory primarily to the defeat of Spain, the success of their national slogan of "McKinley, Conservatism, and Prosperity," the return of many Silver Republicans to their party, and the desertion of conservative Democrats from their party. Other significant factors were the appeals of Father Peter C. Yorke, a popular labor crusader of San Francisco, to the Catholic vote to defeat Maguire; the organization of railroad employees into political clubs; and the preponderant influence of Republican newspapers. In a victory statement Governor-elect Gage said: "The intelligent and thinking people of California have placed the stamp of disapproval upon the principles of the single tax and all other propositions advanced by theorists that have a tendency to lead to social revolution. This is what I would say was one of the great causes of the political avalanche in California in 1898 in favor of the Republican State Ticket. . . ."

On January 5, 1899, Gage was installed into office in an impressive ceremony. Gage, accompanied by retiring Governor Budd and other dignitaries, entered a carriage in front of the Golden Eagle Hotel. The streets were crowded as thousands of Californians viewed the parade of the gubernatorial party escorted by the national guard to the Assembly chamber in the capitol. Before the joint convention of the legislature, Associate Justice Frederick W. Henshaw administered the oath in a moment of dignity and solemnity. Then a band in the corridor played "Hail to the Chief," as heavy guns outside fired a salute. Ex-Governor Budd spoke kindly about his successor and said: "I predict for him an honorable and able administration." Then turning to Gage, he concluded: "Governor Gage, I introduce you to the people."

Gage then read his inaugural address to the large and attentive crowd. After discussing the victory over Spain, he contended that the United States should annex the Philippines. In part Governor Gage stated:

The center of commerce must move westward. California, favorably situated, will, among other advantages, reap the harvest of trade with these new territories, developing our many, varied and growing resources, creating a Western merchant marine for the carriage of our imports and exports, and luring to our markets the nations of the world.

The new governor reviewed state finances and the cost of state government in great detail. To end over-legislation and extravagance in administration he recommended that sessions be held every four years instead of every two years. He criticized excessive appropriations of the past, which had been caused by legislative bartering, and urged that appropriations should be made payable immediately instead of from future revenue.

Gage mentioned that the state printing office had been closed in Budd's administration and that the expense of its reopening would be shifted to his incoming administration. He protested the waste of public offices in printing excessive copies of documents which were usually too voluminous. Then he said: "I find that conciseness is a rare rhetorical beauty in official reports." In reference to yet another subject—which he called "Stale Claims"—Gage presented the following commentary on lobbying:

> With each new administration there is a revival of stale claims which former Governors have vetoed, or former Legislatures disapproved.
> Strenuous efforts have been made to lobby through each new Legislature the bills which have failed to pass each preceding session of the Legislature. The spirit of lobbying is too prevalent, and should be checked.
> It fosters a corrupt sentiment that it is lawful to rob the State.

As a case in point Gage referred to the claims on coyote scalps that were likely to be presented at the current session despite repeal of the act providing for bounties. He criticized county officials for making claims against the state for commissions in collecting state taxes. However, when it came to the question of California's claims against the federal government for equipping and paying volunteers during the Civil War, which totaled over $4,000,000, Gage stated these war claims were just and should be paid.

In a discussion of irrigation, Gage asserted that the expense of storing mountain waters and winter rains for irrigation should be paid by Congress since this would facilitate recla-

mation and sale of federal arid lands within California. He
then stated that land owners had not generally benefited by the
irrigation districts established under terms of the Wright Act.
He claimed that the measure had imposed additional taxes and
litigation while it had only benefited certain portions of California.

As mentioned previously, the gubernatorial campaign of
1898 and the United States senatorial campaign of 1899 were
closely interwoven. In 1898, former Governor George C. Perkins was Senator from the northern section and Stephen M.
White was Senator from the South. In February, White announced that he would retire. At first the leading senatorial
contenders were Robert N. Bulla, a corporation lawyer and
state senator from Los Angeles, and Ulysses S. Grant, Jr., a San
Diego millionaire and son of the former president. Both men
were anti-machine. The Southern Pacific supported Daniel M.
Burns, Republican boss of San Francisco, thereby disregarding
the party compact of not having two Senators from the North.

After his election as governor, Gage supported Burns, instead
of Michael De Young of the *Chronicle*. William Herrin now
apparently would not support De Young. John D. Spreckels
of the *San Francisco Call* joined De Young in an attack upon
Burns accusing him of conspiring with Gage and Herrin.
Harrison Gray Otis of the *Los Angeles Times* joined Spreckels
and De Young in their battle. When the senatorial contest
came up in the legislature in January, 1899, Burns and Grant
were the leading contenders. After 104 ballots, no decision
could be reached, and California remained with only one
United States Senator. This contest continued to dominate
political affairs in California for the first part of the Gage
administration.

In the first legislative session of Gage's term two anti-news-
paper bills were introduced which were related to the senatorial
contest, and probably inspired to suppress newspaper opposition to Burns. On February 23, 1899, Gage signed the "anti-
cartoon bill," and on March 22, he signed the "signature bill,"
which required that all newspaper articles tending to question
the integrity, honesty, or reputation of any individual must be
signed. During the session Gage vetoed excessive and inexpedi-
ent appropriations in his avowed effort to implement his pledge
of economy.

On January 3, 1900, Gage called a special session of the legislature and presented a sixteen-point program. Its primary objective according to his proclamation was to fill the vacancy in the Senate. He declared that the Pacific Coast should be fully represented in Congress during the crucial days of deciding the fate of new possessions gained from Spain. Among a few of Gage's other purposes were to improve San Francisco harbor, to create a commission of public works, and to empower the governor to remove appointees for cause.

The senatorial issue was finally settled on February 7, when Thomas R. Bard, a Ventura banker and rancher, was elected. The defeat of Burns weakened the railroad machine. Henceforth Gage was put on the defensive and newspapers became more vindictive toward him. Although his candidate for the Senate was defeated, the legislature enacted the more important laws recommended by Gage. For example, the port facilities of San Francisco were improved which prepared the city for the expected increase in trade with the Orient.

In addition to the senatorial contest, the Gage administration was harassed by the so-called bubonic plague incident. In March, 1900, the plague broke out in San Francisco Chinatown. Although it was confined to that quarter of the city, it became a state and even national issue. When the first case was reported by Dr. Joseph J. Kinyoun, a federal quarantine officer, Mayor James D. Phelan, the local board of health, and federal health officers endeavored to enforce emergency sanitary measures. However, San Francisco merchants and the local press denied the existence of a plague, fearing a loss of trade.

Governor Gage intervened and publicly stated that reports of the plague were fallacious. When Kinyoun imposed a quarantine on the city, Gage appealed to President McKinley to rescind the order, which the latter did. But next year a federal commission investigated and confirmed Kinyoun's reports. Gage finally granted some financial aid to the city. Federal health officials assisted in cleaning up Chinatown under Kinyoun's direction. The entire affair demonstrated Gage's inability to cope with an emergency.

In his first biennial message of January 7, 1901, Gage reiterated the need for economy because of the recent adoption of constitutional amendments, exempting religious buildings and some private school properties from taxation. As the first governor of the new century Gage perpetuated the typical anti-Oriental attitude of nineteenth century California governors when he said: "The people of California, from their experience in the past, and in view of their prominent seacoast with respect to the ports of the Orient, have reason to dread the immigration of Chinese and Japanese laborers into this State, a fear justly founded and shared in by the American workmen of other States."

In referring to correctional institutions Gage noted that only nineteen women were at San Quentin and said: "This exceeding small number of female convicts, unparalleled in any State in the Union, is a splendid testimonial to the character of the women of California." The governor concluded his message by praising the foreign and domestic policies of McKinley and by predicting that the recent annexation of the Philippines would enrich the varied industries of California.

During the thirty-fourth legislative session several bills were enacted aiding railroads. One measure allowed the Santa Fe Railroad Company to build a terminal and sea wall at China Basin in San Francisco. Gage vetoed a Senate conservation bill because of its large appropriation. However, he approved a measure appropriating $250,000 to purchase Big Basin in Santa Cruz County as a state park. This law also created the California Redwood Park Commission of five members, including the governor. Two other measures of significance were passed by the 1901 legislature. One established the California Polytechnic School at San Luis Obispo. The other was a primary election law which required that primaries be held on the same day under strict supervision in the twelve leading cities.

Gage was the first California governor to mediate a major labor dispute. Following the Spanish-American War a militant labor movement arose in San Francisco where the California State Federation of Labor, representing sixty-one unions, held its first convention in January, 1901. For several years skilled labor had bargained successfully with employers and now a sustained effort was made to organize the unskilled and to convert San Francisco into a closed-shop city. On May 1, cooks and waiters went on strike and were soon joined by the carriage and wagonmakers, machinists, and teamsters. When the Employers' Association brought in strikebreakers and special police, the City Front Federation, comprising eighteen water-

front unions, staged a sympathy strike. Over half the business
of San Francisco came to a standstill as capital and labor resorted to violence.

James D. Phelan, the reform mayor of San Francisco, failed
in his attempts to mediate and only antagonized the labor elements who charged him with using the police to harm their
cause. When President Norton P. Chipman of the California
State Board of Trade demanded that Governor Gage call out
the state militia, he refused and replied:

> Civil Government should not be supplanted except in cases of
> public necessity and in times of actual public danger. The National
> Guard, taken from the body of our citizens, from all ranks of
> business, labor and professions, cannot be made, by a mere pre-
> text, the sanguinary tribunal for the settlement of peaceable dis-
> putes between capital and labor.

As the summer wore on, anti-unionists persisted in demanding that the militia be called out. Governor Gage consulted with
his personal friend, Father Peter C. Yorke, who advised Gage
not to use the militia against the workingmen. At a conference
held in the Palace Hotel on October 2, 1901, the strike was
finally settled when Gage told both factions either to settle the
dispute or accept martial law.

Gradually the workers returned to their jobs and on two
occasions Governor Gage disguised himself as a stevedore and
personally inspected the San Francisco waterfront to observe
whether there were any signs of violence by the workers. After
Gage satisfied himself that all was peaceful, he departed for
Sacramento. While the so-called teamster-waterfront strike of
1901 ended in a stalemate, Gage's intervention probably averted
a general strike. Although the governor threatened to declare
martial law, he actually refused to use his military power to
protect the movement of goods by strikebreakers. While organized labor won no immediately visible gains in the settlement,
the principle of the open-shop was defeated.

By 1902, if not before, Gage had already committed a sufficient number of political errors—if not blunders—to preclude
his renomination. From the start he had antagonized the press
and the senatorial contest had further split the Republican
party. Moreover, in making appointments he customarily selected personal friends and party workers, usually to reward
political services. His former law partner and private secretary,

William I. Foley, was appointed attorney for the board of public health. Gage appointed his law partner and political manager, Daniel Kevane, as secretary of the state board of examiners. As such, Kevane became Gage's main budget adviser, but he lacked business acumen. The tax revenue was reduced below expenditures causing the General Fund to become virtually exhausted by the end of Gage's term. Budd's surplus was depleted and the state treasury was empty.

In his second biennial message of January 5, 1903, Gage boasted that his administration had the lowest tax rate in California history and he claimed that the state was on a "business basis." Like Budd, he pleaded with legislators to extend the time allowed a governor to act on bills and as evidence he stated:

> During the last week of the session hundreds of bills, many of them very lengthy, and nearly all involving intricate questions of law as well as of policy, are thrust upon the wearied Executive, and it is expected that he can determine these many vexed problems within this narrow constitutional limit of ten days.

Gage repeated earlier charges about "unfounded reports" of the plague in the Chinese quarter of San Francisco. He referred to the area as an unsanitary menace and even suggested considering measures to change the location of Chinatown.

In closing, Gage expressed his fear of the growth of municipal leagues. He was probably concerned about the League of California Municipalities, which had been organized in 1898, to foster greater home rule for the cities. Gage brooded that cities were gaining sovereignty at the expense of the state and expressed dissatisfaction as follows: "I regard this excessive growth of municipal power as a peaceful mode of secession from the State, and an unconscious blow against the State's integrity, and, indirectly, an unpatriotic assault upon national existence."

Meanwhile, opposition to Gage mounted. He further lost popularity when he refused to attend a meeting of the California Republican Club at San Jose on April 14, 1902. An anti-Gage Republican Club was organized in Sacramento with Mayor George Clark and Hiram W. Johnson leading the movement. In speeches Johnson vehemently attacked Herrin, Gage, and the manipulations of the Southern Pacific machine. Other groups joined the move to block Gage's renomination by the machine. In San Francisco the Republican Primary League was formed with the blessings of Michael De Young and John D. Spreckels. The *San Francisco Call* made charges that Governor Gage was personally receiving convict-made furniture and articles. Gage then swore complaints against Spreckels and W. S. Leake of the *Call*. In retaliation Spreckels and Leake charged they had been criminally libeled and obtained a bench warrant for Governor Gage's arrest.

In the county primaries for convention delegates held in August, 1902, the Gage forces won in the large cities, but lost in rural areas. Actually Gage lacked sufficient votes at the Republican state convention to win and his opponents merely had to combine their delegations in support of another candidate to defeat him. Finally on August 27, the Southern Pacific machine shifted its support from Gage to Pardee, who was then nominated. The next day in an editorial entitled, "The Right Has Prevailed," the *San Diego Union* stated:

> The campaign of bluff and bluster, the carefully laid plans of schemers, and the conspiracy to force upon the Republican party of the state a nomination that would entail disgrace and disaster, have all come to naught. Henry T. Gage and the malodorous gang of practical politicians who shared his fortunes, have sustained a crushing defeat. And a more sweeping victory for honest politics over machine methods has rarely been achieved in any state of the union.

One of Gage's campaign supporters of 1898 neatly summarized the situation in 1902 when he said: "I can't see how such a man can be renominated for he has raised up an army of enemies."

Gage's greatest weakness was his failure to maintain unity in his own party. As factional disputes and party feuds developed, he attempted to build a personal machine, particularly by distributing patronage among the county bosses to no avail. As a result he became preoccupied with purely political matters and failed to supervise the state administration in a satisfactory way. The few achievements of Gage's administration were offset by political strife and scandals which were probably overplayed by a vindictive press. His economy program failed and management of the normal schools, insane asylums, and dental and pharmacy boards remained static.

In his exercise of the pardoning power Gage was a most conservative governor. He granted only eight pardons, six commutations, and five reprieves. He once complained that a judge would often impose a severe sentence and then would petition the governor to mitigate it by a pardon or commutation.

Gage's honest errors were often viewed as corruption. He left a depleted treasury and a demoralized civil service. Gage tended to overemphasize foreign affairs, perhaps because California was on the periphery of the new American empire. His fear that greater home rule for cities was a danger proved groundless.

After leaving Sacramento, Gage returned to his law practice in Los Angeles. At times certain politicians considered him as a possibility for governor again or United States Senator. In 1909, President Taft appointed Gage as Envoy Extraordinary and Minister Plenipotentiary to Portugal. He was the fifth former governor of California to enter a diplomatic career in the tradition of Bigler, Weller, Low, and Pacheco. In 1911, he resigned the post because of his wife's poor health. He resumed his law practice and remained active in Republican party circles in Los Angeles, where he died on August 28, 1924.

BIBLIOGRAPHY

CONTEMPORARY ACCOUNTS
Assembly Journal, 35th Sess., 1903.
Journals of the Senate and Assembly, Extra Sess., 33rd Sess., 1900.
Senate Journal, 33rd-35th Sess., 1899-1903.
Todd, Frank M., *Eradicating Plague from San Francisco, Report of the Citizens Health Committee and An Account of Its Work* (San Francisco, 1909).

SECONDARY SOURCES
Bates, J.C., ed., *History of the Bench and Bar of California* (San Francisco, 1912).
Cronin, Bernard C., *Father Yorke and the Labor Movement in San Francisco, 1900-1910* (Washington, D.C., 1943).
Knight, Robert, *Industrial Relations in the San Francisco Bay Area, 1900-1918* (Berkeley, 1960).
Robinson, W.W., *Lawyers of Los Angeles* (Los Angeles, 1959).

NEWSPAPERS
Sacramento Record-Union, Jan. 5, 1899, describes Gage's inaugural ceremonies, and has the full text of his address, which is not printed in the legislative journals.
San Diego Union, Aug. 10 and 12, 1902, has data on the attempt to arrest Gage; Aug. 28, 1902, has an editorial criticizing Gage.

Calendar of Events

July 25, 1857	Pardee born at San Francisco.
1879	Pardee graduated from the University of California.
1885	Pardee received M.D. degree from the University of Leipzig.
1893	Pardee elected Mayor of Oakland.
January 8, 1903	Pardee inaugurated Governor.
July 3, 1903	Governor's mansion purchased by State of California.
April 18, 1906	San Francisco earthquake and fire.
October 11, 1906	San Francisco Board of Education ordered separate schools for Orientals.
1911	Pardee appointed by Governor Johnson as chairman of the State Conservation Commission.
1919	Pardee appointed by Governor Stephens as chairman of the State Forestry Commission.
1932	Pardee awarded a Doctor of Laws degree by University of California.
September 1, 1941	Pardee died in Oakland.

George C. Pardee

21ST GOVERNOR—REPUBLICAN
BORN: JULY 25, 1857   DIED: SEPTEMBER 1, 1941
TERM OF OFFICE: JANUARY 8, 1903—JANUARY 9, 1907

GEORGE COOPER PARDEE WAS BORN in San Francisco July 25, 1857, the first of five governors born in California since admission to statehood. Governor Pacheco, also a native Californian, had been born before statehood. As a youth, Pardee attended public and private schools in San Francisco and then Oakland High School when the family moved to that city. In 1875, he entered the University of California, graduating with a Bachelor of Philosophy degree in 1879. In 1881, he earned a Master of Arts degree. He next attended Cooper Medical College for two years. Following this, Pardee went to the University of Leipzig, Germany, where in 1885, he received his degree of Doctor of Medicine.

That same year he joined his father's ear and eye practice in Oakland. His father, also an active figure in state politics, served as mayor of Oakland and as a state senator. In 1887, George Pardee married Helen Newhall Penniman. From this marriage four daughters were born. Pardee first entered local politics in Oakland in 1889, when he was appointed a member of the board of health for two years. In 1891, he was elected to a two year term to the Oakland City Council. In 1893, he was elected mayor of Oakland for a two year term. As mayor, he led a fight for the reduction of water rates and earned an undeserved reputation as an anti-labor man as he stepped into the national railroad strike of 1894 to preserve the peace in Oakland. In 1898, he was a candidate for the Republican gubernatorial nomination but stepped aside for Henry T. Gage. Gage appointed Pardee in 1899 a regent of the University of California. He served as a regent until his election as governor and he automatically continued as an ex officio member of the board.

By 1900, California was the setting of the increasing political power struggle between the Southern Pacific machine and the developing reform element. These two factions after some preliminary skirmishes found themselves deadlocked as the Republican state convention of 1902 approached. The regular Republicans found that they would not be able to renominate their man, Governor Gage, and, hoping to stalemate the reform wing, threw support to George Pardee, an independent in the party's internal struggle. Pardee thus won nomination because of the Southern Pacific machine, but he constantly repeated that his only pledged commitment was to give the people of California good government.

Both during the campaign and the four years as governor, Pardee discovered that he was not the leader of the Republican party. Rather he served merely as a counterbalance between the two wings. Hence he had a difficult gubernatorial campaign. He was forced to answer charges that as a leader against the strikers of Oakland in 1894, he had ordered out fire hoses and pick handles to break up the strike. The truth of the matter was that Pardee had been ill at Castle Craigs at that particular time. He also had to convince reform elements in the state that he was not another tool of the railroad machine. In the November general election, Pardee received 146,322 votes. His nearest opponent, Democrat Franklin Lane, garnered 143,783 votes. Pardee's margin was only 2,539 and after it was revealed that some 5,000 ballots in Los Angeles and Oakland had been disallowed, his victory was in doubt. The State Supreme Court settled the resulting election dispute and Pardee was elected.

Contemporaries of the new governor held that Pardee had great ability and a perceptive mind. He projected a philosophic reflectiveness in both conversation and correspondence. One weakness was his willingness to procrastinate; this trait coupled with a cautious temperament tended to keep him from becoming a dynamic leader. Associates found that he had a kindly disposition and a quiet reserved manner. Some called him urbane while others who did not know him well found him aloof. A common view of Pardee was that he lacked a colorful and outgoing personality which detracted from his image as governor. Physically, Pardee had a medium build. He had very dark hair and a neatly trimmed beard. He wore steel rimmed spectacles. In dress, he showed a fondness for frock coats, white ties, and slouch brim hats. It has been reported that as governor he continued to practice medicine in Sacramento, and that his black bag could often be seen on a table in the hallway of the mansion, ready for the moment when he might be summoned for a house call.

On January 8, 1903, George C. Pardee took his oath as governor. His inaugural address indicated that he knew he was not the leader of the party. The moderate speech enunciated the broad principles which were to govern his actions as chief executive. Pardee warned against the dangers that lurked from class struggle, calling upon labor and capital to work for a common end. He discussed capital's newly found weapon against labor, the injunction. Warning of the danger of its overuse, Pardee also urged caution against hasty legislation that might improperly curb the injunction.

Reciting the national tradition of separation of powers in the federal government, the incoming governor announced that he would maintain the same separation while giving wholehearted cooperation with the other two branches of state government. Pardee's message then reviewed the state's major industries. He stressed the fact that California, in 1903, remained basically a producer of agricultural crops and raw materials. He asked that proven success of the miner and the farmer be given continued support by the state government through research and legislation.

One of the highlights of this first address concerned the state's natural resources. Pardee noted that the forest resources were constantly dwindling and pointed out resulting dangers in terms of inadequate future timber reserves and possible floods created by denuded mountain slopes. With reference to irrigation and water laws, Pardee called for close state cooperation with the federal government in implementing the national 1902 Newlands Act.

With regard to public education, the governor commented particularly on the recent constitutional amendment which approved special state taxes for support of high schools. He asked also for construction of sufficient school rooms to allow every California child at least six years of education. As a corollary to his commitment of educating the state's youth, he urged the legislature to curb the growth of child labor in California.

In his discussion of state mental hospitals, Pardee observed that the number of patients was bound to increase, but the most efficient way to handle the influx was, he felt, to expand existing facilities instead of building new hospitals. He called for separating the criminally insane into two categories: those with infectious diseases such as tuberculosis and those physically well. Reviewing briefly the penal system, he complimented the prison board of directors on its past work while noting that the need still existed to separate youthful offenders from hardened criminals. He suggested creation of a special juvenile court in larger cities.

Pardee agreed with Governor Gage that laws controlling the ballot needed improvement to protect the wishes of the voters. Pardee hoped that recent legalization of voting machines would settle much of the controversy. In passing, Pardee spoke briefly about state civil service and expressed the hope that the public could soon be educated to the values of such a system which must be the basis of California government.

He reserved the major focus of his inaugural address for state finances, particularly the tax problem. Criticizing the last legislature for setting too low a tax rate to provide adequate revenue, he commented that his administration would be confronted with economic difficulties in maintaining state institutions and services. He observed that between July and December, 1903, the General Fund would become exhausted and borrowing from other funds would be the consequence. While he did not say so, this had long been the expedient used by other administrations. The real tragedy, Pardee felt, was that an exhausted General Fund meant that new taxes would have to be higher, but the real problem was that the rate could not be set at a high enough level in the coming year to rebuild the fund. To keep taxes within bounds while replenishing the fund, Pardee demanded that the legislators practice real economy in financing the state's operations.

He also believed that the existing state tax system was not working properly. The general property tax, from the taxpayers' view, was unfair and unjust; from the state's view, it did not produce enough revenue. While the state's prosperity grew, county assessors reported little of this wealth on assessment lists—the basis upon which the state property tax was paid. Pardee felt that there had been too great a reduction in personal property taxation where the state's real wealth lay hidden. He felt that a reappraisal of tax laws needed to take into account this wealth as well as the obvious property wealth of the farmer.

During the 1902 campaign, Pardee instituted the practice of sitting in an open room and meeting all comers there. While governor he continued to keep the door to the governor's office open. He attempted to deal fairly with all legislators without making commitments. During sessions, legislators received priority over other visitors, except certain state officials, as Pardee sought to gain the views of lawmakers on certain bills, or to explain why he had approved or had vetoed certain bills. California newspapers were highly complimentary of this open door policy, contrasting it with Gage's rather high handed manner of dealing with visitors.

The 1903 session enacted much of his program without undue executive pressure. State cooperation with the federal government regarding natural resources, if not all Pardee had hoped for, was at last started. Appropriate legislation for establishing high school districts was passed as well as approval to expand university facilities. Governor Pardee also approved the legislature's designation of the Golden Poppy to be California's official state flower.

Of great importance to the state were Pardee's efforts in replenishing the state treasury and launching an economy program. Both in 1903 and 1905, Pardee exercised personal direction in the realm of state finances. For the first time in many years the legislature received a detailed budget from the governor. Pardee's plan was to push through a general appropriations measure first so that he could then freely veto pork barrel bills. The budget, totaling $5,470,976, gained acceptance and allowed the lawmakers to approve an extremely large number of special interest bills with the knowledge that Pardee would have to bear the blame of not heeding the wishes of the various sections of the state if he used his veto.

The legislature increased the tax levy per $100 from Gage's 1902 low rate of 38.2 cents to 56.1 cents from 1903. This was the highest rate during Pardee's four years as taxes thereafter were reduced annually to a level of 47.6 cents by 1906.

Pardee's economy program and the increased tax rate successfully carried the state through its financial crisis and by June, 1904, the General Fund had a balance of $2,000,000, and by December, 1904, all special funds had been repaid with the General Fund still in good condition. Pardee's course of moderation accomplished his 1903 financial program of rebuilding the treasury. Although economy was the watchword, state services and facilities increased.

However, Pardee found that he could not impose his idea of frugality on the legislature. While he preached and practiced economy in state administration, he urged the lawmakers to follow suit. They instead increased patronage costs. In the Assembly, expenses rose from the 1901 daily cost of $580 to $1,350 by 1907. In the Senate, the 1901 daily bill was $610 as compared to $985 for 1907. The legislators also rejected Pardee's request to withdraw state lands from private entry and his idea of holding the state general election in September to afford incoming governors an opportunity to prepare for office.

While complimenting the 1903 legislators for their efforts at enacting a good program, he vetoed 111 bills, ninety-three of these by pocket veto. In general the press applauded Pardee's firm use of the veto power. He objected to those measures returned because they opposed the best interest of the public or because they were pork barrel bills.

During the 1903 session, the governor grappled with other pressing matters. One of these was his admission in January that there was evidence of bubonic plague in San Francisco, thus opening the way for state cooperation with the federal government to stamp out the disease. Governor Gage had earlier denied the existence of plague and had refused to cooperate. Pardee announced in February, 1903, that the situation had been controlled.

Of concern also to Pardee were conditions in the state printing office which had been a perennial political controversy. The urgency for reform came because the state was in the process of selecting new textbooks to be produced in large numbers. Reform was started and by 1907 the printing office was the largest book manufacturer in the West and the only printer of school books west of Cincinnati.

Textbook selection occupied much of Pardee's time. He was

one of a three-man committee charged with revision and selection. He also became quite active on the state normal school board of trustees. In general, he did much to advance the cause of public education at all levels during his term.

In June, 1903, Governor Pardee toured California, visiting state agencies to learn their problems and to instill into administrative heads the need for economy and efficiency. He was well on his way to becoming a popular governor. When Theodore Roosevelt visited the state in 1903, Pardee was mentioned as a possible 1904 vice presidential candidate, but he scotched these rumors by issuing a statement that he would not be a candidate for that honor, preferring to remain California's governor.

The restoration of public faith in the governor's office developed with Pardee's appointment of capable men to key administrative positions. His appointees formed a council which carried out his economy program. These men were not tied to the Southern Pacific machine and in some cases were anti-machine. The advice of this council to the governor caused Pardee in time to move from a middle of the road position into the outskirts of the Progressive camp.

One of Pardee's important contributions to California, while governor and for many years after, was his deep interest in and his action for conservation. In 1903, he was a delegate to the National Irrigation Congress and selected as vice-president. In 1904, he was elected president of this congress.

On January 3, 1905, Governor Pardee sent his first biennial message to the legislators. He noted first the general prosperity of the state and commented on the recent large influx of new residents to California. While he did not say so, the prosperous condition of the economy made his financial program succeed. He urged a continuation of wise but frugal legislation to improve the fiscal condition. He called for enactment of only necessary laws and these needed to be composed in a clear manner. He claimed that many bills, which he had vetoed in 1903, had been either obscure in meaning or improperly written.

The major emphasis of his message reviewed state finances. He happily reported that the General Fund had improved to a satisfactory level while the public building program had been extended at the same time. He adopted Governor Waterman's suggestion that state funds be taken from the vaults and deposited with various banks to earn interest, thus allowing these funds to increase rather than lie dormant. Submitted by the legislature as a constitutional amendment, this proposal gained the voters' approval.

In a discussion of taxation, a prime topic of his inaugural address, Pardee reviewed the history of state taxation while observing that the 1903 legislators had not coped with the question. The governor, after personally investigating in 1904 how eastern states handled their tax problems, made definite recommendations in 1905. He stated that the general property tax program was outmoded. Legislators should develop other state taxes and the property tax should cease as a source of state revenue, to be reserved for local taxation. He recommended a corporation tax and a graduated direct inheritance tax.

Pardee also examined the state financial structure of public education. He believed that while California had been very liberal in school aid, the gravest educational problem was teacher salaries. Commenting on the difficulty of finding the needed 8,000 teachers, he suggested two reasons caused the shortage—the requiring of better and more educational preparation, and inadequate salaries. Salaries could be improved if the state school fund were distributed in a more equitable manner. He noted that richer school districts received more state money for salaries than did poorer ones. At the same time, poorer districts had the highest county school tax rates. Yet all counties paid at the same fixed rate into the state treasury for education. He recommended a fairer division of the school fund and the legislature made a start in this direction. He asked that a college of agriculture, separate from the University of California, be created and in 1905 Davis was selected as the site.

Pardee called attention to irrigation problems and demanded the development of a state irrigation code. Commenting on state cooperation with the federal government on water and forestry matters, he announced that a definite state forest policy would be submitted during the session. This proposal led to the re-creation of the state board of forestry and the beginning of a state system of forest fire prevention.

By 1905, California had six normal schools and a university

dedicated to higher education. Thirteen institutions cared for
wards of the state. There were two prisons, two reformatories,
one veterans' home, two institutions for the handicapped, and
six mental hospitals. With the exception of the prisons and the
reformatories, Pardee felt all were well-managed and operated
economically.

Pardee agreed with recent legislative findings that the prisons
were no credit to California. He observed that their major
failing had been discernible since 1872, namely improper
classification and segregation of prisoners. He maintained that
San Quentin and Folsom had become "schools of vice and universities of crime." Pardee offered no new solution but urged
more facilities to enable classification. Second only to prisoner
reformation was inadequate utilization of prison labor. San
Quentin jute and Folsom granite had not made the prisons
self-supporting and he recommended the New York state system
of manufacturing items for use in other state institutions. This
allowed for diversification of labor as well as avoiding competition with free labor. Pardee praised highly the board of charities and corrections, established in 1903. Through an investigation of all state institutions and county jails, it made many
positive recommendations for legislative consideration.

At the conclusion of the 1905 legislature, the governor sent
a farewell message to the legislators thanking them for a profitable session and for the initiation of a number of new state
programs. Specifically he was pleased with the creation of the
Sacramento Valley drainage district, aimed at flood control
and reclamation, and the development of the Klamath Lake
district in cooperation with the federal government for irrigation purposes. Pardee concluded with the belief that perhaps
the greatest legislative accomplishment of 1905 had been the
revision of the state civil and penal codes.

During the session it had become apparent that the governor's
tax program would not pass and it was pushed through piecemeal. A commission on revenue and taxation was formed to
report to the 1907 legislature. Taxes on corporation licenses,
insurance premiums, and direct inheritances on a graduated
scale were enacted. Proposed by the administration, but not
passed, was a liquor tax. From these 1905 beginnings of tax
reform the road led slowly to the King tax bill of 1921, three
administrations later.

The major points demanded by Pardee in his 1905 biennial message, such as prison reform and distribution of school funds, became law. Pardee, well thought of as governor, had earned by 1905 the reputation of being an able executive. The *Sacramento Union* claimed that "his work is well done, laboriously done, conscientiously done, without ulterior aims or objects, ironclad against sordid interests or personal greed."

The most dramatic event of the Pardee administration occurred April 18, 1906, when northern California—and San Francisco in particular—was rocked by the great earthquake and fire. Governor Pardee went to Oakland to assess the damage and to mobilize resources. He resisted immediate pressure for an extra session of the legislature until a complete survey of damage could be made. As he took personal charge of sanitary regulations for San Francisco, he immediately declared a legal holiday, at the request of the bank commission, to protect commercial interests and allow banks to dig out their vaults and reorganize. For six weeks he continued declaring daily legal holidays.

On June 1, for the first time since the disaster, Pardee returned to Sacramento and called an extra session to legislate emergency measures. In eleven days the lawmakers enacted much of what he asked. Pardee listed thirty-four topics for consideration and thirty became law. Emergency and remedial legislation to tide over San Francisco—California's financial center—were rushed through as well as programs to re-establish local and state government there.

As the state recovered from the earthquake, the political wheels continued to turn as county politicians made ready to select delegates for the coming state conventions. During June and July, rumors spread that Pardee was losing ground in his chance for renomination. Yet the press generally held that his administration had proven exceptionally able and that he would be renominated and re-elected.

The last Republican state convention was held at Santa Cruz in September, 1906, with Pardee and James N. Gillett the leading contenders. Gillett was nominated on the first ballot. Shortly after the convention, Pardee let it be known that he had every reason to feel that the Southern Pacific machine and Boss Abe Ruef of San Francisco had combined to defeat his renomination. In the campaign that followed, Pardee gave little help to Gillett, who was victorious in November.

The Republican party split during the 1906 campaign. Governor Pardee, for one, moved completely into the Progressive fold. As outgoing governor he had the opportunity to make some last minute four year appointments. Pardee seized the chance to fill these vacancies with anti-machine men and precipitated a political war which lasted through Gillett's term.

On January 10, 1907, Governor Pardee sent his second biennial message to the legislature. This remarkable document was in its own way the initial stage of the Progressives' battle for control of the government of California and a beginning of the reform movement.

He again commented on the continued prosperity of the state. He noted that the Bay Area was rapidly recovering from the earthquake disaster. Pleased with the fine start made in tax reform in the past four years, he summarized the findings of the commission on revenue and taxation. In general, the commission recommended the same points expressed by Pardee earlier.

He then turned to the need to reform primary elections and conventions. He called specific attention to the well established power clique which ran the Republican party and dominated its conventions. He believed as a consequence candidates were no longer being selected by delegates who expressed the wishes of the various counties, but were being decided as a result of trading between various interest groups. He concluded, perhaps from his recent personal experience, that the California nomination process needed great improvement and urged as the first major step the direct election of delegates to conventions.

Pardee reported that state finances had greatly improved despite the earthquake and fire. The treasury in 1907 had a $1,000,000 surplus. While accumulating this surplus, the state continued developing public works. In fact, his administration spent almost as much for improvements as the three preceding administrations. The four year average tax rate during Pardee's term was 51.5 cents which compared favorably with Gage's four year average of 49 cents. Pardee, however, severely criticized the legislature for its inability or lack of interest in economizing its own operations.

He stated that the state prison population had increased to the point where still more facilities would be needed even though prison construction had been accelerated in the last two years. He then noted two areas of experimentation in rehabilitation of prisoners: (1) an extended parole system with a parole officer at each prison to guide men in and out of prison to rebuild their lives and (2) an indeterminate sentencing for those whose good conduct and the original nature of the conviction merited a second opportunity in society. These techniques would, he maintained, reduce prison costs. Pardee urged establishment of an effective convict work program and employment of penology specialists in the prisons rather than politicians. During his four years, Pardee used the pardoning power with more discretion than had other chief executives. He issued ten pardons, 100 commutations of sentence, eighteen reprieves, and thirteen restorations to citizenship.

In discussing mental institutions, he reflected changing views about treating patients and the hope of rehabilitation for some. He also reported that the Agnews state hospital had been totally destroyed in the earthquake with some deaths resulting. He hinted that the lesson learned from the Agnews disaster was that the original construction had been defective and he urged rigid supervision of all future public construction.

He also observed that public education had continued to progress and complimented the legislature for its role. He called attention to the need to rebuild San Jose State Normal School, also destroyed by the earthquake. He asked again for salary increases for the university and public school faculties.

Pardee reviewed state salaries in general, observing that as governor he had received $6,000 a year, $2,500 a year for expenses, and the right to live rent free in the governor's mansion. He had been unable to live on this income, and so it was, he said, with other state officials and employees. He urged an across-the-board salary increase. Pardee's family became the first to reside in the governor's mansion. The governor's mansion had been built in 1877 by N. D. Goodell for Albert Gallatin. Gallatin sold his Victorian mansion to Joseph Steffens, the father of Lincoln Steffens, in 1888. Joseph Steffens, in turn, sold the mansion to the State of California on July 9, 1903, for $32,588.53.

The outgoing governor then discussed the growth of trusts in California. He deplored the widespread practice of railroad rate discrimination. He suggested that Standard Oil had killed off competition in the oil fields by gaining a rate preference from California railroads. Pardee demanded remedial legislation concerning railroad rates and trust regulations aimed specifically at Standard Oil. During his term, he had actively supported the Western Pacific railroad as one means of neutralizing the Southern Pacific monopoly.

Pardee called the railroad commission an abject failure. This had also been the view of Perkins and Stoneman after the commission was instituted under the second constitution. Pardee recommended a constitutional amendment abolishing the board.

While showing concern over the rise of monopolies and the great strength of the railroad in politics, Pardee charged that waterfronts had been monopolized also. Calling for a general investigation, he told the legislators to remember that the San Francisco harbor and waterfront belonged to the people of the state and should be administered for their interests and rights.

Pardee gave his views on the rising Japanese question which had exploded during the last three months of his administration. The San Francisco board of education had ordered all Japanese students to attend the Chinese school regardless of where they lived in San Francisco. Theodore Roosevelt had criticized the action of the board, but Pardee announced that he disagreed with the President who did not understand California's problems. The governor restated the old arguments which had earlier been used against the Chinese, but now with reference to the Japanese. Regardless of training, education, or political background, a majority of white Californians had the same view concerning Asiatics. Congressional action in 1902 had completed the exclusion of Chinese labor from the United States. In California by 1907, opposition had focused upon the increasing Japanese population.

Pardee's second biennial message ended abruptly, a sharp departure from his previous communications. In all other messages he had voiced appreciation for help, advice, and cooperation. On this occasion he presented no such sentiment.

George Pardee then returned to Oakland to reopen his medical practice. For a time there was a movement to elect Pardee United States Senator, but this was unsuccessful. He spent the rest of his life serving on various boards and commissions relating to conservation and natural resources. From 1907 to 1911, he was a member of the National Conservation

Commission and in 1911, Governor Hiram Johnson appointed
Pardee chairman of the state conservation commission. In
1919, Governor William Stephens named him chairman of the
state forestry commission and Governor Clement Young reappointed him in 1928 to serve another two years.

In national politics, Pardee was a delegate to Republican
national conventions in 1900, 1904, 1912, and 1924. In 1912,
he bolted the party to follow Roosevelt and Johnson to the
Progressive party and was a delegate to that party's 1912 convention. He was named a presidential elector in 1912 and 1924.

His home community, Oakland, also pressed him into public
service. He was president of the board of directors of the East
Bay Municipal Utility District from 1914 to May, 1941. He
was for a time chairman of the laws and legislation committee
of the Oakland Chamber of Commerce. From 1927 to May,
1941, he was a member of the Oakland Port Commission. He
resigned from all positions in 1941 because of failing health.
In 1932, the University of California honored its 1879 graduate with an honorary Doctor of Laws degree. The same year, he
was named the "outstanding Oakland citizen."

Dr. George C. Pardee died September 1, 1941, at his Oakland
home at the age of eighty-four. By the time of his death, his
service as governor had been forgotten by all but a few. He was
then remembered for his efforts during the earthquake and fire
and for his constant public service in behalf of the citizens of
California and the East Bay.

In a very real sense Pardee laid the foundations in California
upon which the Progressive party built during Hiram Johnson's
administration. Pardee's term in the governor's chair marked
a definite break with the past. The railroad political machine
for the first time in many administrations was unable to influence the executive branch. While Pardee was not a vigorous
opponent of the machine, he was not its tool either. He was an
astute politician who, while not in command of a powerful
political force, was able, through mediation and by playing one
side against the other, to move his program through the legislature. State government took several positive steps under his
leadership.

BIBLIOGRAPHY

MANUSCRIPTS
Pardee, George, "Correspondence and Papers," (Bancroft Library).
————, "Record Executive Department Administration of George C. Pardee," (California State Archives).

CONTEMPORARY ACCOUNTS
Assembly Journal, 35th-37th Sess., 1903-1907.
Senate Journal, 35th-37th Sess., 1903-1907.
Republican Party. Alameda County Committee. *Governor Pardee and His Administration. A Record of Events for consideration by the voters of California* (1906).

SECONDARY SOURCES
Baker, J.E., *Past and Present of Alameda County.*
Mowry, G.E., *The California Progressives.*

NEWSPAPERS
Humboldt Standard (Eureka), April 21, 1906, Pardee reported to state about earthquake damage; Dec. 8, 1906, Pardee stated his position on Japanese question.
Sacramento Union, Feb. 18, 1906, described how Pardee spent his days in his office; June 2, 1906, reported Pardee's call for extra session to consider the recent earthquake disaster. Sept. 7, 1906, had editorial praising Pardee; Jan. 9, 1907, reported on second biennial message.
San Francisco Call, Jan. 8, 1903, reported on inauguration; Jan. 10, 1907, praised second biennial message.
San Francisco Chronicle, Aug. 28, 1902, sketched his career; Oct. 10, 1902, reported on major campaign tour; Jan. 8, 1903, discussed inauguration; Jan. 4, 1905, reported on first biennial message; Sept. 2-4, 1941, had his obituary and editorial.

THESES
Rose, Alice M., "Rise of California Insurgency, Origins of the League of Lincoln-Roosevelt Republican Clubs, 1900-1907" (Ph.D., Stanford University, 1942).
Staniford, Edward F., "Governor in the Middle—The Administration of George C. Pardee, Governor of California, 1903-1907" (Ph.D., University of California, 1955).

Calendar of Events

September 20, 1860   Gillett born at Viroqua, Wisconsin.
1881   Gillett admitted to Wisconsin bar.
1884   Gillett arrived in Eureka, California.
1888   Gillett elected Eureka City Attorney.
November 3, 1896   Gillett elected to Senate, representing Del Norte and Humboldt Counties.
November 4, 1902   Gillett elected a Republican member of the House of Representatives.
January 9, 1907   Gillett inaugurated Governor.
October 31, 1907   Gillett declared bank holiday to offset Panic of 1907.
1909   Legislature passed Direct Primary Law.
September, 1910   Legislature authorized funds for the Panama-Pacific International Exposition.
April 20, 1937   Gillett died in Oakland.

James N. Gillett

22ND GOVERNOR—REPUBLICAN
BORN: SEPTEMBER 20, 1860   DIED: APRIL 20, 1937
TERM OF OFFICE: JANUARY 9, 1907—JANUARY 3, 1911

JAMES NORRIS GILLETT WAS BORN in Viroqua, Wisconsin, on September 20, 1860. His family moved to Sparta, Wisconsin, in 1865, where he attended elementary school and entered high school. In December, 1878, he left school to study law. He was admitted to the Wisconsin bar in 1881. In the spring of 1883, Gillett started west, working for a time in a Bozeman, Montana, sawmill. After a stay of but a few months, he moved to Seattle. He then worked briefly at the nearby Port Gamble mill of Pope, Talbot and Company.

Early in 1884, Gillett moved to Eureka, California, working in the redwood lumber industry. After earning sufficient money, he opened a law practice, forming a lifelong partnership with Judge Fletcher A. Cutler.

In 1888, Gillett ran successfully for the office of Eureka City Attorney. He was re-elected twice to the office, serving until 1894. In 1896, as a Republican, he won election to the state Senate from Del Norte and Humboldt Counties. His most important assignment during this one term in the Senate was chairman of the judiciary committee. Following this, he returned to his Eureka law practice.

In 1886, James Gillett married Adelaide Pratt and had three children. His wife died in 1896. In 1898, Gillett married Elizabeth Erzaber of San Francisco and from this union a son was born.

In 1902, Gillett gained the Republican nomination for representative from the first Congressional district, which encompassed nineteen counties from Del Norte and Humboldt through

the northern tier of counties of California and down the backbone of the Sierra Nevada with Mariposa and Mono Counties
forming the southern boundary. Gillett, victorious in his bid
for election to the fifty-eighth Congress, was re-elected to the
fifty-ninth in 1904.

In the gubernatorial year of 1906, Gillett early announced
his desire for the Republican nomination. There has always
been considerable confusion about Gillett and his relationship
with the Southern Pacific machine. The question of Gillett's
owing his nomination to the machine has never been objectively
answered, nor have the reasons he desired to become governor
been made clear. His contemporaries, including George C. Perkins and George C. Pardee, believed that Gillett hoped to use the
governorship as a stepping stone to the United States Senate.

When the Republican delegates met in Santa Cruz in September, 1906, Gillett and Pardee were the two leaders for the nomination. It had long been apparent that the railroad machine did
not want Pardee under any circumstances and was therefore
willing to back Gillett; in fact, the machine bosses had decided
that Gillett was the only candidate who could beat Pardee. The
only obstacle to the machine plan lay in the San Francisco bloc
of votes, controlled by Boss Abe Ruef. As the convention un-
folded, delegates became aware that a deal had been made
between William Herrin of the Southern Pacific Political Bureau
and Boss Ruef, Gillett was nominated on the first ballot. Pardee exclaimed to a *San Francisco Call* reporter after the selection that, "We have met the enemy and we were his on the first
ballot. . . It is evident that the railroad machine and Ruef did
not want me to be Governor again, and as they were in control of
the convention what kick have I coming?" Pardee's views were
typical of those Republicans not committed to the machine. But
what was the opinion of these politicians? Was Gillett a tool of
the Southern Pacific machine? Apparently not—in fact, Pardee
while criticizing machine power commented:

> What do I think of Gillett? A good man, . . . Will he make a
> good Governor? Yes, he will if he follows his own personal in-
> clination and is, as I have tried to be, the Governor himself. No,
> I don't think he is a man who can be influenced to do the bidding
> of those who nominated him.

Pardee's views became the rationale of progressive Republicans who could not tolerate the Southern Pacific machine but

still wanted their party to win. They hoped that Gillett would not be a pawn of the machine and would make a good governor, but they still deplored the method by which he received the nomination.

In the years that followed, however, Gillett's acceptance of railroad support was held against him as it was in the campaign of 1906. However, until 1906, this acceptance by political aspirants had been neither unusual nor shocking. Most California politicians accepted and recognized railroad power. Pardee in 1902 had owed his nomination to it. Gillett, not adverse to railroad support, did not count on it alone. He received considerable support from some anti-machine people dissatisfied with Pardee.

Gillett was quite aware of antagonistic feelings within and outside his party over the operation of the 1906 convention. He constantly reiterated that:

> I have made no pledges, bargains or promises respecting State patronage. I am free to give to the people of this State an honest and businesslike administration of public affairs. It will be my aim to serve the people of California, irrespective of the party affiliation, to the best of my ability.

His major opponent, Democrat Theodore Bell of Napa, attacked the railroad's political power. His campaign centered on whether the people of California or the corporations were to control the destiny of the state.

Bell did not receive exactly the answer he had hoped for in November, and yet the people in electing Gillett gave him a lackluster plurality. Gillett ran far behind every other elective office on his ticket. His victory came largely because of a Democratic party split when William Randolph Hearst formed the Independence League and supported William H. Langdon for governor. Hearst's endorsement cost Bell the election. The final vote count was James N. Gillett, 125,887; Theodore Bell, 117,645; William H. Langdon, 45,008; and Socialist Austin Lewis, 16,036. Langdon's votes provided the margin of victory for Gillett who received 40 percent of the popular vote.

People who viewed Gillett during the 1906 campaign saw a successful rural lawyer and politician. This was the general impression he made. He met people gracefully and easily. He had a ready smile and a warm handshake. He spoke usually in low tones. He discussed personal topics in a light and vivacious manner but when he turned to public matters, he became oratorical and stilted in his speech. Gillett had a large physical frame over which his clothes fitted loosely. Gillett came to office under the dark shadow of machine politics. One of his close advisers, to offset this impression, stated that the incoming governor was anxious to prove that he was not controlled by the railroad and would do all possible to run his office as he saw fit.

Gillett's inaugural address was received with mixed feelings throughout the state. The message showed the kind of administration Gillett hoped to establish during the next four years. In many ways, he tried to emulate Pardee's stand of 1903. The speech, an essay in political tact, was delivered at a time when the two opposing forces in California government were in mortal combat for survival. Eventually, the new governor would have to commit himself to one of the two camps. The inaugural message, however, was a sincere effort to placate the factions.

He encouraged the coming of more railroads to California to foster economic growth. He added that railroad companies needed to be treated fairly and not held as the common enemy. However, he opposed excessive rates and discriminatory practices such as rebates, and maintained that the state must move against such practices. Californians could find whatever they wanted in his views on the railroad. Talking of river transportation, Gillett reflected some of his congressional interests as he called for improvement of the major rivers to provide free and inexpensive transportation.

In a brief discussion of capital and labor, he vaguely adhered to the standard conservative position. He asked both for laws of equality protecting individuals in their property and personal rights, and for laws protecting corporate interests so that labor and capital could develop together.

Gillett, restating an observation made in the summer of 1906, declared that one of the congressional milestones of that year had been the passage of the Pure Food and Drug Act. Noting that the federal law applied only to interstate commerce, the governor urgently requested a similar law for additional intrastate regulation. While public health was the major reason, Gillett pointed out that the fruit and wine industries would benefit from such a law. He gave as one example the current mislabeling of cottonseed oil as pure California olive oil.

Governor Gillett avoided taking a stand on one of the most controversial issues, the direct primary, telling the legislature:

There is much that can be said in favor of a direct primary law, and there are many good arguments against it. Of course, upon these you are to pass.

He then quoted the *San Francisco Call* as to why the direct primary was a necessity and recited only favorable reasons for such a law. He advised that a constitutional amendment was necessary to create the direct primary. He found the existing law governing conventions too cumbersome and felt a uniform system was needed.

Gillett agreed completely with Pardee and the revenue and tax commission that tax procedures were out-dated. He asked for adoption of the proposal eliminating the general property tax as a state tax and establishing a dual taxation program. Gillett also agreed with Pardee about the monopolization of state harbors. He demanded an immediate legislative investigation as well as a survey of needed improvements.

The last specific topic of his inaugural dealt with insurance companies and the difficulties experienced following the earthquake and fire. He suggested enactment of a code of insurance laws to protect the public from subtle technicalities and to make certain that sufficient funds were maintained for payment of claims. The legislature concurred and created such a code.

Gillett concluded with a plea for wise and economical allocation of funds to carry out varied services. He observed that:

A State's administration is what its public officials make it. If it is an honest and just one, it will meet with their commendation. The people expect of us an economic administration, that only just laws shall be passed, and that the needs of the State shall be judiciously provided for.

In this first official message Gillett attempted to steer the middle course. Opponents called him a "trimmer" in his efforts to stay clear of political controversies. Perhaps the most important indication that he did not intend to be an aggressive administrator was his failure even to mention the furious international conflict which had developed over San Francisco's segregation of Japanese school children. He explained a few days later that he had not mentioned the topic in order not to embarrass the national government in any treaty negotiations that might be underway. He indicated that he would not discuss the subject further until it was raised in the legislature. The lawmakers, not so reluctant, introduced several anti-Japanese bills.

Gillett's handling of patronage caused the anti-machine group early to lose confidence in him. In November, 1906, he had announced that he would not use his power to punish political or personal enemies. Yet, as January approached, the *San Francisco Call* reported that the chairman of the Republican state committee had prepared a black-list of Pardee men who had worked against Gillett's election and some of these would be turned out of office. Gillett still persisted in his November statement as late as January 15, 1907, and yet on the seventeenth, in a special message to the Senate he withdrew Pardee's appointments, claiming that he was following an established precedent and that he wished personally to investigate the qualifications of these people. In time he made his own appointments, several of which had been previously named by Pardee.

The 1907 legislative session began poorly for Gillett as the Republican majority in both houses voted for an unprecedented patronage increase. Before his inauguration Gillett urged the legislature to be moderate in its use of patronage, for increased demands on state funds would start his administration in a bad light. He made a second appeal after taking office but to no avail. He then protested publicly against the legislative raid on state funds and claimed "this army of employed job holders organized by the Legislature is a disgrace and I fully endorse the press denunciation of this unparalleled patronage grab." However, he made no effort to exert executive pressure on the lawmakers. He informed the newspapers that because of the nature of the bills presented to him he was powerless to veto them. He ignored, however, suggestions that he prepare a special message on the entire matter. The final test of his sincerity about patronage came when he approved a measure granting $25,000 for additional legislative employees. There were no riders or other issues in this measure. The intent was clear and Gillett gave his approval, indicating that he would not stand in the way of the legislature.

In 1907, reform measures were, for the most part, shunted to one side. However, a constitutional amendment establishing direct primary elections was passed. The voters approved this in 1908. One of Gillett's major inaugural proposals—pure food regulation—was enacted and a department of pure food and drugs was established. An anti-trust act was also passed defining trusts, providing regulations, and setting penalties for violations. As a result of the activities of this legislature, the Lincoln-Roosevelt League emerged with the goal of purging the Republican party of the railroad element.

The 1907 legislature, following the opinions of Pardee, reorganized the state prison system with a new board of directors. Included in the act was a schedule of credits allowing deduction of time from sentences for good conduct by prisoners. Also passed was a constitutional amendment increasing executive officers' salaries. The governor received $10,000 a year after the amendment received voter approval. One administrative change established the department of engineering to replace the department of highways, the board of public works, and the various state road commissions.

However, these gains were more than offset by the generally negative attitude of the legislature. Anti-railroad bills were squashed. Anti-racing and anti-gambling measures introduced by Assemblyman John Eshleman were defeated. Perhaps the most blatant affront was the forcing through both houses of a constitutional amendment removing the state capital from Sacramento to Berkeley. Gillett was caught off guard by the resolution, having refused to consider it seriously. When confronted with it, he quickly approved, announcing that he would leave the settlement of the matter to the people. Once again Gillett refused to take a positive stand as chief executive but tried to pass on his responsibility to someone else—in this case the California voter.

In the closing days of the session, he received adverse criticism when he approved an act revising the 1872 railroad corporation act. The new act, better known as the four track bill, granted the Southern Pacific control of the mountain passes, cutting off any incoming competition.

As the Japanese question continued to rage, Governor Gillett tried to remain neutral, acting as the middle man between President Roosevelt and the California legislature. Early in the session, an anti-Japanese resolution was introduced in the Assembly. On January 30, 1907, Gillett made his first official statement on this issue when he sent both houses a copy of a telegram received from the California congressional dele-

gation asking that all legislative action be deferred until after
the meeting of the San Francisco school board with Roosevelt.
The California lawmakers agreed. However, as the session
drew to a close, the state Senate passed an anti-Japanese school
bill which was the signal for a direct telegram from Roosevelt to
Gillett asking suspension of further action. The governor re-
layed this message to the Assembly observing it was important
that no action be taken on the Senate bill which might jeopardize
the federal government's recent immigration arrangements with
Japan. The Assembly agreed to a moratorium for the remainder of the session.

In 1907, Gillett vetoed several measures, most of which
were neither important issues nor new innovations in state
government. During its last hours, the Assembly had a surprise
visitor as Gillett appeared unannounced and unexpectedly on
the floor. After being invited to the Speaker's chair, he recited
the positive gains made and upbraided the press for its attacks
on the legislature. He believed that charges of "needless extravagance and wanton disregard of the people's interests"
were unfair since funds for state institutions had been increased
while at the same time the tax levy had been reduced. He concluded that "the legislature will go down in history as one of
the best that ever met in the state capitol." From this statement his critics concluded that Gillett was either an inept
politician, or another representative of the railroad machine,
or still trying to serve as a counterbalance, and in this latter instance wooing the legislature.

Although the press thoroughly denounced the 1907 legislators, Governor Gillett still retained his popularity. While there
was a growing uneasiness in some quarters, he was generally
regarded, according to the *Fresno Republican,* to be "in the
class with some of the good laws passed by this bad legislature.
He was the creditable product of a discreditable convention."

The 1907 financial panic, which had earlier hit New York
banking institutions, reached California in October. On October 31, Gillett declared a legal holiday to protect local banks
from excessive withdrawals and to avert a panic. The holidays
continued day by day during the first part of November with
the governor issuing reassuring statements about the satisfactory
condition of California banks.

The crisis did not quickly pass and some San Francisco

banks failed. On November 15, Gillett called a special session to consider possible remedies. His November 19th message to the legislature claimed that the panic had resulted from over-speculation, while in reality the nation and the state were indeed quite prosperous. The legislature had to help restore financial confidence and provide protection for California bank depositors. He proposed extending the due period of the first installment of taxes and the beginning of a long range revision of state banking regulations. He asked for the power to declare commercial legal holidays with the courts exempted in order to clear their calendars. He also suggested enactment of proposed San Francisco charter revisions. Finally he reported on the malfeasance of Andrew M. Wilson, railroad commissioner of the second district, who had publicly admitted taking bribes, but had refused to resign even after being indicted. The governor recommended that the legislature investigate, and, if convinced of Wilson's guilt, remove him from office. Wilson, under this pressure, resigned November 19, the first day of the session.

The extra session lasted from November 19 through the morning of the twenty-third. All that Gillett had requested was enacted except ratification of the San Francisco charter amendments. Consequently, Gillett called a second extra session to convene at 1:00 P.M., November 23, to consider these. They received approval that afternoon and the session ended.

The presidential election year of 1908 found Gillett engaged in many duties. In February he conferred with President Roosevelt and with congressional committees in the national capital. Apart from discussions about the Japanese question and California politics, the purpose of Gillett's trip was to appear before the congressional rivers and harbors committee. He hoped to convince that body of the need of federal money to deepen the Sacramento River. In May, Gillett had the pleasant duty of welcoming the "White Fleet" to California as it made its way around the world.

During October, Gillett campaigned actively for the Republican state and national ticket. However, during the campaign and after, he became more and more the target of those newspaper men who endorsed the stand of the Lincoln-Roosevelt League.

On January 4, 1909, the governor presented his first biennial message which mostly recounted the conduct of state affairs over the previous two years. Very little in the way of a legislative program was requested. He happily reported that the fiscal crisis of 1907 had ended and that the state treasury had a surplus after a reduction of the tax rate in 1908 to 40 cents per $100.

Gillett, in discussing his pardoning power, regretted that he had not found sufficient time to handle the backlog of clemency applications. He reported that the recently installed credit system for good behavior had helped instill good conduct among the prisoners. He believed that more assistance to the individual discharged prisoner was needed.

Governor Gillett held high hopes for the parole system as the answer to improved rehabilitation. State experiments in this area had been so gratifying that the governor had adopted two rules relating to paroles. First, any first-time offender with a two year record of good conduct was eligible for parole upon recommendation of the board of prison directors. Second, any person eligible for a pardon would not receive one until first paroled, unless proven innocent of the crime. He recommended that second termers also be given a chance for parole consideration. Gillett indicated that the governor should no longer be asked to consider pardons for inmates of county and city prisons, as this was an impossible burden, and he recommended that boards of supervisors or parole officers assume this duty.

One of his few suggestions for new legislation concerned the railroad. He advocated that California adopt the regulatory procedures of other states. He held that California authorities had been remiss in not enforcing existing constitutional provisos. Gillett felt that if the constitution had been followed no major complaints would have existed. Yet he noted that no law enforcing the constitutional sections had been enacted since 1880 when the railroad board had been created. He urged stronger legislation to end rebates and other discriminations, such as the free pass and free transportation.

State revenue and taxation received considerable attention. He lamented—as had Pardee—about the inequality of tax levies among the various counties due to differing assessment rates. He felt the recent defeat of the dual taxation plan, ending the general property tax as a state revenue, had been caused by a lack of understanding by the voters. He still believed that revision was what the people really wanted. His 1909 message concluded:

> There are many other matters of greater or less interest to the people of this State, but which on account of my physical condition I am unable to submit to you at this time. From time to time as occasion requires I will be pleased to submit to you those matters I deem to be of especial importance.

Some of the matters of "greater or less interest" were the direct primary procedures, anti-gambling measures, and the Japanese question. Gillett, meanwhile, had suffered from influenza and the constant threat of pneumonia. He was never in good health during his term. As in 1907, the 1909 legislature played a greater role in directing the course of state government than did Governor Gillett, although much of what he did recommend received favorable action.

Gillett, early in the 1909 session, found himself caught between President Roosevelt and the legislature regarding anti-Japanese measures. Roosevelt, on January 16, sent both a telegram and a letter explaining his views. Gillett conferred with legislative leaders and announced on January 20, that no discriminatory measures aimed at the Japanese would be passed. Yet two days later, an anti-Japanese school bill was introduced in the Assembly extending and strengthening the state law under which the San Francisco school board had acted in 1906. Gillett then in a special message reviewed the past and present of the situation and again pleaded that no embarrassing measures be passed. The Senate agreed to this request.

The Assembly, however, was not pacified. On February 4, it passed the anti-Japanese school bill which caused the sending of another presidential telegram to Gillett. He sent the telegram to the legislature and urged reconsideration or withdrawal of the bill. In this fight, he clashed with Grove Johnson, the iron-willed Sacramento Assemblyman, who gave no quarter and asked none. Neither Gillett nor Roosevelt were able to force Johnson to retreat from his position. Gillett next held a lengthy conference with Speaker Philip A. Stanton, who went onto the Assembly floor and spoke against the bill which led to shelving the measure.

Some significant measures were enacted during this session. A direct primary law, implementing the 1908 constitutional amendment, placed the nomination of elected local and state officials in the hands of the voters. The real importance of this act was in laying the groundwork for the 1910 election and the eventual triumph of the reform forces. A second reform measure, not called for by Gillett, was the anti-race track gambling bill, which received his signature, preventing bookmaking and pool-selling. Even though he signed the bill, reformers accused him of delaying nine days to allow the Emeryville track the opportunity to finish its season before the measure went into effect.

At Gillett's insistence, the attorney-general's office prepared a bill incorporating the gubernatorial view on railroad regulation but this measure was defeated. The weaker Wright bill, which passed, provided only a fine for violating existing law; the railroad commission was to set maximum rates, but not an absolute rate, and it could not interfere unless the charge of unfair discrimination was proven. A reciprocal demurrage bill designed to end discrimination against certain shippers also passed.

The legislature submitted to the voters a highway bond issue and a corporation taxation amendment. Both measures were accepted. Curiously, the taxation amendment was written in such a fashion that corporations were to be taxed on receipts for only December 31. Left out had been the words, "the year ending" on December 31. Gillett called a special session in October, 1910, to add these words. The legislature agreed to this but it then decreased the corporation tax rate and increased the bank tax rate.

By the end of the thirty-eighth session of 1909, speculation began as to whether Gillett would seek a second term. Publications of the Lincoln-Roosevelt League launched an attack against him although he had gained stature by rejecting several bad bills.

On January 29, 1910, Governor Gillett formally announced that he would not seek re-election. He based his decision upon the wishes of his family and his own desire to return to private law practice. He intimated that he could not afford the financial sacrifice of another four years. Both Pardee and Hiram Johnson made similar statements about their personal monetary losses.

Following the August, 1910, direct primary election, Gillett wired Hiram Johnson, congratulating him upon winning the

Republican nomination for governor. Gillett indicated he was ready to campaign for Johnson but no request came for his help.

Between the primary and November general election, Gillett called two special sessions. The first session, in September, 1910, authorized the state and the city of San Francisco to raise money for the Panama-Pacific International Exposition. The second session, in October, revised the faulty taxation amendment.

His last message to the 1911 lawmakers—his second biennial message—was largely confined to reporting on the condition of the state government. He listed the major accomplishments of his administration. He was proud of the highway act which he hoped would increase prosperity. He commented that this measure had been drawn with much care and it could well serve as the model for all future bond issues regarding highway construction. Other milestones which he reviewed with satisfaction were banking, pure food, railroad rate, reciprocal demurrage, employers' liability, anti-trust, anti-gambling, and direct primary laws, and the establishment of the department of engineering.

Gillett was pleased with his financial record. State services had continued to expand. For example, the Santa Barbara Normal School of Manual Arts and Home Economics and the state farm at Davis were completed. One of Gillett's hopes had been realized as the 1909 legislature had approved a California State Trades and Training School for orphans and other minor wards of the state to be located in Sonoma County. He listed many other improvements. San Jose State Normal School and Agnews State Hospital had been rebuilt, and at other institutions, new facilities had been added. All of this had been done with a constant yearly lowering of the state tax rate. The rate average for his four years was 39 cents, the lowest of the last five administrations. He reported a treasury balance of $2,-000,000, which exceeded Pardee's by one million, and was the largest to that date.

Stating that he would leave legislative recommendations to Johnson, he observed that some changes were needed. He advocated voluntary commitments to mental hospitals be allowed in addition to the usual court commitments. Satisfied with the parole system, he urged that no changes be made in the pro-

gram of interrelating pardons and paroles. He endeavored to
be careful in the use of his pardoning power. During his four
years he granted 159 pardons, fifty-one commutations, and
thirteen reprieves.

Gillett revealed a viewpoint that soon became obsolete with
reference to appointive commissions. He held that the governor
was responsible for the successful performance of public affairs
even though the execution of duty might be in the hands of a
commission. The only power that a governor had over a commission lay in appointment. But once appointed, the commission did fairly much as it pleased. As a result of his own
disappointment with the commission form of state administration, he had seen to it that the governor was directly responsible
for the state highway program.

After thanking the legislature for its service and cooperation,
his public career closed. He returned to his law practice, opening offices in San Francisco while establishing his residence in
Berkeley. In 1914, with the completion of the Northwestern
Pacific railroad to Eureka, Gillett was retained as counsel for
the road.

For a time he was a lobbyist for the Oil Industry Association
of California in Washington, D.C., trying in 1916 and 1917
to regain for private use land set aside by the Navy Department
as oil reserves. In 1934, Gillett started a law partnership with
his son in Oakland, which lasted until his death. He died on
April 21, 1937, at the age of seventy-six from heart disease.

Governor James N. Gillett was the last governor nominated
by the convention system and the last to be picked with the
Southern Pacific machine in control. He was a conservative
who accepted unblinkingly the place of the machine in politics
at the very time when the Progressives were moving in the
opposite direction. Gillett has had to bear, perhaps, too much
criticism for this. He was not an aggressive governor but
neither was he an unintelligent one. Gillett was one of the last
governors who accepted the nineteenth century view of complete separation of powers. His difficulty came when he tried,
as Pardee had done with success, the middle course. With the
rise of the Lincoln-Roosevelt League, and its opposition to the
machine and to all who owed their position to it, Gillett was
vilified. It has been long overlooked that while the legislature
was looting the till and hampering many progressive measures,

the state administration was carried on efficiently and economically. Various progressive measures were passed, and Gillett's role in some of these cannot be lightly dismissed. Perhaps his greatest monument was the creation of the state highway system which pioneered the vast transportation network of California. Also overlooked has been his contribution to the parole system. Gillett was a successful governor from the administrative aspect of his office. His major difficulty lay in the fact that he was unwilling to push a legislative program. This lack of vigor and his unwillingness to oppose the legislature caused him to lose favor with the California Progressives. After his term, it came to be expected that governors would be more vigorous in developing and leading legislative programs.

BIBLIOGRAPHY

MANUSCRIPTS
"City of Eureka Charter Book," (Eureka City Clerk's Office).
Johnson, Hiram, "Correspondence and Letters," (Bancroft Library).
Rowell, Chester, "Papers," (Bancroft Library).

CONTEMPORARY ACCOUNTS
Assembly Journal, 37th-39th Sess., 1907-11.
Senate Journal, 33rd, 37th-39th Sess., 1899, 1907-11.
Congressional Directory, 59th Cong., 1st Sess., 1906.
Gillett, James N., "Autobiography" in Richards, Randolph A., ed., *History of Monroe County, Wisconsin* (1912).
Morison, Elting E., ed., *Letters of Theodore Roosevelt* (8 vols., Cambridge, 1954).

SECONDARY SOURCES
Bailey, Thomas A., *Theodore Roosevelt and the Japanese-American Crises* (Stanford University Press, 1934).
Bates, Joseph C., ed., *History of the Bench and Bar of California* (San Francisco, 1912).
Davis' *Commercial Encyclopedia of the Pacific Southwest* (Berkeley, 1914).
Hichborn, Franklin, *Story of the Session of the California Legislature of 1909* (San Francisco, 1909).
Hudson, J. James, "The McCloud River Affair of 1909," *California Historical Society Quarterly,* XXXV (1956), 29-35.
Mowry, George, *The California Progressives.*
Plehn, Carl C., "Tax Reform in California," *Review of Reviews,* XLIII (1911), 85-87.
Wolfe, Wellington C., ed., *Men of California* (San Francisco, 1925).

NEWSPAPERS

Humboldt Standard, July 16, 1906, has sketch of Gillett's life.

Sacramento Union, Sept. 3, 1906, has sketch of his life; Sept. 8, 1906, has editorial on his candidacy; Nov. 4, 1906, endorses Gillett for governor; Jan. 10, 1907, describes inauguration.

San Diego Union, Jan. 10, 1907, reports favorably on first message.

San Francisco Call, Nov. 4, 1906, endorses Gillett; Jan. 11, 1907, reports Gillett's stand on direct primary; Dec. 12, 1907, commends Gillett's role in bank crisis; Aug. 7, 1908, anti-gambling forces disgusted with Gillett's vacillation; Jan. 8, 1909, reports favorably on second message; Jan. 30, 1910, reports that Gillett would not seek second term.

San Francisco Chronicle, Jan. 11, 1907, has favorable editorial on first message; Jan. 4, 1911, praises Gillett's administration; April 21, 1937, has his obituary.

San Francisco News, April 21, 1937, has his obituary.

THESIS

Rose, Alice, "Rise of California Insurgency. . ."

OTHER SOURCES

The California Weekly, I (1909). This was a Progressive publication that attacked the Gillett administration.

The Mansion and Grounds of Leland Stanford, Governor of California, Sacramento. The Stanford Mansion, located at Eighth and N streets, now called the Stanford-Lathrop memorial home, was erected in 1860. It was occupied by Governor Stanford as his home 1861-1874. It was given by Mrs. Stanford to the Catholic Diocese of Sacramento in 1900, and was used for many years as an orphanage. It has been occupied and cared for by the Sisters of Social Service since 1936. It is a State Historical Landmark.

Calendar of Events

September 2, 1866	Johnson born at Sacramento.
1888	Johnson admitted to California bar.
1905	Johnson joined San Francisco District Attorney's staff
1906	Johnson participated in the prosecution of the San Francisco graft trials.
August 16, 1910	California held its first direct primary election.
January 4, 1911	Johnson inaugurated Governor.
August 7, 1912	Johnson nominated by Progressive Party for Vice President.
January 6, 1913	Johnson became first Governor in the United States to present an executive budget to the legislature.
1913	Cross-filing law passed.
May 19, 1913	Johnson signed Webb alien land bill.
November 3, 1914	Johnson, running as a Progressive, became second California Governor to be re-elected.
November 7, 1916	Johnson elected United States Senator.
March 15, 1917	Johnson resigned as Governor to assume Senate seat.
November 7, 1922	Johnson re-elected United States Senator, the first of four times.
August 27, 1940	Johnson won re-election in the direct primaries, receiving nominations of both Democrats and Republicans.
August 6, 1945	Johnson died at Bethesda Naval Hospital, Maryland.

Hiram W. Johnson

23RD GOVERNOR—REPUBLICAN—PROGRESSIVE
BORN: SEPTEMBER 2, 1866   DIED: AUGUST 6, 1945
TERM OF OFFICE: JANUARY 4, 1911—MARCH 15, 1917

HIRAM JOHNSON'S ELECTION IN 1910 marked the beginning of a new era in California politics. With his victory at the polls, Johnson launched the most successful career in public office in the history of the state, serving as governor and United States Senator for a total of thirty-four years. During his tenure as governor, he broke what had almost become a California tradition as he became the first governor since John Bigler in 1853 to be re-elected and the first four-year term governor to accomplish this.

Hiram Johnson, the third native son to serve as governor, was born in Sacramento, September 2, 1866. He was educated in the Sacramento schools, graduating from high school at sixteen. He worked in his father's law office for one year as a stenographer. In 1884, he entered the University of California, but left in his junior year to marry Minnie L. McNeal of Sacramento. Two sons were born to the Johnsons. In 1886 and 1887, he worked as a shorthand reporter and studied law in his father's office. Admitted to the California bar in 1888, he joined in partnership with his father, Grove L. and his brother, Albert, in the capital. This venture ended in 1896, as the sons broke with their father over divergent political views and his ties with the Southern Pacific Company. This feud flared openly in 1900, as Hiram Johnson successfully backed George H. Clark as a reform candidate for mayor of Sacramento against the regular Republican machine which had re-elected Grove Johnson to the Assembly. For his support, Hiram Johnson was appointed corporation counsel for the city at $75.00 a month.

In 1902, the two brothers moved to San Francisco to open a law office. By 1904, Hiram Johnson was practicing on his own and by 1905 had become associated with William H. Langdon, San Francisco's district attorney. In 1906, he became involved in the famous city graft trials. Johnson moved into the public eye after Francis J. Heney, the prosecuting attorney from the district attorney's office, was shot in open court. Johnson agreed to take over the case and won, leading to the conviction of Boss Abe Ruef.

Johnson was sought out by the Lincoln-Roosevelt League to be its reform candidate for governor in 1910. Refusing at first, Johnson reluctantly accepted in February, stating:

> It seems to be my turn to make the sacrifice and I am going to make it. For two months the utmost pressure had been brought to bear on me. I had steadfastly refused to become a candidate, but it was placed before me in such a fashion that I was forced to fail in my duty or accept. So I am going ahead making the fight as a progressive Republican on the Roosevelt lines.
>
> I am going to make this fight in an endeavor to return the government of California to the people and take it away from the political bureau of the Southern Pacific railway company. If nothing else is accomplished, we can teach the people the lesson talked by our last president and that is being talked today to the people of the United States by La Follette.

The gubernatorial campaign of 1910 must rank with the election of 1849 and 1878 as one of the significant state elections. In 1910, the direct primary was used for the first time and the power of the Southern Pacific Political Bureau was broken. Additionally, Johnson's election meant that California joined the national Progressive movement.

In the Republican primary, which was aimed at securing the nomination directly from the voters instead of convention delegates, Johnson campaigned on the slogan, "Kick Herrin and the Southern Pacific out of the government of the state." Johnson paid scant attention to progressive issues but confined himself to attacking the railroad. To avoid the appearance of the slightest obligation to the Southern Pacific, Johnson toured California in a bright red Locomobile. In August, Johnson and other candidates of the Lincoln-Roosevelt League virtually swept the Republican nominations. The Republicans drafted a progressive platform for the November general election. Johnson chose not to follow the platform, but again hammered against the political power of the Southern Pacific, an issue with proven high emotional appeal. In the general election, Johnson was elected with a plurality, receiving 177,191 votes to Democratic Theodore Bell's 154,835. The Socialist and Prohibition tickets together polled 53,626.

Johnson's contemporaries during the campaign and his occupancy of the gubernatorial chair found him a vigorous fighter who did not understand the use of finesse but who preferred head-on confrontation. Coupled with this aggressiveness was a steadfastness to purpose and a narrowness of vision in understanding problems. Johnson adopted a stand, fought for it, and maintained it, regardless of consequences or subsequent facts that should have changed his position.

Physically, Johnson was short and stocky. He had a round florid face that portrayed his pugnacious character. Publicly, he appeared determined and tense as he approached audiences to orate his views. In private he was much more relaxed, pleasant, and informal. He has been described as a basically insecure person who tended to look upon life pessimistically. Some people found him a difficult taskmaster since he was also supremely egotistical and extremely ambitious. As early as 1910, for example, Johnson had ambitions to become United States Senator and had been assured that the governorship was but a stepping stone to the office he really wanted.

As with all people, Johnson had flaws in his personality and yet he had the necessary characteristics which made him one of the great governors of California. While he drove himself and his followers without restraint, and while he was unpredictable in his relationships with people, his administration changed the character and the structure of California life and politics. Some of his personal liabilities became at times political assets. The fact that he was the determined fighter gave the Progressives the leader who would work long and willingly for their program. While Johnson did not understand all of the nuances of the movement, he proved the visible leader whom the public understood. In a brief period of time, Johnson came to believe in his own mind that he was the leader of righteousness and any who were opposed to Progressive ideals represented forces of evil. He subsequently attacked vigorously and bitterly those political opponents who stood in the way.

As governor, Johnson stood apart from the usual type of man

who had occupied that office. His desire of public service for the people was communicated to and understood by the voters. He was a natural orator who easily found the temper of his audience and then played upon its emotions. Above all, he was courageous in his stands and incorruptible in performing his duties. Johnson represented to Californians a new high in public morality. He kept this deserved reputation although it placed his personal finances in jeopardy.

In January, 1918, Johnson had arranged for an Eastern lecture tour the following fall to recoup the financial losses he had suffered while governor in order that he would have sufficient capital to undertake his new position as Senator in December, 1918. In March, 1918, in the face of his personal hardship, he demonstrated his integrity when he returned a $5,000 unsolicited check to Harris Weinstock, saying:

> I chose the particular path in life in which I now find myself. I chose it when an earning capacity had opened for me that would have led, undoubtedly, to financial ease and comfort. I made my choice, knowing the difficulties that lay in my way and that there were many things I could not hope for, if I continued in political activity. Having made my choice, I feel that I must not only take the advantages, but without repining, must accept the disadvantages.
>
> I am returning to you, therefore, your $5,000 check. Your letter and your offer have a value for me that could never be measured by any amount financially, however great.

To the public, Johnson epitomized the ideal politician. He was the man who restored their government to them. The faith of the voters in Hiram Johnson lasted through two gubernatorial elections and five senatorial contests.

On January 4, 1911, Hiram Johnson took his oath of office and delivered his first inaugural address. At once he tackled the problem of government by privilege and special interests. He claimed that "successful and permanent government must rest primarily on recognition of men and the absolute sovereignty of the people. Upon these principles is based the superstructure of our republic." He said that the state government would be made responsible to the will of the people. As the years passed, one criticism which developed was that Johnson and the Progressives had built a new political machine in California which assumed for itself the role of deciding what was the will of the people.

Johnson's address, restating much of the 1910 Republican

platform, called for the initiative, referendum, and recall. He urged that civil service and the merit system be installed to end governmental control by the special interests. He tackled the railroad rates issue as he, like Gillett and Pardee, asked that the railroad commission be strengthened to control the Southern Pacific properly. He also asked that the direct primary law be amended to allow for voter preference in the choice of United States Senator. He requested that most state elective officers become gubernatorial appointments along the lines of the president's cabinet.

Other Progressive reforms were advanced. One called for county home rule, removing legislative control from internal county affairs. Johnson also demanded extension of national conservation practices as outlined by Gifford Pinchot, particularly with reference to water resources. He recommended workmen's compensation in the form of an employer's liability law. In the field of penology, he felt there should be a reformatory for first offenders.

At the end of the 1911 session, which was controlled by reformers, Johnson sent a congratulatory message claiming that:

> Never before has such wondrous work been so well performed by any legislature; never has been evinced in the history of our State such a steadfastness of purpose and such fidelity to promises made to the people. Not a single promise is to-night left unfilled.

Johnson noted twenty-one specific areas of importance enacted in 1911. In addition to his program, stated in his inaugural, he had successfully led in gaining state control of public utilities under the direction of the railroad commission. He had also been instrumental in establishing the board of control which abolished the state board of examiners and paved the way for administrative budgets.

During the session, Johnson differed with some Progressives on the issue of an eight hour day for women. He approved this measure over the objection of the Lincoln-Roosevelt League. A constitutional amendment was also passed giving women the right to vote although Johnson did not mention this in his review of significant legislative items. The legislature rejected the idea of a gubernatorial appointive cabinet. However, it did endorse the principle of executive administration through state commissions and the groundwork was laid for creation of a large number of these agencies during Johnson's term. The

1911 legislative session, with an energetic governor in charge, breathed new life into California's state government and it moved a long way toward accomplishing the goals of responsive and responsible government.

Governor Johnson called the legislature into two special sessions in November and December, 1911. The purpose of the first extra session was to recommend immediate passage of twenty-six matters, most of which involved implementation of recently approved constitutional amendments, such as granting women's suffrage, establishing the railroad commission's regulation of public utilities, and providing free state textbooks. On December 24, the second extra session enacted supplementary horticultural regulations to protect California agriculture.

During 1911 and 1912, Hiram Johnson, who had become a friend of Theodore Roosevelt, was one of those who urged him to run for the Republican presidential nomination on the Progressive principles in which they both believed. Johnson was successful in having a California Roosevelt slate nominated, which he led to the convention. Behind the scenes in California a strong movement developed to have Johnson nominated for vice president. When the Taft forces emerged victorious, Johnson headed the California movement to gain the nomination of the Progressive party for Roosevelt, and reluctantly agreed to be the vice presidential nominee. Although the Bull Moose ticket failed nationally, it did carry California but by only an 174 vote margin. Roosevelt received 283,610 votes to Woodrow Wilson's 283,436. Others garnered 110,898 votes. Johnson returned to the governor's mansion angered by the political attacks made upon him and fearful that Progressive ideals were in danger.

By 1913, the governor's well-ordered political machine, based upon allegiance to him, was carrying out its dedication to the principle of a people's government. Johnson sent to California's first bifurcated legislature his first biennial message on January 6, 1913. Compared to his several messages of 1911, this 1913 message did not contain such sweeping recommendations. Instead he confined himself largely to a review of accomplishments and suggested how the job of reform should be completed. Two major proposals involved state finance and centralization of supervision of administration in the state agencies.

After a 1910 amendment separated state and local tax sources, the state government had gone through a period of uncertain revenue which dictated rigid state economy. Johnson felt in 1913, that the existing tax structure would not yield sufficient revenue during the next biennium. The flaw in the present system was that corporations had not been required to pay their tax share and he urged a raising of their rates. In a later special message he again called specific attention to this matter. The 1913 legislature did make some slight raises, but failed to solve the problem.

In discussing the reorganization of state government, Johnson enthusiastically praised the success of the board of control. To guarantee efficient gubernatorial administrations, he averred, two regulatory agencies were needed: one, the board of control to supervise fiscal matters, and the other, a centralized body with equal power to supervise administrative matters. This plan was not adopted by the legislature.

Johnson's leadership in the Progressive movement reached its apex during 1913, when the remaining objectives of the reformers were enacted. Among those measures enacted in 1913, recommended in his biennial message and in his 1911 inaugural message were a blue sky law to protect investors, a conservation law to regulate state water power, a comprehensive workmen's compensation act, the establishment of the merit system and the state civil service commission, and acts regarding European immigration coming by way of the Panama Canal and establishing an immigration commission. This commission was charged with aiding European immigration, but nothing was done for Asiatics. A red light abatement act was also passed. A host of other measures were passed such as standard weights and measures, minimum hours for women and protection of labor through the creation of the industrial accident commission and the industrial welfare board.

Johnson, in 1913, revealed his strong adherence to the commission form of government, remarking that he had steadfastly refused to override commission decisions for this became a mere substitution of his views and judgment for the commission's thorough investigations.

Governor Johnson became in 1913 the first state executive in history of the United States to prepare and submit a unified budget. Under the board of control's direction, all depart-

mental requests were assembled and studied, and then Johnson
sent his recommended appropriations to the legislature. Prior
to this, the governor had merely passed on the requests of the
separate state agencies. Johnson's and Stephens' administrations continued this procedure which officially became part of
the governor's responsibility by a 1922 constitutional amendment.

One of the most controversial aspects of the Progressive sessions of 1911 and 1913 was anti-Japanese legislation. Governor
Johnson showed in 1911 that he was willing, as had Gillett, to
cooperate with the national Republican administration to avoid
unfavorable legislation aimed at the Japanese. The governor
worked closely with Taft's Secretary of State, Philander C.
Knox, keeping him alerted as bills were introduced on the
subject. Johnson, responding to Knox's requests, sidetracked all
anti-Japanese legislation by assuring the lawmakers that the
pending treaty provided for restriction of immigration by the
Japanese. However, Johnson, foreshadowing events of 1913,
informed the State Department that California had the right to
legislate as it saw fit in the matter of alien ownership of lands.

In the opening days of the 1913 session, both parties favored
passage of an anti-Asiatic land bill. Bills were introduced in
both houses to exclude all aliens from owning land. After the
thirty day recess, demanded by the bifurcated session, both
houses proceeded to pass bills of exclusion against aliens ineligible to citizenship. During the recess Woodrow Wilson
succeeded Taft as president. Wilson, a Democrat, applied pressure to California Democrats, some of whom now began to oppose anti-alien legislation.

As the situation built to a climax with Johnson's attitude
still not clear, even to his close associates, President Wilson on
April 23, telegraphed both houses and Governor Johnson, asking
permission to send his Secretary of State, William Jennings
Bryan to California to counsel with California officials. Johnson invited Bryan to be his guest, noting that he did not know
what the outcome would be in this strictly state affair. The
governor protested that California was not discriminating
against the Japanese in this instance, for the United States had
already declared the Japanese ineligible for citizenship. Bryan
arrived on April 28, and conferred in closed session with the
lawmakers and the governor. After Bryan had presented the

views of the Wilson administration, Johnson claimed the question at issue was not whether Japan was offended, but whether she was justly offended.

Johnson had privately made up his mind at the time of Wilson's request. While Bryan was on his way to California, Johnson conferred with Attorney General Ulysses S. Webb and Francis Heney. These two men, at the governor's behest, drafted a new bill, known as the Webb bill, which stated that only aliens eligible for citizenship could own or lease for three years agricultural lands in California. Even while Bryan was conferring in Sacramento, this bill started through the legislative mill and passed just as Bryan—having failed in his mission —left the capital. When the bill reached Johnson's desk, Bryan telegraphed him urging use of the veto power. Johnson replied that he could not go against the wishes of the elected representatives who had overwhelmingly endorsed the bill and revealed that he was in complete accord with the exclusion movement. The anti-Japanese forces had victoriously climaxed a thirteen year campaign.

While the Progressives had been far from enlightened in their treatment of the Japanese, the internal political structure of government had been drastically reformed. One significant measure, which the Progressives believed to be the heart and soul of good government for California, was the cross-filing procedure which permitted a candidate of one political party to seek the nomination of other parties in the direct primaries. While in later years, this device proved a source of confusion to the voter and a song of lament for the Democratic party, the intent was clear to the Progressives. Cross-filing allowed nomination of the best man regardless of party affiliation and negated the power of political machines. Progressive reasoning demanded that the voice of the people be allowed freedom of selection at the polls. Nonpartisanship, the Progressive goal, had been made available to California voters at the expense of the two major parties.

By 1914, the Progressives in California were faced with the question of what direction they would take in the future. Internal dissensions had developed within the ranks and their dynamic leader had come to believe that he was now the guiding spirit of the California reform program as he wrote in 1914, to Theodore Roosevelt, "I find that we have to be more watchful of the misdirected zeal from within our ranks than of the mendacious bludgeoning from without." In the state elections of 1914, Johnson faced the question of running for a second term or seeking the office of United States Senator. For the first time in California's history, the people themselves, rather than the California legislature, would directly elect a senator. In January, 1914, Johnson indicated an interest in running for the Senate, but he believed that the rank-and-file of the people wanted him to run for re-election. Francis Heney informed the Progressives that he wanted to run for public office, either for governor or for senator, but he did not wish to oppose Johnson. When he asked the governor for a decision, Johnson procrastinated and finally Heney announced his candidacy for the Progressive nomination for senator. This greatly angered Johnson who tried unsuccessfully to build opposition against Heney.

In the primary campaign, while others took advantage of the recent cross-filing provisions in California's election laws, the governor filed only on the Progressive ticket. He was unopposed. In the primary election, Johnson's total Progressive vote fell far short of his major contender, Republican nominee John D. Fredericks. Even after receiving write-in votes on the Republican, Democratic, and Prohibition tickets, Johnson seemed in serious trouble at the coming general election. In both the primary and the general election campaigns, Johnson stood on his past record implying the need to protect past gains. In contrast to other Progressive candidates, he did not advocate any new programs but repeatedly exclaimed about past accomplishments. A veteran campaigner, he slashed at his opposition and emerged victorious in November. Johnson received 460,495 votes, just missing a majority of all votes cast. His nearest opponent, Fredericks, polled 271,990 votes. Of considerable significance, indicating voter approval of the Progressive reforms, was Johnson's increase of votes over his 1910 success when he received 177,191 votes. He was the only Progressive elected governor in the 1914 national elections.

One important sidelight of the 1914 election was the open split which developed in the Progressive camp as Heney charged that Johnson's lack of support in his senatorial fight caused him to lose. This breach was to have repercussions in the 1916 election.

On January 5, 1914, Governor Johnson took his oath of

office beginning his unprecedented second four-year term. He reviewed the benefits accomplished for the citizens. He held that for the next four years the "first duty is to perfect, preserve, and perpetuate the various measures which so recently have had such emphatic sanction. . . ." Johnson offered no definite program, but touched upon rural credits, full employment, irrigation projects, and state nonpartisan election of officials. He called, in conclusion, for the "highest and wisest statesmanship" to maintain Progressive objectives.

The 1915 legislature was unique in comparison with previous sessions, for five political parties, Republican, Democratic, Progressive, Prohibitionist, and Socialist were represented. This fact made the fate of any positive program questionable. Under these circumstances, Johnson on January 6, submitted his second biennial message. The bulk of the message reviewed accomplishments of the various state agencies in implementing the hopes and dreams of the Progressives. As for the immediate future, Johnson offered a five point program.

He first expressed grave and continued concern over the fiscal well-being of the state. The recent abolition of the poll tax by the voters, coupled with the loss of revenue from the temporary invalidation of the corporation license tax, meant a serious loss of funds. At the same time, the voters had endorsed further expansion of state services. Consequently, the governor demanded rigid economy in state affairs and postponement of new services in order to provide funds for existing governmental functions. He reviewed recent attempts at increasing public corporation taxes, still maintaining that they were not paying their proportionate share in comparison to individual property owners. However, he only asked for legislative investigation on how to equalize the tax burden. The legislature in considering this made as little progress as had the 1913 session in solving California's financial matters. Acts of 1915 restored the corporation license tax and raised slightly inheritance taxes.

A second part of Johnson's 1915 program, promised in the 1914 campaign, requested a nonpartisan measure to have all state officers elected without party designation. The purpose, claimed the governor, was to allow the electorate to decide upon the best man for state office, regardless of political affiliation. He based his faith upon the success of city governments whose officials were elected on a nonpartisan basis. The legislature approved his request. Johnson next related that unemployment had increased greatly in the state and he offered as a temporary solution the establishment of free labor exchanges—a state employment service. This proposal was rejected.

Governor Johnson, the advocate of direct legislation, had become appalled, as had many others of the Lincoln-Roosevelt League, to discover that this political technique was a two-edged sword. While it was possible for the reformers to sponsor their propositions by the initiative and the referendum and to use the recall, so could their opposition. Johnson noted that certain abuses of direct legislation had developed and "to permit their use through fraud and forgery is to pollute at its very source our government." He called for an end to these and the legislature enacted measures making such activities criminal and prescribed proper punishment.

He announced finally that he wanted the 1915 legislature to study all aspects of a rural credits program to enable the farmer to become more productive. He did not call for specific legislation but called only for a special committee to make a thorough investigation.

One of the major bills to receive a gubernatorial veto during the 1915 session was the jitney bus bill. Street car lines had suffered a loss of business as gasoline driven buses came into use. The state had suffered a loss of tax revenue as the street cars lost customers and a drive was started to make up the deficit by taxing the jitneys. Franklin Hichborn, in writing of the 1915 session, held that the real objective was to tax the jitneys out of existence. A tax measure passed both houses and Johnson held a hearing on the bill, and after listening to both sides, vetoed it. Following the recess, a second bill to regulate the methods of securing bus franchises was introduced to limit competition. It was also vetoed by the governor.

Even while the legislature was wending its way through the 1915 session, Governor Johnson had set his sights on the forthcoming senatorial election for George Perkins' seat. In the 1916 direct primary, he filed on both the Progressive and the Republican ballots. Although the conservative wing of the California Republican party waged a bitter campaign against the "deserter," Johnson won both nominations and was successful in the famous 1916 general election which saw his election

by a margin of about 300,000 votes while Charles Evans Hughes
lost California to Wilson by some 4,000 votes in the presidential race.

In April, 1916, when Lieutenant Governor John Eshleman
died, Johnson was placed in the position of naming his successor as governor if he won his bid for the Senate. In July, he
appointed Congressman William D. Stephens. After Johnson's
November triumph, a disagreement started as to when Johnson
would resign as governor. What at first was merely a coldness
of attitude between Johnson and Stephens developed into a
heated controversy with neither man speaking to each other.
Stephens' supporters pressured Johnson to resign immediately
after the election but he refused. The situation became more
heated in December when Stephens went to San Francisco to
confer with Johnson on appointments and to reassure the governor that Progressive policies would continue. Stephens then
asked help in writing what he thought was to be his first message to the 1917 legislature in January. At this juncture Johnson informed him that there was no need, for he intended to stay
in office at least during the first half of the session. Hard words
passed between the two and cordiality ended.

On January 8, 1917, Hiram Johnson delivered his fourth
and final biennial message to the legislature. Knowing that it
was his last, he reviewed for the most part his six years in office.
He listed advances made in reforming the state government. He
pointed with pride to the accomplishments of various state
agencies. He noted two new developments since 1915—the use
of convicts for road construction which had given these men a
sense of doing good work while providing roads for the state,
and the development of the state market director's office which
supervised selling of California farm products.

Hiram Johnson used his pardoning power with more reserve
than his predecessor, James Gillett, as from 1911 through 1916,
Johnson granted 135 pardons, sixty-four commutations of sentences, and twenty-seven reprieves.

In March, 1917, President Wilson called Congress into
special session and Johnson was forced reluctantly, on March
12, to announce his resignation as governor, effective March
15. During this period, Johnson and Stephens did not communicate with each other, even through intermediaries. On the fifteenth, Johnson addressed both houses of the legislature again,

listing past victories. While claiming his awareness of the
honor of becoming a senator from California, he stated that
leaving the office of governor was a task which was "the most
difficult of all my life." Johnson paid special tribute to John
Eshleman. He then entrusted the burden of the office to
Stephens, without mentioning the incoming governor's name.
Thus ended Johnson's gubernatorial career. California's great
Progressive march seemed at an end. At least so it seemed to
Johnson who had come to view Stephens—also an ardent Progressive—as an opponent in the developing power struggle.
At a much earlier date, Johnson had come to believe that only
he alone could successfully carry on the Progressive program
from the governor's chair. Largely because of Johnson's at-
titude, and following his resignation, the diverse elements
within the movement fell to fighting each other. Johnson, in
Washington, showed no interest in these bickerings.

United States Senator Johnson in 1917 started a new political
career which lasted the remainder of his life. He was re-
elected four times, serving in all twenty-eight years. During his
years in the Senate, he became one of the major leaders of
isolationism. In passing, it should be noted that in the 1920's
he played a major role in federal immigration legislation which
led to the exclusion of the Japanese from the United States. He
was also an important leader in solving the Colorado River
controversy.

On August 6, 1945, Hiram Johnson died at the Bethesda
Naval Hospital, Maryland, at the age of seventy-nine. He must
rank as one of California's greatest governors. At a time when
California politics were controlled by corporate interests, Johnson had been the perfect choice to carry to success the program
of the Lincoln-Roosevelt League. During Johnson's first term,
his political camp won from Theodore Roosevelt the praise that
there had been enacted in 1911 in California "the most comprehensive legislation ever passed at a single session of any American legislature." Johnson ably led his party in carrying reform
views into law.

Johnson was the first of the California governors who assumed
responsibility of leading a legislative program. Under his administration, state government was reorganized and revitalized.
Out of these years emerged a twentieth century administration
geared to handle contemporary problems.

BIBLIOGRAPHY
MANUSCRIPTS
Johnson, Hiram, "Correspondence and Letters," (Bancroft Library).
————, "Biography and Excerpts from his Speeches and Statements," (Bancroft Library).
Rowell, Chester, "Papers," (Bancroft Library).

CONTEMPORARY ACCOUNTS
Assembly Journal, 39th-42nd Sess., 1911-17.
Senate Journal, 39th-42nd Sess., 1911-17.
California Blue Book, 1911 & 1913-15.
California Progressive Campaign Book for 1914: Three Years of Progressive Administration in California Under Governor Hiram Johnson (San Francisco, 1914).
Creel, George, "What About Hiram Johnson of California," *Everybody's*, XXXI (1914), 448-60.
Holman, A., "The Case of Hiram Johnson: Guilty," *North American Review*, CCV (1917), 186-202.

SECONDARY SOURCES
Daniels, Roger, *The Politics of Prejudice: The Anti-Japanese Movement in California and the Struggle for Japanese Exclusion* (Berkeley, 1962).
Hichborn, Franklin, "The Party, the Machine and the Votes," *California Historical Society Quarterly*, XXXVIII (1959), 345-57 & XXXIX (1960), 19-34.
————, *Story of the Session of the California Legislature, 1911* (San Francisco, 1911).
————, *Story of the Session . . . 1913* (San Francisco, 1913).
————, *Story of the Session . . . 1915* (San Francisco, 1916).
Lincoln, A., "My dear Governor," *CHSQ*, XXXVIII (1959), 229-47.
McKee, Irving, "The Background and Early Career of Hiram Warren Johnson, 1866-1910," *PHR*, XIX (1960), 17-30.
Mowry, George, *The California Progressives*.
Storke, Thomas, *California Editor*.

NEWSPAPERS
Sacramento Union, Jan. 6, 1915, has account of second inaugural; Jan. 9, 1917, has account of last biennial message; March 15, 1917, presents estimate of Johnson as governor.
San Francisco Call, Nov. 9, 1910, reports Johnson's election; Jan. 4, 1911, describes his inauguration.
San Francisco Chronicle, Jan. 5, 1911, reports his inauguration; Aug. 7, 1945, has Johnson's obituary and an eulogy by Chester Rowell.

THESES
Knoche, Viola M., "The Gubernatorial Nomination of Hiram W. Johnson, 1910" (M.A., Stanford University, 1947).
Milias, George W., "Hiram Johnson's Campaign for the Governorship of California in 1910" (M.A., Stanford University, 1944).

Calendar of Events

December 26, 1859	Stephens born at Eaton, Ohio.
1887	Stephens arrived in Los Angeles.
1907	Stephens elected President of Los Angeles Chamber of Commerce and served also on the Board of Education.
March 16, 1909	Stephens elected interim Mayor of Los Angeles by city council.
November 8, 1910	Stephens elected a Republican member of the House of Representatives.
November 3, 1914	Stephens elected to third term in the House of Representatives on Progressive ticket.
July 18, 1916	Stephens appointed Lieutenant Governor by Governor Johnson.
March 15, 1917	Stephens inaugurated Governor to complete Johnson's term.
December 17, 1917	Governor's mansion bombed.
November 5, 1918	Stephens elected Governor, defeating Theodore Bell, Independent.
November 28, 1918	Stephens commuted Tom Mooney's sentence from death to life imprisonment.
January 7, 1919	Stephens inaugurated Governor.
March 20, 1919	Stephens submitted state administrative reorganizational plan.
August 29, 1922	Stephens lost Republican nomination for governor to Friend Richardson.
April 24, 1944	Stephens died in Los Angeles.

William D. Stephens

24TH GOVERNOR—REPUBLICAN
BORN: DECEMBER 26, 1859   DIED: APRIL 24, 1944
TERM OF OFFICE: MARCH 15, 1917—JANUARY 10, 1923

WILLIAM DENNISON STEPHENS, born in Eaton, Ohio, on December 26, 1859, was named for William Dennison, one of the founders of the Republican party and a governor of Ohio. Stephens attended the public schools of Eaton. Graduation from high school in 1876 closed his formal education. During the next four years, Stephens taught school and studied law. Unable to pursue his legal studies, he left home in 1880 to engage in railroad construction in Ohio, Indiana, Iowa, and Louisiana. In 1887, he went with his family to Los Angeles because of his mother's health, and in 1888, he was managing a retail grocery store. From 1891 to 1902, he was a traveling salesman for the wholesale grocery firm of M.A. Newmark and Company. In June, 1891, Stephens married Flora Rawson of Los Angeles. In 1902, he helped create the partnership of Carr and Stephens, wholesale and retail grocers.

By 1902, Stephens had become an important figure in the Los Angeles business world and was named a director of the Los Angeles Chamber of Commerce, serving until 1911. In 1907, he was president of the chamber. In the same year he was a member of the board of education in that city.

The years 1909 and 1910—busy ones for Stephens—saw the launching of his political career. When Los Angeles Mayor Arthur C. Harper resigned under pressure charged with alleged corruption, the city council appointed Stephens interim mayor for two weeks until a new mayor could be elected. He helped carry to completion in 1909 the consolidated harbor district of Los Angeles, a project with which he had been work-

323

ing since 1902. In 1910, he served on the advisory committee
for the building of the Owens River Aqueduct and was president of the board of water commissioners of Los Angeles.

The statewide dreams of the Lincoln-Roosevelt League came
to fruition in 1910. Part of its hopes was realized when
William Stephens defeated the machine-supported congressman
from the tenth district in the Republican primary and the
Democratic nominee in November. He was re-elected in 1912.

In 1914, Stephens showed his faith in the progressive movement as he bolted the Republican party and ran, as did Governor Hiram Johnson, on the Progressive ticket. Stephens was
successful, being returned to his third term in Congress.

Internal California politics in 1916 took Stephens from Congress and placed him in the governor's mansion in 1917. Because of friction within the disintegrating Lincoln-Roosevelt
League and the demand of southern California Progressives
that one of their ranks be named as lieutenant governor, Johnson, to keep harmony, agreed to select his probable successor
from the southern part of the state. After some bickering over
the choice, the southern Progressives prevailed upon an un-
enthusiastic Johnson to accept Stephens. After a meeting between the two men, Johnson on July 18, 1916, announced the
appointment.

When Congress was called into special session in March,
1917, Johnson reluctantly resigned as governor on March 15,
and William Dennison Stephens was installed as governor. On
this occasion, Stephens delivered one of the briefest inaugural
addresses. He promised to carry on the good fight and to protect previous gains while urging the legislature to continue the
advance of progressivism.

On March 23, 1917, Stephens delivered a more lengthy address devoted to legislative topics he deemed important. With
the United States under the shadow of war, the governor's remarks reflected impending hostilities as he asked California
to prepare for war. He tied expansion of highway construction
to military needs. He noted that if war came agriculture would
play a key role. However, since California's agriculture was in
a state of decline, it needed assistance in three areas: land occupancy, marketing, and the extension of state rural credits—
based on firm banking principles.

Because of the imminence of war, Stephens asked that economy become the political watchword. He assured all that he was not advocating retrenchment, but extravagance should not be permitted in the face of the national emergency. While recapitulating the gains made under Johnson, he made additional suggestions in three fields: a program of social insurance to care for the infirm and the aged, an expansion of civil service, and a formalizing into the constitution of the state budget system which had proven so valuable under Johnson.

Stephens came to office late in the 1917 legislative session and not many of his ideas were enacted. A state council of defense and a state defense guard were established. The latter was activated when the national guard was called to federal duty. On April 24, the governor reported that the defense council had been organized and was hard at work.

During the 1917 session, Stephens vetoed twenty bills outright and pocket vetoed many more. He devoted most of his time to the war effort and his re-election as governor.

Following the adjournment of the legislature, Stephens became active as ex officio chairman of the defense council. He toured the state in behalf of the war effort delivering patriotic addresses. In May, 1917, he set up machinery for the selective service program, serving as chairman of the state registration board and appointing physicians to examine men for the local draft boards. Governor Stephens' appeals in behalf of California's war efforts were gathered into a 1920 state document, the *War Addresses of Governor William D. Stephens*, which gave an insight into his leadership during the First World War.

On December 17, 1917, a high explosive bomb destroyed part of the governor's mansion in Sacramento but no one was injured. While the Sacramento police searched for the bombers, Governor Stephens received a letter demanding $50,000 to be delivered by him at a location near Oakland, and threatening that unless the terms were met, several buildings, including the mansion and the capitol building, would be dynamited. On January 17, 1918, a bomb addressed to the governor was intercepted in the San Francisco Ferry Post Office. At first the governor attributed the mansion bombing to pro-Germans who were using terrorism as one of their tactics. Later Stephens accepted the more commonly accepted view that this violence was a manifestation of the extremist activities of the Industrial Workers of the World, better known as the "Wobblies." Out of the Sacramento police investigation of the mansion bombing, fifty-five members of the I.W.W. were arrested by the end of January, 1918. As the months passed, Stephens became an outright foe of this group; part of his 1918 campaign emphasized his leadership in helping to suppress the militant I.W.W.

Governor Stephens early in 1918 announced his candidacy for re-election and took advantage of the then very intricate election code drafted by the Progressives to give direct government to Californians. With the unique system of cross-filing, Stephens filed for the primary nomination on the Republican, Progressive, and Prohibition tickets. In the primary and general elections, Stephens campaigned as "California's War Governor" and used extensively the Lincoln slogan: "It is wise not to swap horses while crossing the river." Stephens advocated prohibition, suppression of the I.W.W., and a continuation of the Johnson principles with some economy in state government.

As the primary campaigns were starting in July, 1918, Stephens was confronted with the Tom Mooney case. Mooney and Warren K. Billings had been arrested and convicted for the San Francisco Preparedness Day bombing, July 22, 1916, which killed ten people. Mooney received the death sentence and Billings life imprisonment. Mooney was scheduled for execution on August 23, 1918, four days before the primary election. On July 27, 1918, Stephens granted a reprieve until December 13, well after the elections, announcing he wanted time to study the case carefully. On November 28, after the United States Supreme Court refused to review the case, Stephens commuted the sentence to life imprisonment. The Mooney case was to haunt California governors until 1939 when Culbert Olson pardoned Mooney and later commuted Billings' sentence.

In the primary election of 1918, five others sought the Republican nomination. Stephens' chief opposition came from James Rolph, Jr., mayor of San Francisco. Francis J. Heney and Rolph, a Republican who had cross-filed, both sought the Democratic nomination with Heney cross-filing on the Progressive ticket.

After the August 27 primary election, confusion prevailed. Stephens had won all three of his nominations while defeating Rolph for the Republican nomination and Heney for the Progressive ticket. Meanwhile, Rolph had defeated Heney for the

Democratic nomination and had emerged with the most votes cast for any one candidate. However primary election laws, dealing with cross-filing, eliminated Rolph as a nominee since as a registered Republican he had failed to carry his own party. Heney was also disqualified to run as a Democrat for he had not secured his party's nomination, placing second. The upshot of the controversy, finally decided in the State Supreme Court, was that the Democrats could not have any candidate's name printed on the general election ballot. Stephens commented after the primary that it looked as though he had been re-elected governor and, speaking from a very favorable position, added that he would be willing to run in November against a Democrat and hoped that one could be put on the ballot.

The 1918 general election was a dull affair after the excitement of the primary election. The best the Democrats could do was to back Theodore Bell as an Independent candidate. Bell had been the unsuccessful Democratic candidate in 1906 and 1910. The outcome was no surprise with Stephens overwhelming Bell 387,547 to 251,189, with other candidates receiving 49,934 votes. Stephens became the first governor since 1898 to be elected by a majority.

On November 25, 1918, Governor Stephens, following an idea expressed in his 1917 message, launched the first comprehensive survey of the state's administrative system. He appointed a committee of efficiency and economy to investigate ways to improve administration of the state's affairs and to recommend possible savings without impairment of service. Progressive reconstruction of the state government, Stephens said, had been carried out in a hurried manner. He charged the committee to find any overlapping or duplicating services and to suggest methods of elimination.

On January 7, 1919, William D. Stephens was inaugurated governor in his own right. In a brief address, full of generalities, he commented on California's contribution to the victorious war effort and then turned to the new problems of a peace time economy. He believed that California stood at the threshold of an industrial expansion which would provide employment to returning veterans. He added that the highway commission would give preference to veterans on road construction jobs. His message concluded with the observation that for the first time in California history women lawmakers sat in the legislature.

The next day, January 8, Stephens returned to the legislature to deliver his first biennial message. He pointed with pride to the work of the land settlement board which had developed reclamation and irrigation projects. The governor hoped that such lands would be made available first to returning veterans.

Stephens related how and why he had appointed a committee to study governmental efficiency. He summed up the problem saying:

> The people of California have demanded that their government shall render certain services and perform certain work. Those services and that work are being performed. The people have a right, as well, to expect and demand that the costs be kept at the lowest possible point consistent with good service.

He also urged modernization of the constitution through revision by amendments and to prepare for the holding of a convention.

The governor hoped that state taxes would not be increased since the federal government would demand high taxes for several years to pay for the war. He advocated cooperation with the National Tax Association in establishing a general program of inheritance taxation.

He advised that the prohibition amendment would be submitted to the 1919 legislature and recommended acceptance. Then alluding to the recent fiasco in the August primaries, he suggested changes to correct defects in the primary election law. His message concluded with the hope the state would continue its forward advance in all areas of activity.

On March 20, 1919, Governor Stephens transmitted the findings of his committee on efficiency and economy of California. The report called for a reorganization of the existing commissions into a system of departments and bureaus, with their heads directly responsible to the governor. Hiram Johnson had been the first governor to ask for this. Stephens observed that there were not enough days remaining in the 1919 session to legislate a complete reorganization program, but he believed that "so far as the people have given this subject thought, I am convinced that they are not interested so much in the structure of government as they are in an immediate reduction of the cost of government while maintaining the same high standards of efficiency." The governor stated that bills would be presented at once to start implementation of the plan, but he urged caution and study with particular reference to the idea of concentrating additional power in the office of governor. He found the report an important step forward which made the goal of reorganization a definite possibility.

Stephens sent two additional messages to the 1919 session. The first endorsed a constitutional amendment providing for an additional $40,000,000 in highway bonds. The measure passed the legislature and received voter endorsement in June. In the second message he warned that the state's fiscal condition was jeopardized by pending appropriations which could draw the treasury surplus below the margin of safety.

The governor noted that despite war-time demands upon state finances, an estimated surplus of $4,219,000 existed in January, 1919. The executive branch had consequently drafted its 1919-20 budget of $47,580,153.66, which was some $389,-336.34 below anticipated revenue. The governor held that if his budget were adopted, the surplus would increase. His budget allowed for normal increases in the cost of state services in education, veterans' affairs, and other state institutions. Stephens' special message held that the legislature was making appropriations beyond the normal increases of the budget and he felt that any additional appropriations would have to be limited by funds available.

Two significant measures, which passed the 1919 legislature with Stephens' support, were ratification of the eighteenth amendment to the United States constitution endorsing prohibition and the criminal syndicalism law. Thus some of Stephen's campaign pledges were kept. In conjunction with ratification of prohibition a state enforcement act received the governor's signature, but a successful referendum petition held up the act. The criminal syndicalism law, which dealt stringently with the I.W.W., reflected growing national reaction to radical movements.

During the 1919 session Stephens returned only two bills to the legislature with veto messages, but used the pocket veto extensively to cut back legislative appropriations. Measures that may be properly called progressive continued to be enacted during 1919. Regulation of irrigation and water power was extended; primary election law difficulties were corrected; new labor legislation included rehabilitation of injured workmen.

In 1919, with the Paris Peace Conference in session, the California legislature again advocated restriction of Japanese immigration, but when the United States Department of State applied pressure, no legislation was enacted. However, Governor Stephens asked the board of control to prepare a study during 1919 and 1920.

In November, 1919, Stephens called the legislature into special session to ratify the nineteenth amendment to the United States constitution granting women's suffrage. The Senate additionally resolved that the governor should call a special session in 1920 to consider the alien land matter in its entirety, but Stephens, in an unpopular decision, refused to act until the board of control reported. Consequently, an initiative measure was circulated to end leasing of farm lands to alien Japanese and to strengthen the Webb Law of 1913.

In June, 1920, the board issued its findings, *California and the Oriental*. Governor Stephens, in transmitting the report to Secretary of State Bainbridge Colby, adopted the traditional anti-Japanese view and urged that the federal government take the lead in eliminating Japanese immigration into the United States. The federal government had gained a concession from Japan that no more passports would be issued to "picture brides." Nevertheless, Californians endorsed the initiative measure at the November general election.

On January 4, 1921, Stephens delivered his second biennial message which was concerned mainly with three topics: revision of criminal trial procedure, development of hydro-electric power and enlargement of irrigation, and state fiscal matters. He also expressed his gratification about the anti-alien land initiative measure. He found the Oriental problem a real and growing menace and reiterated that the final answer, restriction of Japanese immigration, rested with the federal government.

During the 1921 legislative session Stephens worked diligently to consolidate administrative agencies and to increase corporation taxes. On January 18, in a special message, he urged revision of the executive branch of the state government. He presented eight bills to reorganize many agencies into departments, observing that the 1919 creation of the department of agriculture showed what was possible. New departments requested by the governor were finance, education, labor and industrial relations, professional standards, and public works, while many constitutional agencies, such as the board of control and the railroad commission, were to continue as separate entities. Stephens' reorganization plan, except for the professional standards bill, became the law of the state, marking the first successful attempt at a logical and studied revision of the executive branch since the adoption of the 1879 constitution.

The biggest battle of the 1921 session concerned increasing public service corporation taxes. The state board of equalization recommended a tax rate increase of about 33 percent, holding that such an increase was long overdue inasmuch as there had been none since before the First World War. A measure upholding the board's sentiment passed the Senate and failed in the Assembly just before the mandatory interim thirty day adjournment. During this period, Stephens toured the state in behalf of increased taxes. He and his supporters succeeded in forcing through the King tax bill which increased corporation taxes 25 percent to help defray higher costs of government.

Stephens vetoed only two minor measures during the 1921 session. However, he used his pocket veto 237 times, generally against special appropriations bills.

Stephens was a large man—tall and well proportioned. One trademark, or characteristic, of dress for which Stephens became noted was his continued use of the bow tie at a time when most men had commonly adopted the cravat. He had sparkling eyes and an engaging smile. Political contemporaries have recounted that he was honest of purpose, genial, warm-hearted, and easy-going. They have counted these traits as both assets and liabilities for the governor. He readily sought conversation and his position on political issues was well known in advance of final decisions. These very facets also created political enemies of some whose opinions had been asked and then not followed.

Stephens indicated early his intention to run for re-election in 1922, and announced his candidacy in July, filing on the Republican and Prohibition tickets. His one opponent on the Republican ticket was Friend W. Richardson who charged the Stephens' administration with over-extravagance in state expenditures. In the August primary, Stephens won the Prohibition nomination, but lost the Republican nomination to Richardson. Since Stephens was a registered Republican, he was disqualified as the Prohibition nominee. Several factors contributed to Stephens' defeat. One of the major burdens he had to bear was his active support of the King tax bill increasing corporation taxes. The Automobile Club of Southern California opposed his highway program. Its criticism was largely based on the claim that there was already a pressing need for some $65,000,000 for road repairs to maintain highways recently built. He had also to face the opposition of the wine producers and the liquor interests regarding prohibition. It was true that Richardson also supported prohibition, but Stephens had been the governor who had pushed the program. Finally, the Progressive movement, which had lasted longer in California than in the rest of the nation, had dissipated by 1922. Also, it should be remembered that California had re-elected only two previous governors for a second term.

On January 9, 1923, Governor Stephens presented his third biennial message and on January 10, participated in the inaugural ceremonies for incoming Governor Richardson. Also in attendance were two future governors, Lieutenant Governor Clement C. Young and Speaker of the Assembly Frank F. Merriam.

Stephens' last review outlined what he believed the highlights of his administration. He recounted some of the problems he had as a war-time governor. He was proud of the veterans' welfare plan which included relief for the disabled veteran, education, and farm and home loans. He was particularly pleased that prohibition had been introduced and had become a reality during his term. The Oriental question had been a major problem during his six years and he repeated that its ultimate solution rested with Congress.

He then reviewed the administrative reorganization into six executive departments which had cut down the patronage problem by reducing unnecessary positions and increased efficiency while bringing about needed economies. Stephens next commented on state expenditures and the condition of the state treasury. He felt compelled to answer the many charges of waste and extravagance which had been leveled at him by the Richardson camp during the primary campaign. Stephens demonstrated that state finances were in good condition with a large balance to carry it forward the next six months until the beginning of the new fiscal year.

The remainder of his biennial message surveyed various state institutions and services rendered. These he found to be in a satisfactory condition. He called specific attention to the Colorado River Compact which had been approved by state representatives on November 24, 1922, and then urged ratification in order that needed water be secured for Southern California agriculture. Seven states were involved in the compact and all had to agree. Arizona refused and the matter was stalemated.

As he ended his six years as governor, Stephens asked the lawmakers to remember his and Johnson's administrations as having maintained the progressive ideals and to continue building on the foundations so well established.

One of the curious aspects of the Stephens' administration was the many proclamations that the governor made in observance of special days such as "Go to Sunday School Sunday," "Ripe Olive Day," "Gauze Mask Use Day," and "Law and Order Sunday." While governor, Stephens used his pardoning power moderately, issuing ninety-one pardons, seventy-eight commutations, and nineteen reprieves.

Governor Stephens returned to Los Angeles where he entered private law practice. He had been admitted to the California bar while governor. He remained a leading citizen of Los Angeles until his death at the age of eighty-five on April 24, 1944.

The administration of William D. Stephens extended the program of the Johnson Progressives. Reform still continued although Stephens had to solve problems started by his predecessor, particularly in the area of finance. That he confronted and defeated the opposition of the corporate interests against tax increase was perhaps his most courageous act. He was concerned about the increased cost of government. His successful reorganization program was his answer to efficient and economical government. The administrative branch of state government remained organized through 1961 along the lines started in the Stephens' administration. Stephens had kept faith with the California Progressives and had managed to keep the spirit alive long after the flame had diminished elsewhere. He had been a competent administrator and a pleasant, friendly representative of the people.

BIBLIOGRAPHY

MANUSCRIPTS
Fitzhamon, E.G.B., "Collection," (California Historical Society).
Johnson, Hiram, "Correspondence and Letters."
Jones, Herbert C., "Papers," (Borel Collection, Stanford University).
Lissner, Meyer, "Papers," (Borel Collection).
Rowell, Chester, "Papers."
Stephens, William, "Executive Appointments: Administration of Governor William D. Stephens," (California State Archives).

CONTEMPORARY ACCOUNTS
Assembly Journal, 42nd-45th Sess., 1917-23.
Senate Journal, 42nd-45th Sess., 1917-23.
California Blue Book, 1913-15.
Board of Control, *California and the Oriental: Japanese, Chinese, and Hindus.* (Sacramento, 1920).
Report of the Committee on Efficiency and Economy of California to Gov. Wm. D. Stephens (Sacramento, 1919).
Stephens, William D., *California in the War. War addresses, proclamations and patriotic messages of Governor William D. Stephens* (Sacramento, 1921).

SECONDARY SOURCES
Hichborn, Franklin, *Story of the Session of the California Legislature of 1921* (San Francisco, 1922).
Melendy, H. Brett, "California's Cross-Filing Nightmare: The 1918 Gubernatorial Election," *Pacific Historical Review,* XXXIII (1964), 317-30.
Mowry, George, *The California Progressives.*
Wolfe, W.C., ed., *Men of California* (1925).

NEWSPAPERS
Los Angeles Times, April 26, 1944, has Stephens' obituary.
Sacramento Bee, April 26, 1944, has obituary.
Sacramento Union, Dec. 18, 1917, reports bombing of governor's mansion; Jan. 19, 1919, reports first biennial message; Jan. 5, 1921, carries second biennial message; Aug. 19, 1922, praises Stephens' administration; Sept. 1, 1922, has editorial on Stephens' defeat for renomination; Jan. 8, 1923, praises Stephens as he leaves office.
San Diego Union, March 25, 1917, describes problems confronting new governor; Jan. 7, 1921, reports on second biennial message.
San Francisco Bulletin, Aug. 29-30, 1918, has results of 1918 direct primary election; Sept. 2, 1918, has editorial on direct primary.
San Francisco Chronicle, Jan. 10, 1919, has editorial on first biennial message; April 26, 1944, has obituary.

THESIS
Curry, John, "William D. Stephens, Twenty-Fourth Governor of California" (M.A., San Jose State College, 1961).

State Printing Office, Sacramento. The state was building a grand executive mansion for its governors when Newton Booth was inaugurated in 1871. But the legislature failed to appropriate sufficient funds, and the building above was converted eventually into offices for the state printing department. It was located in what today is Capitol Park.

Calendar of Events

December, 1865	Richardson born at Friends Colony, Michigan.
1897	Richardson purchased and published the *San Bernardino Times-Index*.
1901	Richardson purchased and published the *Berkeley Gazette*.
1902	Richardson elected president of the California Press Association, holding this office for forty-one years.
November 23, 1911	Governor Johnson appointed Richardson to vacant post of Superintendent of State Printing.
November 3, 1914	Richardson elected State Treasurer for first of two terms.
January 9, 1923	Richardson inaugurated Governor.
February 1, 1923	Richardson submitted first mandatory executive budget.
August, 1923	Progressive Voters League formed in opposition to Richardson's economy program.
August 31, 1926	Young defeated Richardson for Republican nomination as Governor.
1931	Richardson purchased and published the *Alameda Times-Star*.
January 1, 1932	Governor Rolph appointed Richardson Building and Loan Commissioner.
June 24, 1934	Governor Merriam appointed Richardson Superintendent of Banks.
September 6, 1943	Richardson died in Berkeley.

Friend W. Richardson

25TH GOVERNOR—REPUBLICAN
BORN: DECEMBER, 1865   DIED: SEPTEMBER 6, 1943
TERM OF OFFICE: JANUARY 9, 1923—JANUARY 4, 1927

FRIEND WILLIAM RICHARDSON WAS BORN on a farm in Friends Colony, south of Ypsilanti, Michigan, in December, 1865. He was named William Richardson and after the manner of his Quaker faith was called Friend William. In time he had the name of Friend legalized. When Richardson was quite young, his family moved to San Bernardino where he attended local schools. He attended and graduated from Sturges Academy. He then read law for two years. In 1891, he married Augusta F. Felder of San Bernardino. They had three children.

From 1891 to 1896, Richardson served as San Bernardino County Clerk and law librarian. In 1896, he started working for the *San Bernardino Times-Index*, launching a journalism career which became both his vocation and avocation for the remainder of his life. In 1897, he purchased the paper and published it until 1901. He then moved to Berkeley where he bought the *Berkeley Gazette*, which he published until 1915. In 1902, the California Press Association elected Richardson its president, a position he held for the rest of his life.

In 1910, Richardson was a candidate for superintendent of state printing, but he lost by 309 votes to the incumbent, William Shannon, who had held office since January, 1903. However, during the first year of the Johnson administration Shannon resigned following charges of malfeasance in the state printing office and the governor appointed Richardson to the $5,000 a year position. In 1913, Johnson praised the reorganized printing office and the manner in which it handled the printing of free state text books.

In 1914, Friend Richardson sought and received the nomination for state treasurer from the Progressives, Democrats, and Republicans in the direct primaries, another $5,000 a year job. His August victory through cross-filing assured his November election. Richardson served two terms as state treasurer, being re-elected in 1918. Richardson became aware of both the expansion of state government and increasing costs under the Progressive governors, Johnson and Stephens. He came to believe that the fiscal well-being of California depended upon economy and retrenchment.

First selected for public office in 1911 by the Progressives and then running as a registered Progressive in 1914, Richardson had returned to the Republican fold by the 1918 election. By 1922, he had moved from the progressive wing to the conservative wing of the Republican party. In this election year he became the leader of the conservatives who sought to dethrone Governor Stephens. Richardson campaigned on a policy of retrenchment and an end to the political machine, created by Johnson and sustained by Stephens, which had dominated the state since 1911. A claim of the conservatives was that the Progressives had merely replaced the Southern Pacific machine with their own organization. Richardson indicated that his service as state treasurer had taught him how to cut the budget and still provide the kind of government the people of the state wanted. When the smoke of battle cleared, Richardson had won the Republican nomination and he claimed to have won on the single issue of economy with a mandate to reduce the state budget.

In November, Richardson received 576,445 votes while his Democratic opponent, Thomas Lee Woodbine, received 347,520. Others received 41,809. Thus Richardson became one of the few governors to receive a majority of the votes cast.

Most newspapers stated that Richardson's November triumph showed that the citizens wanted strict economy in government. The press held a common opinion that Stephens' administration had been too expensive and the newly elected Richardson was well qualified to check extravagances. While there were indeed many other reasons for Richardson's victory, it must be remembered that the dominant political view both in California and the nation in the 1920's was one which endorsed a laissez-faire attitude of government regarding business.

Richardson was physically a large person. He was tall and

heavy set. He had bushy eyebrows and mustache. He was a conspicuous and picturesque political figure. According to those who knew him, he manifested a strong vigor coupled with an air of common sense. Personally, he was extremely friendly but taciturn. He seldom displayed anger or impatience, but kept applying pressure to gain his point. He was well known for his bluntness. When he made up his mind about an issue, he spoke forthrightly without regard for consequences. He earned the reputation as a shrewd and capable politician. At the time of his death, the *Sacramento Union* noted that Richardson had been a strong political force in California. He had successfully imparted his philosophy to a group of young men, the most notable being Frank Merriam. Richardson, it was reported, had no illusions about politics, but considered it a business which he learned early and taught his followers to know and understand.

On January 9, 1923, Friend W. Richardson took his oath of office as governor of the state. With his predecessor, William D. Stephens, sitting nearby, Richardson proceeded to criticize the outgoing administration. The new governor stated that "The people by their vote at these two elections indicated that they want the State conducted on an economical, efficient and businesslike basis, that they want to stop the orgy of extravagance which has prevailed during the past few years, and that they want to put out of power the political machine which has dominated the State government." Richardson said the first job to be accomplished was the destruction of the existing political machine, the root of the whole problem. He promised to remove from office all members of the Stephens group and to abolish all unnecessary commissions and offices. Thus the new governor gave notice that the Progressive era had closed.

Richardson specifically charged that the state highway system was in a deplorable condition with millions of dollars having been squandered on inadequate construction. As a consequence, much road building had to be redone. He charged that the highway department had not learned from past experience; meanwhile, the state still waited for good roads.

In his address, Richardson advocated, as had Stephens, aid to farmers, help to veterans, a fair deal for labor, protection of life and property, enforcement of the federal Volstead Act, exclusion of Orientals, and revision of court procedures in the state. He announced that in keeping with the newly adopted constitutional amendment, he would shortly submit his executive budget, which reflecting the wishes of the people, would emphasize economy. He called for fewer and better laws, a familiar request from California governors.

Governor Richardson's choice for Speaker of the Assembly was Frank Merriam, his 1922 campaign manager. After a bitter floor fight, Merriam secured that office. The administration thus was able to control matters in the Assembly where budget issues started. On February 1, 1923, the governor submitted the first mandatory executive budget in the history of the state.

Richardson estimated that 1923-24 expenditures would be $78,974,628 and that income would be $85,237,000. Some $5,200,000 of the income, however, was tied up in litigation over the recent King tax bill which had increased public utility tax rates. He criticized the taxation of these corporations on the grounds that increases were passed on to the public in the form of higher charges. He stated that his budget preparation had been difficult since many department heads were hostile toward him. Nevertheless, he stated:

> I have heeded the voice of the people and made my cuts regardless of any political consequences to myself. I have hewed to the line, letting the political chips fall where they may. The advocates of the "pork barrel" idea in appropriations have been given no consideration, as I have tried to consider the State as a whole and the general needs of the people. My chief purpose has been to relieve the people of their great burden of taxation.

Believing that too much money was being spent for educational purposes, he claimed that "extravagance in educational matters has run riot during the past few years." He recommended closing the California Polytechnic School, saying it did not fit into the scheme of the state educational system. He also announced that Humboldt State Teachers College cost too much per capita in comparison to other colleges, and suggested closing the institution.

His message received mixed reactions throughout the state since his recommendations were more than $13,000,000 below Stephens' 1921 budget. The major reductions were made in salary lists with many positions being eliminated, causing consternation in every department. The governor created many new enemies with his message, but the press commended him for a courageous political act and for standing by his pledge.

During the 1923 legislative session, Richardson sent twenty-two veto messages to the Senate and fifty-three to the Assembly. These vetoes covered all topics ranging from code modifications to rejection of appropriations for new services.

In the last days of the session he sent a special message warning the lawmakers to reapportion legislative districts. This matter had been pending since 1921 and a bill at the 1923 session had already been defeated. Finding the duty of the legislators clear, he stated that he would not call a special session for redistricting.

A major proposal affecting Richardson's ability to administer his program was the Bromley bill, which would make the terms of office of the governor's appointees, except those terms fixed by the constitution, subject to his pleasure. The bill eliminated continuing appointments not only in the "official family," but extended to all boards and commissions whose members had terms lasting longer than the governor's. This bill was an attempt to smash the "Stephens machine" and to fill offices at all levels of the administration with men sympathetic to the incumbent's view. Richardson's measure passed both houses, but he reluctantly withheld approval in the face of a threatened referendum by the Progressive opposition.

Governor Richardson made an all-out effort in his economy program. A form letter was delivered to every officer, elected or appointed, apprising each of the gubernatorial view. One such letter, sent to Chester Rowell, a member of the regents of the University of California, stated:

> The adoption of the economy budget by the legislature and its approval by me is only the first step forward in putting the State on a business basis.
>
> Every officer and employee of the State is asked to cooperate in putting economy in practice. The budget fixes the financial bounds within which the various departments must keep, but they are expected to conserve their funds and see how much they can save. See how little you can spend and maintain the efficiency of your department, and not how much.
>
> Economy is not a campaign slogan, but a policy that must be put into practice.
>
> You are urged to lend your aid in helping me give California an economical, efficient, and businesslike administration.

By March, 1924, criticism of the budget cut was publicly manifested. In an open letter, Will J. French, member of the industrial accident commission, announced his resignation, claiming reductions had hamstrung his commission. The task of that body could not be accomplished and reports could not be completed with only a skeleton crew. French stated that the governor had crippled the commission at the cost of human lives and safety. He held that private business would suffer in the long run. He objected, too, to the appointment of C. B. Day as manager of the state compensation fund at a $6,000 annual salary. French believed that Day had been appointed because he was the stepson of Frank Merriam. In a real sense, French's action was part of the program of the Progressive Voters League, formed in August, 1923, to oppose Governor Richardson and his policies. French later became director of the department of industrial relations during Clement C. Young's administration.

Although the Progressive Voters League in the 1924 election made inroads against the administration's power in the legislature, the Richardson forces maintained control of both houses with Merriam re-elected Speaker of the Assembly. On January 7, 1925, Richardson submitted his first biennial message, which resembled gubernatorial messages of an earlier day. The 1925 message was a review of past events rather than a plan of action for the immediate future.

Richardson re-emphasized that his watchword was economy in government and as a result, $12,000,000 had been saved in two years, leaving a $6,000,000 surplus. The governor interpreted his role as that of state business manager. He had delved into all phases of state operations. While he claimed that his appointments had been on merit, many of his critics did not agree.

He announced that in keeping with the vote of the people in November, 1924, he had appointed the newly formed athletic commission. He stated that he had put aside personal convictions regarding the moral effect of prize fighting and had named reputable business men to the commission.

He called attention to the fact that all bond money for road construction had been expended and that the existing two cent gasoline tax was for road repairs and not for new construction. He indicated that the legislature would have to grapple with financing additional construction. He reminded the lawmakers again that state legislative districts still had to be reapportioned following the 1920 census. He suggested that certain drivers be prohibited from using state highways—those who were either incompetent or were physically disabled—for automobiles had increased at an alarming rate. Here was the first recognition by a governor of a problem that would concern all his successors.

His message concluded with the thought that the humane and progressive laws of the state had been well protected by the various state agencies. As governor, he stood pledged to support all legislation in the best interests of the people.

During the 1925 session Governor Richardson again wielded a heavy hand in vetoing Senate and Assembly bills which either concerned additional appropriations or expanded the powers of the state. In this latter category, he preferred to allow business to manage its own affairs without state regulation. Here Richardson reflected national sentiment about the relationship of business and government.

The governor pressed during the 1925 session for financing of the state highway program. He forwarded the study made by his appointed highway commission which recommended additional bond issues and increased taxes on motor vehicles. The commission also outlined a priority plan of road construction. The program, enacted by the legislature, gained voter approval in the 1926 general election.

Governor Richardson chose to run for re-election in 1926, seeking the Republican nomination. Many small newspapers in the state supported him. His presidency of the California Press Association helped him considerably. The governor defined the issues in the campaign as threefold: California's need and desire for four more years of a sane businesslike constructive administration; a continuance of a government of law and order which had as its policy crime suppression and a refusal to interfere with the sentences of the courts; and an administration which did not yield to political bosses.

He pointed out that the administrative costs were the same as they had been for five years; the fiscal line had been held while the quality of service increased and a treasury surplus accumulated. His administration also pointed with pride to over 300 miles of highways newly paved, the largest amount to date in any administration. Richardson stood on his record and re-emphasized his accomplishment of economy. However, he lost his bid for a second term, but ran a close second to Clement C. Young, losing by 15,272 votes. The Progressive Voters League, the Bank of Italy, and assorted foes in Republican ranks had tipped the balance away from the governor, who had been fairly certain of re-election almost up to the August primary. What remained of the old Johnson Progressives had been able to muster enough strength and to gain allies to run against the national tide of conservatism.

In October, 1926, Governor Richardson called the legislature into special session to ratify the Colorado River Compact upon which the seven western states were still working to find agreement. The lawmakers were quite unhappy about this compact and in a brief session of only four hours rejected it. The compact received a total of only eleven votes from the two houses.

Richardson summed up his administration in his second biennial message on January 4, 1927. He stressed that he had accomplished his prime goal—a state government operated on a business basis with efficiency and economy the major tenets. He was proud that the General Fund had been built to more than $20,000,000 without increased taxation. Richardson's administration had accumulated $14,000,000 by "constant resistance to spendthrifts and vetoing and suppression of legislative bills carrying millions of dollars in appropriations." The remainder of the surplus came from public utility taxes tied up in the King tax bill litigation.

The governor claimed that he had been fortunate in selecting department heads who had been "business men of the highest integrity and ability." He highly commended the board of control and the highway commission. For the most part, the message reviewed the operation of his business administration. As in his first biennial message, Richardson made no major recommendations for a possible legislative program. In 1927, however, with his leaving office, this was more understandable.

Richardson was entirely satisfied that the state had maintained the status quo. While no new services were started, existing facilities were improved. In fact, during the last two years of his term, more money had been appropriated for a building program than at any prior time in state history. While the Richardson years marked time, they allowed some opportunity to consolidate the executive branch.

Governor Richardson in 1925 had related that his pardoning power was wielded in support of his position of sustaining and upholding verdicts of juries and decisions of judges. He said, "The matter of pardons is a grave and arduous duty which I have tried to exercise for the protection of society generally." A firm advocate of capital punishment, he announced in 1925 that he was determined "to stand firmly by the law and not to permit sentiment or political influence or hysterical journalists to prevent a warning being given to would-be criminals."

In 1927, reviewing his use of this power, he stated he had issued pardons "solely to prevent a miscarriage of justice and to be used only in extraordinary cases." He continued:

> Executive clemency should not be exercised to defeat the ends of the law, to override the verdicts of juries or decisions of courts. Only by strict enforcement of the laws and the elimination of sentimentalism in meting out punishment can law and order be maintained.

Consistent with his views, Richardson during his four year term granted eleven pardons, four commutations of sentence, three reprieves and five restorations to citizenship. His total use of the pardoning power was twenty-three, the lowest of any governor since J. Neely Johnson. Richardson was followed closely in this conservative use of the pardon by his successor, C. C. Young, who used the power twenty-seven times.

During Richardson's administration, several advances were made in the state's judicial system. In 1924, the municipal court system was established, and in 1926, the courts were unified under the judicial council. California became the second state to adopt such an arrangement and the first to authorize it by constitutional amendment.

After leaving the gubernatorial chair, Richardson and his wife toured the world in 1927. In 1929, they returned to Europe for a short visit. In 1930 and 1931, he arranged and managed excursions for the California Press Association to Mexico and Hawaii. In 1931 and 1932, he owned and published the *Alameda Times-Star*.

Richardson's political career was revived during the Rolph administration when he was appointed building and loan commissioner on January 1, 1932. He held this position until June, 1934. This office had some difficult times during the depression years, but Richardson, remaining true to his concept of public service, reported that the commission had been operated on an economical basis.

Following Rolph's death in June, 1934, Friend Richardson was appointed by his old ally, Frank Merriam, as superintendent of banks. He remained in this position until the end of the Merriam administration in 1939. Again he reported that he had been able to economize the operations of this office while maintaining efficiency. A small irony developed with Richardson's appointment, for he now supervised the A. P. Giannini banks which had worked against his re-election as governor in 1926.

Upon completion of his term as superintendent of banks, Richardson continued his work as president of the press association. In July, 1943, he had a heart attack from which he never recovered, and died on September 6, 1943, in Berkeley at the age of seventy-eight.

Governor Richardson had often said, "Politics is my meat and bread." In his case this was quite true—he gave California a long life of public service based on his motto for public office "of making good on the job." He was characterized as being a blunt and plain speaker, expressing openly what was on his mind. He was a capable politician who trained many state politicians in his philosophy of government. These men carried on the affairs of California during the difficult 1930's.

The Richardson administration has been called by some a hiatus in the progressive program of Johnson and his followers. In a sense, this was perhaps true, but Friend Richardson's election in 1922 was consistent with the national political scene as the conservative view had become dominant. Liberals criticized him for running counter to their wishes and yet, as a conservative governor, he accomplished what he had promised. Aside from striving for economy in a businesslike government, the major criticism leveled at Richardson was his lack of any other positive program. He left for C. C. Young the necessary reorganizational work to develop both efficiency in government and sufficient funds to operate the state.

It must be remembered, however, that Governor Richardson's economy program created a sizeable surplus in the General Fund and that his program of reducing state personnel made it easier for Governor Young to reorganize and to continue the treasury surplus which buffered the first years of the depression for the state government. He accomplished his goal of introducing business methods into the numerous state agencies. Richardson gave his successor a prosperous ship of state which was operating smoothly and efficiently.

BIBLIOGRAPHY

MANUSCRIPTS
Richardson, Friend, "State Officials' Letter File," (California Section, State Library).
Rowell, Chester, "Papers."
Stephens, Williams, "Executive Appointments: Administration of Governor William D. Stephens," (California State Archives). Richardson's appointments are listed in Stephens' appointment ledger.

CONTEMPORARY ACCOUNTS
Assembly Journal, 45th-47th Sess., 1923-27.
Senate Journal, 45th-47th Sess., 1923-27.
California Blue Book, 1911, 1913-15, & 1924.
Commonwealth Club of California, *Transactions,* XVIII (1923), 1-52.
[French, Will J.], "Open Letter to Gov. Friend W. Richardson" (San Francisco, 1924).

SECONDARY SOURCES
Collins, Frederic L., "Friend Richardson of California," *Woman's Home Companion,* L (1924), 17.
McIntyre, Charles, *Fifty Years Married: Augusta F. Richardson, Friend William Richardson: 1891-1941* (San Francisco, 1941).
Merritt, Frank C., *History of Alameda County, California* (2 vols., Chicago, 1928).
Posner, Russell M., "The Bank of Italy and the 1926 Campaign," *California Historical Society Quarterly,* XXXVII (1958), 267-75, 347-58.
———, "The Progressive Voters League, 1923-26," *CHSQ,* XXXVI (1957), 251-61.
Wolfe, W.C., ed., *Men of California* (1925).
"Economy in California," *American Review of Reviews,* LXVII (1923), 391.
"The Elections," *The Outlook,* CXXXII (1922), 503.

NEWSPAPERS
Sacramento Union, Nov. 9, 1922, has editorial on Richardson's election; Feb. 2, 1923, praises governor's policy for reduced budget; Jan. 9, 1925, has editorial on first biennial message; July 18, 1926, endorses Richardson for renomination; Jan. 2, 1927, gives estimate of Richardson as governor; Sept. 6, 1943, has his obituary.
San Diego Union, Jan. 10, 1923, outlines his inaugural message; Sept. 7, 1943, has his obituary.

Calendar of Events

April 28, 1869	Young born at Lisbon, New Hampshire.
1870	Young family moved to Butte County.
1892	Young graduated from the University of California.
November 3, 1908	Young elected to Assembly from Berkeley.
January 6, 1913	Young elected Speaker of Assembly.
November 5, 1918	Young elected Lieutenant Governor.
January 4, 1927	Young inaugurated Governor.
July 29, 1927	Governor's Council, created by legislature, met for first time.
August 26, 1930	Rolph defeated Young in his bid for renomination.
August 28, 1934	Merriam defeated Young for Republican nomination for Governor.
1939-1940	Young served as president of the Commonwealth Club of California.
January, 1943	Young directed Commonwealth Club's study, *The Legislature of California*.
December 24, 1947	Young died in Berkeley.

Clement C. Young

26TH GOVERNOR—REPUBLICAN
BORN: APRIL 28, 1869   DIED: DECEMBER 24, 1947
TERM OF OFFICE: JANUARY 4, 1927—JANUARY 6, 1931

CLEMENT CALHOUN YOUNG WAS BORN in Lisbon, New Hampshire, on April 28, 1869. When he was one year old, the Young family moved to California, settling in Butte County where he grew to boyhood and attended grammar school. The family next went to San Jose where Young attended high school until 1885. The family again moved, this time to Santa Rosa where he graduated in 1886. In 1887, he secured a teacher's certificate. The following year he enrolled at the University of California, graduating in 1892. He then started his teaching career as vice principal of Santa Rosa High School. In 1893, he moved to Lowell High School in San Francisco where he remained for fourteen years teaching English. While at Lowell, "C-Square" Young, as he was known by the students, co authored in 1904 with Charles Mills Gayley, a textbook, *English Poetry: Its Principles and Progress.* The book became well known as a standard text in California schools.

On March 15, 1902, Young married Lyla Jeannette Vincent of San Francisco. Two daughters were subsequently born of this marriage.

In 1906, following the San Francisco earthquake and fire, Young's teaching career came to an end as he joined the firm of Mason-McDuffie Company of San Francisco and Berkeley, which dealt in real estate, insurance, and loans. He remained with this company—except while governor—for the rest of his life. By the 1920's he had become a vice president in the firm. In 1925, Young joined in organizing the Berkeley Guarantee Savings and Loan Association, serving as vice president from its inception until his death in 1947. Clement Young, while building his political career, also found success in the business world.

In 1908, he won the Assembly seat from the Berkeley area. He gained re-election every two years through 1918, serving in five sessions. From 1913 to the end of his tenure in the Assembly, he served as Speaker, which was a record up to that time.

In the Assembly, Young became identified with the rising Lincoln-Roosevelt League and was one of the leaders in the fight to end the convention system. During Hiram Johnson's administration, he became a prominent sponsor of reform legislation which led to his election as Speaker.

In 1918, he was elected to the office of lieutenant governor. Re-elected four years later, he held that office longer than any of his predecessors. By 1920, Young had given up his Progressive affiliation and had returned to the Republican fold. He served as one of the presidential electors, voting for Harding and Coolidge.

In 1923, Young commenced his second term as lieutenant governor as Friend Richardson entered the governor's office. Young and other former members of the defunct Lincoln-Roosevelt League viewed Richardson's economy program as mistaken policy. Consequently, as the 1923 legislative session drew to its close, several of these men laid plans to combat the Richardson program. In August, 1923, the Progressive Voters League was organized with Young as one of the founders. After gaining some legislative seats in the 1924 election, the league prepared for the 1926 gubernatorial election. It had two choices: Young and Superintendent of Public Instruction Will C. Wood, both of whom were anxious for the chance to run. Yet both were reluctant to announce their availability prematurely. On October 11, 1925, to head off the mayor of Oakland, Young announced that he would seek the Republican nomination. As the 1926 campaign developed, Richardson had the advantage until Hiram Johnson returned from Europe to campaign in Young's behalf. The candidate gained additional support when A. P. Giannini instructed all employees of the Bank of Italy to campaign for Young. The bank's expansion program had not received all that it desired from the Richardson administration. Assured that the bank would receive fair and impartial treatment under a Young government, Giannini sent out his directive. This late support spelled the difference in a close race as Young edged Richardson for the nomination 327,596 to 311,324 votes.

Young's August nomination virtually assured his election as it had for Republicans in other elections. The California state Democratic party for the most of the first half of the twentieth century was ineffectual. When the votes were counted, Young received 814,815 votes to Democratic J. C. Wardell's 282,451. Upton Sinclair, Socialist candidate, received 45,972 votes and there was an additional scattering of 874. Young thus received 71 percent of the vote, the largest margin of victory over any preceding governor.

Governor-elect Young came to office perhaps better qualified for that position than any other governor. Long service in the Assembly and eight years as the presiding officer of the Senate had given him invaluable experience in understanding the intricacies of California government.

Young, as a person, was of medium build with unruly hair and clear penetrating eyes. He was basically a friendly man who talked easily with associates but who appeared austere and reserved to the public. He was known as a fair-minded person with a keen intellect. He gained the reputation of being a very studious person who worked diligently and capably as governor. Those who knew reported that his personal drive for success and hard work inspired others in state government to match his efforts. The *Oakland Tribune* has claimed that while Young's manner was not spectacular, he was sincere, conscientious, and able. These traits, coupled with a sense of high morality and a scrupulous performance of his duty, made him an outstanding governor.

On January 4, 1927, Clement C. Young took his oath of office and briefly stated his philosophy of government and his aims. He claimed that "I accept the result of that election [November] not at all as a personal tribute, but rather as the endorsement of a philosophy of government which I trust has been consistently mine throughout my eighteen years of endeavor to serve the State." Young cited his three principles of government—first, that "we are not afraid to be progressive"; second, that it "will be conceded that we have not entered public service merely for the sake of advancing our own selfish inter-

ests"; and third, "we shall all insist on a 'square deal,' " and
fair and impartial government, devoid of special privilege or
favor. Thus Young reasserted the aims of the Lincoln-Roosevelt League and the Progressive Voters League.

Turning to specific problems of state government, Young
related that since the 1921 adoption of the existing tax program,
expenditures had continued to exceed revenue and that the
state had kept pace by raising public corporation taxes. He
recommended that the legislature appoint a commission to
study the tax structure with an eye to periodic justifiable
public utilities tax increases, that the present session make no
change in the tax structure and observe rigid economies, and
that the existing surplus be held as a reservoir for emergency
use only.

Young urged completing reorganization of the executive
branch started by Stephens. Reorganization was to be the major
accomplishment of his administration. Young, in this first
address, called for the creation of a governor's cabinet and the
consolidation of many departments and bureaus. The legislature enacted measures incorporating these significant ideas.

The governor's message touched on highway construction,
water and forest conservation, law enforcement and prisons,
the continuation of direct primaries, and steady progress in
humanitarian and educational fields.

In conclusion, he asked that, in place of an over-abundance of
needless measures, only well thought out bills be introduced.
He observed that, because past legislators had lacked this self-
control, governors had been forced to assume undue legislative
duties through the use of the veto. Without a word in his message for retiring Governor Richardson, Young told the legislature that "you and I have a splendid task before us. We have
gone a long way forward . . . there must be no backward step."

Two days after his inauguration, Young asked for enabling
legislation to cooperate with the federal government in the development of the Boulder Canyon project on the Colorado
River. This project had had its inception during Stephens' administration when a governors' conference was held at Salt
Lake City in 1919. From this beginning, the Colorado River
Compact was developed in 1922, but Arizona refused to ratify
the agreement. For the next several years, the matter centered
in the United States Congress as Representative Philip D. Swing

of San Bernardino and Senator Hiram Johnson introduced bills to authorize a Colorado project. The Boulder Canyon proposal gained approval of the California legislature in 1927, but it was not until December, 1928, that Congress passed the Swing-Johnson bill authorizing construction of the dam.

On January 19, 1927, Young submitted his budget message. He inferred that while the constitutional amendment of 1922 required the governor to submit a complete plan of all proposed expenditures, Richardson had not done so. Young surveyed the growth of state expenditures since 1915, which had increased every biennium. Young claimed that his proposed budget showed the lowest percentage increase since 1915. Young's position on expenditures was that:

> it will be the policy of this administration to continue holding down these increases to the lowest possible figure. It is of course inevitable that expenses must grow with a growing state, but we must exercise constant care that not a dollar is spent which does not bring back one hundred cents worth of efficient service or of absolutely necessary permanent improvements.

Governor Young proved to be an energetic administrator who ranged far and wide over the affairs of the state. His budget was adopted, and his recommendations regarding taxation and crime resulted in the creation of commissions to study these matters. The legislature also moved along the path of administrative reform requested by Young. Four new administrative departments—industrial relations, natural resources, public health, and social welfare—were added to the existing five.

The keystone of Young's reorganization plan was the governor's council created by the 1927 legislature. With the exception of the director of education, the other eight council members were appointed by the governor, serving at his pleasure. The council first met on July 29, 1927, and thereafter held monthly open meetings. At each meeting, department heads reported on the activities of their areas, creating greater liaison between the various branches of the administration.

Young vetoed several bills of the 1927 legislature. In several instances, he noted inaccuracies in the preparation of the bills. Perhaps, as a former English teacher, he was overly conscious of such matters. Late in the session he asked the Speaker and the President of the Senate to inform members that all bills should be accompanied by a written explanation as to the purpose of the bill for his consideration. This device was also extended to other legislators favoring or opposing a particular bill in order that Young could weigh the evidence.

On April 4, 1927, Young notified the lawmakers that recent court decisions had nullified part of California's tax program by invalidating state corporation license fees and taxation of state banks. Attempts were made to remedy the problem but no permanent solution was effected. As a consequence, Young called the legislature into special session in September, 1928, to consider a new approach to bank taxation and to propose constitutional amendments for the coming November general election. Both houses unanimously passed a 4 percent bank tax on net income. This measure was adopted at the general election.

While the legislature was in special session, Young notified both houses that the legislative counsel's office stood ready to accept drafts of bills and he suggested that the state printing office be authorized to set up galley proofs of bills to be proposed so that regular session business could be expedited. The lawmakers agreed to try this procedure. On January 7, 1929, Governor Young submitted what was perhaps the most comprehensive biennial message to date. He went into intimate detail about the workings of the entire state government. Underlying this message was his theme of "constructive long-time planning" which had to be adopted, he held, if California government were to move forward. He claimed that two year plans were no longer sufficient and that his council had developed a ten year plan.

Young dealt at some length with the old problem of the proper relationship of local governments to state government. Stating that a far reaching constitutional revision was needed, he asked that county government be made more responsive to the wishes of the people.

He devoted considerable attention to the legislative branch, based on his own experience in both houses. He still urged that fewer bills be submitted and these should always be prepared in advance. He expressed some unhappiness over bifurcated sessions as an unnecessary expense for lawmakers.

He then reviewed the state judicial system, noting recent reforms such as reassignment of superior court judges to areas with full dockets to expedite the trying of cases. He stated that recent constitutional changes in the judicial system were all reflections of what he meant by long range planning.

Turning to the executive branch, he discussed the reorganization program and the success of the governor's council. He reported that California led the nation in such planning. After examining the three branches, he analyzed in detail activities of the state agencies. He noted that agriculture, due to diversification, had not suffered as had agriculture nationally. Young considered the two land settlement experiments, started at Durham, Butte County and at Delhi, Merced County, to be failures, having cost the state $3,000,000. Both executive and legislative committees had reached the same conclusion. He asked that the land resettlement program be concluded after readjustments had been made which were fair to both the state and to the project settlers.

Young advocated, as had his predecessors, the necessity of adequate agricultural pest control and quarantine regulations. Worrying about agricultural controls at the state borders with the development of the automobile, he proposed the construction of inspection stations to control and monitor incoming traffic. He announced that the first state forest had been established near Lassen Peak. Commenting on the survey under way to locate suitable state park sites and to plan a bond issue, he believed that the immediate future would find a well developed park system in California.

After a review of various departments and independent agencies, Young commented upon the legislature's investigations of teachers' retirement programs, state employees' pensions, and state aid for the needy. He endorsed all three ideas as in keeping with his theme of building for California's future.

Young considered administrative reorganization to be only in its initial stage as he asked for additional departments of investment, vocational standards, military and veterans' affairs, and penology. He listed also several agencies which should be brought into existing or new departments. The legislature created the four new departments and their heads joined the governor's council.

He concluded that California had an opportunity to launch a government which would influence the history of the state "for a generation to come." Certainly neither this message nor his budget message to follow gave any hint that by the end of 1929 and for the next decade the realms of private and public finance would be sorely tried.

On January 8, 1929, Young submitted his 1929-30 budget, containing three major divisions—the general budget receiving 24 percent of the total, the education budget 32 percent, and the highway budget 44 percent. He reported the items in this manner so that the two largest claimants on the budget could be studied separately. One innovation was to list what each agency had requested and why certain deductions had been made. He called attention for the first time to a problem which plagued succeeding administrations and legislatures. As governor, Young only had direct recommending control over 27.22 percent of the entire budget. The remaining amount was frozen by fixed charges which had been appropriated by legislatures and by expenditures definitely fixed by the constitution or the vote of the people.

California state government had indeed become big business in comparison to the days of the early governors. Young's total budget for his entire administration was $244,075,305.97. Even as late as 1917 the state budget had been only $79,687,-495, but each succeeding biennium had seen increases.

Increased governmental operations were feasible at least during the Young administration because revenues far exceeded spending. When Young came into office the General Fund surplus had been $20,420,983 as of July 1, 1927. He announced that great care had been exercised to live within the state's income and as a result the General Fund had increased to an estimated $29,302,946.40 as of June 30, 1929. He noted that, for the coming two years, 1929-30, anticipated income exceeded expected expenditures by $788,787. In spite of the deepening depression and reduced state income, Young's administration left the state financially strong in 1931.

The accomplishments of Young's 1929 legislative program were best summarized in his 1931 biennial message, which reviewed his four years in office. Great strides were taken during the 1929 session to complete the investigation of the structure of state government. Commissions, comprised of private citizens who gave their time without compensation, had been created to carry out the suggested studies. Four major commissions were initiated in 1929. One was the constitution commission which recommended a revision of the bulky and cumbersome constitution, but nothing materialized from these findings. A commission on county home rule surveyed the need for more county autonomy. The code commission scrutinized every statute with an eye to pruning out dead laws and consolidating duplicates. By 1931, this commission had prepared civil procedures and penal codes. Finally there had been established the commission for the study of education problems which investigated the many phases of public education. In 1929, the school code had been presented to, and adopted by, the legislature. Young reported, too, on the continuing work of the tax commission. In 1931, he reported that its investigations had been more "comprehensive and thoroughgoing" than any study made by any other state. He commented that the source of California's taxes differed from all other states in that the majority of its tax revenue came from public utilities. His 1931 biennial message suggested that public utility tax rates, which had not been raised since 1921, be increased from 30 to 50 percent to equalize the tax burden between those corporations and the private citizens.

Young's review of the 1929 session noted in particular three measures he considered vitally important: construction of a ship-side refrigeration terminal, state supervision of all dam construction work, and creation of a traffic patrol, under civil service, to supervise the use of the state highways.

Governor Young in 1930 sought renomination for a second term. He campaigned on the idea that his administrative reorganization program was but half done and he wished to complete it. He believed that reorganization had been his major accomplishment. He was proud of a far-sighted highway program and of the surplus in the General Fund. His major opponents, Mayor James Rolph, Jr. of San Francisco and Lieutenant Governor Buron Fitts, attacked his program, but no real issue was debated and the campaign came to a finish in August still undecided. However, when the ballots were counted, the colorful campaigner, Rolph, had defeated Young for the Republican nomination by a margin of about 35,000 votes.

In January, 1931, Young sent the legislature his second biennial message which was as comprehensive as his first. His general theme remained long range planning instead of immediate piecemeal legislation. This, Young held, had been the major contribution of his administration as governmental changes and investigations had been effected. He reported that a ten year building program had commenced during his term. He indicated that for the first time in the state history a complete inventory of its property had been made in order to check duplication and waste and to use all property as long as possible.

The governor proudly related that the ten year highway program would create a fine road system. He was pleased that the legislature had curbed its right to create special routes and that the public works department had been allowed to develop a priority system. He suggested that any tax recommended by the tax commission would be proper, for that body had been painstaking in its studies. He also obviously delighted in reporting that the General Fund surplus had increased some $7,500,000 in the last biennium. The Young administration, faced with falling revenues and an expanding state government, had continued to practice economy measures, enabling the surplus to grow.

The nation had suffered through the 1929 stock market crash and the attending depression during the last two years of his term. Young thought that while California had not suffered as much as other parts of the country serious employment problems existed. To overcome these, he advocated first, a greatly expanded public works program to ensure immediate employment, and second, an investigation of the depression so that any future blow to the state's economy might be lessened.

Governor Young complimented the legislature for notable achievements, listing sixty specific measures enacted during the preceding two sessions. He well understood the role of the legislature in making any administrative program succeed as he said, "The service which any Governor can render to his State is largely determined by the legislative sessions during his term in office." He placed these key measures into three categories: governmental, developmental, and miscellaneous. Among governmental acts, executive reorganization headed his list. He also believed the creation of the judicial council to simplify court procedure and of several investigative commissions to be significant. Some of the developmental acts were the long range state building program, financing of highway construction through gasoline taxes, provisions for a California park system, and a program of oil and gas conservation. Among miscellaneous acts were those creating new state institutions—a narcotic hospital, a new penal institution for women, and a nautical school.

At the conclusion of both of his biennial messages, he reported his views concerning the pardoning power. During his term, Young issued seven pardons, six commutations, three reprieves, and twelve restorations to citizenship. He was second only to Richardson in a careful restriction of this power. Young, with reference to executive clemency, considered the effect upon society. He felt that clemency should not be easily obtained by law violators. He was also reluctant to overturn any verdict rendered by a jury or a judge unless new evidence was presented. Young held that a governor should not sit as a thirteenth juror in such cases. He also maintained that no clemency should be granted until a person had been paroled through action of the parole board and had proven that he had become rehabilitated. When this had been done, the person was then subject to be considered by the governor.

In his 1931 report on acts of executive clemency, the governor reviewed at great length the study given to the Tom Mooney case and the reasons for rejecting Mooney's petition. This case was the most controversial incident concerning Young's pardoning power.

Governor Young on January 6, 1931, gave a brief farewell address to the legislature at the inauguration ceremonies of his successor, James Rolph. He restated the principles of good government which he felt had been installed in the preceding four years and claimed that the state was in fine condition and augured well for the incoming administration.

Thus ended Clement Young's long and distinguished elective career. He returned to his former business association, the Mason-McDuffie Company. In 1934, following the death of James Rolph, Young announced his candidacy for the Republican nomination in opposition to the new governor, Frank Merriam, a member of the conservative wing of the Republican party. He was, however, unsuccessful in this attempt, running second in the August primary.

Young's interest in good government did not cease with his retirement from office. He remained an active member of the Commonwealth Club of California, serving as its president in 1939 and 1940. He supervised for the Commonwealth Club a study which was published in January, 1943: *The Legislature of California: Its Membership, Procedure and Work.* It compared the state legislature's activities with other states and presented a factual report of the actual workings of the California legislature.

On Thanksgiving Day, 1947, Young suffered a stroke. He died on Christmas Eve at his Berkeley home at the age of seventy-eight.

His administration must rank as one of the most successful. Efficiency was instilled in state government; many important studies were started and some were completed during his term. The most important aspect of the Young administration was the organization of the governor's council with the consolidation of the many agencies and commissions into a workable and a responsible form of state administration. Clement C. Young proved to be a man of high character and firm resolve. As governor and legislator he served his state well and conscientiously. He was a politician of whom California could justly be proud.

BIBLIOGRAPHY

MANUSCRIPTS
Merriam, Frank, "Papers and Letters" (Bancroft Library).
Rowell, Chester, "Papers."
"Young Biographical Collection," (California Historical Society).

CONTEMPORARY ACCOUNTS
Assembly Journal, 47th-49th Sess., 1927-31.
Senate Journal, 47th-49th Sess., 1927-31.
California Blue Book, 1913-15 & 1924.
Commonwealth Club of California, *Transactions,* XXI (1927), 442-48.
"Sunset's Gallery of Western Governors," *Sunset,* LXVIII (May, 1927), 46.
West, George P., "California's New Governor," *Nation,* CXXIII (1926), 502.
Young, Clement C., "Campaign Letter to the Citizens of California, May 6, 1930."

SECONDARY SOURCES
Posner, R., "The Bank of Italy and the 1926 Campaign . . ." *California Historical Society Quarterly,* XXXVII (1958), 267-75; 347-58.
————, "The Progressive Voters League, 1923-26," *CHSQ,* XXXVI (1957), 251-61.

NEWSPAPERS
Berkeley Gazette, Dec. 26, 1947, has Young's obituary.
Sacramento Bee, Dec. 26, 1947, has obituary.
Sacramento Union, Jan. 5, 1927, reports on Young's inauguration; Jan. 8, 1929, carries story on first biennial message; Dec. 27, 1947, has obituary.
San Diego Union, Jan. 5, 1927, has editorial on inaugural address; Jan. 9, 1929, reports first biennial message.
San Francisco Chronicle, Jan. 5, 1927, has editorial on Young's inauguration; Jan. 9, 1929, reports first biennial message; August 27, 1930, reports Young's defeat for renomination; Jan. 6, 1931, reports Young's last message as governor.

Calendar of Events

August 23, 1869	Rolph born at San Francisco.
1900	Rolph helped found Hind, Rolph and Company.
1911	Rolph elected Mayor of San Francisco and was re-elected to four more terms.
September 24, 1918	Rolph disqualified as candidate for Governor by State Supreme Court.
January 6, 1931	Rolph inaugurated Governor.
October, 1932	The California State Grange proposed recall of Rolph.
March 2-3, 1934	Rolph declared state bank holidays.
May 2, 1933	Legislative special committee presented report critical of Rolph's administration.
1933	State sales tax enacted.
June 2, 1934	Rolph died in Santa Clara County.

James Rolph, Jr.

27TH GOVERNOR—REPUBLICAN
BORN: AUGUST 23, 1869   DIED: JUNE 2, 1934
TERM OF OFFICE: JANUARY 6, 1931—JUNE 2, 1934

JAMES ROLPH, JR. WAS PERHAPS the most picturesque figure to occupy the California governor's chair even though it was his lot to hold office during the dark days of the Great Depression. "Sunny Jim," as he was affectionately called, was the fourth native son governor. Born in San Francisco on August 23, 1869, his life was closely associated with that city. After attending local schools and graduating from Trinity Academy in 1888, Rolph went to work that year as a messenger boy for the shipping firm, DeWitt Kittle and Company. He remained with this firm for twelve years, serving in various capacities.

The year 1900 was an eventful one for James Rolph. First, he married Annie Marshall Reid. Second, he joined his old friend, George U. Hind, in establishing the Hind, Rolph and Company, a shipping concern. Thus was launched a major feature of Rolph's business career. In 1903, he moved into banking circles as he helped found the Mission Bank of which he became president. In 1906, after the earthquake, he became president of the newly formed Mission Savings Bank.

The earthquake and fire became the occasion of Rolph's first public service. As refugees flooded the Mission district, he organized and headed the "Mission Relief Committee." Out of this grew the Mission Promotion Association with Rolph as its president. Later in his life he engaged in other business activities: the Rolph Navigation & Coal Company, the Rolph Shipbuilding Company, and later James Rolph & Company. Rolph found himself in serious financial straits as a result of his wooden ship building venture during the First World War.

Yards had been built on Humboldt Bay at what became known as Rolph. This ship construction venture cost him about a $3,000,000 loss as the ship market collapsed with the end of the war. Not until 1927, was Rolph able to announce that he was financially "out of the woods."

As a consequence of his business and political careers, Rolph found himself a director of the Ship Owners and Merchants Tugboat Company and the San Francisco Chamber of Commerce. He served as vice president of the 1915 Panama-Pacific International Exposition Company and as president of the Merchants Exchange and the Ship Owners Association of the Pacific Coast.

In 1911, James Rolph became a reluctant candidate for San Francisco mayor. He successfully defeated the incumbent, Patrick H. McCarthy, a prominent labor leader in a strong labor city. This victory of "Plain Jim Rolph of the Mission" was but the first of five mayoralty successes as he was re-elected in 1915, 1919, 1923, and 1927. His career as mayor spanned nineteen consecutive years.

San Francisco emerged as a modern city during Rolph's administration. When he took office, the city was emerging from the devastation of the fire and earthquake. By the time he left office, the civic center had been planned with the city hall and auditorium completed. The first municipally owned street car service in the United States had been established. The Hetch Hetchy water system and the Spring Valley Water Company had been secured by the city while a road improvement plan had been carried out with streets paved and the Stockton and Twin Peaks tunnels bored.

In 1918, after a successful first re-election as mayor, Rolph declared himself a candidate for governor as he cross-filed for the Republican and Democratic nominations. The results of the primary election led to great confusion as he won the Democratic nomination, but lost the Republican. A registered Republican, he was consequently disqualified for the November general election which was won by William D. Stephens. Rolph returned to San Francisco politics for the next twelve years.

By 1930, political observers had come to believe that the program of direct primaries had all but destroyed the Democratic party in California at the state level. The real battle for office occurred among the various factions of the Republican party. The Republicans of the state had the usual conservative-liberal split. But in the 1930 campaign there was also bitter conflict over prohibition. The state Anti-Saloon League split with its northern wing supporting Governor Young and the southern wing backing Lieutenant Governor Buron Fitts. The league opposed Rolph, a known "wet."

In the primary campaign, both Rolph and Fitts attacked Young's administrative program. Rolph, relatively unknown outside of the Bay Area, canvassed some 28,000 miles by chartered airplane in an effort to meet the public. Decked out in boots and with a gardenia or carnation in his buttonhole, "Sunny Jim" met his fellow Californians. He showed off his major asset—his winning personality. Rolph emerged from the primary victorious. Some newspapers maintained he won the Republican nomination because he was an avowed "wet," and that his victory repudiated the Anti-Saloon League. It should finally be observed that Rolph did not cross-file in 1930 after his personal disaster in the 1918 gubernatorial race.

The Democrats nominated Milton K. Young, an announced "dry," and Upton Sinclair was again the nominee of the Socialist party. James Rolph, Jr. overwhelmed his opposition at the November polls. He received 999,393 votes; Young garnered 333,973 votes and Sinclair received 50,480. Rolph gained 72 percent of the vote—a sweeping endorsement and the largest majority any governor had received to that time.

As Rolph came to office, Duncan Aikman, writing in *The Nation,* characterized the new governor. The writer claimed that both Johnson and Young had not treated the numerous state political factions too kindly. Aikman held that Rolph's political method was, through a feeling of harmony and tolerance, to create no enemies at all. The writer concluded that the Rolph administration would give little leadership but much radiance.

Rolph took his oath of office January 6, 1931. His inaugural message concerned itself with the effect of the depression upon California: loss of tax revenue, necessary extension of certain state services, and helping the economy to recover. Rolph promulgated no positive legislative program and Governor Young's long range ideas met with scant attention.

He outlined what he called his practical measures. Discussing first the care and treatment of wards of the state, he stated that "the poor, the stricken and the unfortunate shall have a first claim on the consideration of my administration." Although economy in the operation of the state government was necessary, he noted that California could not be niggardly in its care of dependents. Consequently, he advocated repair and expansion of many state facilities.

A major problem was finance. The depression, he reported, had reduced tax revenues at a time when expenditures had sharply increased. Fortunately, the state had a surplus reserve of some $30,000,000. It was natural and proper, he claimed, to expect that the reserve would be used in part to help out in the immediate crisis. He optimistically added:

> A substantial but not excessive surplus should always be maintained, and the surplus, when depleted below the safety point, should be rebuilt. The inroad on the surplus necessitated in the approaching biennium is an emergency and will not recur in the absence of extraordinary conditions.

Rolph claimed that as of January, 1931, there was no need for increasing taxes. Aware that these had become a heavy burden, he pledged: "To keep taxation as low as possible without impairing the service which modern, humane and civilized government ought to render to the public will be my constant concern."

The governor then turned to other problems facing the new administration. He reported that the legislature faced the task of reapportioning legislative districts based on the 1930 census. He urged a fair distribution with no regard to party, sectional, or individual interests. His plea had little effect.

Rolph, in reviewing California's perennial water problem, called for a general unified plan. He, however, offered no new solution. He touched upon the oil and gas industry, relating recent efforts at conservation by the state. He complimented the industry for its voluntary curtailment of production but still maintained that this was a problem for the state to solve.

Rolph touched a tender nerve when he reported that certain distributors had not been paying the 3 cent state gasoline tax. As a result these distributors undersold their competition. He called for remedial legislation.

Rolph reported that while California had an excellent school system, many expenditures could be curtailed. Finding an "oversupply of teachers in the United States," the governor claimed that state teacher colleges need not have their facilities expanded. He further recommended a study of duplication of educational services in the junior colleges, teacher colleges, and the university.

Rolph held that in California, "agriculture is a method of living rather than a business." He thought that the real solution to agriculture's problem was to permit only the state's farmers to enjoy the rich home market. Through enforcement of quarantine laws and other techniques, the governor apparently hoped to restrict competition from abroad and from other states to improve the lot of California farmers.

Governor Rolph maintained that he was friendly to both labor and business. While advocating that labor was entitled to its fair share of industrial production, he announced that he would not stand by and watch a small minority of "hostile" agitators attack the institution of private property. On the other hand, he pledged support to business. Reflecting the conservative position, he observed that "the welfare of business is closely involved with the welfare of the entire population," for these firms employed labor, built the economy, and developed natural resources. Romanticizing for a moment about the fame of California gold, he urged a revival of this once important industry.

Speaking of the state's banks and building and loan associations, Rolph claimed in 1931 that the banks were in excellent condition. However, he found building and loan associations needed to be regulated. His recommendations to codify the laws to strengthen public confidence in these organizations gained subsequent approval.

Governor Rolph, expressing his own personal optimism, urged strong faith in the future:

> All California needs right now to bring about that recovery is a spirit of confidence and quick response to courageous leadership; the state of mind which says, "I will," instead of "I can not." It is my wish to apply such leadership within my province.
> I wish to imbue the people of California with my own faith in California. I wish to begin my administration on a note of hope and confidence. Be prepared by holding such hope and confidence to follow my leadership into the bright days which I see just ahead.

Rolph finished his inaugural address by calling for harmony. His inaugural message was received with mixed reaction throughout the state, reflecting the factional basis of the California political system of his day.

At the start of the 1931 legislative session, Rolph had an unbounded optimism that the depression was about at an end. By the close of the session, however, other elective officers began to have serious doubts about Rolph's views and leadership, and the remainder of his tenure was marked by disharmony. His dream of a tranquil term vanished.

On January 12, 1931, Rolph submitted his first budget message, recommending an outlay of $265,345,955.38. Of this amount, he reported that his office only had direct control of 31.01 percent of the total. He announced that the increase in expenditures was the smallest of any budget presented since 1923. Diminished state income was the grim aspect of his budget. Rolph reported that income in past years had increased at an average of 10.8 percent per biennium. The estimated increase for 1931-32 was only 3.06 percent. In total, state expenditures were estimated to be in excess of anticipated income by $8,440,081.96 which meant that the General Fund reserve would have to make up the deficit. Believing recovery near, Rolph felt that the state could operate for four years without depleting its treasury reserve.

In his budget message, he again recommended funds for permanent improvements in the state institutions to alleviate over-crowding and to curtail unemployment. This proposal was based in large part on Young's ten year building program.

On January 23, 1931, just prior to the mandatory recess, Governor Rolph paid courtesy calls to the Assembly and the Senate. In addressing the Assembly, he stated:

> It has never been my conception of government that the Chief Executive should interfere with the conduct of the government to satisfy the people. He is the head of the government and he should not exert himself in the matters pertaining to the economics of the Senate and the Assembly. He should not use a "big stick." He should not carry on politics. He is the representative of that branch of government which is supreme authority for the State and therefore you have seen nothing in the shape of politics; you have seen nothing in the shape of interference; I have done nothing on my part, except as I saw it.

Here was a key to the difficulties that Rolph later encountered. Refusing to provide legislative leadership, he consequently came to grief when the fiscal crisis deepened. After 1931, the legislature disdained his opinions and provided its own leadership.

Rolph sent the report of his water conservation committee to the 1931 legislature. In essence, the report contained the bold outline of what later became the Central Valley Project. At the same time, Rolph reported on the progress of public works as he listed contracts which had been let for highway construction and for public buildings. To reduce unemployment, this public works program had been greatly accelerated.

As the 1931 session ended, State Treasurer Charles Johnson announced that he foresaw a deficit of from $5,000,000 to $10,000,000 by June, 1933. Johnson charged that state government was being managed by inexperienced hands. In response to this attack, Rolph asked his director of finance, Roland A. Vandergrift, to submit a reply to the legislature. Vandergrift in May, 1931, estimated that by June, 1933, there would be a treasury surplus of about $14,000,000, which would reduce existing funds by $16,000,000. The director commented the Rolph budget had necessitated using some $9,000,000 of the reserve. He reported that the lawmakers had additionally enacted special appropriations in excess of $6,000,000. The responsibility of reducing the reserve to such a low point in the final analysis lay with the legislature. Vandergrift held that the safety margin of the reserve was $15,000,000 and the legislature had been the one to pull it below this point. His summary of the situation was that either Johnson had been misquoted or that he did not have all the information that the department of finance had.

Apart from a public construction program, there were few accomplishments in this session. Certain administrative changes were enacted. The legislature created the new department of motor vehicles, showing the growing importance of the automobile in California's economy. A new building and loan association act replaced the 1911 law. The state park system recommended during the Young administration was established.

Growing disenchantment with Rolph developed during the remainder of 1931 and the next year. The governor, however, outwardly appeared undisturbed by the mounting criticism. He continued to travel about the state as its carefree ceremonial chieftain. He apparently felt that his fellow citizens should share his good times. In August, 1931, he proposed that everyone take a six day holiday from September 4 through September 9. This was so startling a proposal that it met more with amazement than protest. Rolph, meanwhile, went on a fishing trip and the proposal came to an end, but not without people wondering what kind of man would suggest a holiday in such difficult times.

While mayor of San Francisco, Rolph had developed good political relationships with labor. However, in 1932, labor leaders began to lose faith in him as he followed the precedent of other governors in refusing to pardon Tom Mooney. On April 22, 1932, he announced that he could find no basis for a pardon and that he believed in Mooney's guilt.

The gathering storm of protest broke in October, 1932. However, the *New York Times* reported that Rolph, a constant rodeo attender, had learned how to ride out rough going in the political arena. In October, the California State Grange instituted a recall resolution against the governor and demanded investigations of the departments of agriculture, finance, and public works. The Grange adopted a general resolution that the legislature make a thorough investigation.

The background of the Grange incident, according to the *New York Times,* was the fact that Rolph had allowed dissension within his political family. For weeks the press had been aware of a fight behind the scenes and then came the Grange's outburst. There had been some vague allegations of irregularities in granting the contract for 1933 auto license tags. This charge brought from the governor a blast against his critics and the dismissal of some of his aides. He demanded the resignations of Walter E. Garrison, director of the department of public works and James I. Herz, his chief deputy. Rolph claimed that the two dismissed men had been leaking gossip about his administration. Garrison charged that he had been fired because he refused to channel business opportunities to a trucking company friendly to the governor.

At the same time, Charles Johnson charged that the director of finance, Vandergrift, had incurred a $100,000 loss to California by selling state and municipal bonds below the current market price and then buying the bonds back at a higher price. Vandergrift claimed that this had long been normal procedure and that in reality he had made about $500,000 for the state. At a later date, Rolph discharged his director of agriculture,

Dudley Moulton, as a result of criticism over state and federal cooperation in agriculture.

The *New York Times* observed that "since the removal of Garrison . . . Every day had brought out a new set of allegations of some sort of skullduggery in one or another branch . . . Patronage, rake-off on surety bonds for public contractors, brokerage or the buying and selling of securities in the State Treasury have figured in the allegations. Relatives of the Governor have been mentioned as beneficiaries of business thrown their way as the result of official pressure." In the face of such turmoil, the governor continued to fly about the state visiting fairs and carrying on his role of public functionary with no visible concern about the criticism heaped upon him.

Thus was the stage set for an eventful legislative session in 1933. The state government was overwhelmed by the economic disaster which confronted it. Much feuding occurred between the governor and the lawmakers regarding the means of solving the financial crisis and by the end of the session, they were at loggerheads.

Governor Rolph's 1933 biennial message disclosed his own uncertainties. His optimistic thoughts of 1931 had not been borne out by subsequent events, and Charles Johnson had proved an able prophet about the General Fund. Rolph reported a deficit of about $9,500,000.

The depleted treasury haunted Rolph as he delivered this message. At a moment when vigorous new planning seemed to be needed, the governor expressed outmoded ideas about relief and aid to the distressed in California. He indicated that the state could no longer carry out its many public services. In 1933, he advocated that the counties would have to reassume these duties and shoulder their responsibilities for the sake of economy. Still holding that California had its duty to care for its own, he found the state's ability was not "as unlimited as our zeal." He added that there was a "natural division of such humane responsibilities between the state and local government."

He believed that the 1933 legislature met in "the midst of the most momentous economic prostration that has afflicted mankind since the commencement of the age of machinery." His solution, one reflecting his frustration, was for the people of California to continue having hope and faith in the future.

This was a restatement of his 1931 position, but in 1933, it seemed stated more in desperation.

Turning to the financial condition of California, he claimed to be proud of the fiscal accomplishments of the past two years. Despite increased demands on state aid, such as old age pensions, he announced that there had been a reduction in the per capita cost of government and that his administration had cut expenditures about $4,000,000. In spite of this, the 1931 General Fund surplus had become a deficit of some $9,500,000. That it had not been more, Rolph said, was due to careful administration. Fiscal collapse came as tax sources withered away, far below 1931 budget estimates. He called for a 1933 balanced budget based on state economies and further reduced tax revenues. One possible solution, he claimed, was "on the one side drastic economies; on the other side heavy additional taxes."

The governor again surveyed the depletion of the General Fund and tried to explain away the difficulties ensnaring his administration. He announced plans to re-establish the surplus as soon as possible. If his budget recommendations were followed, there would be no need for new taxes and he claimed that the deficit would be wiped out! If nothing else, such an attitude pronounced Rolph as a confirmed optimist.

He then outlined specific proposals. He suggested that a special election be held in February to authorize reduction of constitutional charges which made specific levies on the budget. He had in mind reducing school support from $30.00 to $24.00 per pupil and removing constitutional control of fixed school appropriations. Such control, he felt, should be delegated to the legislature. The alternative to this proposal, he warned, was increased taxes. He also asked that there be a constitutional amendment to allow borrowing from the perpetual school fund.

He advocated that fixed budget charges which had been enacted by legislative statute be reduced, such as state aid to public tuberculosis wards. He devoted considerable attention to controlling state aid to the aged. He thought the state had reached its financial limit here and that the counties should make up the difference in costs. He urged reduction of vocational education costs by 25 percent. He concluded with a reiteration that a balanced budget was possible.

Reacting to the Grange's criticism of the department of agriculture, the governor carefully noted advances by that agency. He listed among its accomplishments a surplus food distribution plan, eradication of various animal diseases, and effective control of certain plant insects and diseases. He pointed particularly to the establishment in the San Joaquin valley of two labor camps which provided employment for 200 men.

With reference to labor and unemployment, Rolph called for constructive remedial legislation to return people to work. An immediate solution, already started, preceding the Civil Conservation Corps of the federal government, had been the establishment of camps for unemployed single men. These men were put to work constructing firebreaks and improving watersheds. Rolph found that national publicity about these camps had reduced the influx of unemployed to California. He reviewed the conditions of banks and building and loan associations. Some failures had occurred but he added all depositors needed to have faith that in time their savings would be returned. He concluded his message by once more urging that a spirit of good will prevail.

His message was coldly received by the legislature. The *Sacramento Union* was extremely critical of the message and the governor as it wrote:

> Rolph may be proud of the fiscal administration of the past two years but he is sadly in the minority.
> He shows a lack of knowledge of current trends of thought throughout his message. He has evidently listened only to those with good things to say. He has not heard the undercurrent of dissent.
>
> *   *   *
>
> Flitting from place to place and lighting like a butterfly has not enriched the governor's knowledge of state affairs. He has sipped only the honey and has not tasted the bitterness everywhere present. It is amazing that he could remain so ignorant of real conditions as his message shows him to be.
> The legislature should take the message for what it is worth and try to extract from it such wisdom as it can find. It will need all the help it can get to put the state back on its feet.
> The message proves beyond a shadow of doubt that the governor in spite of two years' experience is entirely innocent of public trends of thought. He is too naive to be real.

Throughout the 1933 session—a lengthy one—state finance was of major concern. On January 12, Governor Rolph submitted his budget message. He observed that no governor, since budget reporting had become mandatory, had been faced with presenting a balanced budget in the light of uncertain income. He again stated that either there must be economy in expenditures or increases in taxation. He related that his program of reducing legally fixed charges and strict adherence to his requests were the only way to a balanced budget without additional taxes. To accomplish the needed reductions, he proposed a seven step program. In addition to those constitutional changes urged in his biennial message, he advocated reimbursement from the General Fund for money previously diverted to highways, approval of recommended appropriations, and reduction by law of fixed statutory charges.

He outlined possible new tax sources if his economy program was not adopted. In opposition to increasing the tax load of those already carrying a heavy burden, he suggested widening the tax base in order to include those people who were in no way contributing to state finances. He listed tobacco, beer, beverages, confections, and certain luxury items as possible areas of taxation.

Rolph's recommended 1933-34 budget was $258,655,163.47, a reduction of more than $24,000,000 over his previous budget. He paid close attention to ways of reducing current expenditures. He did not outline expected revenues but noted estimated income was to be about $92,300,000.

During January, the governor reported that the Reconstruction Finance Corporation had approved support funds for the state's labor camps and the San Francisco Bay Bridge. Late in the month, while confined to the St. Francis Hospital in San Francisco, he wrote the lawmakers thanking them for passing the necessary measures to start work on the bridge.

Although ill, Rolph later sent a sharp note to the legislature as it prepared for its constitutional recess. He complained that his budget plan had only been studied haphazardly. He charged that no steps had been taken to meet the deficit in the General Fund and his plan for a special election had been sidetracked as the lawmakers had surrendered to lobbyists. He claimed the only remaining option was increased taxes. He placed the blame on the legislature and stated that since they had not followed his lead, it was charged with finding a solution to the problem.

On January 30, the State Grange announced that it had

petitions of recall ready to circulate. The petition stated that
Rolph was incompetent. At this point, the governor found himself caught between the recall movement and a special Senate
investigation committee, which was then holding hearings into
the conduct of his administration. Although Rolph was ill at
his Santa Clara County ranch, he released countercharges
against Senators J. M. Inman and Herbert C. Jones which put
the committee on the defensive. On February 23, the Grange
dropped its recall plan.

On February 28, as the legislature reconvened, Governor
Rolph addressed a joint convention of the lawmakers. He outlined the state fiscal picture as they returned to work. Since
they had rejected his proposals, he said it should be determined whether the people opposed new taxes, particularly an
ad valorem tax, or whether they would accept economies in
government. He now stated that he opposed increasing taxes.

California, like the rest of the nation, faced a banking crisis.
Rolph in a proclamation said that the national crisis had adversely affected California banks with heavy withdrawals of
funds leaving the state. To protect the institutions and the depositors, he declared March 2 and March 3 as legal holidays.
President Roosevelt, after taking office, declared a national
bank holiday. Governor Rolph on March 8, prior to the passage
of the federal emergency banking act, extended the holiday in
California through March 11.

On March 9, the Senate fact-finding committee, searching for
economies in government, submitted its report on the constitu-
tionally elected officers. It reported that the budget request for
support of the governor's office was $154,840. Of this, $20,000
was the governor's salary. The state had been asked to provide
$36,340 to maintain the governor's mansion. For the gover-
nor's office, $88,500 had been proposed. An additional $10,000
had been requested for a special contingent expense which, the
committee indicated, was for paying secret service agents. The
committee reported that the cost of the office for 1923-25 had
been $98,680. Recommendations were made that operational
costs of the office and mansion be reduced.

Governor Rolph was constantly aware of the special investigating committee which was looking into the conduct of his
administration and from time to time he issued complaints
about the committee. On May 2, the committee issued its final

report. It was extremely critical of Rolph's reported use of influence to determine the route of secondary roads to benefit political friends. It also criticized the fact that the firm of Rolph, Landis and Ellis, of which the governor had been a former partner, had written an unduly large amount of indemnity bonds for state agencies and individuals. The report suggested that "if these facts tend to cast reflection upon any State official then the fault lies with such an official."

On May 11, Rolph replied to the charges. He assailed the report as being venomous. He asserted the committee had been packed by Lieutenant Governor Frank Merriam, an "avowed candidate" for governor. He called the investigation led by Inman and his office associate, Sheridan Downey, an effort "to poison" public opinion against the governor. He then related the specific charges he had earlier made against Inman and Jones. He answered point by point the criticisms leveled against the various departments and himself. This was the end of public name calling by the two sides but personal animosities were not easily forgotten.

The bill incorporating the governor's budget finally passed the Assembly, but was rejected by the Senate. A second budget bill, drafted by legislative leaders, passed both houses and was presented to the governor to sign. On May 11, he signed, but noted that it did nothing more than provide for the operation of the government. No provisions had been made either to meet the current deficit or to provide for revenues to meet approved appropriations. He then criticized the lawmakers for planning to take an unprecedented recess until July 17 with major problems still confronting them. He stated that since they had rejected his program, the solution lay with them.

During this fiftieth session, the legislature enacted a state income tax bill which Rolph vetoed. He agreed to the passage of a state sales tax which levied a 2.5 percent tax on retail items except gasoline. While this was in keeping with Rolph's view that all people ought to contribute to the cost of state government, he lost favor with wage earners who were the hardest hit by the new program. People sarcastically referred to the new tax as "Pennies for Sunny Jim."

For the bulk of the session, the governor and the legislature were unable to cooperate on fiscal problems. However, in other state affairs, the legislature did not repudiate his leadership.

While it was in session, Rolph vetoed fifty-six Assembly bills; only eight were not sustained. He returned forty-three Senate bills of which seven vetoes were overridden. During the session, Rolph appointed many investigating committees to study the economic crisis, but little action was forthcoming.

During his tenure, Governor Rolph made liberal use of his pardoning power. He granted 374 pardons; 351 of these were for people who had violated laws enforcing prohibition. When these laws had been repealed in 1933, those convicted under them were released.

In December, 1933, Rolph found himself once more in the national spotlight when two men were taken from jail and lynched by a mob in San Jose. He had been asked to provide troops to protect the two kidnappers, but refused. Afterwards, *The Nation* quoted the governor as saying:

> Why should I call out troops to protect those two fellows? The people make the laws, don't they? Well; if people have confidence that troops will not be called out to mow them down when they seek to protect themselves against kidnappers, there is liable to be swifter justice and fewer kidnappings.

The governor's claim that the hangings had provided a good lesson for the country brought him extremely bad publicity. He was dubbed "Governor Lynch."

In February, 1934, he commenced mending political fences for the forthcoming gubernatorial campaign. On February 28, he collapsed at Marysville and was rushed by ambulance to San Francisco. After weeks of serious illness, complicated by a previous attack of pneumonia, he was allowed to go to his Santa Clara County ranch, and later to his San Francisco office. On May 3, he collapsed again. Upon recovering, he announced that after the conclusion of his current term he would retire from public office. He went to the Walter Linforth ranch in Santa Clara County in a vain effort to recuperate. On June 2, James Rolph, Jr. died at the age of sixty-four of a heart ailment.

No one would deny that James Rolph had come to the governor's chair at a most difficult time. He firmly believed the office of governor of California to be one of the highest offices in the United States. By 1933, he was aware that his boundless optimism was not sufficient. He could not cope with the disaster that lay ahead. Faith and hope alone did not solve problems and he—along with other elected officials—lacked the personal characteristics to provide needed leadership. Governor Rolph did his best but the economic crisis overwhelmed him. In spite of this, the *Sacramento Union,* an extreme critic of his gubernatorial career, expressed the feelings of most Californians when it stated that he was loved simply for being himself.

BIBLIOGRAPHY

MANUSCRIPTS
Rolph, James, Jr., "State Officials Letter File," (California Section, State Library).

CONTEMPORARY ACCOUNTS
Assembly Journal, 49th-50th Sess., 1931-33.
Senate Journal, 49th-50th Sess., 1931-33.
California Blue Book, 1932.

SECONDARY SOURCES
Aikman, Duncan, "California's Sun God," *Nation,* CXXXII (1931), 35-37.
"Governor Lynch and His Mob," *Nation,* CXXXVII (1933), 666.
"Mayor Jimmie Rolph—an Institution," *Sunset,* L (June, 1928), 16-18, 54.
Taylor, David W., *The Life of James Rolph, Jr.* (San Francisco, 1934).
Wolfe, W.C., ed., *Men of California* (1925).

NEWSPAPERS
Sacramento Bee, Jan. 4, 1933, reports on Rolph's only biennial message; Jan. 12, 1933, has story on his controversial budget.
Sacramento Union, Aug. 24, 1930, studies candidates in 1930 gubernatorial campaign; June 3, 1934, has Rolph's obituary.
San Diego Union, Jan. 7, 1931, reports Rolph's inauguration; June 3, 1934, has his obituary.
San Francisco Chronicle, Jan. 7, 1931, has the inauguration; Jan. 5, 1933, is critical of Rolph's biennial message; June 3, 1934, has his obituary.
San Jose Mercury, June 3, 1934, has his obituary.
New York Times, Oct. 23, 1932, reports on California Grange recall movement and relates the background for the charges; Feb. 23, 1934, indicates recall program dropped.

THESIS
Goldbeck, Herman G., "The Political Career of James Rolph, Jr.: A Preliminary Study" (M.A., University of California, 1936).

Governors Mansion, Sacramento. The above engraving was made for Thompson and West's *History of Sacramento County* in 1880 when the mansion was the home of Albert Gallatin. Gallatin, an associate with Huntington, Hopkins and Company, built the home in the mid 1870's. Located on the southwest corner of 16th and H, it became the official home for California governors in 1903, and has been the home of eleven chief executives.

Calendar of Events

December 22, 1865	Merriam born at Hopkinton, Iowa.
1888	Merriam graduated from Lennox College, Hopkinton.
1896	Merriam elected to Iowa House of Representatives.
1898	Merriam elected Iowa State Auditor.
1904	Merriam moved to Oklahoma Indian Territory.
1910	Merriam moved to Long Beach.
November 7, 1916	Merriam elected to Assembly from Long Beach for the first of five terms.
January 8, 1923	Merriam elected Speaker of Assembly.
August 31, 1926	Buron Fitts defeated Merriam for Republican nomination for Lieutenant Governor.
November 4, 1930	Merriam elected Lieutenant Governor.
June 2, 1934	Merriam became Governor, following death of Rolph.
January 8, 1935	Merriam inaugurated Governor.
1935	State income tax enacted.
November 8, 1938	Olson defeated Merriam.
April 25, 1955	Merriam died in Long Beach.

Frank F. Merriam

28TH GOVERNOR—REPUBLICAN
BORN: DECEMBER 22, 1865   DIED: APRIL 25, 1955
TERM OF OFFICE: JUNE 2, 1934—JANUARY 2, 1939

FRANK FINLEY MERRIAM WAS BORN December 22, 1865, at Hopkinton, Iowa, a small community near Dubuque. He attended the local schools and in 1888 graduated from Lennox College at Hopkinton with a B.S. degree. He then became principal of the Hopkinton school for two years. He served for one year as superintendent of schools at Postville. He next became the editor of the *Hopkinton Leader*.

His successful Iowa political career started in the early nineties as he served first on the Republican state central committee. In 1892, he was appointed clerk of the Iowa House appropriations committee and in 1894 was appointed clerk of the Iowa Senate judiciary committee. Profiting from his experience with the legislature, Merriam in 1896 was elected as representative from Delaware County. He was re-elected in 1898. In his first session, he was a member of a three man commission, which investigated all Iowa state agencies. From this study came the law creating the Iowa board of control.

In 1898, he was a candidate for Iowa state auditor, gaining the Republican nomination without opposition. Success in this election led to his resignation from the House; he served two terms as auditor.

In 1901, he married Mrs. Nellie Day. In 1904, Merriam moved to the Oklahoma Indian Territory where he tried unsuccessfully to acquire free land. While in the territory, he owned and published the *Muskogee Evening Times*. In 1910, Merriam and his wife left for California, arriving at Long Beach where he joined the *Long Beach Press* advertising de-

381

partment. In time he became its business executive. Merriam's wife died July 7, 1931. On January 25, 1936, he married Mrs. Jessie Lipsey, becoming the first governor to be married in office.

Merriam's long California political career began in 1916, when he ran for the Assembly for the Long Beach district. This was the first of his five terms in that body. In 1922, he managed successfully Friend Richardson's campaign for governor and, in turn supported by the governor, was selected as Speaker for the 1923 and 1925 sessions. He was one of the main legislative leaders of the Richardson economy program. As Speaker, Merriam gained prominence and was known as an aggressive leader of the Republican right wing.

In 1926, Merriam sought the Republican nomination for lieutenant governor but lost to Buron Fitts. However, this was but a momentary set-back in his political career. In 1928, as chairman of the Republican state central committee, he managed Hoover's presidential campaign in California. He was also elected in 1928 to the State Senate where he served two years.

In 1930, he again was a candidate for lieutenant governor and this time won. Merriam has been the only governor to have served in the Assembly, both as a member and Speaker, and in the Senate, both as a member and presiding officer. In 1930, Merriam polled 879,597 votes as opposed to 445,470 for his two rivals. Merriam served as lieutenant governor until June 2, 1934, when Governor Rolph died. In reality, Merriam continued as lieutenant governor and served as acting governor for the duration of Rolph's term which expired in January, 1935. Based on a supreme court decision, after James Budd's attempted appointment of a lieutenant governor was disallowed, it was held that the lieutenant governor performed the functions of the two offices. The same ruling had also been applied in 1917 when Lieutenant Governor Stephens assumed the duties of governor.

Rolph's death disrupted normal administrative affairs, and, occurring in a gubernatorial election year, threw the Republican party into confusion. Merriam at once became the leading contender.

Merriam's first official act was to close all state offices until after the funeral of Rolph. On June 5, Merriam announced "the state's business will be conducted from the seat of govern-

ment and not from Long Beach or any other city in the state."
This was a direct slap at Rolph who had made San Francisco
his main headquarters. In preparing for the August primaries,
Merriam gave some appointments to men sympathetic with his
policies.

The threat of possible violence along the San Francisco
waterfront confronted Merriam's administration immediately.
Longshoremen had been on strike since May 9, 1934, and the
crisis was slowly building; in addition, there were other labor
disturbances in the state. On June 12, Merriam issued a statement pledging that the state government would resist to the
utmost the "subversive activities of avowed Communists" and
fomentors of industrial hatred.

On July 5, following an effort to break the San Francisco
strike, violent fighting broke out. Merriam called out the national guard to protect state property and in particular the
state owned Belt Line Railway. The governor's vigorous stand
against the strikers gained him conservative support throughout
the state as large numbers of Californians viewed with concern
the widespread labor unrest.

These same Californians soon found another threat to their
point of view. In the August primaries while Merriam defeated
three other Republicans for nomination, including ex-Governor
C. C. Young, Upton Sinclair captured the Democratic nomination, receiving more votes than Merriam. Political sages commonly held that if Sinclair received the endorsement of President Roosevelt, he would win the November general election.

With the full effect of the depression being felt in every
corner of the state, an air of desperation lay over California.
Under these circumstances the 1934 general election was conducted. Upton Sinclair, long time Socialist, had just a few
months earlier switched to the Democratic party. He had
written much about the problems of capitalism, and in 1934
he came forward with a program called End Poverty in California. Better known as EPIC, this was Sinclair's solution to
the depression. Political opponents, both in and out of his
party, waged a campaign of fear. Merriam through the fall
months found gathered in his camp all those groups who feared
the consequences of a Sinclair victory.

Based partly on Sinclair's threat to his election and partly
on the real need of the people of California, Merriam called the

legislature into special session in September. The purpose
was to enact bond measures for the ballot in the coming election. These measures had been drafted in keeping with recommendations by federal relief authorities as representing California's share in recovery and relief programs. Merriam stated:

> There can be no question of the fact that a very broad and far-
> reaching program must be carried out by the State government of
> California looking not only to the care of the unemployed, the sick
> and disabled, and the aged, but also to the establishment of
> agencies concerned with the restoration of sound economic con-
> ditions throughout the state.
>
> Greater social justice, guaranteed by statute and by State policy,
> must be our determined purpose.

Many of Sinclair's points were neutralized to some degree
by measures passed in this session. It was also apparent that
Roosevelt's New Deal gained some acceptance in California as
the state government found that state resources could not meet
the crisis alone. The legislature accepted Merriam's program
with only minor reservations.

The 1934 California general election saw three major candidates with Raymond L. Haight running on a strong Progressive
ticket. This Progressive party was composed primarily of
moderate and liberal Democrats opposed both to Sinclair and
Merriam. The November election results showed Merriam
winning with 1,138,620 votes. Sinclair received 879,537 votes,
and Haight received 302,599. Other candidates received 9,046
scattered votes. California politics continued to confound
political experts as the state returned a Republican governor in
the face of national Democratic gains under the New Deal.

Merriam was physically a large man. His rotund, genial
face was accentuated by his baldness. Early in life, Merriam
had been characterized by acquaintances as having a strong
personality and popularity. As he grew older, he became more
conservative in his political views and more retiring in his
personality. As governor, he was known to be sincere, honest
of purpose, and forthright and devoted in defense of his beliefs.

On January 8, 1935, Frank Finley Merriam, standing before
the joint convention of the legislature, took the oath of office to
become governor in his own right. In a brief inaugural address,
Merriam, outlining his philosophy of government and plans
to combat the depression, called for complete cooperation and

confidence by the legislature. The major task facing the government of California was, he claimed, to restore employment, provide relief for the destitute and the suffering, and promote fuller enjoyment of the "full range of social justice and basic human needs."

The future of the state's economy looked bright to Merriam despite the depression. To attain high employment levels, he claimed, the state government had to provide necessary public services. Merriam revealed his conservatism as he stated that in times of emergency it was natural for people to look to all levels of government for aid and support—"but as fondly as some may believe, and as earnestly as others may hope, government itself can not indefinitely assume the responsibility for meeting all the demands of this depression and this emergency." He continued this theme by stating that "government cannot permanently assume responsibilities which the private citizen and private business must eventually discharge if our people are to remain free and independent."

Merriam held that the key to recovery in the state was "placing the government of California on a sound financial basis." He advocated, as had his predecessors, a stringent reduction of expenditures. He added that no burdensome taxes should be imposed; any new ones should be distributed on an equitable basis and not aimed at any particular segment of the population. He pointed out that despite a program of retrenchment and economy, the fiscal deficit had continued to mount.

The governor reported that the state had cooperated with the federal government's relief program. Merriam held that California had never fully understood its responsibility for the handicapped and that society would have to assume this obligation. His inaugural ended with the thought that the legislature should guide its own affairs in the crisis ahead and not respond to special interest groups.

On January 22, 1935, Merriam appeared before the legislative joint convention to deliver his first budget message which also served in part as a biennial message as he recommended fiscal and legislative programs. He called attention to the deepening economic crisis as he stated:

> There is no precedent in this State for the financial difficulties
> in which we find ourselves. State revenues have decreased marked
> ly during the last few years. At the same time, due in part to

emergency demands arising from the extended economic depression, it has not been possible to accomplish any great reduction in governmental costs.

We now come face to face with the fact that the disparity between the income of the State and the expenditures of the State has reached a point of real danger.

In the face of greatly curtailed tax revenues, Merriam maintained that the governor and the legislature had to "provide means and adopt policies that will cause the State itself to observe the ordinary precautions of the prudent citizen who does not spend more than he may reasonably expect to earn, and who does not borrow more than he may ultimately be able to repay." The state fiscal situation was so bad that even if all agencies supported by the General Fund were eliminated, the budget still would not be balanced. He claimed that "the people, who expect no such impossible action nevertheless demand that we, as their chosen representatives, shall cut out all needless costs; that we shall place the government on a sound footing of economy and efficiency, and that we shall obtain maximum returns from the expenditure of public funds."

He summarized the minimum budget requirements for 1935-1937 as being in excess of $228,200,000, which did not include the anticipated deficit of about $29,000,000. The other aspect of this dark picture indicated the estimated revenue for the two year period would be about $132,600,000. Thus California by 1937 would find its fiscal sheet out of balance by $124,600,000, unless precautionary steps were taken.

The governor proposed that the deficit be handled separately from the budget through an amortization plan over a period of years. To offset declining tax income, Merriam proposed nine new sources of tax revenue. The greatest departure from previous tax suggestions was his recommendation and subsequent adoption by the legislature of a state personal income tax. Following his recommendation, an alcoholic beverage control act established rates on hard liquors and raised rates on beer as well as implementing methods of regulating alcoholic sales.

The legislature adopted some of his recommendations and enacted additional taxes which gained Merriam's signature. Confronted with inadequate revenue, the governor demonstrated his devotion to the political views of Friend Richardson by subscribing to a program of rigid economy and high efficiency.

Governor Merriam reviewed conditions in the various state institutions. He found all to be overcrowded. A recent San Quentin prison break was a manifestation of this condition. He claimed that this prison was a blight on the record of the state. It was no place, he said, to send first offenders, for they were not segregated from the more confirmed criminal. To alleviate this, he called for a new institution in the southern part of the state. Subsequently, the prison at Chino was built.

Conditions in state hospitals were deplorable with many temporary housing facilities, built in 1918, still in use. The governor proposed a minimum construction program. Both hospital and prison building proposals, he noted, could possibly be financed by federal public works funds.

He called for a new department of public safety to combine the many law enforcement agencies. He hoped that the state would become "unpopular with the gangster, the criminal, and the thug. . . ." He believed that such a department would curb organized crime in the state, but his proposal was rejected.

His message next discussed California's water and power problem. He held that restating the issues would only add to the confusion and the prejudices surrounding the topic. He called for a commission to investigate the water and power program. His proposal on electrical power was based on the federal government's recently enacted Tennessee Valley Authority. He alluded to the fact California had two large power systems—one privately owned and the other publicly owned. As a result of TVA, the governor was uncertain as to the status of private power and he wanted the citizens informed. There was no doubt that he sympathized with the private power position. He tied the problem of electrical power to that of water resources, recognizing that the two could not be separated.

Governor Merriam's message in 1935 clearly foresaw California's water problem. Outlining the fact that parts of the state had surplus water while the rest had scant supplies, he urged that long range planning be continued. Apart from mentioning plans for the Central Valley Project, he did not elaborate on what the immediate course should be. In accordance with Roosevelt's position on public works, Merriam stated that California could obtain unemployment relief funds to make the Central Valley Project a reality.

Merriam, turning to social security legislation, quoted at

length from President Roosevelt's outline of federal social security. Merriam, in complete agreement with Roosevelt, announced that once Congress had acted he would ask for enactment of measures permitting California to participate in the program. The 1935 legislative session passed the necessary laws.

The governor also suggested that the legislature devise a state program of unemployment insurance to meet future crises. He endorsed the old age pension plan advocated by Dr. Francis Townsend of Long Beach as potentially practical. His suggestion that the legislature memorialize Congress to investigate the merits of the plan was adopted.

In a discussion of the state highway system, Governor Merriam urged abandoning the dual system of state and county highways to create a single state system to save countless tax dollars. His proposal that cities receive an additional ¼ cent from the existing 3 cent gasoline tax to be used to construct and maintain city streets other than those designated as state highways was adopted by the legislature.

Another area of importance in California politics was oil production. Merriam's budget message noted that private regulation of crude oil production had not been satisfactory and he urged state controls to protect small producers who were being forced out of business by large ones. The oil lobby exerted powerful influence on the lawmakers and during the 1935 session the governor's request for a severance and processing tax on oil came to naught. The tidelands oil controversy loomed as a major issue. A 1935 measure gave owners of the littoral land exclusive right to obtain leases to slant drill tideland oil reserves. Merriam killed this bill with a pocket veto. In November, 1935, speaking informally before a meeting of oil producers, Merriam, however, rebutted his earlier position as he suggested that oil producers be given the opportunity to regulate production without federal or state interference.

Merriam's 1935 budget message was not well received. It was apparent to most observers that state finances were in a critical condition. In mid-January, he delivered his version of a "fireside chat" to Californians in which he discussed fiscal problems and asked that citizens forward ideas about any new taxes. He immediately provoked a vast majority of citizens with his program of "consumer and nuisance taxes." Following his budget message, a coalition of progressive Republicans and EPIC Democrats revolted against his tax proposals. A joint legislative committee took leadership out of the hands of the governor and developed a compromise tax program between Merriam's position and that of the EPIC group. The legislature passed a personal income tax at 25 percent of the federal income tax levy; the state sales tax was increased from 2.5 to 3 percent; inheritance and bank and corporation taxes were sharply increased.

As the 1935 session ended, the *New York Times* provided an estimate of Merriam's encounter with the lawmakers. The newspaper noted that the 1935 legislature needed leadership more desperately than any other in California history. However, even before Merriam took his oath of office, it was apparent that even his own party was not pleased with him as governor. To many voters, he had been the lesser of two evils in the November election. From the beginning of his four year term, he lacked popular support.

During the session, Merriam alienated both conservatives and liberals in and out of the legislature. He began by irking conservatives with his open stand for the Townsend plan. In June, he antagonized liberal elements when he vetoed the Nielsen bill, which authorized creation of local public utility commissions to distribute the electrical power and water from the Central Valley Project. Merriam based his veto on the fact that only a simple majority vote in a proposed district was needed to endorse such undertakings. He held that the usual procedure of a two-thirds majority should be mandatory. This bill had passed the Senate without a dissenting vote and had received a two-thirds vote in the Assembly. The private power lobby had been particularly active in trying to defeat the bill and Merriam's veto appeared to many as an indication that he had joined ranks with the power group. A *New York Times* correspondent claimed that "Governor Merriam remains an amiable and somewhat neutral figure. California has no strong feelings about him one way or the other. He has turned out to be about what was expected."

Serious strikes continued to plague the Merriam administration. In September, 1936, Merriam helped break a Salinas area lettuce strike when he ordered in 150 highway patrolmen who used sticks and tear gas. The press, noting that the patrol had been expressly forbidden by law to do strike duty, called the governor no friend of labor.

On January 14, 1937, Governor Merriam broke with tradition when he presented his budget message. He did not deliver the usual biennial message, but combined fiscal affairs and legislative suggestions into the one message.

He stated that in the past two years, California had made a steady recovery from the depression. He claimed that the state had a balanced budget while the estimated 1935-37 deficit was about $18,000,000. He held that if his budget were adopted the government by 1939 would again find itself with a General Fund surplus in excess of $21,000,000. His 1937-38 budget called for estimated expenditures of $446,476,507.34 with income predicted at $487,440,131. He reported that the 1935 revenue estimates had been too conservative and that increased state revenue reflected the general upturn in business conditions.

The governor consequently felt that no new taxes need be levied. Economies carried out by his administration and the rapid improvement of business, he claimed, made this possible. Once more expressing the philosophy of his mentor, Friend Richardson, Merriam said, "by spending less than we collect, by saving all that we can, by increasing efficiency without unnecessarily adding to expenses, we shall eventually take the next great step in a return to the normal functions of good government—a reduction in taxation." The governor added that voter rejection of the 1935 state bond issues for construction of new state buildings proved that citizens endorsed the idea of curtailing indebtedness.

A major stress on budgets of the 1930's was unemployment relief. Merriam requested $48,000,000 to sustain this program for 1937-38. After reviewing the history of relief financing from 1933 to 1936, Merriam revealed that California and the United States together had spent $158,816,551 in 1935 and 1936 for state relief.

In 1937, for the most part, official communication between the governor and the legislature consisted of a series of veto messages signed by Merriam. These showed Merriam's determination to hold the line against increased state expenditures as he rejected increases for salaries, services, and taxes.

During the 1937 session, Senator Culbert Olson led in the passage of a tidelands oil measure. His bill, placed on the

November, 1938, ballot as a referendum measure, was rejected. The tidelands oil matter and some other issues were debated in a special session of the legislature in March, 1938. In calling the meeting, Merriam listed thirty-six points to be considered. He claimed that no partisan issues were involved in problems confronting the state. He related the need for a measure to protect oil deposits. The legislature passed, and he signed, an act creating the state land commission which could authorize slant drilling only in the tidelands.

He reiterated the urgent necessity of housing bills. He also commented on the rise of unemployment which had altered the estimated expenditures for relief. To help those state agencies concerned, he asked for an additional $4,900,000. He requested another $3,000,000 for the emergency fund to meet any subsequent demands.

In 1938, Merriam was a candidate to succeed himself as governor. Many in the Republican party wishing to unseat him rallied behind Lieutenant Governor George J. Hatfield of San Francisco. A bitter intra-party feud developed and while Merriam was successful in overwhelming Hatfield in the August primary, the party remained badly split. This factionalism, along with Merriam's lackluster personality and the national tide of Democratic victories during the 1930's led to the governor's defeat in November by Culbert Olson.

Merriam proved to be more liberal than most twentieth century governors in the use of his pardoning power. He issued from July, 1934, to the end of his term 139 pardons, forty-three commutations of sentence, forty-two reprieves, and one restoration of citizenship. However, like his four predecessors, he refused to pardon Tom Mooney.

On January 2, 1939, at the inaugural ceremonies of Olson, Frank Merriam said his farewells as his long career of public service came to a close. He said that he naturally had regrets about leaving but he had satisfactions also. He noted that he had been governor during a most difficult period. He claimed that:

it is the duty of an official to do the best he can—and permit his own conscience to judge his acts.

In the long run there comes a satisfaction from having done the right as you have seen the right; in attempting to serve the best interests of all the people, in trying to deal fairly according to your own sense of fair play and justice.

Merriam returned to his Long Beach home where he became active in real estate. He also acquired a ranch and peach orchard. In 1951, he became seriously ill and never completely recovered. He died in Long Beach April 25, 1955, at the age of eighty-nine.

Merriam was remembered at the time of his death by most state newspapers as being the governor who had handled the San Francisco waterfront strike with firmness. The *Sacramento Union* added that "a grateful state will long remember him for his honesty of purpose, his sincerity, his devotion to principle, and his constant forthright stand against the vicious element."

Governor Frank Merriam managed the state's administration during some of its most difficult years. He remained faithful to his political philosophy. Unfortunately, Governor Merriam, as with many of his contemporaries in office, had a static political view more in keeping with the concept of duty held by nineteenth century governors. He was unable to provide the state with the executive ability which was needed during the crisis of the 1930's. He also found himself in political difficulties with his strongest supporters when he cooperated with New Deal programs of relief and recovery in order to gain federal funds to help replenish state coffers. Merriam offered no positive program to the legislature and he provided no leadership in advocating measures to ameliorate conditions in the state.

BIBLIOGRAPHY

MANUSCRIPTS
Merriam, Frank, "Papers and Letters," (Bancroft Library).
―――, "State Officials Letter File," (California Section, State Library).

CONTEMPORARY ACCOUNTS
Assembly Journal, 51st-52nd Sess., 1935-37.
Senate Journal, 51st-52nd Sess., 1935-37.
California Blue Book, 1932 & 1938.
Sinclair, Upton, *The Autobiography of Upton Sinclair* (New York, 1962).
―――, *I, Candidate For Governor And How I Got Licked* (Los Angeles, 1934).

SECONDARY SOURCES
Burke, Robert E., *Olson's New Deal for California* (Berkeley, 1953).
Larsen, Charles, "The Epic Campaign of 1934," *Pacific Historical Review,* XXVII (1958), 127-47.
Wolfe, W.C., ed. *Men of California* (1925).

NEWSPAPERS
Long Beach Press-Telegram, April 26, 1955, has Merriam's obituary.
Sacramento Bee, Jan. 23, 1935, has Merriam's first budget message; Jan. 14, 1937, reports Merriam's combined biennial and budget message; April 26, 1955, has his obituary.
Sacramento Union, June 5, 1934, has Merriam's statement upon taking office; April 26, 1955, has obituary.
San Francisco Chronicle, June 24, 1934, gives estimate of Merriam's new administration, based on statewide editorials; Oct.-Nov., 1934, reports bitter gubernatorial campaign; Jan. 9, 1935, has Merriam's inaugural message; April 26, 1955, has obituary.

Calendar of Events

November 7, 1876	Olson born near Fillmore, Utah.
1895-1896	Olson attended Brigham Young University.
1897	Olson served as secretary to Congressman John H. King.
May 28, 1901	Olson graduated from Columbian University Law School.
1904	Olson defeated as a candidate for the Utah Assembly.
1916	Olson elected to the Utah Senate.
1920	Olson served as a delegate to the Democratic National Convention.
1920	Olson moved to Los Angeles.
1934	Olson elected to the California Senate.
1934	Olson appointed State Chairman of the California Democratic Party.
January 2, 1939	Olson took office as Governor.
January 7, 1939	Olson pardoned Tom Mooney.
November 7, 1939	"Ham and Eggs" pension scheme defeated in a special election.
November 3, 1942	Olson defeated by Warren.
1943	Olson resumed law practice in Los Angeles.
October 30, 1947	Olson addressed Committee on Revision of the State Constitution at Santa Barbara.
April 13, 1962	Olson died in Los Angeles.

Culbert L. Olson

29TH GOVERNOR—DEMOCRAT
BORN: NOVEMBER 7, 1876   DIED: APRIL 13, 1962
TERM OF OFFICE: JANUARY 2, 1939—JANUARY 4, 1943

CULBERT L. OLSON WAS THE FIRST Democratic governor of California in the twentieth century and the first since the administration of James H. Budd. A handsome and white haired 62-year old man of large stature, Olson was a sincere person with a strong sense of social justice. Although he had been an effective campaigner and speaker in the past, he began to show signs of exhaustion and nervousness as early as his gubernatorial campaign of 1938. After he took office, his health began to suffer and handicapped his administration.

A nonconformist in many respects, Olson ranks among the most controversial California governors. For several decades California had been a one-party state under Republican dominance. Olson was not only a Democrat, but a liberal who had been influenced by the political philosophy of evolutionary socialism. Despite his idealism, he was no visionary dreamer but a practical businessman with broad legal experience. To many Olson appeared a threat to the status quo and was branded radical.

Olson was born November 7, 1876, on a farm near Fillmore, Utah Territory. His parents were Daniel and Delilah King Olson. His mother was active in the women's suffrage movement, and after her husband's death, she became the first woman elected to public office in Utah, serving as treasurer and recorder of Millard County. Before his fourteenth birthday, Olson had worked on a farm and on several construction jobs. Then he worked for the Denver and Rio Grande Railroad. While attending high school and college, he was a telegraph

395

operator for Western Union. He completed a two-year course of study at Brigham Young University in 1895. The next year he worked as a reporter and city editor for the *Ogden Standard*. Although he was too young to vote, he supported William Jennings Bryan during the 1896 presidential campaign.

In 1897, he moved to Washington, D.C. and served as secretary to his cousin, Congressman William H. King. At the same time he attended Columbian University Law School, later George Washington University, from 1897 until 1901, except for an interim of one year's study at the University of Michigan. On May 28, 1901, he obtained a degree of Bachelor of Laws at Columbian University, and began practicing law in Salt Lake City.

In 1905, Olson married Kate Jeremy and they were the parents of three sons. From the influence of his mother and his early training Olson acquired a liberal philosophy, becoming a Democrat. In 1904, he was an unsuccessful candidate for the Utah Assembly. While his law practice flourished he participated in civic and commercial affairs. He developed mining projects, built hotels in Idaho and Nevada, and organized two banks, the Price Commercial and Savings Bank at Price, Utah, and the First National Bank of Burley, Idaho.

In 1916, Olson was elected to the Utah Senate where he sponsored considerable progressive legislation. Four years later he attended the Democratic national convention in San Francisco as a delegate-at-large from Utah. In an address to the platform committee he urged his party to repudiate imperialism and the policy of laissez faire. He favored labor reforms, expansion of government ownership and control of public utilities and natural resources, and governmental regulation of agriculture and industry. These concepts were fundamental to Olson's political philosophy.

In 1920, he relinquished his political interests in Utah and decided to move to Los Angeles. Through his law practice Olson fought against fraudulent business practices and worthless stock promoters in Los Angeles during the booming twenties. In 1924, he campaigned for Robert M. LaFollette, the Progressive presidential nominee. When the disorganized Democratic party of California revived during the depression, Olson was a founder of the Los Angeles Democratic Club and its president. He contemplated running for governor in 1934, but instead ran for the State Senate. Although he did not join the powerful End Poverty in California movement, he supported Upton Sinclair in the gubernatorial campaign.

In the Democratic senatorial primary Olson with EPIC support polled 149,177 votes while his seven opponents totaled 139,335 votes. In September, Olson played a part in drafting the Democratic state platform. Sinclair appointed Olson state chairman of the Democratic party and he managed the campaign for the general election. Despite Sinclair's defeat, Olson was more successful in his own behalf, winning a Senate seat in November.

Olson eventually obtained control of the Epic-Democratic bloc in the 1935 legislature. He endeavored to convert the emotional approach to reform of the EPICS into something more practical and to integrate them with the liberals among the Democrats. As leader of the Merriam opposition, Olson began a series of nightly fifteen-minute radio broadcasts over a state-wide hookup. The liberals led in defeating part of Merriam's tax legislation and Olson won abolition of sales tax on food for home consumption. Olson also involved himself in the tidelands oil controversy and his fight against the oil monopolists was his major contribution as Senator. In 1935 and 1936, Olson started preparations for his gubernatorial campaign and opposed Senator William G. McAdoo's influence in the California Democratic party.

After the 1936 elections, Olson seemed to lead the diverse liberal forces. He announced his candidacy for governor on September 4, 1937. Among leading Democrats who followed suit were John F. Dockweiler, a Los Angeles Congressman, Sheriff Daniel C. Murphy of San Francisco, J. F. T. O'Connor, former comptroller of the currency, and Herbert C. Legg, chairman of the Los Angeles County board of supervisors.

On April 18, 1938, Olson issued a platform in which he indicted the "moribund Merriam-Hatfield regime" and advocated public ownership of public utilities, financial reforms, "production-for-use," slum clearance, and protection of labor's rights.

The main interest in the 1938 campaign was an initiative amendment, popularly known as the "Ham and Eggs" or "Thirty-Dollars-Every Thursday" pension plan. Congressman Dockweiler supported the measure. While Olson did not endorse "Ham and Eggs," he emphasized the constitutional right of the people to vote on the issue, making it appear that he favored the pension. In the primary election Olson won, receiving 483,483 votes to 218,342 for Dockweiler, his closest rival. More surprising than Olson's victory was McAdoo's defeat by Sheridan Downey in the senatorial race. The Democratic victor as lieutenant governor was Ellis E. Patterson.

In the general election Olson faced the weak incumbent, Merriam, who was also his opposite in political philosophy. In September and October, Olson was on the offensive. The Republicans officially denounced "Ham and Eggs," but Merriam asked the legislature to urge Congress to enact the Townsend Plan. Business and industrial leaders generally supported Merriam, but in 1938, there was not the great effort to defeat Olson as had been the case in 1934 to defeat Upton Sinclair. On October 18, Raymond Haight—the Progressive candidate—withdrew, but refused to support either Olson or Merriam.

The final vote on November 8, gave Olson 1,391,734 votes and Merriam 1,171,019 votes. Ellis Patterson defeated Walter S. Franklin for lieutenant governor to become the only other Democratic state officer in the Olson administration. Olson gained victory because he did not directly oppose the defeated "Ham and Eggs" referendum measure, denounced an anti-labor proposition on the ballot, and staged an able campaign. Moreover, the split in Republican ranks and the National Democratic trend aided his cause.

Governor Olson delivered his inaugural address before a joint session of the Assembly and Senate on January 2, 1939. In a conciliatory manner he assured Californians that he entered office free of prejudice even against his opponents. He appeared friendly toward business except in referring to lobbying and the utility companies. He alluded to advances in science and to increased facility for manufacturing, but stated that the problem of distribution had not been solved. Olson praised the New Deal of Franklin Roosevelt and asserted that the people of California wanted similar measures on a state level. He requested legislative cooperation in achieving these objectives, stating: "the people of California want employment, a decent standard of living, education, opportunities for youth, social security, old age retirement, protection against pauperism and starvation."

Olson indicated that California had inherited a large deficit from the last two administrations. To prevent a heavy tax burden he proposed relief through self-employment. To raise the morale of all concerned he recommended a substitution of the present small cash doles by a system of productive work for the unemployed. He also urged labor legislation, liberal old age pensions, several specific plans to aid the farmers, and government ownership of public utilities.

Olson then drew an analogy between the present change in administration with that of 1910. He related how the people had ended the domination of state government by the principal public utility, only to have it replaced by other privately owned public utilities. Olson claimed that water, power, oil, and gas resources had not been protected or regulated and then charged: "with the aid of a subsidized daily press, and cleverly designed and costly publicity methods, they have from time to time influenced the people to vote against their own interests, through false and misleading propaganda."

Olson proposed that the state be prepared with public agencies to receive the power of the Shasta Dam of the Central Valley Project. Then he concluded by stating that pre-election battles were over and requested a solution of problems through liberal government.

The *Sacramento Union* on the day of the inaugural predicted that Olson: "will be as hide-bound . . . as the most conservative Yankee of New England . . . he will be no different than Governor Merriam. . . . The man has to fit the office. The office isn't changed to fit the man." From the start Olson faced serious problems. In the matter of patronage there were few jobs to award to eager Democrats while thousands anticipated them. While the Democrats had a small majority in the Assembly, the Republicans maintained a small majority in the Senate. Paul Peek, an Olson supporter, was elected Speaker of the Assembly, but in the Senate, Republicans stripped Lieutenant Governor Patterson of his appointive power.

The first major move of the Olson administration was the pardoning of Tom Mooney, the "labor martyr," who had been convicted for the San Francisco Preparedness Day bombing in 1916. On January 7, 1939, in the crowded Assembly chamber Olson granted Mooney a full and unconditional pardon during proceedings that were dramatized in a national broadcast. For his clemency Olson was both highly praised and violently censured.

At the end of his first week in office, Olson suffered a nervous collapse and was hospitalized. During his sickness Olson's executive secretary, Ralph Evans, announced that a committee on policy or "regency" would act during the governor's absence. Olson did not regain his strength until the next month. Before his illness the governor had begun preparation of the budget. When submitted with proposed expenditures of $557,163,355, it met opposition from the "economy bloc," composed of both Democrats and Republicans, who wanted to curb relief programs, decrease spending, and prevent tax increases.

In the first week of April, the Republicans accused the state relief administration of being a dumping ground "for both Olson supporters and left-wing fanatics." The economy bloc was able to remove the entire relief appropriation from the budget in order to consider it separately as well as reduce other items. The budget as finally adopted amounted to $468,071,-624, and was signed by Olson on June 3. On June 22, the legislature passed a $35,525,000 relief bill and adjourned. Only 40 percent of this amount could be expected in the first two quarters of the new fiscal year. This meant that Olson would have to reconvene the legislature, after six or seven months, to obtain more money and that the economy bloc intended to keep a close check upon relief expenditures. Olson also suffered other legislative defeats in 1939. He failed to gain cooperation from his opponents in the legislature and the press generally opposed his entire program. As a solution to the conservative bloc three remedies were advanced to no avail. These were a restriction of lobbying, a unicameral legislature, and a punishment of "obstructionists" at the polls in 1940.

The first extraordinary session of the fifty-third legislature convened on January 29, 1940, with the economy bloc intent on opposing the state relief administration. In his message Olson reported that the last relief appropriation would be expended by February 5, and that the sum of $95,500,000 was needed for the remainder of the biennium because of an increased case load and curtailment of W.P.A. projects. The legislature appropriated only $12,200,000, over Olson's veto, to carry the relief load until June 1, and attached amendments to prohibit political activities by the relief administration. After a legislative recess, the administration woefully accepted an additional $24,347,000 to cover the period June 1, 1940 to March 31, 1941.

In the meantime, the "Ham and Eggs" pension movement, after its defeat at the polls in 1938, continued to plague Olson. Petitions were taken to the governor's office and on May 18, 1939, Olson promised to call a special election. On July 1, he issued a proclamation, fixing the regular election day on November 7, 1939. Despite his sympathy for pensions, Olson denounced this program as impractical. Yet he reasoned that a third of the voters could not be ignored and he did not want the scheme to complicate the 1940 election. Actually Olson's proclamation satisfied neither side on the pension issue. After the pension proposal was defeated in the 1939 special election, Willis Allen and Roy G. Owens, two leaders of the "Ham and Eggers," denounced Olson and began to circulate petitions for his recall. Many of Olson's erstwhile opponents came to his defense. For example, the *San Francisco Examiner* congratulated Olson for his stand on "Ham and Eggs" and favored a vote of confidence in him. Earlier in 1939, J. A. Murphy, a Los Angeles politician, and James W. Mellen, leader of the "Jeffersonian Democrats of California," had launched the first recall movement charging Olson with incompetence, lack of leadership in the Democratic party, and with dragging relief into politics. Whereas the first recall movement was weak, the second was stronger, but it also vanished because of general disfavor. During 1940 a third recall movement was sponsored by the "Olson Recall Committee, Inc.," which had first operated in southern California and then opened a headquarters in San Francisco early in March. It was largely backed by independent oil companies, but the movement again failed because of public disapproval and the national emergency arising from the invasion of France by the Nazis. All the recall attempts met opposition from bipartisan groups and Olson even had the support of former Republican governors, George Pardee and Clement C. Young.

As Olson began his second year as governor in 1940, he faced a difficult situation with his legislative program stalled. Besides attacks by recall groups, he was being deserted by his party colleagues. In December, 1939, Olson publicly backed Roosevelt for a third term and in the Democratic presidential preference primary on May 7, 1940, the Roosevelt-Olson slate won a great victory. However, this victory came only after a bitter factional dispute within the California Democratic party in which Olson and Lieutenant Governor Patterson exchanged invectives. Olson headed the California delegation to the Democratic national convention in Chicago and was selected as a national committeeman.

When Olson returned from Chicago, he was concerned with the August primary election. He tried to remove his legislative opponents and at times campaigned in particular districts. The results of the primary and general elections were a political disaster to Olson's program. The Republicans controlled the Senate, and Republicans and anti-Olson Democrats had gained a majority in the Assembly.

In his first biennial message of January 6, 1941, Governor Olson announced an improvement in state finances resulting from the stimulus of defense industries. He related that anticipated current revenues would meet the expenditures of his prospective new budget as well as reduce the remaining deficit. Thus he saw no need for additional taxes. However, it should be mentioned that the 1939-40 state deficit was the largest of any of the past decade. After discussing the various departments of state government, he made several recommendations. Again Olson appealed for relief work instead of the cash dole. He suggested means by which utilities could be publicly owned. He repeated earlier requests for universal compulsory health insurance, a state housing authority, soil conservation legislation, a reorganization of state agencies, and a labor relations act. To secure improved liquor regulation he asked for its control by an agency other than the board of equalization. In conclusion he warned that defense spending was only a temporary and partial solution to the serious problem of mass unemployment.

Olson had more success with his 1941 budget than with the previous one. While reduction of items was smaller, relief appropriations were again made separately. The legislature endeavored to decentralize relief in 1941, by enacting a measure that provided for county administration. Olson vetoed the bill and the Senate failed to override his veto. Since employment was increasing, the legislature adjourned leaving the state relief administration with only enough funds for four additional days of operation.

During the second half of his administration Olson faced the serious problems of defense and war. In June, 1940, he established the California state council of defense, but at first the legislature refused to provide funds. A year later the governor was authorized to organize a state guard. After the United States was in the war, Olson had difficulties over the state guard and some of his opponents charged that it was "Olson's Army." Olson was accused of using the state guard to build a political machine for his re-election. Unfortunately, Olson and Attorney General Earl Warren feuded over defense matters. Olson failed to consult openly with Warren, who criticized Olson's "state of emergency" proclamation of December 14, 1941. The views of Warren and Olson on their respective roles in the war effort were at variance and an atmosphere of mutual distrust developed. Another problem of Olson's final year in office was Japanese evacuation. The Japanese were relocated on the grounds of "military necessity." Although Governor Olson had no voice in the decision, he did not oppose the move.

In his fight for re-election, Olson faced Earl Warren who sought the governorship as a nonpartisan despite his long Republican background. Warren cross-filed on the Democratic ticket and his campaign was managed by the professional public relations firm, Whitaker and Baxter. "Leadership, Not Politics" became the keynote of his effort. Warren toured the state in company with the movie actor, Leo Carrillo. In the primary campaign the Republicans criticized the scandals of the state relief administration and accused Olson of failing to build an adequate state guard.

Since Olson did not cross-file, he had no need to conduct a vigorous primary campaign, but he justified his defense and war policies. He also defended his fiscal policies and linked his administration to that of Roosevelt. The results of the August 25th election were disastrous for the Democrats despite their 900,000 superiority in party registration. Warren won the Republican nomination over nominal opposition, but amazingly gained 404,778 votes in the Democratic party compared with Olson's vote of 514,144. Warren's votes in both parties totaled 1,040,008.

In the final campaign, organized labor made a tremendous effort and in the general election Olson came within 342,292 votes of Warren. Yet Warren won a decisive victory receiving 57 percent of the total vote, winning in fifty-seven counties. The main factors causing Olson's defeat were the ineptness of the Democratic party and widespread newspaper support for the Republican opponent. Warren successfully portrayed himself as nonpartisan which proved to be an effective war-time theme. Moreover, Olson had antagonized many powerful interest groups. From the beginning of the campaign he had been on the defensive and probably the military reverses of 1942 were suggestive of a change of power. In a letter of November 18, to the chairman of the Los Angeles County Democratic central committee, Governor Olson explained the defeat in the following way:

> There is no question that the primary cause of our defeat was the unfortunate national trend against the national administration, due to dissatisfaction with the war and its consequences, and to the unusually light vote cast. Of course, as to myself, the local factors of the terrific drive of the predatory interests and their newspapers, directed at me, and in building up their man, together with the hatreds inspired among the remaining followers of the Ham and Egg racketeers, played an effective part. Under all the circumstances, the fact that nearly a million voters withstood the attack and the trend is the assurance we have of the Party's comeback in the future and the maintenance of the mission of the Democratic Party, which must be that of a liberal democracy, internationally and internally, along the lines of economic planning, with a clear-cut and forthright declaration of procedures and objectives.

Olson became governor in 1939, offering the people of California a comprehensive reform program that promised to curb monopoly, to help labor, to end the dole, and to curtail lobbying. While his election was in large measure made possible by the spectre of the Great Depression, he assumed office when the depression was less severe. His program was not implemented because of factionalism among the liberals and pension groups and because of a hostile legislature and the general indifference of the people. On March 29, 1960, former Governor Olson in a letter said in part:

> Achievements of a governor's administration are connoted with the enactment of legislation approved by the governor with little or no reference to any executive accomplishments of the administration. If my recommendations to the legislature had been adopted there would have been a number of what I would designate as

major achievements. But, unfortunately, I had to deal with an opposition party-controlled legislature determined to prevent the enactment of measures which I recommended and would regard as achievements.

Later in an interview on April 14, 1960, Olson expressed disappointment about his inability to achieve a substitute for the dole system and his inability to distribute electric power at cost. He expressed a sense of pride in establishing the state guard at the moment the national guard was called into federal service. He was proud of the role of the state guard in coastal defense during World War II. Olson viewed his reforms at San Quentin prison as an achievement and he praised the work of the warden, Clinton T. Duffy. He emphasized special pride in converting Chino into a minimum security prison where first offenders were sent for rehabilitation. With a smile on his face Olson mentioned a signed letter of appreciation from all the inmates at Chino, telling him how the institution had aided their lives.

Despite the lack of harmony with the legislature, Olson was able to make some prison reforms through his use of executive powers. Also accomplishments were made in public transportation; for example, the state purchased the Carquinez Bridge and toll charges were reduced on the San Francisco-Oakland Bridge. During the Olson administration the California Youth Authority was established by the legislature in 1941 to care for juvenile offenders. The establishment of the Langley Porter Clinic in 1941 at San Francisco was an achievement in the field of mental health.

Olson's efforts at reform undoubtedly came too late, for California became engrossed with problems of defense and war after his election. Besides other handicaps already mentioned, Olson suffered from his own sickness and the death of his wife in 1939. He was unable to implement his broader programs and failed to win over his opponents. He lacked the necessary tact of a successful administrator. Nonetheless, several of his recommendations were adopted by later governors. For example, one suggestion which was realized in the 1950's was the creation of a liquor control agency separate from the board of equalization.

In retrospect the Olson administration seemed almost doomed from its start. The coalition of organized labor, liberal groups, radicals, and pension advocates that backed him in 1938 quickly fell apart. Although the California economy had been stimulated by the general national recovery and by defense industries, unemployment, agricultural distress, and the social strife of the early thirties remained. The relief problem was acute and its administration became an issue of conflict. While the press, business and industrial organizations, and the Farm Bureau and Associated Farmers attacked Olson because of his proposed economic program, the pension advocates and militant left-wingers turned against him. Olson also became involved in the then existing battles between the AFL and the CIO. Not only was Olson a Democratic executive whose legislative program was blocked, but other constitutional officers, except for the lieutenant governor, were Republican. Factionalism within the Democratic party also caused Lieutenant Governor Patterson to break with Olson in the selection of delegates for the Democratic presidential preference primary of 1940. Although the inept Democratic honeymoon faded away, Olson's greatest contribution was that he brought attention or at least more attention to the deep-rooted economic and social problems facing California.

At the close of his term Olson returned to his home in Los Angeles and resumed his law practice. He served as Democratic national committeeman until 1944, but his power in the party quickly disappeared. In 1944 rumors appeared in the press that he might be appointed governor of the Virgin Islands or ambassador to Mexico, but no appointment materialized.

On October 30, 1947, Olson addressed a session of the legislative committee on revision of the state constitution meeting at Santa Barbara. He pointed out the need for revising and simplifying the California constitution. He reiterated his support of a unicameral legislature which he had favored as state senator and as governor. Olson stated that unicameralism would bring about closer cooperation between the executive and legislative branches. He also proposed that the constitution allow the governor and heads of executive departments to sit with the legislature and participate in its discussions of proposed laws, but not to vote. Furthermore, he suggested making the state treasurer, secretary of state, and attorney general appointive instead of elective offices. In the concluding paragraph of his address the following comment provided an interesting view of his difficulties as governor:

> It is my thought that when a majority of the voters vote for the policies and policy-making candidates of one party, the elected officials of that party should have a free hand to discharge the responsibilities they have undertaken and to carry out the policies the majority have voted for without checks and balances to prevent their doing so, except the checks and balances reserved to the people by the Recall, the Referendum, and the Initiative petition.

During his retirement years Olson made two trips to Europe and the Near East. He occasionally authored political articles and delivered lectures. Since his early teens Olson had been a freethinker. His views about religion were not generally known while he was governor. He later was active in the United Secularists of America and served as president of its board of trustees. In May, 1959, he published an address entitled, "The Problem of Separation of Church and State," in this organization's magazine, the *Progressive World*. Olson claimed that he had intended to deliver the address before the Commonwealth Club of California, but was denied permission once his subject was known. Shortly thereafter Olson presented his freethought views on a television program. Failing health caused Olson to move to a rest home. On April 13, 1962, he died in Los Angeles at the age of eighty-five.

BIBLIOGRAPHY

MANUSCRIPTS
Olson, Culbert L., "Papers," (Bancroft Library).
Letters from Culbert L. Olson to B. F. Gilbert, Dec. 5 and 6, 1959;
    March 29, 1960.

CONTEMPORARY ACCOUNTS
California Blue Book, 1942 (Sacramento, 1942).
Mosk, Stanley, comp., *State Papers and Public Addresses, Governor
    Culbert L. Olson* (Sacramento, 1942).
Olson, Culbert L., "Democracy and Efficiency, An address at a plen-
    ary Session of the Committee of the California Legislature on Re-
    vision of the State Constitution, at Santa Barbara, October 30th,
    1947" (Mimeographed).
————, "The Problem of Separation of Church and State," *Progressive
    World,* XIII, 1959), 6-16.
Scully, Frank, *The Next Governor of California* (c. 1938).
*Speaker's Manual for Governor Culbert L. Olson's Re-Election Cam-
    paign of 1942* (c. 1942).
Young, Jack. *The People Be Damned; A Record of the 53d Session of
    the State Legislature of California* (San Francisco, 1939).

SECONDARY SOURCES
Barrett, Edward L., Jr., *The Tenney Committee: Legislative Investi-
    gation of Subversive Activities in California* (Ithaca, 1951).
Burke, R.E., *Olson's New Deal for California.*
Chambers, Clarke A., *California Farm Organizations, A Historical
    Study of the Grange, the Farm Bureau, and the Associated Farmers,
    1929-1941* (Berkeley, 1952).
Perry, Louis B. and Richard S., *A History of the Los Angeles Labor
    Movement, 1911-1941* (Berkeley, 1963).

NEWSPAPERS
Los Angeles Times, April 14, 1962, has a sketch and obituary of Olson.
San Francisco Chronicle, April 14, 1962, has a sketch and obituary.

THESIS
Goodman, T. William, "Culbert L. Olson and California Politics, 1933-
    1943" (M.A., University of California at Los Angeles, 1948).

INTERVIEW
Culbert L. Olson by B.F. Gilbert, April 14, 1960.

Capitol Building, Sacramento. The present Capitol, at L street in Sacramento, was occupied in 1869. Ground was first broken on September 24, 1860, and while under construction was inundated by floods in 1862. Work was intermittent and was finally completed after 14 years in 1874. The above engraving is from Thompson and West's *History of Sacramento County*.

Calendar of Events

March 19, 1891	Warren born in Los Angeles.
1912	Warren graduated from the University of California.
1914	Warren graduated from Boalt Hall of Law.
1919	Warren served as clerk of the Judiciary Committee of the Assembly.
1926	Warren elected District Attorney of Alameda County.
1928	Warren served as an alternate delegate to the Republican National Convention.
1930	Warren re-elected District Attorney of Alameda County.
June, 1932	Warren served as a delegate to the Republican National Convention.
1934	Warren re-elected District Attorney of Alameda County for the second time.
1934-1936	Warren served as chairman of the Republican State Central Committee.
November 8, 1938	Warren elected Attorney General.
January 4, 1943	Warren took office as Governor.
June 4, 1946	Warren won both the Republican and Democratic nominations in his first re-election.
November 7, 1950	Warren re-elected for a third term.
September 30, 1953	President Eisenhower appointed Warren as Chief Justice.
October 4, 1953	Warren resigned as Governor.
May 17, 1954	Supreme Court outlawed segregation in public schools.
November 29, 1963	President Johnson appointed the Warren Commission.
September 24, 1964	Warren Commission Report issued.

Earl Warren

30TH GOVERNOR—REPUBLICAN
BORN: MARCH 19, 1891
TERM OF OFFICE: JANUARY 4, 1943—OCTOBER 4, 1953

EARL WARREN WAS ELECTED California governor three times, holding that office longer than any other. He had the distinction of being the only governor ever elected in a state primary. He has been the only native Californian ever elevated to the United States Supreme Court. He was born March 19, 1891, in Los Angeles, the son of Methias H. and Crystal Hernlund Warren. After attending the public schools of Bakersfield, he enrolled at the University of California at the age of seventeen where he majored in political science. In 1914, he graduated from Boalt Hall of Law and was admitted to the state bar. For a year he worked in law offices of the Associated Oil Company in San Francisco. He was later employed in an Oakland law firm. In August, 1917, he enlisted in the army as a private and received basic training at Camp Lewis in Washington. He was assigned to the 91st Division and qualified for officers' training school. At the war's end he was discharged as a first lieutenant.

In the 1919 legislature Warren served as clerk of the judiciary committee of the Assembly. For a time he was a deputy city attorney in Oakland and then served as deputy district attorney in Alameda County. In 1925, at the age of thirty-three he was appointed district attorney of Alameda County. There he married Nina Palmquist Meyers, and six children were born of the marriage.

Warren was elected to the same office in 1926 and re-elected in 1930 and 1934. As district attorney he fought bootleggers, the bail-bond racket, and crooked investment companies. He exposed health insurance rackets and helped to end graft in the

411

sheriff's office. For his reforms Warren gained a national reputation and became president of the State Association of District Attorneys.

After Ulysses S. Webb decided to retire from his long tenure as attorney general of California, Warren sought that office. In the 1938 campaign through the cross-filing device, he gained the nominations of the Republicans, Democrats, and Progressives, assuring his victory at the general election. This popular triumph presaged his 1946 gubernatorial election feat in the primary.

Warren reorganized the office of attorney general, departmentalizing the work load into divisions. A central filing system was devised to coordinate information. Warren fought bookmakers and gamblers and brought dog racing tracks under supervision. He closed down the nefarious operations of the luxury gambling ship, the *Rex*, lying off Long Beach beyond the three-mile limit. Mustering a fleet of fire-fighting ships and fish and game commission cutters, he dispatched law-enforcement officers out to the *Rex* to destroy all gambling equipment aboard the vessel. In 1940 Warren became president of the National Association of Attorney Generals.

When the select committee investigating national defense migration, chaired by Congressman John H. Tolan, held hearings at San Francisco on February 21 and 23, 1942, Attorney General Warren was asked to testify. He expressed approval of the executive order recently signed by President Franklin D. Roosevelt authorizing the War Department to exclude any persons from prescribed military areas. He also gave the committee data about the location of Japanese adjacent to strategic military installations and industrial plants, and warned of the dangers of possible sabotage and subversive activities.

In the twenties Warren had been active in the Republican party. He was an alternate delegate to the 1928 national convention and full delegate in 1932. From 1934 to 1936, he was chairman of the Republican state central committee. The feud between Warren and Olson over civil defense was a factor in Warren's decision to become a gubernatorial candidate in 1942. Although he was a registered Republican, he operated his campaign in an independent manner. He detached himself from other candidates and stood on his own views and record in winning election.

Instead of experience as a legislator, Warren had been a devoted career public servant. He was a salaried man of middle-income status with a large and happy family. A tall, broad figured, and friendly man, he possessed a pleasing personality. Quiet and stolid in temperament, he was somewhat cautious but did not lack political acumen. With his record of performance and a practical legal mind, he made no utopian promises. He was to bring a measure of "judicial quality" to the office of governor.

On January 4, 1943, Chief Justice Phil S. Gibson administered the oaths of office to Earl Warren as governor and to Frederick F. Houser as lieutenant governor. In his inaugural address Warren informed the legislators that clear thinking was necessary to cope with the problems of war and to alleviate postwar uncertainties. He stressed the need for protecting public health caused by population shifts and the need for a child welfare program. He recommended a streamlining of government and a revamping of the parole system.

Referring to man-power utilization, he favored an increased flexibility in all state agencies not yet fully participating in the war effort. He also pointed out the necessity of a postwar program to sustain the new shipbuilding, aircraft, and other war industries and to prevent a return to the relief dole. Since Californians resided in a "theater of war," he recommended a reorganization of civil defense. In the matter of the treasury surplus resulting from taxes on war industries he urged its conservation or use for essential projects.

Warren's first two years in office increased his popularity. His relations with the legislature were effective. He succeeded in reducing the income tax, sales tax, and bank and corporation franchise taxes because of the booming economy and expanding tax base. He was able to increase old age pensions and maintained a truce with organized labor. Unemployment insurance coverage was widened to include employees of small establishments. The state guard was reorganized and appropriations were made for its postwar development. Also created were the departments of corrections and justice. Warren's initial program of 1943 was more conservative than his programs of later years. At first he had to concentrate on defense and mobilization, but he recognized the need for future economic and social growth.

In 1944, Earl Warren was the keynote speaker at the Republican national convention at Chicago where he delivered what was probably his most partisan political speech. In part he said:

> It is the purpose of this convention to put the public welfare above private self-interest; to put the nation above the party; to put the progress of the whole American community above special privilege or any part of it; to put INDISPENSABLE PRINCIPLES —ONCE AND FOR ALL—ABOVE INDISPENSABLE MEN.
>
> In Washington, where the bureaucrats live, there is still a Democrat in the White House. But out there where the people live, the country is predominantly Republican.

Warren argued that the New Deal destroyed representative government and the two party system, established a bureaucracy, and injected politics into relief and social welfare. During the campaign Warren gave five speeches supporting Dewey and Bricker, and charged that the Democratic party was comprised of left-wingers, conservative Southerners, machine politicians, and impractical idealists.

In his biennial message of January 8, 1945, to the fifty-sixth legislature Warren said: "when victory has been achieved in Europe, California will serve as the funnel through which will flow the strength for final victory in the Pacific." He told the legislators that plans must be made for the return of California's 850,000 service men and women who would want employment, a health program, recreation, and a high standard of educational opportunity. Governor Warren recommended a prepaid medical service, stating that only the wealthy and indigent were obtaining adequate care. He suggested a system of pay roll deduction from both employer and employee in order to spread the cost of medical care among all people. He favored modernizing the mental health program and recommended a further increase in old age assistance as well as an extension of unemployment insurance. He proposed the establishment of a commission on political and economic quality to study minority problems and a commission to study housing problems. He suggested a continuation of the 1943 tax reductions during the next biennium and requested an agency to centralize all veterans' services since the previous legislature had enacted various benefits for returning servicemen.

Warren's program was the most comprehensive to be offered since Hiram Johnson's administration. A number of recommendations were approved, but the 1945 legislature, controlled by conservative Republicans, defeated compulsory prepaid medical care, a widening of unemployment insurance, and the concept of a commission to study minority problems.

On July 15, 1945, Governor Warren moved his office to Columbia and for a single day this Mother Lode town, once called the "Gem of the Southern Mines," was made capital of California. Before a crowd of residents, officials, and many visitors, Warren signed the bill making Columbia a state park. According to local legend Columbia in its heyday had been a contender for the state capital. Although no one could prove the legend, the occasion represented the realization of a long cherished dream. Columbia Historic State Park has since been partially restored and made the best preserved of the Gold Rush towns.

With the return of peace in August, 1945, war workers remained in California and the veterans came home. Many servicemen trained in California military installations during the war also returned and the population boom continued. Warren called a special session in January, 1946, to deal with the resulting problems. He announced that the most critical one was housing and said: "Men who fought in foxholes have returned to find less of a home here than they had Over There." He recommended an appropriation to implement an urban development act and asked the legislators to decide what to do with the public works money set aside during the war years. He urged an extension of unemployment compensation to the sick. In recognition of the new air age he recommended establishing an aviation commission to assist the state in continuing as an airplane manufacturing center and an important point on the air routes of the world.

The legislature responded generously to Warren's requests of 1946, and in March, he announced that he would cross-file in seeking a second term. Now he relied on his record and made no new promises. Warren stated that his relations with the legislature were excellent and that ninety of his recommendations had been approved. He stressed that he had no political machine and said: "No man should be permitted to be both Governor and a political boss. I repeat the promise I made four years ago—that whenever I leave the Governor's Chair, I will return it to the people unencumbered, and without any political strings around it."

Attorney General Robert W. Kenny, a Democrat, announced that he would oppose Warren and cross-file on the Republican primary ballot. Kenny attacked the Warren record, charging that his administration was guilty of a "muddling through" policy, that it had no "blueprint" for solving postwar problems, and that it was based upon "pure opportunism." He also chided Warren for not securing passage of a number of "liberal" measures, claiming that the governor lacked sufficient party leadership in the legislative process. "Individual careerism," Kenny asserted, was not good enough for effective government in California.

Warren defended "open dealing" with the legislators and condemned "boss" rule and the "package deal." He also stated that he would never be a part of any attempt to force upon the people a "disciplined" legislature. In his campaign speeches Warren reviewed the measures he had sponsored such as the establishment of the department of mental hygiene, the reorganization of the department of public health, increases in unemployment insurance and workmen's compensation, and the conservation of a financial surplus.

Most voters, satisfied with Warren's record, seemed to share the opinions of the *San Francisco Chronicle;* in its May 17th issue the newspaper editorialized:

> A big man with mature concepts, Earl Warren brought to the Governorship a philosophy which placed the welfare and progress of California well above any small consideration of party or group. In the implementation of that philosophy he has exerted a quiet, steady pressure toward his objectives, refusing to be jarred off the course by hysterical pleadings of special interests or lured off the deep end by plausible propositions which attached rewards to compromises of principle.

After listing random illustrations of his "long program of progressive policies," the *Chronicle* concluded:

> It is this implacable dynamism, this liberalism of deed rather than word, that has made Earl Warren one of the outstanding Governors in California history. It is The Chronicle's considered opinion that such a Governor as Earl Warren should receive an overwhelming mandate of the people to continue in office.

Warren won an unprecedented victory in the primaries of June 4, 1946, receiving both the Republican and Democratic nominations. By polling 1,367,682 votes, he had a comfortable majority of 766,383. In the general election on November 5, Warren amassed 2,344,542 votes against Henry R. Schmidt, the Prohibition party candidate. In 1946, the lieutenant governorship went to Judge Goodwin J. Knight who defeated John F. Shelley of San Francisco.

Governor Warren delivered his second inaugural address at the first regular postwar session of the legislature on January 6, 1947. He requested cooperation in solving problems which transcended partisanship and he pointed out the need of adapting state services to the two million new people added to the seven million who had resided in California prior to 1940. Again he recommended an aviation commission to make California "the peacetime capital of the aviation world." He also requested highway, health, and other improvements.

As the session proceeded, special interest groups opposed some of Warren's favorite proposals. The governor lost on his re-introduced program of prepaid public health insurance, but he won the fight to increase the gasoline tax and other highway user taxes designed to finance an improved system of roads. The highway battle lasted six months, for the oil and trucking lobbies opposed him. According to Herbert L. Phillips, political editor of the McClatchy chain of newspapers, the highway battle was a "parliamentary contest" in which Warren lashed out against the lobbyists who had much influence in the Assembly.

In other matters Warren put through major bills without serious difficulty. He gained more funds for local health departments, hospital construction, and additional mental health clinics. Aeronautics and recreation commissions were established. A better law for the mediation of labor disputes was enacted and he signed a bill outlawing jurisdictional strikes. Many anti-labor bills were defeated. But labor became angered when he permitted a bill allowing permanent prohibition against secondary boycotts and hot cargo practices to become law without his signature. In actuality Warren doubted its constitutionality and let it become law so that the judiciary might consider it. Eventually this particular act was declared invalid.

In 1948, Warren was mentioned as a possible presidential

nominee and his name was put before the Republican national convention at Philadelphia by President Robert Sproul of the University of California. Instead, he received the vice presidential nomination. Although Thomas E. Dewey and Warren were unsuccessful, national attention was focused on Warren.

During the regular session of the 1949 legislature, Warren discussed the state's continuing growth. He informed the legislators that postwar conditions had delayed construction of new facilities required for schools, prisons, and hospitals. He also related that the current highway program had been started in time to meet the need for increased transportation facilities.

Next Warren mentioned progress in the field of public health, but said: "We have not, however, come to grips with the fundamental problem of bringing good medical care within the financial means of the average family." He repeated his recom·mendations of 1945 and 1947 for a system of universal health insurance and attempted to reassure the legislature that it could be accomplished without socializing medicine.

Warren's medical plan had been defeated in the Assembly by one vote in 1945, and by a larger margin in 1947. In 1949 and 1950, it was defeated again after the medical profession hired the public relations firm of Whitaker and Baxter to organize a campaign against it. This was the same public relations firm that had managed Warren's successful campaign for the governorship against Olson.

On December 12, 1949, Warren called a special session of the legislature. Point five of his program called for legislation relating to lobbying. Startling exposés of the methods of the arch-lobbyist, Artie Samish, had been made in *The Nation* by Carey McWilliams and in two issues of *Collier's* by Lester Velvie. An act was passed requiring lobbyists to make financial reports. The next year further legislation was enacted to regulate lobbying.

In 1950, Governor Warren presented a budget of $971,000,-000. It was a balanced budget without new taxes and he indicated that there should be a small surplus at the end of the fiscal year. Warren said: "It retains intact our Rainy Day Fund of $75,000,000 as a cushion against any recession." However, in his analysis of the budget he noted proposed appropriations for the construction of buildings. He revealed that this sum constituted most of the remainder of the building

reserves. Then he warned that the day of surpluses in state
government was over and that conditions called for economy
since some of the spending formulae established by the constitution and by statutes would probably accelerate expenditures
faster than revenue intake.

Since in even-numbered years the legislative session was
restricted to budgetary and financial matters, Warren in 1950
convened a special session to consider problems he regarded
as too urgent to wait until the 1951 general session. These
concerned social welfare, air pollution, gambling, public works,
and lobbying.

On February 1, 1950, Warren announced his candidacy for
a third term and said:

> I will keep my administration honest, free from every subversive
> influence and from every predatory interest. I will not permit it to
> be encumbered by any entrenched political machine. I will devote
> all of my waking hours to programs which will enable us to catch
> up, step by step, with the problems caused by our unprecedented
> growth.

The Democratic opponent in the election of 1950, James
Roosevelt, charged that the Warren administration had failed
to stimulate any additional employment opportunities. Roosevelt implied there was a danger of unemployment and to attract new industry he favored a California development agency.
At one time Roosevelt stated: "My opponent has chosen to
talk about his record, which is strange; for the record is a
record of non-performance. It is a record of pretense, of delay,
of evasion, and of shirking responsibility." On June 2, Warren
referred to Roosevelt as "a prophet of doom." He tried to link
his opponent with the pension promoter, George McLain, while
defending the California pension system which had increased
the maximum benefit from $40 to $75 per month.

The outbreak of the Korean War in June, 1950, created a
situation similar to that of 1942. On October 20, Warren
stated: "During these days of world tension, Mr. James Roosevelt would divide us—party by party, group by group." Although Roosevelt was able to win the Democratic nomination,
Warren's majority in the general election was 1,127,898 votes.

Warren began his unprecedented third term in January,
1951, as the shadow of a possible third world war hung over
the state. Since war production centers were located in Cali-

fornia, he called civil defense the foremost problem. He urged
the legislature to extend Second World War veterans' benefits
to those in service. To facilitate the defense program and to
prepare for the reconversion period after the Korean War, he
recommended a state planning commission similar to the reconstruction and re-employment commission which had termi-
nated in 1947. He again recommended a commission on political and economic equality. He also suggested further improvements in social welfare. He recommended a study of health
insurance, but indicated that he would not resubmit an administrative bill.

In 1952, Governor Warren presented a budget of $1,185,-
379,270. He stated that large postwar increases in the birthrate
and in-migration had created a need for more schools. During
the year he called extra sessions of the legislature to attend to
such problems as civil defense, capital outlay for schools, and
earthquake relief in Kern County.

The year 1953 proved to be Warren's last in the governor's
chair. In his annual message to the legislature he said: "We
must cultivate our growth to insure healthy growth, looking forward to the day which is rapidly approaching when California,
now second, will be the most populous state in the Union." He
recommended a program for the care of the senile and an extension of social security to aid the permanently and totally
disabled. Once more he proposed health insurance. He urged
extending educational benefits to Korean veterans. He praised
the Feather River Project authorized in 1951, and asked for
the completion of both federal and state projects as well as the
launching of new projects to develop and conserve water resources.

Warren emphasized the need for more highway capacity.
He related that the Collier-Burns Act of 1947 had provided
additional funds for roads, but that progress was not fast
enough. He stressed that California was "a state on wheels"
and its economy was based "around the motorcar." Hence he
proposed a one billion dollar ten-year program to overcome the
accumulated backlog of freeway construction.

The 1953 legislature responded to only a few of Warren's
recommendations. The governor viewed the highway bill as
the only legislation of major significance. Among other measures he was pleased to sign were an appropriation for two new

mental hospitals, a bill extending the educational program to Korean veterans, and a bill allowing the state department of public health to render services in smaller counties. However, he was disappointed that the legislature did not attempt to solve problems concerning natural resources, human relations, and governmental reorganization. In protest he said: "It was a session devoted largely to trying to stand still." Warren—like Olson—also favored separating liquor control from the board of equalization, but also failed. It remained for his successor to achieve this reform.

Despite his long tenure as governor, Warren had few critics. Some elements within the Republican party protested his emphasis on social problems and particularly his program for health insurance. Warren often had Democratic support for his program, but many Democrats objected to what they considered his mythical nonpartisanship, pointing out that in presidential years he was purely Republican. Some liberals charged that he owed much to Joseph Knowland of the *Oakland Tribune* and to Norman Chandler of the *Los Angeles Times*. The liberals criticized his appointment of William Knowland to the United States Senate. They also criticized his attitude toward the Japanese-Americans after the bombing of Pearl Harbor. Others charged that he avoided controversy and never crusaded for a single piece of progressive legislation. Some opponents asserted that his administration spent too much and imposed needless taxation while others stated that he delayed sponsoring a school bond issue until five years after the war. Whatever might be attributed to Warren, it was probably something more than prosperity and the impotency of political parties in California that elected him to the governorship three times.

Warren had no political machine and he maintained a campaign organization only during an election. Using a pragmatic approach, he believed that government should be active and positive in serving the people and he held that the governor should administer on a nonpartisan basis. In building his staff he searched for competence rather than political qualifications. He built his staff from three associates and one Olson appointee, William J. Cecil, to a staff of fifty-six. His long incumbency provided continuity and stability in administration. Warren considerably altered the office of California governor by introducing the administrative staff on an expanded scale. While he relied upon others to collect and analyze facts and to make recommendations, he made decisions.

Warren did not place great faith in consulting either Republican or Democratic party officials for ideas concerning legislation. In recognition of the heterogeneous population of California and its diverse economic and social thought, Warren consulted citizens' conferences, advisory committees, and investigative commissions as a basic source for legislative proposals. Civil servants of the executive branch and members of his staff constituted another major source of advice. Moreover, he revived the governor's council and utilized it for information and coordination with monthly meetings. This practice, although mandatory by law, had not been adhered to since the Young administration. By 1947, the council was meeting regularly and operating efficiently. During Warren's tenure five additional departments were created—corrections, justice, mental hygiene, highway patrol, and fish and game. Another innovation Warren introduced was to request elective constitutional officers and others not designated by statute to participate in council meetings.

Governor Warren recognized the independence of the legislature and warned his department heads not to lobby. He did not use threats, but made personal visits to individual and groups of legislators. As stated before, Warren's initial platform of 1943 was not as liberal as those which followed. By 1948, a group of southern California Republicans opposed Warren's nonpartisanship and "New Dealism." In some ways Warren changed the Republican party of California from a conservative force in 1943 to a moderate force by the time he left office in 1953.

On September 3, 1953, Earl Warren announced: "I will not be a candidate for the governorship next year and the people of California should be the first to know that fact in order to have ample time for the selection of my successor." He based his decision on the belief that a periodic change was needed. When he announced that he would not seek a fourth term, Warren did not realize that the highest judicial post in the nation would be offered him. Five days later Chief Justice Fred Vinson died. On September 30, President Eisenhower appointed Warren as Chief Justice of the United States Supreme Court. At first he held a recess appointment since the Senate was not in session. Early the next year his appointment was confirmed.

On October 4, Warren resigned as governor. In an emotional farewell address he urged the state government to maintain pace with continued growth and criticized opponents of his program of enlarging and improving hospitals, schools, prisons, and highways. On the occasion he also said: "I do not intend to cut my moorings from my state."

Earl Warren became the fourteenth Chief Justice. Ninety years earlier President Lincoln had appointed another Californian, by residence and not birth, as a justice of the Supreme Court. He was Stephen J. Field, who had been a Marysville alcalde, Yuba County Assemblyman, and a state justice of California.

On May 17, 1954, Chief Justice Warren read the historic decision holding that racial segregation in public schools was unconstitutional. The decision has had a widespread social impact upon the nation. In his opinions Warren has usually been on the liberal side of the court. For this Warren has been the subject of intense criticism, and in some quarters his impeachment has been demanded.

On November 29, 1963, one week after the assassination of President John F. Kennedy in Dallas, President Lyndon B. Johnson appointed Earl Warren as chairman of The President's Commission on the Assassination of President Kennedy. While this assignment might seem a peculiar role for a chief justice, the choice of Warren was logical because of his background of investigatory work. His long tenure as district attorney of Alameda County and his four years as attorney general gave Warren diversified and extensive experience as an investigator.

For ten months the Warren Commission investigated the assassination and made its report to President Johnson on September 24, 1964. Warren then returned to California on one of his annual visits. At Sacramento while in the capitol he described the investigation as "a long and depressing job." On October 1, 1964, he made his first public appearance since the release of the Warren Commission report. Warren and John A. Carver, Jr., assistant secretary of the interior, participated in the dedication ceremonies at Victorian Park in San Francisco, when the city's cable car system was designated a national landmark.

Warren paid tribute to Andrew Smith Hallidie, inventor of the cable car, and recollected his own first ride on a San Francisco cable car when he was a freshman at the University of California. In January, 1965, Warren was one of the official representatives of the United States at the funeral of Sir Winston Churchill in London.

When Warren resigned as governor, he placed his private papers collected during his three terms in the state archives to be sealed for ten years or until his death. He thus established a precedent for a more careful preserving of gubernatorial papers in the future. In 1963, Warren requested that the secretary of state keep the records under seal until further notice. With the Warren papers closed, a thorough assessment has been impossible; however, it may be stated that Warren has been considered one of the most popular governors of California and a political legend in his own time. Moreover, his candidacy for Vice President of the United States and his elevation to Chief Justice of the United States Supreme Court have added prestige to the office of California governor.

BIBLIOGRAPHY

CONTEMPORARY ACCOUNTS
Assembly Journal, 55th-56th Sess., 1943-45; 1947-53 Sess.
Senate Journal, 55th-56th Sess., 1943-45; 1947-53 Sess.
The Adjutant General, *History of the California State Guard* (Sacramento, 1946).
California Blue Book, 1946 (Sacramento, 1946).
"Highlights of Monthly Governor's Council Reports, June 1947-Dec., 1952," (Documents Section, State Library).
Report of the President's Commission on the Assassination of President John F. Kennedy (Washington, D.C., 1964).
Select Committee Investigating National Defense Migration, H. of R., 77th Cong., 2d Sess., Part 29, "San Francisco Hearings," Feb. 21 and 23, 1942 (Washington, D.C., 1942).
Christman, Henry M., ed., *The Public Papers of Chief Justice Earl Warren* (New York, 1959).
Warren, Earl, "War-Time Martial Rule in California," *Journal of the State Bar of California,* XVII (1942), 185-204.
———, (As told to Milton Silverman), "Why I'm Fighting for My Health Plan," *Look Magazine,* XVI (May 6, 1952), 105-106, 108.
"Press Releases" (Warren), 1950, 1953 (Documents Section, State Library).

SECONDARY SOURCES
Barclay, Thomas S., "Earl Warren, 'So-Called Nonpartisan,' " in J.
   T. Salter, ed., *Public Men in and out of Office* (Chapel Hill, 1946).
McWilliams, Carey, "Warren of California," *New Republic*, CIX (Oct.
   18, 1943), 514-17.
Moley, Raymond, *27 Masters of Politics, In A Personal Perspective*
   (New York, 1949).
Phillips, Herbert L., "Warren of California," *Nation*, CLXXIV (May
   24, 1952), 495-97.
Post, Langdon, "Warren: The Myth and His Record," *New Republic*,
   CXXVI (June 23, 1952), 11-13.
Scoggins, Verne, "Earl Warren, A Biography" (Mimeographed, 1952).
————, *It Happened in California* (1953).
Stone, Irving, *Earl Warren, A Great American Story* (New York, 1948).

NEWSPAPERS
Christian Science Monitor, Dec. 23, 1958, has an article, "Earl Warren
   and the Supreme Court," by Erwin N. Griswold.
Sacramento Union, Oct. 4, 1953, has data about Warren's appointment
   to the Supreme Court.
San Francisco Chronicle, Oct. 15, 1963, has data about Warren's gubernatorial papers.
San Jose Mercury, Oct. 3, 1953, has data on Warren's farewell address
   to the people of California.

THESES
Bell, James R., "The Executive Office of the California Governor under
   Earl Warren, 1943-1953" (Ph.D., University of California, 1956).
Harvey, Richard B., "The Political Approach of Earl Warren, Governor
   of California" (Ph.D., University of California at Los Angeles, 1959).
Pederscn, Richard F., "Governor Earl Warren, As Seen through His
   Speeches" (M.A., Stanford University, 1947).

Calendar of Events

December 9, 1896	Knight born in Provo, Utah.
1904	Knight moved to Los Angeles.
January, 1918	Knight enlisted in the Navy.
January, 1919	Knight discharged from the Navy.
June, 1919	Knight graduated from Stanford University.
March 28, 1921	Knight admitted to the State Bar.
September 20, 1935	Knight appointed a Judge of the Los Angeles County Superior Court.
August, 1936	Knight elected as a Judge.
August, 1942	Knight re-elected as a Judge.
November 5, 1946	Knight elected Lieutenant Governor.
June 6, 1950	Knight re-elected Lieutenant Governor by winning nominations of both major parties in the primary.
October 5, 1953	Knight succeeded Warren.
1953	California Democratic Council formed.
November 2, 1954	Knight elected Governor.
January 3, 1955	Knight inaugurated as Governor.
November 4, 1958	Knight defeated in his bid for the United States Senate.

Goodwin J. Knight

31st Governor—Republican
Born: December 9, 1896
Term of Office: October 5, 1953—January 4, 1959

Goodwin J. Knight, the son of Jesse and Lillie Milner Knight, was born in Provo, Utah, on December 9, 1896. His father was a lawyer and mining engineer. The family moved from Provo to Los Angeles in 1904. As a boy, Goodwin Knight participated in Hiram Johnson's gubernatorial campaigns. He was well acquainted with Governor Johnson's campaign manager and close associate, Meyer Lissner. After graduating from Manual Arts High School in Los Angeles, Knight worked for a year in lead and zinc mines in southern Nevada. He was later a reporter on the *Los Angeles News* and for a time worked as a grocery clerk.

In 1915, he entered Stanford University, but the First World War interrupted his college education. In January, 1918, he enlisted in the Navy as an apprentice seaman. He served aboard a sub-chaser and was discharged in January, 1919, as a seaman 2nd class. He then returned to Stanford, completing his A.B. degree. Knight was selected for the Telluride scholarship at Cornell University where he devoted one year to graduate study in political science and law. When his scholarship money was depleted, Knight could not complete his law degree. He next worked as a clerk in a Los Angeles law office and was admitted to the bar on March 28, 1921. At first he engaged in his own law practice, but later formed a partnership with Thomas Reynolds. In 1925, he married Arvilla Cooley and they had two daughters. His wife died when he was lieutenant governor. In 1954, Governor Knight married Virginia Carlson.

In the early thirties Knight purchased the Elephant-Eagle

427

gold mines in Kern County, which proved to be a profitable investment. He continued his prosperous law practice until September, 1935, when Governor Merriam appointed him to fill a vacancy on the Los Angeles County Superior Court. Judge Knight was elected to the same post in 1936 and re-elected in 1942, serving ten years. During his judicial tenure he rendered 7,000 decisions and only a few were reversed by higher courts.

From his youth Knight demonstrated a love of politics. As a boy he had distributed handbills in Governor Johnson's first campaign. In 1920, he worked in the Johnson-for-President campaign headquarters in New York City and four years later campaigned for Senator Hiram Johnson in Los Angeles County. He was keynote speaker at the Republican state convention at Sacramento in 1934, and participated actively in Merriam's campaign against the EPIC movement.

To extricate himself from the relative obscurity of a judgeship, Knight participated in an educational radio program, The Open Forum, beginning in 1941. Knight became well known to Los Angeles listeners as program moderator. Then he sought a wider audience and for a time moderated The Round Table at San Francisco on Saturdays.

In 1944, Knight was one of several Republicans who considered running for the United States Senate. However, Republican leaders endorsed Lieutenant Governor Frederick N. Houser and Knight withdrew. In the election incumbent Sheridan Downey defeated Houser. Two years later Knight decided to run for lieutenant governor and Houser became a candidate for Knight's judicial post.

In his 1946 campaign Knight employed the professional campaign management firm of Whitaker and Baxter and he conducted a vigorous campaign in fifty counties. He urged economy in government and a greater development of water resources. In the November election, Knight defeated his opponent, State Senator John F. Shelley of San Francisco, by a large majority. Four years later, without the aid of a private campaign firm, Knight won both the Republican and Democratic nominations for the lieutenant governorship, receiving 68 per cent of the primary vote. Knight had split Democratic opposition, defeating ex-Lieutenant Governor Ellis E. Patterson and State Senator George Miller, Jr. He made a better showing in 1950 than in 1946. In fact his victory marked the only time that the lieutenant governorship was won in the primary. In the November election, Knight obtained 3,089,278 votes, a record high for any state official.

Lieutenant Governor Knight worked diligently to give his position added prestige and more duties were assigned to the office. He was appointed to the state land commission, state disaster council, board of regents of the University of California, toll bridge authority, and committee for interstate cooperation. When Knight entered office the monthly salary was $330 and when he left, it was $1,000, after three pay raises.

In the 1948 presidential campaign Knight supported the Dewey-Warren ticket—when the governorship was almost within his grasp—but the Republican defeat ended his hopes temporarily. In 1950, rumors circulated that Knight would oppose Warren and a group of county central committees endorsed him. Knight and Warren had differed on such matters as state health insurance, loyalty oaths, and fiscal matters. Knight made a few speeches against Warren's policies, but withdrew from the political race for the sake of party harmony.

On September 16, 1953, Knight officially announced that he would run for governor, thirteen days after Warren had stated that he would not seek a fourth term. Knight indicated that he would maintain a "business-like administration with emphasis on reduced spending." His opportunity came somewhat earlier, when Warren was elevated to the Supreme Court. On October 5, 1953, Knight became the ninth lieutenant governor to succeed to the governorship. For a while there were fears that Knight might upset Warren's administrative machine, but he decided to retain Warren's experienced appointees.

It is said that Knight began his campaign for governor when only eighteen years old and that he copied William Jennings Bryan on the rostrum and studied the career of Theodore Roosevelt for political guidance. Hospitable and friendly, "Goodie" Knight with his husky physique and impressive appearance was artful and astute at politics. Although in his fifties, Knight was trim and physically fit for the office.

Knight was well-qualified for his new post, for he had served a total of 420 days as acting governor during Warren's absences. In fact he even had the unusual duty of signing legislative bills with Warren's approval during the important closing days of the 1952 session while Warren was attending the English coronation.

The new governor delighted in flying aboard his plane, *The Grizzly*, to deliver forceful speeches in his pleasant and sonorous voice. During his first fifty-nine days in office Governor Knight gave eighty-four speeches. After serving three months, Knight in a "Report to the People" broadcast stated that the number one problem in California was its "almost unbelievable growth." In an address before the Newspaper Publishers Association convention at Los Angeles, Knight told his audience about the varied duties and excitement of the California governorship. His typical day included receipt and preparation of about 250 incoming and outgoing letters, 200 telephone calls, thirty visitors, and twenty-five invitations to speak. In addition, there were press conferences, meetings of commissions and committees, conferences with department heads, and pardon and extradition hearings. He indicated that his most pressing problem was the preparation of the state budget and that his fiscal policy was to adhere to a strict economy without compromising essential public services and to pay for all necessary expenditures without new taxes. Knight commented that the problem was complicated by the fact that the largest items such as welfare, schools, and highways were fixed into the budget by law.

On March 1, 1954, Governor Knight delivered his budget and special session messages. He had called a special session to meet concurrently with the budget session, but indicated that this should not be construed as the beginning of a policy of making each or any budget session the reason for discussing numerous issues which properly belonged to a general session. He also opined that the transition from one administration to another had been achieved in an efficient manner.

Knight presented a budget of $1,423,345,684 as compared to the previous budget of $1,429,615,586. He pointed out that it required no new taxes and that it was one of the few budgets calling for a reduction in expenditures. Additions were made to the budget for the department of mental hygiene, youth authority, department of corrections, state colleges, and the University of California. Knight stated that the budget did not make any inroads on the so-called "Rainy Day" fund and that it was designed neither to incur heavy deficits nor to accumulate large surpluses.

The first item Governor Knight included among the emergency matters for the extra session was alcoholic beverage control. He recommended a new structure and a single authority with full responsibility. The second item recommended an increase in the maximum weekly unemployment insurance payment and the third item was an additional bond issue for veterans' farms and homes. Another item requested an additional bond issue for school construction while most of the remaining items were of a specialized or local nature. Knight achieved his major aims with the 1954 legislature which agreed to place the liquor reorganization proposal on the ballot and also voted to increase the maximum weekly unemployment payment from $25 to $30.

Governor Knight faced his 1954 campaign with confidence. He did not deviate much from the Warren campaign approach as he sought election in his own right. A long series of Democratic defeats for state offices and the Republican sweep of 1952 discouraged potential candidates from opposing Knight.

The gubernatorial election of 1954 was unusual in several respects. In 1952, California voters adopted a measure requiring the designation of a candidate's party registration on the ballot, but at the same time disapproved an initiative measure to abolish cross-filing. This was followed by the rise of Democratic clubs, and in 1953 the California Democratic Council was formed. The Democrats now had an extra-legal body similar to the California Republican Assembly with which to endorse candidates before the direct primary election.

In February, 1954, the California Democratic Council and the Dime A Day for Democracy organization jointly held a pre-primary convention at Fresno and endorsed a slate for nomination in the coming primary. With the aid of George Miller, Jr., and Glenn Anderson, Richard P. Graves was recommended as gubernatorial candidate. Graves had recently changed his party affiliation from Republican to Democratic. He was executive director of the League of California Cities, but had never held political office. Graves had been close to Warren and had worked with him on civil defense matters. For lieutenant governor the Democrats endorsed Edward Roybal, Los Angeles councilman.

A coalition of Knight and William Knowland forces—assisted by United States Senator Thomas H. Kuchel—directed the loosely knit California Republican party organization with Knight in control of the state central committee. Whitaker and Baxter guided Knight's campaign and obtained endorsement of over one hundred mayors in a Mayors-of-California Non-Partisan Committee. To weaken Graves, the Democratic Conference Against Radical Party Leadership was formed in San Francisco on May 31, and Graves charged that it was a hoax to defeat him for the Democratic nomination. Knight and his running mate, Harold J. Powers, obtained official AFL endorsement. However, an independent union group along with the CIO supported Graves.

Knight hoped to capture both the Republican and Democratic nominations in the primary, but Graves defeated Knight by a slight margin on the Democratic ticket while Knight defeated Graves by a 10-1 margin on the Republican ticket.

After the primary, Knight let his opponent battle in the dark and seldom mentioned his name. Graves endeavored to present a broad program including water and power development, industrial expansion, and smog control. Graves also supported fair employment practices legislation and opposed special loyalty oaths. Moreover, he expressed the belief that the budget should be balanced by increased liquor and racetrack taxes instead of using "Rainy Day" reserves.

The final campaign was described by many as issueless and lackluster. For a time Graves was ill and had to direct his campaign from a hospital bed. As a candidate in 1954, Knight was known as a former lieutenant governor and successor to Warren. However, the voters had to be persuaded that he was able to perform the job. In a sense his opponent was not Graves, but the former governor. As the returns came in, the *San Francisco Chronicle* in an editorial of November 3, stated in part:

> Running the executive administration of California is one of the top responsibilities in the country. It was not easy, you will have to concede for Goodie Knight to step into Earl Warren's shoes and show in a year's time that he was just the man for this responsibility. But he has managed to satisfy a good 55 per cent of the voters, according to the trend of the returns last night.

Actually Knight's victory was an easy one. He polled a 551,000 majority, when Republicans elsewhere suffered a poor political year. His natural campaigning abilities, his promise to veto any anti-labor legislation, and the fact that he had not varied much from the Warren approach were factors which probably explain his victory.

In his message to the legislature on January 3, 1955, Knight stated that economy was essential, but not at the "sacrifice of important services." After mentioning the part of his 1954 budget message in which he had emphasized long-term planning for state facilities, he pointed out the need for training additional teachers. Next he urged an effective and immediate solution to the problem of air pollution. Knight asked the legislature to raise funds for constructing the Feather River project and he recommended a joint resolution urging Congress to start the Trinity River project. Also he proposed a coordinated water resources department.

In a discussion of labor-management relations he mentioned his "duty to discourage any form of punitive legislation which shackles labor or management and pits one against the other in economic and social warfare, often at considerable expense and inconvenience to the general public." Knight described unemployment insurance as a great achievement and suggested an increase of at least $5 per week in disability allowances as well as more liberal death benefits in cases involving fatal industrial accidents.

Knight praised the legislature for proposing the liquor control measure at the special session the previous year. Then he recommended establishing a control advisory council whose members would be appointed by the governor and be representative of all sections and interested groups. Furthermore, he suggested a revision of the election code and the passage of an effective fair campaigns practices act.

In December, 1955, fifty-three California counties were hit by devastating floods. When the budget session and a concurrent extraordinary session met in March, 1956, Governor Knight proposed rehabilitating public facilities which had been damaged by the floods. Also he recommended an increase in the emergency fund because of the flood disaster and stated that the December floods had demonstrated the urgency for an early start of the Feather River project. Knight submitted a budget of $1,736,112,983, without new or higher taxes, which was an increase of 8.1 percent over the 1955-56 budget. The new budget provided for a capital outlay of $358,000,000 for highways, buildings, beach and park program, 1960 Winter Olympics, wild life conservation, flood control, and the Feather River project. The extraordinary session created the department of water resources with a director appointed by the governor subject to confirmation by the Senate.

When the regular session convened in January, 1957, Knight requested the adoption of a water development program. He pointed out that the most pressing problem was to formulate adequate constitutional provisions and legislative enactments in order to protect areas of origin and to reserve water for future needs. Knight indicated that the problem was largely one of the mechanics of control, conservation, and transportation of the existing rich water resources. Then he recommended establishing a water development fund to be supported by long-range financing. Moreover, he suggested that the state assist local agencies in developing their own water resources by providing loans on a long-term and low interest rate basis.

Governor Knight also proposed various labor and welfare reforms and legislation to prohibit alcoholic beverage licensees from contributing to gubernatorial campaigns. In his annual budget message he presented a budget of $1,947,964,993 to finance state operations during the next fiscal year.

The 1957 legislature adopted several of Knight's recommendations regarding the water program. Improvements were authorized in the field of mental health and increases were made in unemployment benefits, workmen's compensation benefits, and old age pensions. Also a measure was signed establishing child care centers on a permanent basis.

In his budget message of 1958, Knight indicated that revenue yields would be considerably below the trend of previous years because of the recent recession. He explained that expenditures were reduced because of the sale of bonds for capital outlay and because the budget temporarily omitted needed expenditures for water development. Knight expressed the view that taxes should not be increased in view of the economic situation and he related that a revenue deficiency now existed. Hence he requested use of the "Rainy Day" Fund to fulfill its intended purpose. Furthermore, he stated that even with an upswing in business, future budgets would face a large deficiency of revenues. Knight explained that the tax structure was twenty years old and that new burdens and inflation had outmoded it.

On August 19, 1957, Knight officially announced his intention to seek re-election. He remarked that the office of governor should not be used as a stepping stone to any other office. Political commentators assumed that he was referring to United States Senator William F. Knowland, who was expected to be a gubernatorial candidate. As the year progressed Knight and Knowland clashed on the "right-to-work" issue and Knight warned that the injection of the issue into the 1958 campaign could disturb the industrial peace of California. As the prospect of a bitter primary fight between Governor Knight and Senator Knowland developed, rumors circulated late in October, 1957 that Knight had decided to run for the Senate and leave a clear field for Knowland in the gubernatorial race. In the meantime, three Republicans had already announced their candidacy for Knowland's seat. They were Mayor George Christopher of San Francisco, State Controller Robert Kirkwood, and Warren Atherton, a Stockton lawyer.

After the actual candidacy switch occurred, some journalists contended that Richard Nixon played a role in making the change in order to prevent a struggle between Knight and Knowland over the governorship which would give the victory to Attorney General Edmund G. Brown and the Democrats. In the campaign of 1958, Knowland urged Knight's election to the Senate, but Knight did not support Knowland. In the November election the Republicans met a serious defeat. Clair Engle won over Knight in the senatorial race and Knowland was defeated in his bid for the governorship by Edmund G. Brown. On December 6, 1958, Knight spoke before the board of directors banquet meeting of the California Republican Assembly and told his listeners there was much to learn in defeat. He urged that Republicans forget the causes of defeat and work to rebuild their party.

At his final press conference on January 2, 1959, Governor Knight related that he had no regrets concerning his administration. However, he warned against what he considered a "dilution" of gubernatorial powers by the legislature. He indicated that more of the governor's appointments were required to be confirmed by the Senate. Although he had no difficulties with his appointments, he believed that in the future the legislature might have unwarranted control over the executive by withholding confirmations.

Before he left office Governor Knight was mentioned for an

appointment as a federal district judge. In April, 1959, former Governor Knight told California Republicans that they would have to liberalize their party in order to make a political comeback. On July 1, some Republican leaders of southern California suggested Knight for a cabinet position, but he discounted the possibility. Later in the month Knight, who was now active in business enterprises in southern California, announced that he would support Nixon for the Republican nomination as President. In October, Knight began participation in a television show called "Judge for Yourself," which explained legal problems to the layman. In 1960, Knight was a member of the Nixon-for-President delegation at the Republican national convention. On August 24, 1960, the press announced that Knight had been named president of an insurance company. While occupied in business, former Governor Knight has maintained an active interest in politics.

Among the major achievements of the Knight administration were those in the field of water development. Water agencies were combined under a single organization and beginnings were made on the Feather River project and on the Whale Rock project in San Luis Obispo County. Also a program was enacted to aid local water conservation efforts. Overcrowded conditions in the state prisons were improved by new construction and by remodeling. Long-range planning in public works was conceived and a better college building program was launched. In the matter of liquor control Knight was successful in achieving a reorganization after his two predecessors had failed to gain the cooperation of the legislature. A department of alcoholic beverage control, approved by the voters in November, 1954, was created on January 1, 1955.

On September 11, 1961, ex-Governor Knight announced at a press conference in Los Angeles that he would seek the Republican gubernatorial nomination in 1962. He became one of the few former governors to seek a return to the office, but illness soon forced him to withdraw as a candidate. Knight has since regained his health and appears as active as when he was governor. On April 7, 1965, he informed members of the Republican legislative caucus that he might run for governor in the June, 1966, primary if conditions were favorable.

Bibliography

MANUSCRIPTS
Letters from Goodwin J. Knight to B.F. Gilbert, Dec. 8, 1959 and May 30, 1960.

CONTEMPORARY ACCOUNTS
Assembly Journal, 1954-58 Sess.
California Blue Book, 1954 (Sacramento, 1954).
"Legislative Accomplishments under the Program of Governor Goodwin J. Knight," 1957, (Documents Section, State Library).
"Press Releases" (Knight), 1953-58.

SECONDARY SOURCES
Barclay, Thomas S., "The 1954 Election in California," *Western Political Quarterly,* VII (1954), 597-604.
Champion, Hale, "California's Governor Knight: Balance of Republican Power?" *Reporter,* XIV (Feb. 23, 1956), 20-24.
Friedman, Ralph, "The Gay Beaver," *Frontier,* IX (June, 1958), 10-19.
Taylor, Frank J., "How to Run for Office," *Saturday Evening Post,* CCXXVIII (Oct. 29, 1955), 34-36, 76, 80, 82.
Pony Express Courier, XV (Feb., 1949), 11-12, has a biographical sketch of Knight, when he was lieutenant governor.
Who's Who in California (Los Angeles, 1941, 1956).

NEWSPAPERS
Sacramento Union, Jan. 26, 1947, has an article about Knight as lieutenant governor.
San Francisco Chronicle, Nov. 1 and 2, 1957, has articles about Knight as a candidate for the United States Senate; Aug. 25, 1960, has an article entitled, "Knight to Head Insurance Firm."
San Jose Mercury, Nov. 6, 1955, has an article on the Knight-Nixon struggle within the Republican party.

Calendar of Events

April 21, 1905	Brown born in San Francisco.
1927	Brown awarded LL.B. degree by San Francisco College of Law.
1928	Brown defeated as a Republican candidate for the Assembly.
1934	Brown changed his political affiliation to Democratic and elected to County Central Committee in San Francisco.
1939	Brown defeated in his first bid for District Attorney of San Francisco.
January 8, 1944	Brown inaugurated as District Attorney of San Francisco.
November 5, 1946	Brown defeated in race for Attorney General.
1947	Brown re-elected as District Attorney of San Francisco.
November 7, 1950	Brown elected Attorney General.
November 2, 1954	Brown re-elected Attorney General.
October 30, 1957	Brown announced his candidacy for the governorship.
January 5, 1959	Brown inaugurated as Governor.
1959	Cross-filing abolished.
November 8, 1960	Water bond issue approved by voters.
1961	Legislature overhauled the executive branch creating the Agency Plan and the Governor's Cabinet.
November 6, 1962	Brown defeated Richard M. Nixon and was re-elected Governor.

Edmund G. Brown

32ND GOVERNOR—DEMOCRAT
BORN: APRIL 21, 1905
TERM OF OFFICE: JANUARY 5, 1959—

EDMUND G. "PAT" BROWN, CALIFORNIA'S thirty-second governor, is the second Democrat to occupy the office in the twentieth century and unlike Olson has the advantage of a legislature of his own party. Born April 21, 1905, in San Francisco, he is a second generation Californian. His father, Edmund J. Brown, died in 1943, and his mother, Ida Shuckman Brown, resides in San Francisco.

During World War I, when a seventh-grade pupil at Fremont Grammar School, young Edmund Brown delivered a fiery speech to sell liberty bonds, climaxing it with the shout: "Give me liberty or give me death." His classmates nicknamed him "Patrick Henry" Brown. Afterwards his friends dubbed him "Pat" and the name stuck through his rise in California politics.

As a boy residing in San Francisco's Western Addition, he earned his own spending money by delivering the *Call* and the *Chronicle*. After graduating from Lowell High School, he worked in his father's store and attended San Francisco College of Law. At the same time he took courses at the University of California Extension Division. Eventually he found employment with a blind lawyer, Milton L. Schmitt, while attending law college. He obtained his LL.B. degree in 1927, and passed the California state bar examination in the same year. From 1927 to 1943, he engaged in private law practice in San Francisco. On October 30, 1930, Edmund Brown married Bernice Layne, daughter of a San Francisco police captain. They are the parents of three daughters and one son.

Pat Brown first ventured into politics as a Republican when California was virtually a one-party state. At twenty-three he ran unsuccessfully for the Assembly in the 26th district. In the early 1930's, Brown assisted in organizing the Order of Cincinnatus, a nonpartisan group of young voters sponsoring good city government. In 1934, he changed his party affiliation to Democratic and was elected to that party's county central committee. The next year he served as president of the Order of Cincinnatus and in 1936, he participated in the San Francisco municipal campaign.

In 1939, Brown contested the veteran incumbent, District Attorney Matthew Brady, but lost; four years later he defeated him. Brown was sworn into office on January 8, 1944, in joint ceremonies with Mayor Roger Lapham. In his inaugural address at city hall Brown said:

> The office of District Attorney inevitably deals with human nature at its worst . . . with crime, vice, and humanity gone wrong. Its primary obligation is to protect society from its rebellious and predatory members. It must move vigorously and impartially in the prosecution of crime. It must seek the full penalty of the law against the deliberate malicious, and unrepentant offenders.

However, he continued: "the office should not become an agency of grim, blind, and implacable justice."

In war-time San Francisco, Brown brought a sense of objectivity and fairness to his office. He gathered a trained staff and with community support launched a juvenile crime prevention program. He minimized gambling and waged a campaign against prostitution and the abortion racket. Moreover, he instituted the practice of screening cases thereby protecting people from false charges.

In 1946, Brown won the Democratic nomination for attorney general of California, but lost in the general election to Fred N. Howser, district attorney of Los Angeles County. In 1947, Brown won his second four-year term as district attorney of San Francisco. In a second attempt Brown won the attorney generalship in 1950, being the only Democrat to win statewide office, when Earl Warren gained his third term as governor. In 1954, Brown obtained the nominations of both parties in an overwhelming victory for a second term. In the Republican primary he defeated his former opponent of 1946. Brown considered running for governor in 1954, but preferred to keep his post of attorney general.

Brown made an impressive record and cooperated whole-heartedly with Warren's administration during eight years as attorney general. When the State Supreme Court in the Ivanhoe case removed the 160-acre irrigation limitation on federal reclamation projects, Brown joined in an appeal to the United States Supreme Court which resulted in a reversed decision. Brown's opinions concerning civil rights and the protection of minorities were commendable. In a question over religious instruction in public schools he upheld the principle of separation of church and state.

At a press conference, held in Los Angeles on October 30, 1957, Brown officially announced his candidacy for the governorship. He stated that he would run whether his opponent were Governor Goodwin J. Knight or Senator William F. Knowland, but believed that Knight would be persuaded to run for the United States Senate. Knowland became the Republican party's gubernatorial candidate and supported Proposition 18, the "right-to-work" amendment, which tended to antagonize organized labor. During his campaign Brown promised to solve the water problem, to implement a fair employment practices act, to sponsor legislation guaranteeing democracy in unions, and to reorganize state government.

In the general election Brown was victorious with a million vote majority. Congressman Clair Engle defeated Governor Knight for Knowland's former Senate seat and Glenn Anderson unseated incumbent Lieutenant Governor Harold Powers. The California Democrats won all statewide offices except one and achieved their first majorities in both legislative branches since 1889.

The Republican party failed to present a united front to the voters, with the moderate wing of the party preferring to sit out the election. Knowland became the focus and target of a campaign by organized labor and its sympathizers to defeat the "right-to-work" amendment.

The California political pattern reversed itself, bringing about Democratic solidarity and Republican factionalism. In the closing days of the Republican campaign, the *San Francisco Chronicle* withdrew its endorsement of Knowland. In an editorial on the Republican defeat, the *Chronicle* of November 7, theorized:

An extreme group in the California Republican party decided over a year ago to take California back into the 19th Century, away from the "modern Republicanism" that the members of the group so heartily loathe; away from the progressive tradition and spirit of the great Republican governorships of Hiram Johnson, C. C. Young and Earl Warren; away from Goodwin Knight, whom they hold in contempt for his odd notion that the way for Republican candidates to win is to try to gain support from all elements of the public, including labor.

The 1958 gubernatorial election marked the return of the two-party system to California. The Democratic party once again had adequate financing and it was revitalized with energetic leadership. Brown was the first Democratic candidate in many years to muster considerable support from the press. He successfully exploited the Knowland-Knight feud and charged that Knowland coveted the governorship as a stepping stone to the presidency.

In his inaugural address of January 5, 1959, Governor Edmund G. Brown related that the voters had rejected "reaction by the radical right" and said: "our duty is to bring to California the forward force of responsible liberalism." Such a government, he asserted, would not pamper its citizens or threaten solvency. He defined liberal government as one concerned with people first and as one spurning special privilege. Governor Brown then stated:

In the path of responsible liberalism, we walk in the giant footsteps of such memorable governors as Hughes and Roosevelt in New York, Wilson in New Jersey, LaFollette in Wisconsin, Altgeld and Stevenson in Illinois, and Johnson and Warren in California. Let us mark their example and set our sights to match their achievements.

Governor Brown made twelve specific recommendations. He first called for legislation to prevent discrimination by an employer or by a labor union on the basis of race, creed, national origin, or age. Next he urged protection of consumers, the establishment of an agency for economic development, and a strengthening of the collective bargaining process. Moreover, he favored increases in unemployment insurance and other welfare benefits as well as a minimum wage of $1.25 an hour for workers not covered by federal law. To reform election practices he recommended abolishing cross-filing, improving legislation on the disclosure of campaign funds, and using electronic computers to count votes. He proposed a reorganization of state government, requesting that the governor be authorized to prepare such plans to submit to the legislature.

Brown also suggested improvements in crime prevention and narcotic control. He pointed out the need for more good teachers and for additional educational facilities. He proposed more research on smog control and the establishment of a coordinator of atomic energy development. To alleviate the backlog in the courts he suggested creating an automobile accident commission. In conclusion, Brown proposed studies of long-term problems such as health insurance, discrimination in housing, and crowded airways.

On January 20, Governor Brown in a special message requested further regulation of labor-management relations. Two days later the legislature met to hear his significant water message in which he pleaded for an end to delay and deadlock. He recommended use of the "investment fund" to begin a construction program and declared: "it is time to start moving dirt and stop throwing mud." He proposed a general obligation bond issue and urged encouragement of federal financing of projects for navigation, flood control, and irrigation. Furthermore, he asked for development of water resources on a statewide integrated basis to avoid "Balkanizing our state into competing water provinces." Water resources, he related, should be available to every part of California and the goal was obtainable either with or without a constitutional amendment. On January 27, Brown submitted a $2,188,000,000 budget and requested a $202,000,000 program of increased taxes to return California to solvency.

The 1959 legislature was responsive, enacting thirty-five of the forty major measures supported by the governor. The Burns-Porter Act submitted a $1,750,000,000 water bond issue to the voters for decision in November, 1960. In addition the $172,000,000 investment fund was earmarked for water development, and $85,000,000 was appropriated for water projects in the next fiscal year.

A fair employment practices act was passed. Maximum unemployment insurance was increased from $40 to $55 a week and increases were also made in disability and workmen's compensation benefits. A consumers' counsel was established to protect the consumer from false labeling and deceptive carrying charges on installment credit purchases. Moreover, the consumers' counsel was empowered to advance the consumers' interests by public education and by representation before governmental agencies. An economic development agency was created to implement long-range planning to attract new industries and employment.

The legislature enacted new revenue measures such as the cigarette tax to solve the problem of deficit spending. The Democrats succeeded in abolishing cross-filing which had tended to weaken the partisan responsibility of political parties. Cross-filing, it will be remembered, had been instituted by the Progressives in 1913 and went into practice the next year. This procedure, however, historically had worked against the Democratic party in California. In 1952, the voters had disapproved an initiative measure to abolish cross-filing, but at the same time had modified the procedure by approving an amendment which required the party affiliation of each candidate to be placed on the ballot after his name. Although more Democrats than Republicans began to win both nominations in the primaries, Governor Brown moved to abolish cross-filing completely. Brown's only major defeats during the session were the failure of the legislature to pass a minimum wage act and a fair labor standards act.

Governor Brown described the passage of the water bond issue as the "crowning achievement" of the 1959 session when he signed the Burns-Porter Act. Meanwhile, in April, 1959, he called upon California educators to devise a master plan for higher education. Moreover, he instituted two major studies on governmental reorganization in 1959 in accordance with his campaign pledge.

On November 1, 1959, Governor Brown attended the inauguration of Governor Eligio Esquivel Mendez of Baja California. It will be remembered that several Spanish governors and one Mexican governor had ruled simultaneously over both Californias. By 1959 California had been one of the United States for 109 years, but now Baja California was the newest Mexican state. Governor Brown appropriately remarked:

> The early history of Alta California is inseparably tied to yours. Our missions, the names of our streets and cities and mountains and valleys, our architecture, all reflect our debt to your culture.

North of the border we are proud of the close cultural ties that bind us to our southern neighbor.

In his first anniversary report as governor, given on January 5, 1960, Brown announced that he would convene a special session of the legislature in March to consider the problems of smog control and improvement of education. On February 1, the governor submitted a record budget of $2,477,121,574 for the next fiscal year. Because of the increasing population of California, the inflationary trend, and pyramiding costs of education, highways, social welfare, parks, and other public services, each of Governor Brown's budgets has shown an increase. On February 19, he granted Caryl Chessman of death-row fame a sixty-day reprieve. At the same time Brown proposed that the legislature consider the abolition of capital punishment at the special session. This caused an uproar in the legislature—other business was delayed while the death penalty issue was debated. An anti-capital punishment bill was killed by the Senate judiciary committee. The legislature then returned to the budget and proposed tax cuts made by the Republicans were defeated. An important master plan for higher education designed to bring improvements and cooperation among the state university, state colleges, and junior colleges was adopted and a $300,000,000 school construction bond issue was approved.

In the presidential primary election held on June 7, 1960, Brown won control of the California Democratic delegation, but George McLain, the pension promoter, displayed an unexpected strength in the so-called "gray-haired revolt." On July 7, Brown announced his support for Senator John F. Kennedy for president and released his delegates. But at the Democratic national convention in Los Angeles, Brown was unable to deliver the entire California delegation to Kennedy. In the November election Richard M. Nixon narrowly won California's thirty-two electoral votes after a count of the absentee ballots. Some political commentators contended that Brown and the California Democrats were losing prestige with the electorate. Nonetheless, the voters in approving the water bond issue despite formidable opposition gave Governor Brown a victory for one of his favorite proposals.

In 1961, the Democrats controlled the legislature with 47 Democrats and 33 Republicans in the Assembly and 30 Democrats and 10 Republicans in the Senate. On January 3, Brown delivered his biennial message urging a continuation of "responsible liberalism." After outlining his program in general terms, he first discussed education. He recommended adoption of the state board of education and the state department of education proposals to reduce the types of teaching credentials "from a bewildering 40 to a basic 5" and to require teachers to major in an academic subject. He also recommended an emphasis on "solid" subjects and increased assistance to special programs for gifted children. To reduce crime he recommended harsher penalties for narcotic peddlers. In the field of social welfare he proposed an increase in maximum benefits to the aged and a modification of the relatives' responsibility law. In order to consider the need for more representation in urban areas, Brown requested the appointment of a commission to study State Senate reapportionment.

Other problems Governor Brown considered worthy of attention were civil rights, labor-management relationships, and consumer protection. He saw no need for new taxes and recommended that prescription drugs be exempted from the sales tax. On January 25, Brown submitted a budget of $2,592,304,521 which was $115,182,947 more than his previous budget.

The 1961 legislature undertook the first major overhaul of the executive branch in over thirty years. Since the Young administration the governorship had been weakened by diffusion of authority—department directors, boards, and commissions were unable to communicate adequately with the governor. The governor's council, created in 1927, while it had served a useful purpose for the exchange of information, failed to fulfill its original function as a policy advisory group. In 1959 an advisory committee on organization of state government, appointed by Brown, devised "The Agency Plan for California." It proposed grouping the numerous administrative departments into eight agencies and heading each with an administrator who would be a member of the governor's cabinet.

On February 13, 1961, Governor Brown transmitted the government reorganization program to the legislature. He referred to the present structure as "jerry-built" and "often haphazard" with about 360 boards, commissions, and agencies. To simplify the unwieldy structure Brown asked for the establishment of the agency plan. He suggested that the legislature approach the problem slowly to circumvent any drastic change and to avoid a gigantic superstructure. Hence he only asked for the creation of four agencies at that time. Brown proposed that "the plan must be so worded as to retain the full power of the Legislature over the organization of the executive branch, and it must also conserve our fundamental division of government into three co-equal branches by denying to the chief executive any authority to reorganize either our judicial system or to affect our Legislature and its staff agencies." Despite Brown's assurances, some Republican legislators charged that the reorganization would reduce the power of the legislature and create a "super-government." In an editorial of February 15, the *San Francisco Chronicle* came to the governor's defense, stating in part as follows: "Legislators who are sounding off against this idea merely because Pat Brown is a Democrat would be well advised to approach less partisanly a goal that is, after all, virtuous and very important."

In accordance with the governor's wishes the 1961 legislature created four agencies: natural resources, health and welfare, youth and adult corrections, and highway transportation. To complete the agency plan Governor Brown established four additional agencies by executive order as follows: revenue and management, business and commerce, employment relations, and public safety. Two years later the legislature decided not to give these agencies statutory status, but they were continued under executive order. However, the legislature established two new departments: general services and rehabilitation. The agency plan and the governor's cabinet were designed to create defined lines of responsibility and to reduce the cost of state government in responding more effectively to the needs of the people. While Governor Brown felt that the agency plan was essential for responsible government, opponents have charged that it was super-government.

Brown was the first California governor to submit a thorough anti-narcotics program to the legislature. The 1961 session enacted harsher penalties and authorized an institution for narcotic addicts. Moreover, the legislature revamped the state juvenile court act. Upon the advice of a committee appointed by Governor Brown, the legislature reduced the types of teaching credentials from over forty to five and gave greater emphasis to content in teacher training. Several changes in welfare benefits were made and unemployment insurance and disability benefits were liberalized.

Besides government reorganization, bitter legislative battles occurred in 1961 over the water problem and reapportionment. The $1,750,000,000 California water project which the voters had narrowly approved in November was now considered by the legislature. It was questioned whether or not the project might eventually plunge the state into deficit financing. Some legislators were not sure that the rights of the water-originating northern counties were protected and were fearful that these might be subverted to the claims of southern California users. A third major question bore upon adequate flood control. During hearings held by a Senate fact-finding committee, protests were made by San Joaquin Valley water users that northern California farmers had been "priced out" of the state water plan by a contract signed by Governor Brown with the Metropolitan Water District of Southern California just before the November election.

Despite powerful opposition the legislature retained intact the $1,750,000,000 California water project proposal. Later that fall when Governor Brown touched off a dynamite blast marking the start of the Oroville Dam, he stated that it would end the long water war between the northern and southern sections of the state. While the governor called the project "monumental," others foresaw high water costs, law suits, and ultimately a northern California water shortage.

The 1961 legislature approved a Democratic plan to realign Congressional and Assembly districts for the next decade. Some Republican leaders expected to destroy the Democratic plan by a statewide referendum. In an editorial of June 15, entitled, "Is a Referendum Going to Help?" the *San Francisco Chronicle* concluded: "Connoisseurs of reapportionment procedures over the years are unable to conclude that the Democrats this year rigged the new districts any more conspicuously than the Republicans rigged them in 1951." In its editorial, "The Sighs at Adjournment," the *Los Angeles Times* of June 20, stated: "And although the gerrymander's claws tore at the Assembly redistricting map, the Legislature also approved the formation of a commission to consider the need and means of reapportioning the State Senate."

On February 5, 1962, Governor Brown presented the legislature with a $2,885,523,247 budget. It was his fourth balanced budget and third that required no new taxes; however, it included $141,000,000 in bonds to finance state buildings. The budget as approved by the legislature the following April was slightly higher. Brown's State Senate reapportionment plan, giving Los Angeles County more Senators, was defeated by the 1962 session.

Meanwhile, in October, 1961, Richard M. Nixon, former Vice President of the United States, had decided to run for the governorship and a long and bitter campaign ensued. In the June, 1962 primary Nixon defeated his Republican opponent, Joseph C. Shell, by a two to one margin. In the general election of November, Brown defeated Nixon by approximately 300,-000 votes. Diligent precinct work by Democratic party workers and by the political forces of organized labor caused a heavy turnout of voters and was a major factor in Brown's re-election. The Democrats were well organized and retained control of the legislature.

During his first term Governor Brown had carried out many of his 1958 campaign pledges. Cross-filing had been abolished and significant changes were made in the fields of education, governmental reorganization, and water conservation. While some of his proposed reforms in the areas of civil rights, labor benefits, and political practices were not adopted, others were.

Governor Brown delivered his second inaugural message on January 7, 1963. He reviewed what he considered accomplishments of the past four years made under "the banner of responsible liberalism." Proudly, he said: "The California Water Project, which once threatened to divide our state, now unites it." He referred in optimistic terms to the new master plans for education, highways and parks, and hospitals and mental health clinics. And he praised the prosperous economy of California and her leadership in the space industry.

Among the governor's new major proposals were an "Office of California Development," a scenic highway system, and a more comprehensive park and beach program. He also recommended a revision of criminal law and procedure, a removal of discriminatory practices in housing and of de facto segregation in public schools, and a further reorganization of state government. He concluded his inaugural with these words:

Let us accept no limitations except those of our own imagination and enterprise. Let us say: This golden state—a symbol of man's striving toward a better life—shall not only lead our nation, but deserve to lead, in the challenging time before us. Let us determine, with God's guidance, to be equal to this splendid prospect.

On February 4, Governor Brown submitted a narrowly balanced budget of $3,250,401,969, the largest state budget in the history of any state. The 1963 regular and concurrent special sessions saw the passage of the Rumford Fair Housing Act, social welfare aid, consumer protection laws, savings and loan reforms, and educational aid for "culturally deprived" children. The Rumford Act outlawed racial discrimination in most private and public housing and directed the fair employment practices commission to hear complaints and enforce decisions, if necessary, in court. The legislature created an automation commission to study the impact of technological changes on the California economy and labor force, a coordinating council on urban policy to study urban growth problems, and a fine arts commission to inventory the state's artistic resources.

On February 3, 1964, Governor Brown submitted his sixth budget to the legislature. It called for an expenditure program of $3,260,000,000 from current sources which represented an increase of $129,000,000 or 4 per cent over the 1963-64 revised operating budget. In addition, it proposed $398,000,-000 bond financing for capital construction facilities of the state water plan and for state institutions, principally of higher education. Meanwhile, in compliance with an earlier legislative measure, Brown on March 2, transmitted the first economic report of any governor. This document was a detailed analysis of the California economy, evaluating both its strengths and its weaknesses. It marked the implementation of a declared policy by the legislature that the state should "foster and promote full employment and increased productivity, income, and purchasing power." In June, Brown signed the 1964-65 budget bill for $3,652,384,869. The new budget brought the state's total spending to about 6.6 per cent over the previous year's spending program.

When the 1964 session closed, Brown praised the legislators for enacting "a sound and progressive budget, an excellent school finance measure, a vastly improved method of sharing tidelands oil revenue and a host of other measures responsive to the needs of this most dynamic of American states." Of the sixty items the governor placed on the special session call, only four were defeated. Among the major legislative accomplishments were the passage of a savings and loan holding company disclosure act, the creation of an office of tourism and visitor services, and the establishment of rapid transit districts in Los Angeles, Marin, and San Mateo Counties.

Several times in 1964 the press hinted at rumors of a widening breach between Governor Brown and Assembly Speaker Jesse M. Unruh. During the primary campaign Brown supported Controller Alan Cranston for the United States Senate to succeed ailing Senator Clair Engle, while Unruh supported Pierre Salinger, former presidential press secretary. Salinger's victory over Cranston was viewed as a defeat for Brown. After Engle's death, the governor appointed Salinger to the vacant Senate seat. In the general election Salinger was defeated by his Republican opponent, George M. Murphy. Some observers of the political scene felt that the feud between Brown and Unruh had been intensified by alleged differences between the two Democratic chiefs in the management of the general election.

The 1964 California election was not all too pleasing to Brown and the Democrats. While President Johnson easily carried the state and Democratic majorities were returned to the state legislature and the California Congressional delegation, California now had two Republican United States Senators. Moreover, the Rumford Fair Housing Act, a source of pride to the Brown administration, was repealed by the passage of the controversial initiative measure, Proposition 14, which also outlawed any future anti-discriminatory housing legislation.

On the national scene Governor Brown was a staunch supporter of the late President John F. Kennedy and of President Lyndon B. Johnson. On August 26, 1964, in an unprecedented double-nominating ceremony Governor Brown and Governor John B. Connally of Texas shared the honors of placing President Johnson in nomination at the Democratic national convention in Atlantic City. Meanwhile, rumors circulated that Brown might be appointed either Attorney General of the United States or to the United States Supreme Court.

After President Johnson's sweeping victory over Republican

Barry Goldwater, Governor Brown in a press conference at Sacramento on November 10, 1964, revealed that President Johnson wanted him to run for a third term in 1966. It was speculated that a "power vacuum" within the California Democratic party might be created if Brown did not run. Shortly thereafter rumors circulated in Washington, D.C. that Speaker Unruh had offered to support Republican Senator Thomas Kuchel for the governorship in 1966. These rumors were quickly denied and Brown announced that Unruh had pledged to back him in 1966. Some Sacramento observers believed that if Brown won a third term, an intra-party battle would develop in determining a successor.

When Governor Brown appeared before the 1965 legislature on January 5, he announced that the two most urgent tasks were reapportionment and revenue. He expressed regret that "the United States Supreme Court has left the people of California no voice in the apportionment formula of their Senate." The court's rule of "one citizen, one vote" was described by Brown as "simple and rigid." Brown hoped for the adoption of a reapportionment plan that would be fair and promised help to the legislature in the matter. Turning to the revenue problem, Brown said: "Tax increases became inevitable last year when the legislature gave bipartisan support to increases in local schools to improve our school systems and help ease the burden on local property owners."

Brown stated that he favored the recommendation of the commission on California state government organization and economy that a single department of revenue be created. Moreover, he stated that he would ask for a business and commerce agency consolidating such departments as real estate, savings and loan, banking, corporations, and insurance. And he favored combining the recreation and park commissions into a single body.

Brown proposed that the legislature raise the unemployment insurance maximum because the average weekly wage had increased over $17 since 1959. He also stated that he would submit legislation to extend unemployment insurance to agricultural workers and that he would ask for increased workmen's compensation benefits. He recommended a constitutional amendment to remove the need for a two-thirds vote in each legislative branch to approve the annual budget. While he stressed the value of the initiative in allowing citizens to right any wrong, he said: "I believe legislation is needed to prevent special interests from turning the initiative to private gain through the use of professional petition circulators and large sums of money." Finally, Governor Brown called for annual legislative sessions and increased salaries for legislators.

On January 25, 1965, Governor Brown submitted his seventh budget to the legislature. While he emphasized economy, he quoted Edmund Burke's distinction and said: "I trust we will not confuse economy with parsimony. . . ." A spending program of over $4,000,000,000 with an increase in taxes was proposed for the fiscal year 1965-66. Brown again proposed payroll deduction of state income taxes, which the legislators had turned down in 1963.

On January 28, Hale Champion, state finance director, reported to the legislature that state social welfare program costs would be $367,260,400 in 1965-66, which was $16,148,000 above budget estimates. The welfare programs included aid to the blind, aid to the potentially self-supporting blind, aid to the disabled, aid to families with dependent children, old age security, and medical assistance for the aged.

A serious economic problem faced by gubernatorial administrations since the Great Depression has been the increasing costs of social welfare. In 1954-55, California public assistance expenditures totaled $340,237,879, not counting administrative overhead. The state's share of this cost was $137,-688,985 while the federal government expended $148,475,472 and county governments expended $54,073,422. By the fiscal year 1960-61, total welfare expenditures in California had risen to $575,722,157. The next fiscal year they amounted to $647,479,523. In 1962-63, total welfare expenditures were $752,454,211 with the federal share amounting to $324,581,-794, the state share to $278,259,265, and the county share to $149,613, 152. For the fiscal year 1962-63, welfare constituted 9.7% of total state expenditures.

The influx of population, increasing life spans, rising costs, and automation were among some of the factors causing increased expenditures for social welfare. In 1963, legislation was passed to organize a community work and training program to give adult welfare recipients training in the development of new or improved skills. Once the program was implemented, federal, state, and local agencies found employment for about 13,000 trainees within an eight-month period. It has been recognized that solution to welfare remains a pressing and urgent problem. Increasing social welfare costs in California as elsewhere in the nation have made the problem a subject of active political controversy.

On February 1, 1965, Governor Brown proposed a program of aid to flood-stricken areas in northern California which had been hit by disaster the previous December. On the fifteenth, Brown won his first major victory of the session when the Assembly passed an emergency bill to increase disability insurance taxes.

When the 1965 legislature opened, there were hints that a bipartisan economy bloc comparable to the one which had harassed the Olson administration might develop. While the legislators seemed cool to some of Brown's plans, particularly to the abolition of the death penalty and to repeal of the constitutional requirement of a two-thirds vote in both the Assembly and the Senate for passage of the budget, even the Republican minorities did not consider the administration program entirely bad. Moreover, it appeared that some legislators were anxious to reverse the trend toward centralization of executive powers and to curtail expansion of the agency plan.

Although Governor Brown's image has had its ups and downs, his political approach has been generally successful. He has withstood some bitter press opposition, occasional charges of nepotism, and intra-party conflicts. Brown intensely enjoys public life and the law. When he finally decided to run for governor, his wife opposed the step. Although Mrs. Brown probably would never have chosen politics as her husband's career—had the choice been hers — California's first lady has assumed a more important role in an informal way among women's groups and Democratic party workers. During evening moments of relaxation in the executive mansion, Governor Brown has read about the careers of early California governors in the volumes authored by Theodore H. Hittell. Brown has ambitions to write and he does keep a diary. While his office is demanding, Governor Brown seems to find it rewarding. For recreation he golfs and hunts and one of his companions when duck hunting occasionally is Chief Justice Earl Warren.

Since 1903, the California governors have resided in the

executive mansion, located on the southwest corner of 16th and H Streets in Sacramento. In 1962, it seemed that work might begin on a new mansion closer to the capitol after a design had been selected from 197 entries. The next year, when estimated costs of the project rose from $470,000 to about $875,000, a controversy arose over the new home for California governors. The legislature rejected requests for building funds, and only permitted the architects' fees to be paid. In the meantime, the old Victorian mansion has been remodeled. Gold and white flocked wallpaper and new paint have been added to the downstairs parlors, dining room, and music room. On the walls hang paintings by California artists which are on loan from several museums. Governor Brown's room is now done in a deep blue with flocked wallpaper, a thick blue carpet, and white canvas drapes while the first lady's room is painted in raspberry red with white wallpaper covered with large pink flowers. Prior to the remodeling, the upstairs bedroom walls were cracked and peeling from the vibration of heavy street traffic. Despite its elegance, the mansion is considered a fire hazard. From the upstairs bedrooms there is a rope fire escape and the Browns are not permitted to use the six Italian marble fireplaces downstairs.

Most political writers view Brown as a governor who follows the middle of the road on major issues and within his own party. After Brown had been in office eighteen months, a British journal, *The Economist,* stated:

> In governing California he has relied on personal appeals to leaders of the opposition and on quiet trading with the pressure groups which must be balanced off against each other, and defied when necessary, in a state where the Governor has little patronage with which to exert pressure of his own.

During his years in office Governor Brown has learned many valuable lessons and some of these he has expressed. In an article, "How to Put the States Back in Business," appearing in *Harper's Magazine* of September, 1964, Governor Brown proposed two revisions in federal-state relationships. First, he pointed out the need for a council of governors; and secondly, he recommended federal legislation to create formal regional structures. Brown voiced his belief that many problems such as education, employment, welfare, civil rights, and urban growth occurring in states and cities are national in scope and cannot be solved entirely on the local level. He explained that while many government services are administered jointly by the states and the federal government, the governor is only given an informal and infrequent voice in administration. Brown felt that although the American state governor is the "people's advocate," he must consult at the national level through intermediaries. To overcome this handicap he favored a council to give governors a true voice in national affairs. Hence Brown proposed a council of five governors appointed by the president with "rotating regional representation on a bipartisan basis."

Despite a large turnover of close advisers, particularly in his first term, Governor Brown has brought young talent to his staff. Through the efforts of his staff and the use of representative citizens' conferences, such as Warren used, there has existed an awareness of the complexities of California's rapid growth as it became the most populous state. To meet these problems and to maintain financial solvency, Governor Brown urged increased revenues as early as his first year in office. Most opposition to Brown has centered on issues such as tax increases, welfare costs, reapportionment, the water plan, capital punishment, government reorganization, and fair housing. Although he moves cautiously, he never seems to compromise with his basic principles. While his growth in political stature as governor has been debated, his image was improved by defeating a strong opponent in 1962.

Governor Brown has attempted to improve minority group relations, particularly in the fields of housing and labor. To supplement the efforts of the legislature and the courts, in 1963 he issued an executive order establishing the first code of fair practices in an attempt to end discrimination in all operations of state government.

More than any previous governor, Brown has been directly involved in a constructive way with foreign affairs. Particularly outstanding has been the Chile-California Program of the Alliance for Progress, functioning under contracts negotiated together by the federal government, California, and Chile. For example, California has aided Chile in planning the multipurpose development of water resources in her Maule River Basin. California has also helped Chile to establish a better agricultural extension service and more effective rural cooperatives and credit institutions. On June 25, 1964, Governor Brown and the late Governor Eligio Esquivel Mendez of Baja California signed a friendship pact at the Calexico-Mexicali border. The legislature created a "sister-state" commission and on August 7, Governor Brown appointed the members of the commission whose duties were to strengthen the economic and cultural ties of California with Baja California.

At the time of his second gubernatorial campaign Brown was referred to as a puppet of the "left wing" California Democratic Council and he was accused of importing Tammany Hall political tactics in an alleged attempt to end the nonpartisan tradition of California state government. Those charges were hurled in the heat of political battle. Although Brown is a Democrat and is obviously more partisan than the Progressives of the early part of the century, he has in a sense inherited the political mantle of Hiram Johnson and William D. Stephens and of Earl Warren. Brown as a liberal is a proponent of civil rights and of social welfare. He has supported the concepts of the "New Frontier" of President Kennedy and of the "Great Society" of President Johnson.

Although it is too early to assess the Brown administration in historical perspective, some aspects are sufficiently advanced to warrant a partial evaluation. Of all the Democratic administrations in California history, Brown's has been the most successful in terms of realizing its legislative objectives. Moreover, major changes have occurred in the executive branch with the creation of the agency plan and the governor's cabinet. Much attention has been paid to sectional problems involving water distribution and legislative reapportionment. Brown has prepared courses of action to meet California's growing stake in foreign trade and to participate in President Johnson's antipoverty program.

During the Brown administration the California governorship has gained in importance not only within the state, but also on national and international levels. Whether or not one agrees with Governor Brown's policies, it may safely be said that he is energetic, aware of political and economic problems, and has a great concern for his native state.

BIBLIOGRAPHY

CONTEMPORARY ACCOUNTS

Brown, Edmund G., *Inaugural Message,* Jan. 5, 1959 (Sacramento, 1959), *Inaugural Message,* Jan. 7, 1963 (Sacramento, 1963) ; *Mesnomic Report of the Governor* (Sacramento, 1964) ; *Budget Messages,* Jan. 5, 1965 (Sacramento, 1965) ; *Governor's Code of Fair Practices* (Sacramento, 1963) ; *Statement on Capital Punishment* (Sacramento, 1963) ; *Statement on Social Welfare* (Sacramento, 1963) ; *Statement on Government Reorganization* (Sacramento, 1963) ; *Economic Report of the Governor* (Sacramento, 1964) ; *Budget Messages,* 1959-1965 (Sacramento, 1959-65).

——, "How to Put the States Back in Business," *Harper's Magazine,* CCXXIX (Sept., 1964), 98-103.

"Press Releases" (Brown), 1958-1965.

Pitts, Thomas L., *Labor Legislation, Report on 1963 Regular Session of the California Legislature and 1963 First Extraordinary Session* (San Francisco, 1963).

The Agency Plan for California (Sacramento, 1959).

California Blue Book, 1961 (Sacramento, 1961).

Committee to Re-elect Governor Brown, *Record of Achievement: Administration of Edmund G. Brown, Governor, 1959-1962* (10 vols., San Francisco and Los Angeles, 1962).

Report to the Governor on Reorganization of State Government by the Task Forces (Sacramento, 1959).

Report of the Study Commission on Senate Apportionment (Sacramento, 1962).

Senate Interim Committee on Governmental Reorganization, *Organization of the Executive Branch of State Government* (Sacramento, 1958).

SECONDARY SOURCES

Anderson, Totten J., "The 1958 Election in California," *Western Political Quarterly,* XII (1959), 276-300.

—— and Lee, Eugene C., "The 1962 Election in California," *WPQ,* XVI (1963), 396-420.

Champion, Hale, "To the Victors Belongs the Empty Treasury," *Reporter,* XIX (Nov. 27, 1958), 17-18.

Lee, Eugene C. and Buchanan, William, "The 1960 Election in California," *WPQ,* XIV, Pt. 2 (1961), 309-326.

Marine, Gene, "This is 'Pat' Brown . . . The Man with the House Percentage," *Frontier,* IX (1958), 6-12.

"Man in the Middle," *The Economist,* CXCVI (July 9, 1960), 150.

NEWSPAPERS

San Francisco Chronicle, July 29, 1935, and Dec. 29, 1936, has data on Brown's activity in the Order of Cincinnatus; Jan. 9, 1944, has data on Brown's inauguration as District Attorney of San Francisco.

INTERVIEW

Governor Edmund G. Brown by B.F. Gilbert, June 13, 1960.

Epilogue

THE OFFICE OF CALIFORNIA GOVERNOR as an institution is almost two hundred years old. Once entrusted to Spanish and Mexican officials and then to United States Navy and Army officers, the governorship has been held by thirty-two men since California gained statehood. The administrations from Burnett to Brown achieved great prestige and vast powers while guiding California's destiny. It has become one of the more important elective offices in the United States. All thirty-two governors have had similar administrative problems with solutions to these reflecting the eras in which they lived. All have had to present a philosophy of government, to find answers to state finance, and to provide administrative leadership and organization.

Nineteenth century governors, both Democrats and Republicans, possessed strong beliefs in Jeffersonian democracy. In the twentieth century, governors such as Pardee, Johnson, Stephens, and Young, extremely conscious of how industrialization had changed life in California, followed Progressive views with the goal to reforming political and social institutions in the state. Since the 1930's more recent administrations have accepted much of what has been called the New Deal philosophy. Since Olson's administration, the governors have assumed that the state had an obligation in such areas as employment, industrial relations, public health, and social welfare. However, regardless of political philosophy, all thirty-two governors have named economy as the watchword of their respective administrations. In this instance, some were much more successful than others.

Until recent times, the governors tended to judge their own success in terms of private business practices. A fairly common ideal, these men held, was to have a "business-like administration." Their goal was to live within the state's income while maintaining and expanding state services. The fiscal programs of the governors related to economy and to the condition of the state debt. Obviously those administrations with little or

459

no debt were able either to reduce expenditures, if this were
their bent, or to extend state services more easily. Nineteenth
century governors commonly believed in "pay as you go"
financing. This meant limitation of services, and in many
instances, increase in taxes, unpopular both to politicians and
to voters. As a consequence, twentieth century gubernatorial
administrations have resorted more and more to bond issues,
rather than asking for tax increases, as a means of securing
desired institutions and services. The problem of adequate
state revenue has plagued most of the governors.

Ever since California's admission as a state, many governors
have been dissatisfied with the constitution and the organization
of the executive branch. Several called for conventions to revise
the Constitution of 1849 and the unwieldy Constitution of
1879. The twentieth century saw the executive branch vastly
expanded to meet mushrooming problems confronting state
government. Stephens and Young developed successful reorganization programs which lasted until the administration of
Governor Brown. He initiated plans for a new executive
organization.

Another change has occurred in the relationship of the governor with the legislature. All nineteenth century governors believed in separation of powers with their prime function being
to enforce those laws passed. Few of these men believed that
a governor should plan and lead in the enactment of a legislative program. Most twentieth century governors, beginning
with Hiram Johnson, labored diligently to implement their
programs, utilizing their political powers to the utmost.

Although these men possessed different backgrounds and
training and held diverse concepts of the office, the California
governorship has grown in significance through the years. Some
of the governors were much more positive in their approach to
state administration and more vigorous in developing their
philosophies of government. Yet in their various ways, the
California governors contributed to the development of the
office and to the growth of the state.

Notes on Sources

MANUSCRIPTS

Fairly complete gubernatorial papers exist for only a few California governors. The Hiram Johnson, Merriam, Olson, and Pardee papers in the Bancroft Library at the University of California and the Haight and Markham papers in the Henry E. Huntington Library at San Marino, California are the most extensive and useful. Manuscripts relating to Latham's career are deposited in the Huntington Library, Stanford University Library, and California Historical Society Library in San Francisco. Miscellaneous manuscripts of Bartlett, Burnett, Low, and McDougal are also in the Bancroft Library. Papers of Perkins and Rolph at the California Historical Society and of Waterman at the Bancroft Library were not made available. The Warren and Knight gubernatorial papers, entrusted to the California State Archives in Sacramento, remain under seal. Some executive papers and letters of several governors are available in the State Archives. In 1952, J. N. Bowman compiled the more important of these in "The Early Governors of California: Records Showing the Kinds of Men They Were," which is deposited in the State Archives.

Besides gubernatorial papers, other manuscripts contribute significantly to an understanding of the governors. The Cassius T. Ryland papers in the Bancroft Library were consulted for Governor Burnett as were the Chester Rowell papers in the same depository for Governors Hiram Johnson, Gillett, Stephens, and Richardson. The Herbert C. Jones papers and the Meyer Lissner papers at Stanford University Library were used for Governor Stephens. For governors such as Bigler, Markham, and Stoneman, who had diplomatic, congressional, or military service, miscellaneous manuscripts about their careers are in the National Archives in Washington, D.C. Also in this depository is much correspondence between federal officials and California governors relating to the Asiatic question. Certain presidential papers in the Library of Congress in Washington, D.C., such as those of Theodore Roosevelt and Woodrow Wilson, shed light on the relationships of California governors with the presidency.

AUTOBIOGRAPHIES, PUBLIC PAPERS, SPEECHES, AND REMINISCENCES

Robert H. Becker has edited *Some Reflections of An Early California Governor* . . . (Sacramento, 1959), containing a memoir dictated by Governor Frederick F. Low and an interview of Low by H.H. Bancroft. These are valuable because they give information on Low's attitude toward his office as well as his impressions of several early governors. Peter H. Burnett in his *Recollections and Opinions of An Old Pioneer* (New York, 1880) devoted a few pages to his governorship. Governor James N. Gillett wrote a brief "Autobiography," which appeared in

R.A. Richards' *History of Monroe County, Wisconsin* (1912).

Lauren E. Crane edited *Newton Booth of California, His Speeches and Addresses* (New York, 1894). *Letters of Theodore Roosevelt* (8 vols., Cambridge, 1951-54), edited by Elting E. Morison, give insights into the controversies between Roosevelt and Governors Pardee, Gillett, and Hiram Johnson over the Japanese question. Papers of the First World War governor were compiled in *California in the War: War Addresses, Proclamations, and Patriotic Messages of Governor William D. Stephens* (Sacramento, 1921). Governor Olson's *State Papers and Public Addresses* (Sacramento, 1942) as selected by his executive secretary, Stanley Mosk, have been put into book form by the State Printing Office. *The Public Papers of Chief Justice Earl Warren* (New York, 1959) have been edited by Henry M. Christman. Only the first part of its four parts relate to the period when Warren was governor.

The Memoirs of Elisha Oscar Crosby, Reminiscences of California and Guatemala from 1849 to 1864 (San Marino, 1945), edited by Charles A. Barker, have miscellaneous data on the military governor, General Bennett Riley, as well as on Governors Burnett and McDougal. Harris Newmark in his *Sixty Years in Southern California, 1853-1913* (New York, 2nd ed., 1926), edited by Maurice H. and Marco R. Newmark, has much of interest about Governor Downey and some data about Governors Gage, Low, and Markham. In 1896, Colonel James J. Ayers wrote his *Gold and Sunshine: Reminiscences of Early California* (Boston, 1922). A journalist and politician, who resided in California for forty-seven years and served as state printer in the Stoneman administration, Ayers discussed Stoneman and several other governors, particularly those of the Civil War. Unfortunately, few memoirs by Californians exist for the twentieth century; however, Thomas Storke has written his *California Editor* (Los Angeles, 1958), which has some useful data about Governors Merriam, Olson, and Warren.

STATE AND FEDERAL DOCUMENTS

J. Ross Browne compiled the *Report of the Debates in the Convention of California on the Formation of the State Constitution* (Washington, D.C., 1850), which has Governor Riley's proclamation calling the convention, the proceedings of the convention, and a list of delegates. Its appendix has a copy of the Constitution of 1849, the memorial of the United States Senators and Congressmen-elect from California, a digest of Mexican laws in effect in 1849, and the official correspondence of Governor Riley relating to the convention. *California and New Mexico*, Ho. of R., 31st Cong., 1st Sess., Ex. Doc. 17 (Washington, D.C., 1850) has significant correspondence and documents issued by the military governors.

Inaugural addresses, messages, veto messages, and special communications and reports of the governors appear in the *Assembly Journal* and *Senate Journal* and their appendices which have been printed since 1850 as have the *Statutes*. Some of the governors' messages have been printed separately; for example, the inaugural address and first and second biennial messages of Governor Markham were printed in

1895. E.B. Willis and P.K. Stockton have compiled the *Debates and Proceedings of the Constitutional Convention* (3 vols., Sacramento, 1880-81), which reflect the opinions of the delegates who drafted the Constitution of 1879. The *California Blue Books*, appearing for many of the years since 1893, are important contemporary and historical volumes of reference that pertain to the structure of state government. Most significant for nineteenth century gubernatorial and other campaigns, including party platforms and election results, is the *History of Political Conventions in California, 1849-1892* (Sacramento, 1893) by Winfield J. Davis. This valuable compilation was published by the California State Library; regrettably, nothing comparable exists for the present century.

GUBERNATORIAL CAMPAIGN LITERATURE

These significant materials are not abundant because of their ephemeral nature, but some have been preserved among various gubernatorial papers and in scrapbooks. Pamphlets, handbooks, manuals, and posters relating to campaigns are more plentiful for the twentieth century. A good example is the *California Progressive Campaign Book for 1914: Three Years of Progressive Administration under Governor Hiram W. Johnson* (San Francisco, 1914). Mention might also be made of *The Story of the Legislature of 1909* (San Francisco, 1910) and other volumes on the California legislative sessions of 1911, 1913, 1915, and 1921 by Franklin Hichborn, the newspaperman. In a sense these five volumes were campaign literature for the Progressives. Moreover, they provide analyses both of key legislative measures and political forces at work.

For the 1934 gubernatorial campaign Upton Sinclair's pamphlet, *I, Governor of California: And How I Ended Poverty* (Los Angeles, 1934) and its sequel in book form, *I, Candidate for Governor: And How I Got Licked* (Los Angeles, 1935) are important for the program of a defeated candidate. Frank Scully's *The Next Governor of California* (c. 1938) is an example of campaign propaganda for Olson's election. Four years later appeared *Speakers' Manual for Governor Culbert L. Olson's Re-Election Campaign of 1942*. The Committee to Re-elect Governor Brown issued the *Record of Achievement: Administration of Edmund G. Brown, Governor, 1959-1962* (10 vols., San Francisco and Los Angeles, 1962). This mimeographed set has been deposited in the California Section of the State Library.

NEWSPAPERS AND PRESS RELEASES

Newspapers were invaluable in obtaining biographical data about the governors, interesting incidents in their lives, coverage of their campaigns and elections, insights into their administrations, and editorial opinions about their executive abilities. The various indices to newspaper files in the California Section of the State Library facilitated their use, particularly for Sacramento and San Francisco newspapers. In the research on Governor Budd an index in the Stockton Public Library made it easier to consult several Stockton newspapers. The files of over twenty-five California newspapers extending from Eureka to San Diego were consulted. Among the more important newspapers were the *Daily Alta California* and *Daily California Chronicle* of San Francisco, *Humboldt Standard, Los Angeles Times, Sacramento Bee, Sacramento Union, San Diego Union, San Francisco Bulletin, San Francisco Call, San Francisco Chronicle, San Francisco Examiner, San Francisco News, San Jose Mercury, Stockton Evening Mail,* and *Stockton Independent.* The most useful newspapers of other states consulted were the *New Orleans Times, New York Herald, New York Times,* and *New York Tribune.*

Some press releases of the Warren and Knight administrations were located in the Documents Section of the California State Library. Press releases of the Brown administration were also a significant source. The value of the press releases is that they are often more detailed than newspaper accounts.

GENERAL WORKS

Theodore H. Hittell's *History of California* (4 vols., San Francisco, 1885-97) discussed in considerable detail the Spanish, Mexican, United States military, and nineteenth century civil governors through 1887. The volumes comprising Hubert Howe Bancroft's *History of California* (7 vols., San Francisco, 1886-90), while containing some useful data on the governors, are not as accurate or valuable as those by Hittell. Both of these multi-volume sets are important in setting a historical framework for the nineteenth century governors. H.H. Bancroft's *Popular Tribunals* (2 vols., San Francisco, 1887) are valuable for understanding the confrontations that Governor McDougal had with the Vigilance Committee of 1851 and that Governor J. Neely Johnson had with the Vigilance Committee of 1856. Franklin Tuthill's one volume *History of California* (San Francisco, 1866), despite its journalistic quality, was helpful in studying Governor Downey's problem with the bulkheaders at the San Francisco embarcadero. Other general histories of California shed little light upon the governors, but Charles E. Chapman's *A History of California, The Spanish Period* (New York, 1921) is of value on the Spanish governors.

BIOGRAPHIES OF GOVERNORS

The scarcity of biographies on the California governors is appalling; however, several excellent studies exist for the Mexican and military governors. Two of these are George L. Harding's *Don Agustín V. Zamorano, Statesman, Soldier, Craftsman, and California's First Printer* (Los Angeles, 1934) and Dwight L. Clarke's *Stephen Watts Kearny, Soldier of the West* (Norman, 1961). The best biography of a California civil governor is George T. Clarke's *Leland Stanford* (Stanford University Press, 1931). Although it has little about his gubernatorial career, another study is Hubert H. Bancroft's *History of the Life of Leland Stanford* (Oakland, 1952). Robert E. Burke's *Olson's New Deal for California* (Berkeley, 1953), though largely an administrative account, contains important biographical facts about Governor Olson. Irving Stone's *Earl Warren, A Great American Story* (New York, 1948) was published when Warren was the Republican vice presidential candidate. It is more of the nature of a campaign biography. David W. Taylor wrote *The Life of James Rolph, Jr.* (San Francisco, 1934), an eulogy. A worthwhile booklet, published by the Society of California Pioneers, and entitled, *Memorial of the Life and Services of Washington Bartlett, Late Governor of California* (San Francisco, 1888), is a good biography. Peter T. Conmy has authored a brief but useful pamphlet about *Romualdo Pacheco: Distinguished Californian of the Mexican and American Periods* (San Francisco, 1957), which was published by the Native Sons of the Golden West.

Important facts concerning the nineteenth century governors are recorded in several biographical compilations such as Hubert H. Bancroft's *Chronicles of the Builders of the Commonwealth* (8 vols., San Francisco, 1891-92), Alonzo Phelps' *Contemporary Biography of California's Representative Men* (2 vols, San Francisco, 1881-82) and Oscar T. Shuck's *Representative and Leading Men of the Pacific* (San Francisco, 1870) and *History of the Bench and Bar of California* (Los Angeles, 1901). The various regional studies of California by James M. Guinn have biographical accounts of several governors; for example, the *History of the State of California and Biographical Record of San Joaquin County* (2 vols., Los Angeles, 1909) has a sketch of Governor Budd.

The Dictionary of American Biography (22 vols., New York, 1928-44), edited by Allen Johnson and Dumas Malone, has biographical sketches of Burnett, Bigler, Latham, Stanford, Low, Haight, Pacheco, Stoneman, and Perkins. Recognized scholars such as Edgar E. Robinson, who wrote on Latham and Haight, authored these biographical portraits. Of the twentieth century governors, only a biography of Rolph written by Dean E. McHenry is published in this set, appearing in the first supplemental volume. For those governors with careers in Congress, sketches appear in the *Biographical Directory of the American Congress, 1774-1949* (Washington, D.C., 1950).

Paradoxically, the best studies of individual California governors are secreted away in graduate theses in the colleges and universities. To date only one of these, Burke's study on Olson, has been published as a book. Parts of some of these theses have appeared in scholarly periodical articles. An excellent study on the beginnings of the Progressive movement with important data pertaining to Governors Pardee and Gillett is Alice M. Rose's "Rise of California Insurgency, Origins of the League of Lincoln-Roosevelt Republican Clubs, 1900-1907," (Ph.D., Stanford University, 1942).

MONOGRAPHS

Unfortunately, no monograph has been written about Spanish and Mexican rule in California. For the best coverage of the governors from 1769 to 1846, one must consult the general work by T.H. Hittell, *History of California*. Theodore Grivas' *Military Governments in California, 1846-1850* (Glendale, 1963) is useful for an understanding of the role of the military governors. Cardinal Goodwin's *The Establishment of State Government in California, 1846-1850* (New York, 1914) discusses the period of military rule, the Monterey constitutional convention of 1849, and the organization of state government. For the first decade of statehood the best study is William H. Ellison, *A Self-governing Dominion: California, 1849-1860* (Berkeley, 1950). Much about Governor McDougal's difficulties with extra-legal government is found in Mary F. Williams, *History of the San Francisco Committee of Vigilance of 1851* (Berkeley, 1921). The relations of California with the federal government are adequately covered in *California and the Nation, 1850-1869* (Berkeley, 1927) by Joseph Ellison.

The most helpful study for California administrative history from 1849 to 1933, is the excellent monograph by Gerald D. Nash, *State Government and Economic Development* (Berkeley, 1964). An economic history concerned with public revenues, debts, and expenditures from Spanish rule to 1910 is William C. Fankhauser's *A Financial History of California* (Berkeley, 1913). The history of public welfare in California is covered by Frances Cahn and Valeska Bary in *Welfare Activities of Federal, State, and Local Governments in California, 1850-1934* (Berkeley, 1936).

The story of the movement to emancipate California from corporate rule and political corruption in the period from 1900 to 1920, is told in George E. Mowry's *The California Progressives* (Berkeley, 1951). Two books, Thomas A. Bailey's *Theodore Roosevelt and the Japanese-American Crises* (Stanford University Press, 1934) and Roger Daniels' *The Politics of Prejudice* (Berkeley, 1962), discuss in part the involvement of California governors in the Japanese question from 1906 to the 1920's.

PERIODICAL ARTICLES

Several important articles relating to the governors have appeared in scholarly historical journals. Their number are woefully limited, but a few examples may be given. Raymond K. Morrison authored "Luís Antonio Argüello: First Mexican Governor of California," in the *Journal of the West*, II (1963), 193-204, 347-61. Irving McKee's "The Background and Early Career of Hiram Johnson, 1866-1910," appeared in the *Pacific Historical Review*, XIX (1950), 17-30. In the same journal H. Brett Melendy has recently clarified identities of two governors in "Who was John McDougal?" XXIX (1960), 231-43 and in "California's Washington Bartletts," XXXI (1962), 139-42. William E. Franklin authored "Peter H. Burnett and the Provisional Government Movement," in the *California Historical Society Quarterly*, XL (1961), 123-36. A. Lincoln in "My dear Governor," in the same journal, XXXVIII (1959), 229-47, discussed the correspondence between Hiram Johnson and Theodore Roosevelt.

Articles concerning some of the twentieth century governors have appeared in popular magazines. George Creel wrote "What about Hiram Johnson of California" in *Everybody's*, XXXI (1914), 448-60; Rolph is portrayed in Duncan Aikman's "California's Sun God" in *The Nation*, CXXXII (Jan. 14, 1931), 35-37; and Carey McWilliams authored "Warren of California" in the *New Republic*, CIX (Oct. 18, 1943), 514-17.

Index

87, 95, 103, 112
Terry, David S., 83, 96
"Thirty - Dollars - Every - Thursday," — see Ham and Eggs Movement
Tidelands oil controversy, 388, 391, 397
Tolan, John H., 412
Torres y Tortolero, Luis de, 13
Townsend, Francis, 388
Townsend Plan, 389, 398
Tracy, Frederick P., 117
Transportation Commissioners, 178, 182
Trinity River Project, 433
Turner, Eugene S., 115
Twain, Mark, 123, 132

Union Party, 120, 135-6, 145-6; Convention of 1863, 122, 131, 168; of 1867, 145, 168; see also Democratic Party, Republican Party
United States Military Governors, 19-22
United States Sanitary Commission—see Sanitary Commission
University of California, 150, 151, 162, 170, 234, 247, 254, 256, 280, 341
University of Southern California, 112
Unruh, Jesse M., 451, 452

Wagon roads, 56, 84, 85
Waldo, William, 52
Walkup, Joseph, 83, 85
Wardell, J. C., 351
Warner, Juan José, 111
Warren, Earl, 403-4, 429, 454; early life and education, 411; District Attorney of Alameda County, 411-2; Attorney General, 412; elected Governor, 403-4; re-elected in 1946, 417; re-elected in 1950, 419; as Governor, 413 - 23; views on Japanese, 412; resigned as Governor, 423; appointed Chief Justice, 422-3; Warren Com-

mission, 423; estimate of, 421-2
Washburn, Charles A., 159
Water resources, 420, 433, 434, 436, 443, 448, 449; see also Central Valley Project, Irrigation
Waterman, Robert W., 279; early life, 227; mining career, 228; elected Lieutenant Governor, 228-9; as Governor, 229-34; death, 234; estimate of, 234
Waterman, Theodore, 227
Webb, Ulysses S., 315, 412
Webb Anti-Alien Land Law of 1913, 315, 330
Webster, Jonathan V., 248
Weinstock, Harris, 310
Welfare, 183, 373, 385, 387-8, 390, 391, 397-8, 399, 400-1, 403, 413, 414, 415, 420, 421, 431, 433, 434, 442, 443, 446, 452, 453-4; see also Institutions
Weller, Charles L., 82
Weller, John B., 94, 130; early life and education, 81-2; Ohio Congressman, 81; on International Boundary Commission, 82-3; U.S. Senator from California, 83; elected Governor, 83; as Governor, 83-8; Minister to Mexico, 88; alleged Confederate sympathies, 89; later life and death, 89; estimate of, 89
Weller, John B., Jr., 82
Wells, Alexander, 143
West Coast Land Co., 191
Western Pacific Railroad, 137, 285
Whale Rock Project, 436
Whig Party, 68, 69, 78
Whitaker and Baxter, 403, 418, 428, 432
White, Stephen M., 229, 262, 265
Whiteside, N. E., 88
Whitman, George W., 75
Whitney, Josiah D., 111, 134
Whittaker, Samuel, 44
Wigginton, Peter D., 171
Wight, Lymon, 26
Wilmington Harbor, 171, 238

Designed and printed
in an edition limited to 1,000 copies
at The Talisman Press, Georgetown, California.

December, 1965